W9-BYK-836

www.wadsworth.com

wadsworth.com is the World Wide Web site for Wadsworth and is your direct source to dozens of online resources.

At *wadsworth.com* you can find out about supplements, demonstration software, and student resources. You can also send email to many of our authors and preview new publications and exciting new technologies.

wadsworth.com
Changing the way the world learns®

The Wadsworth Contemporary Issues in Crime and Justice Series

Todd Clear, Series Editor

1997 Golden: *Disposable Youth: America's Child Welfare System*
Hickey: *Serial Murderers and Their Victims*, Second Edition
Irwin/Austin: *It's About Time: America's Imprisement Binge*, Second Edition
Messner/Rosenfeld: *Crime and the American Dream*, Second Edition
Shelden/Tracy/Brown: *Youth Gangs in American Society*

1998 Bailey/Hale: *Popular Culture, Crime, and Justice*
Chesney-Lind/Shelden: *Girls, Delinquency, and Juvenile Justice*, Second Edition
Johnson: *Death Work: A Study of the Modern Execution Process*, Second Edition
Pollock: *Ethics, Crime, and Justice: Dilemmas and Decisions*, Third Edition
Rosenbaum/Lurigio/Davis: *The Prevention of Crime: Social and Situational Strategies*
Surette: *Media, Crime, and Criminal Justice: Images and Realities*, Second Edition
Walker: *Sense and Nonsense About Crime and Drugs: A Policy Guide*, Fourth Edition
White: *Terrorism: An Introduction*, Second Edition

1999 Arrigo: *Social Justice/Criminal Justice: The Maturation of Critical Theory in Law, Crime, and Deviance*

2000 Walker/Spohn/DeLone: *The Color of Justice: Race, Ethnicity, and Crime in America*, Second Edition

2001 Austin/Irwin: *It's About Time: America's Imprisonment Binge*, Third Edition
Belknap: *The Invisible Woman: Gender, Crime, and Justice*, Second Edition
Karmen: *Crime Victims: An Introduction to Victimology*, Fourth Edition
Shelden/Tracy/Brown: *Youth Gangs in American Society*, Second Edition
Pope/Lovell/Brandl: *Voices from the Field: Readings in Criminal Justice Research*
Walker: *Sense and Nonsense About Crime and Drugs: A Policy Guide*, Fifth Edition
Wooden/Blazak: *Renegade Kids, Suburban Outlaws: From Youth Culture to Delinquency*, Second Edition

2002 Alvarez/Bachman: *Murder American Style*
Hickey: *Serial Murderers and Their Victims*, Third Edition
Johnson: *Hard Time: Understanding and Reforming the Prison*, Third Edition
Pollock: *Women, Prison and Crime*, Second Edition
Ross/Richards: *Convict Criminology*
Sacco/Kennedy: *The Criminal Event: An Introduction to Criminology*, Second Edition
White: *Terrorism: An Introduction*, Third Edition

Terrorism

An Introduction

THIRD EDITION

JONATHAN R. WHITE
Grand Valley State University

Australia • Canada • Mexico • Singapore • Spain • United Kingdom • United States

WADSWORTH

THOMSON LEARNING

Criminal Justice Editor: Shelley Murphy
Development Editor: Terri Edwards
Assistant Editor: Dawn Mesa
Editorial Assistant: Lee McCracken
Marketing Manager: Jennifer Somerville
Marketing Assistant: Neena Chandra
Print/Media Buyer: Tandra Jorgensen

Permissions Editor: Stephanie Keough-Hedges
Production Service: Scott Rohr/Buuji, Inc.
Copy Editor: Alan DeNiro
Cover Designer: Laurie Anderson
Cover Image: PhotoDisc
Compositor: Buuji, Inc.
Printer: WebCom, Ltd.

Printed in Canada
3 4 5 6 7 05 04 03 02

For permission to use material from this text, contact us by
Web: http://www.thomsonrights.com
Fax: 1-800-730-2215
Phone: 1-800-730-2214

Wadsworth Thomson Learning
10 Davis Drive
Belmont, CA 94002-3098
USA

For more information about our products, contact us:
Thomson Learning Academic Resource Center
1-800-423-0563
http://www.wadsworth.com

International Headquarters
Thomson Learning
International Division
290 Harbor Drive, 2nd Floor
Stamford, CT 06902-7477
USA

UK/Europe/Middle East/South Africa
Thomson Learning
Berkshire House
168-173 High Holborn
London WC1V 7AA
United Kingdom

Asia
Thomson Learning
60 Albert Street, #15-01
Albert Complex
Singapore 189969

Canada
Nelson Thomson Learning
1120 Birchmount Road
Toronto, Ontario M1K 5G4
Canada

Library of Congress Cataloging-in-Publication Data
White, Jonathan Randall.
    Terrorism: an introduction / Jonathan R. White. —3rd ed.
      p.   cm.
    Includes bibliographical references and index.
    ISBN 0-534-57331-2 (alk. paper)
    1. Terrorism. I. Title.
    HV6431 .W48 2001
    363.3'2—dc21
                                                         2001026219

To Jean Marie White with love

Come, behold the works of the Lord . . .
The Lord makes wars to cease to the end of the earth;
The Lord breaks the bow, and shatters the spear;
The Lord burns the shields with fire.
"Be still, and know that I am God!"

Selections from Psalm 46

Contents

Foreword

As I write, we are less than a week from the execution of Timothy McVeigh for the bombing of the federal building in Oklahoma City and the murder of over 100 of its occupants, a terrorist act of astonishing enormity. His act, and his execution, reminds us of our everyday vulnerability to violence, and the hard truth that we can never be completely protected from the sporadic extremist willing to wreak havoc for a political cause.

The very word *terrorism* holds us at attention. To be terrified is a dreadful experience; someone who is willing to use terror to achieve personal aims stands exposed as a dreadful person. Terror is an alarming emotion, and to provoke it is to invite alarm. When terror is used a tool for social change, it invites among us a kind of social alarm, a disturbance of the basic sense of social order. What happened in Oklahoma City was a personal tragedy of unimaginable proportion for the families and friends of the victims, but it was also a social calamity, shaking us at the very level of the possibility for a civil society.

That is why the study of terrorism is important. It is not because terrorism is, in the broad scheme of things, a common event. Thankfully, it is not. Very, very few of us will ever experience terrorism directly. Rather, we study terrorism because, despite its rarity, whenever it happens it is a momentous social event. In a sense, any act of terrorism has two sets of victims. One set is comprised of the people who suffer injury as a consequence of the terroristic crime—in Oklahoma City, the occupants of that building and their family and friends. The larger victim, however, is all of us, who lose a sense of security and a confidence in social order. We all become victimized by a horrific act of seemingly senseless violence against strangers for political ends, for we have to wonder, seeing these crimes, if our society is in some way falling apart.

Terrorism: An Introduction, by Jonathan R. White, now in its third edition, is the best basic study of terrorism available today. As editor of the Wadsworth Series on Contemporary Issues in Crime and Justice, I am pleased to announce this new edition and welcome its arrival in the series. The series is dedicated to the exploration of important issues in crime and justice that receive limited attention in textbooks, but deserve closer study. Books appearing in this series are used by students to deepen their understanding of important questions facing the fields of criminology and criminal justice, and we are proud to say that the series has, over the years, published some of the most important books on current topics of interest to the field. This book fits is of one of them.

Professor White has written a thoroughly researched, carefully documented analysis of the current status of terrorism across the globe. The breadth of coverage is extremely helpful, and anyone interested in gaining a working knowledge of the nature and degree of terroristic activity in the world today will find this book to be essential reading. What sets this book apart from others that deal with this subject matter is the holistic way in which terrorism is presented as a worldwide phenomenon. This book also provides broad coverage of all major forms of terrorism, and highlights the patterns of similarity, as well as the important differences, that one finds in the use of terror to accomplish political aims. To this thoroughness, the third edition has added several new sections, including a discussion of cyberterrorism, a chapter on religiously based terrorism, and updated material throughout.

This book, like many treatments of terrorism, is extremely topical: today's headlines become the data to be analyzed. But Professor White has taken his analysis further, and located our understanding of terrorism within the context of what we know about individual and collective behavior, so we may understand how disputes or grievances can mutate into terrorist movements. In this way, Professor White helps us to see terrorism as not simply a set of disconnected events or a series of news stories, but a part of the landscape and inherent capacity—albeit a negative one—of the human condition. The new chapter on religion adds to the discussion of social behavior to show how society can easily find itself giving birth to the circumstances that allow terrorism to emerge.

The middle chapters of this book are fascinating, reliable treatments of contentious events and situations that have spawned terrorism in different settings. The student will find there is much to be learned from the similarities in these descriptions, and there is much grist for the intellectual mill in the differences Professor White exposes. The closing chapters, which open a window to the future of terrorism and the attempts to control it, will be equally stimulating to those who will find themselves living in that future.

Professor White has written an essential book for those who want to understand today's world through the lens of violent political action. The world of terrorism is extraordinarily complex, and therefore it requires a first-class understanding of the topic to provide us with an eloquent and effortless explanation of the present situation and future prospects of terror. I admire Professor White for his depth of understanding, and congratulate him for a book of immense usefulness to those who want to improve their knowledge of this problem of terrorism in the world today. With great pleasure, I welcome this new edition to the series and commend it to the reader.

Todd R. Clear
New York City
May 10, 2001

Preface

Comments from an Air Force officer charged with counterterrorism spawned the first edition of *Terrorism* more than a decade ago. He told me he wanted a basic introduction his troops could understand—a practical work that could provide the basis for understanding theoretical perspectives. That principle guided the first edition and has been the dominating factor in the subsequent revisions.

The main purpose of this book is to provide basic information in a college-style text. It is written specifically for criminal justice majors, but it should continue to have some value for other disciplines, such as political science and history. The book has proven to be of value to military and security forces, and it will hopefully continue to be helpful to these audiences.

Regardless of where the book is utilized, the basic premise remains the same. It is designed to introduce students who may have little understanding of international politics and history to the world of terrorism. It is an elementary introduction to domestic and international terrorism. There are other works that go into great detail, but this book provides the basics. It is designed to enable students to move on to more complicated works.

Several professors have kindly forwarded suggestions about the revision of the text, and I have included a number of their suggestions. This new edition has a number of enhancements to help nonspecialists understand terrorism. It includes:

1. **A section titled "Essential Background."** This section allows students to study the emergence of modern terrorism from several different areas of the world. It demonstrates the relationship of developments in terrorist philosophy and how the history of terrorism influenced subsequent movements. It also provides several elementary historical sketches needed to understand modern terrorism.

2. **New sections on Weapons of Mass Destruction (WMD).** WMDs are introduced in the third part of the text, as well as descriptions of nuclear, chemical, and biological weapons, and their effects on human beings. The book also discusses policy, planning, security, and civil liberties.

3. **A new section on cyberterrorism.** In the information age, virtual terrorism is a reality. This edition examines the use of computers in terrorist activities, as well as threats to the management and flow of information.

4. **Expanded discussions of technological terrorism.** Although it has become popular to use computer terminology to refer to mass destruction, modern terrorism has become a problem because of its relationship to technology. Cyberterrorism and WMDs are treated within the context of technology, the energy industry, and media coverage.

5. **A new chapter on religion and terrorism.** Religion has become the dominating factor in domestic and international terrorism. This chapter explains basic theological concepts in nonspecialized language. It shows how religious motivation can transform into terrorist action.

6. **New material on the Middle East.** Many criminal justice professors stated that they spent the majority of their time in terrorism classes explaining the history and politics of the Middle East. This new edition expands the amount of background material on the region, and it is presented for students who may have limited knowledge of the history of the Middle East.

7. **A new section at the end of each chapter titled "Food for Thought."** These snippets raise practical issues about each chapter. They may be used for student reflection, essays, class discussions, or as the basis for research papers.

8. **A simple point-by-point summary of each chapter.** To make sure a student has the opportunity to grasp the major points, each subtopic in every chapter is summarized in outline form. If students use the objectives at the beginning of each chapter in conjunction with the summary, they should be able to master the material, even if they have no background in the area.

Information from earlier editions has also been included to help students understand the complex world of modern terrorism, including:

1. Maps and diagrams to simplify complex concepts

2. Suggestions for further reading

3. Diagrams and summaries to outline complex points

4. Historical time lines to demonstrate the development of terrorism

LEARNING AIDS

The text contains a number of features designed to help students understand the complex nature of terrorism, including:

1. Maps located throughout the text

2. Objectives at the beginning of each chapter

3. Subheadings based on chapter objectives

4. Boxes summarizing text material

5. Point-by-point summaries of chapter objectives

6. Several time lines to assist nonhistorians

7. A dictionary of prominent terrorist groups

8. Bibliographic and Internet references for further study

These aids are designed to help readers organize information without over-simplifying it.

ACKNOWLEDGMENTS

Terrorism is a complicated subject that crosses disciplines as freely as it does jurisdictional boundaries. Trying to summarize information for those concerned with security was an arduous task, which many people lightened by supplying tapes, files, background information, training, critiques, and interviews. I am grateful to a great many people for their willingness to share information and evaluate concepts.

Many colleagues made themselves available to listen to ideas, discuss certain aspects of terrorism, attend panels at conferences, critique papers, or share their work. I am grateful to the following academic colleagues: Rev. Dr. Thomas Boogaart, Western Theological Seminary; Dr. Hugh Stephens, University of Houston; Dr. Robert Taylor, University of North Texas; Dr. Richard Holden, Central Missouri State University; Dr. Mujo Mustafa and Dean Ibrahim Bokich, University of Sarajevo; Dr. Mark Pitcavage, the Militia Watchdog; Dr. Jeffery Ian Ross, University of Baltimore; Dr. Rick Lovell, University of Wisconsin–Milwaukee; Dr. H. H. A. Cooper, University of Texas at Dallas; and Dr. Mahendra Singh, Grambling State University; Dr. Harvey Kushner, Long Island University; Dr. Brent Smith, University of Alabama at Birmingham; Dr. Thomas R. Phelps, California State University at Sacramento.

The help of colleagues from the law enforcement field is deeply appreciated. I am thankful for the assistance of D. Douglas Bodrero, William Dyson, Emory Williams, Jennifer Turner, Marcy Kilgore, and William Reed (in memoriam) of the Institute for Intergovernmental Research; Attorney General Heidi Heitkamp of North Dakota; Peter Howse, Brian Robinson, and Brian McDonnell of the United Kingdom's RMH and Associates; Superintendent Peter Ryan of the New South Wales Constabulary in Australia; Sheriff Blaine Koops and Undersheriff Terry Fisk of the Allegan County Sheriffs Department in Michigan; Special Agent Bryan Costigan of the Montana Bureau of Criminal Investigation; Special Agents Mark Hady, Stanley Zimmerman, Timothy Sullivan (ret.), William Durham, Charles Houser, and Mark Siebert of the Bureau of Alcohol, Tobacco, and Firearms; fellow Cleveland Browns fan Colonel Kenneth Morckel of the Ohio State Highway

Patrol; Colonel Michael Robinson, Lieutenant Colonel James Bolger (ret.), First Lieutenant Marshall Johnson, and First Lieutenant Brian Ray of the Michigan State Police; Chief Richard Olson of the North Dakota Bureau of Criminal Investigation; Colonel Roger Hlavcka and Captain Robert Bereiter of the Wisconsin Highway Patrol; Superintendent James MacMahon of the New York State Police; Deputy Director (ret.) Oliver B. "Buck" Revell of the Federal Bureau of Investigation; former New York City Police Commissioner and U.S. Marshals Service Deputy Director Howard Safir; John Kendall and Robert DuHadway of DuHadway, Kendall, and Associates; and United States Marshal for Western Michigan (and Grand Valley State Criminal Justice alum) Barbara Lee.

I am also grateful to the staff of the following institutions: the Federal Bureau of Investigation; the United States Marshals Service; the Northwestern University Traffic Institute's School of Police Command; the alumni of the Federal Bureau of Investigation's National Academies in Michigan, Wisconsin, and Indiana; several FBI Joint Terrorism Task Forces; the Bureau of Alcohol, Tobacco, and Firearms; the International Association of Chiefs of Police; the United Kingdom's Bramshill Police Staff College; Bosnia's College of Criminal Science at the University of Sarajevo; the Norfolk Constabulary in the United Kingdom; and the Institute for Intergovernmental Research.

As always, Marcia, thank you. You have been with me in every book I have written, gently reminding me that things never slow down and I always over-commit. If the world could be ruled by the love and peace you bring to others, there would be no need to study this terrible topic or write a new edition of this book. I pray that such gentleness may be realized by all.

A NOTE TO STUDENTS

This text is designed to give you essential background information about terrorism. When you start a chapter, read the objectives at the beginning. The information in each chapter is based on these objectives, and the subtitles show you where the information is located. If you desire, you can even develop an outline of the chapter using the objectives and subtitles to guide your reading. This approach will ensure that you get every piece of information provided in the text. Each chapter also has a summary of information—a handy aid when reviewing for an examination.

Also, keep in mind that this is an introduction, not the definitive word on terrorism. My purpose is to introduce you to new concepts. Use the reading guides at the end of each chapter to begin exploring topics in-depth. You might also find these reading guides are handy aids in starting a term paper.

When you study terrorism, you are bombarded with the names and acronyms of dozens of terrorist groups. The dictionary in the appendix is designed to help you keep track of the major terrorist groups. Making frequent use of the appendix will help you become familiar with many different groups.

The book is organized in the following manner:

Part I The Criminology of Terrorism

This part focuses on the manner in which terrorism is changing, the dynamics of individual and group behavior, and the ways terrorists organize themselves. It also incorporates an extensive discussion of the relationship between religion and terrorism.

Part II Essential Background

Modern terrorism developed on a path that can be traced through Europe, Latin America, the United States, and the Middle East. This part of the book describes the history of terrorism and the ways terrorist movements in various parts of the world and at various times influence one another.

Part III Modern Terrorism

This part of the book relates the previous historical section to the practice of contemporary terrorism. It covers domestic and international terrorism.

Part IV Issues in Modern Terrorism

The book closes with the issues that dominate modern terrorism. These issues appear in all parts of the world, in all types of governmental systems.

Finally, I have tried to be objective about this topic, but its very nature produces deep-seated feelings. In addition, I write from a law enforcement bias. I did not write this book for terrorists. I wrote it for the police, military, and security personnel who fight terrorists. My opinions and assumptions are summarized in the following points:

1. Terrorism is a tactical phenomenon that fluctuates according to geographical and cultural variables. It cannot be strictly defined because it is intangible. Typologies do not account for all forms of terrorism.

2. Terrorism is sometimes a tool for revolutionaries and nationalists, but it is most frequently used by governments to maintain state power.

3. Terrorism can be used as a tactic in guerrilla campaigns, but most guerrillas are not terrorists.

4. Ideological terrorism is not the exclusive property of the revolutionary left.

5. The use of terrorism to repress populations is not exclusive to the reactionary right.

6. Some forms of criminality cannot and should not be distinguished from terrorism.

7. Some forms of terrorism cannot and should not be distinguished from warfare.

8. Terrorism is not necessarily revolution, and revolution is not necessarily terrorism.

9. The theory and rhetoric of revolution are even further removed from terrorism than revolutionary acts.

10. Just about everybody is willing to support some forms of terrorism. (To understand this, we must realize that terrorism comes in a variety of forms.)

11. Terrorism is difficult to study objectively, because it evokes deep-seated political emotions.

12. Terrorism is essentially a minor threat unless it is allowed to escalate.

13. The American political, military, and criminal justice systems need to develop an understanding of terrorism.

14. Specific terrorists can be defeated with logical policies and tactics, but incidents of terrorism will continue. No policy or tactic will completely eliminate terrorism.

These are my opinions, and they do not have to reflect your ideas. Please keep my biases in mind as you read the text. Use them, along with the opinions of others, as a backboard against which to volley your own inferences.

Jonathan R. White

✳

PART I

The Criminology of Terrorism

1

✳

Mutating Forms
of Terrorism

Y ou have probably heard and may have used the word *terrorism* prior to
reading this book. If you have, then you had an image in your mind
when you discussed it. Other people have used the word, and they also
project their own meanings into the term *terrorism*. This creates a problem.
Nobody has been able to produce an exact definition of the subject. As a result,
terrorism means different things to different people. To make matters worse,
the nature of terrorism has changed over the course of history. Violent activity
at one point in time may be called terrorism, while the same action may be
deemed war, liberation, or crime in another period of history. Religion has
come to play an important part of some forms of terrorism in the past few
years. The purpose of this chapter is to introduce methods for understanding
terrorism and the tactics terrorists use.

After reading this chapter, you should be able to:

1. Describe the problems of the contextual meaning of terrorism.
2. List and define some of the contexts of terrorism.
3. List and summarize some common definitions of terrorism.
4. Explain the strengths and weaknesses of typologies of terrorism.
5. Describe a tactical typology of terrorism.
6. List and summarize the five basic tactical forms of terrorism.

THE CONTEXT OF TERRORISM

Terrorism beams into our homes through television screens, it assaults us in newspapers and magazines, and it sometimes touches our lives in more direct manners. People do not seem to worry about the definition of terrorism at such times. They simply feel terror when they see the violence. Sometimes it seems as though the event itself defines terrorism. For example, when a plane is destroyed by a bomb, it is frequently called *terrorism,* but when military forces shoot down a civilian aircraft, it can be deemed an unfortunate mistake. The United States may launch missiles at a suspected terrorist base and claim it is defending national interests. Yet, it may condemn another country for doing the same thing in another part of the world. Dual standards and contradictions lead to confusion any time the term *terrorism* is employed.

The term *terrorism* has spawned heated debate. Instead of agreeing on the definition of terrorism, social scientists, policymakers, lawyers, and security specialists often argue about the meaning of the term. H. H. A. Cooper (1978, 2001), a renowned terrorist expert from the University of Texas at Dallas, aptly summarizes the problem. There is, Cooper says, "a problem in the problem definition." We can agree that terrorism is a problem, but we cannot agree on what terrorism is.

There are several reasons for confusion. First, terrorism is difficult to define because it has a pejorative connotation. (Pejorative means that it is emotionally charged.) A person is politically and socially degraded when labeled a terrorist, and the same thing happens when an organization is called a terrorist group. Routine crimes assume greater social importance when they are described as terrorism, and political movements can be hampered when their followers are believed to be terrorists.

Further confusion arises when people intertwine the terms *terror* and *terrorism.* The object of military force, for example, is to strike terror into the heart of the enemy, and systematic terror has been a basic weapon in conflicts throughout history. Some people argue that there is no difference between military force and terrorism. Many members of the antinuclear movement have extended this argument by claiming that maintaining ready-to-use nuclear weapons is an extension of terrorism. Others use the same logic when claiming that street gangs and criminals terrorize neighborhoods. If you think that anything that creates terror is terrorism, the scope of potential definitions becomes limitless.

One of the primary reasons terrorism is difficult to define is that the meaning changes within social and historical contexts. This is not to suggest that "one person's terrorist is another person's freedom fighter," but it does suggest the meaning fluctuates. Change in the meaning occurs because terrorism is not a solid entity. Like crime, it is socially defined, and the meaning changes with social change.

This chapter examines some common definitions of terrorism. These definitions are worth reviewing, but it is more important to understand that definitions of terrorism are not very helpful. You need to understand the context of the definition before applying the term. The definition of terrorism always changes with social and historical circumstances. As a result, terrorism presents a problem. Akin to the Supreme Court's definition of pornography, we do not know how to define terrorism, but we know what it is when we see it. It seems that H. H. A. Cooper is indeed correct. We have a problem in the problem definition.

Some Common Contexts of Terrorism

Before reviewing definitions of terrorism, it is helpful to examine the meaning of terrorism within specific frameworks. It is more helpful to list the context of terrorism than to memorize a variety of definitions. The following are some contextual issues to consider.

History   The meaning of terrorism has changed over time. It is almost impossible to talk about terrorism without discussing the historical context of the terrorist campaign. This is so important that the second part of the text is designed to familiarize you with historical developments in world history.

Modern terrorism originated from the French Revolution (1789–1795). It was used as a term to describe the actions of the French government. By 1848, the meaning of the term changed. It was employed to describe violent revolutionaries who revolted against governments. By the end of the 1800s and early 1900s, terrorism was used to describe the violent activities of a number of groups including: labor organizations, anarchists, nationalist groups revolting against foreign powers, and ultranationalist political organizations.

After World War II (1939–1945), the meaning changed again. As people revolted from European domination of the world, nationalistic groups were deemed to be terrorist groups. From about 1964 to the early 1980s, the term *terrorism* was also applied to violent left-wing groups, as well as nationalists. In the mid-1980s, the meaning changed again. In the United States, some of the violent activity of the hate movement was defined as terrorism. Internationally, terrorism was viewed as subnational warfare. Terrorists were sponsored by rogue regimes.

As the millennium changed, the definitions of terrorism also changed. Today terrorism also refers to large groups who are independent from a state, violent religious fanatics, and violent groups who terrorize for a particular cause such as the environment. It is important to realize that any definition is influenced by the historical context of terrorism.

Conflict   The meaning of terrorism fluctuates around various types of war. In times of conventional war, armies use commando tactics that look very much like terrorism. In the American Civil War, the Federal Army unleashed Major John Anderson to destroy Confederate railroads. The Confederates captured Anderson and accused him of being a spy, but he remained a hero in the North. He did not wear a uniform, and he did not fight by the accepted norm.

Armies routinely use such tactics in times of war and never define their actions as terrorism.

In guerrilla war, guerrillas use terrorist tactics against their enemies and may terrorize their supporters into submission. In total war, air forces may destroy entire cities with fire. The German Air Force (*Luftwaffe*) did so at Stalingrad in 1942, and the British and American Air Forces did the same at Dresden in 1945. Neither side believed it was practicing terrorism. While it is possible to cite many other examples and endless contradictions, you should realize that the definition of terrorism changes with the nature of conflict. The term *terrorism* is more likely to be employed to describe violent activity that explodes during a peaceful period.

Political Power   The definition of terrorism depends on political power. Governments can increase their power when they label opponents as "terrorists." Citizens seem willing to accept more abuses of governmental power when a counterterrorist campaign is in progress. "Terrorists" do not enjoy the same humanitarian privileges as "people." In the public mind, illegal arrest and sometimes even torture and murder are acceptable methods for dealing with terrorists. Labeling can have deadly results.

Repression   Closely related to the issue of power is the concept of repression. Some governments routinely use terrorism to keep their citizens in line. Such repression can sometimes be seen in the political structure of the country as leaders use secret police forces to maintain power. Joseph Stalin (1879–1953) ruled the Soviet Union from 1924 to 1953 through terror, and Saddam Hussein rules Iraq by similar methods. Latin America has witnessed several rulers who maintain power through repression, many times with help from the United States. Repression can also develop outside formal political structures. This is called *extrajuridical* repression. It refers to repressive groups who terrorize others into certain forms of behavior. Political repression is a form of terrorism, but people seldom refer to this form of violence when defining terrorism.

Media   Journalists and television reporters frequently use the term *terrorism* to define political violence. However, there is no consistent standard guiding them in the application of the definition. Many times they employ the term to attract attention to a story. Terrorism, when defined by the media, is relatively meaningless.

Crime   You might think that criminals and terrorists represent two different types of violent behavior. Some analysts would agree, but confusion remains. A few years ago, a Presidential Commission on criminal justice stated that it was necessary to look at the motivation of a criminal act to determine whether it was a terrorist action (National Advisory Committee on Criminal Justice Standards and Goals, 1976). When a crime is politically motivated, the report says it is terrorism. The problem with this approach is that a crime is a crime no matter what motivation lies behind the action. Except in times of conflict or government repression, all terrorism involves criminal activity. Even in the United States, the Federal Bureau of Investigation does not file most political crimes under the heading of terrorism in its *Uniform Crime Reports.*

Religion In recent years, religion has played a more significant role in the process of terrorism. This is fully examined in Chapter 4, but it is important to understand that extreme religious beliefs provide a context for defining terrorism. Religious violence centers around three sources (White, 2000). First, some religious groups feel they must purify the world for a new epoch. This can be defined as *violent eschatology*. Second, some groups feel they are chosen and may destroy other people in the cause of righteousness. This type of attitude can lead to violent intolerance and religious war. Finally, other people may become so consumed with a particular cause that they create a surrogate religion and take violent action to advance their beliefs. Ecological terrorists serve as an example of this type of pseudoreligious terrorism.

Specific Forms Sometimes the term *terrorism* is defined within a specific context. A detailed look at weapons of mass destruction is presented later in this book under the heading of *technological terrorism*. Another specific form of terrorism refers to computer attacks, viruses, or destruction of an information infrastructure. This is called *cyberterrorism*. Finally, drug organizations frequently use terrorist tactics, and some terrorist organizations sell drugs to support their political activities. Some analysts use the term *narcoterrorism* to describe this type of violence. Retired FBI counterterrorist specialist William Dyson (2000, in press) argues these issues are not separate forms of terrorism. Rather, they are modes of attack used by political terrorists.

Changing Contexts

Can you think of other contextual factors that influence the definition of terrorism? The list is probably endless. Regardless, it is enough to be aware that the definition of terrorism changes with political and social contexts. Terrorist analyst Alex Schmid (1983) says no matter how we define terrorism, the definition will always fluctuate because the context of violent activity changes. We cannot define terrorism. With that weakness in mind, it is time to look at some of the more popular definitions.

SOME COMMON DEFINITIONS

The most widely used definition in criminal justice, military, and security circles is a rather simple view fostered by Brian Jenkins, a widely known counterterrorist security specialist, and Walter Laqueur, another leading authority from Georgetown University. They defined terrorism separately but arrived at remarkably similar conclusions.

Jenkins offers a definition he has frequently used while consulting with security forces. Jenkins (1984) calls terrorism the use or threatened use of force designed to bring about a political change. In a definition closely related to that of Jenkins, Laqueur (1987, p. 72) says terrorism constitutes the illegitimate use of force to achieve a political objective by targeting innocent people. He adds that attempts to move beyond the simple definition are fruitless because the term is so controversial. Volumes can be written on the definition of terrorism, Laqueur writes in a footnote, but they will not add one iota to our understanding of the topic. In a later work, Laqueur (1999, pp. 8–10) promotes a simple definition, only arguing that meanings and definitions fluctuate with history.

Both Jenkins and Laqueur freely admit problems with their simple approach. Neither definition limits the topic, and there is no meaningful way to apply a simple definition to specific acts of terrorism. Simple definitions also leave academicians, policymakers, and social scientists frustrated. In short, simplicity does not solve the problem presented by Professor Cooper.

Yet, Laqueur intimates, it is necessary to live with the problems and weaknesses of the simple definition because terrorism will always mean different things to different people. With this in mind, examine the positions of Laqueur and Jenkins. From a security perspective, Laqueur's conclusion makes sense: terrorism is a form of political or criminal violence using military tactics to change behavior through fear. This simple approach does not solve the political problems of definition, but it allows security personnel to move beyond endless debates. Anyone charged with counterterrorism is trying to prevent military-style criminal attacks against innocent people in a noncombat area.

But definitions hardly stop with pragmatic simplicity. Germany, the United Kingdom, and Spain outlawed terrorism more than a decade ago, and America has examined the idea of a legal definition (Mullendore & White, 1996). The beauty of legal definitions is they give governments specific crimes that can be used to take action against terrorist activities. Beyond that, they are quite useless because they account for neither the social nor the political nature of terrorism. More important, they can be misused. Violence is the result of complex social factors that range beyond narrow legal limitations and foreign policy restrictions. Political violence often occurs during the struggle for legitimacy. For example, American patriots fought the British before the United States government was recognized.

Legal definitions also contain internal contradictions. Under the legal guidelines of the United States, for example, *some groups can be labeled as terrorists, while other groups engaged in the same activities may be described as legitimate revolutionaries.* In addition, governments friendly to the United States in Latin America have committed some of the worst atrocities in the history of the world in the name of counterterrorism. Ironically, some Latin American revolutionaries who oppose our repressive friends espouse the rights expressed in the U.S. Declaration of Independence and Constitution, yet we refer to them as terrorists. Legal definitions are frequently shortsighted.

Martha Crenshaw (1983) says terrorism cannot be defined unless the act, target, and possibility of success are analyzed. Under this approach, freedom fighters use legitimate military methods to attack legitimate political targets. Their actions are further legitimized when they have some possibility of winning the conflict. Terrorists fail to meet the legitimacy test in one of the three categories: military methods, military targets, and some chance of victory.

Crenshaw also suggests revolutionary violence should not be confused with terrorism. To Crenshaw, terrorism means socially and politically unacceptable violence aimed at an innocent target to achieve a psychological effect. Such analytical distinctions have helped make Crenshaw a leading authority on terrorism, but two problems remain. Whoever has the political power to define "legitimacy" has the power to define terrorism. In addition, the analytical definition has not moved far from the simple definition.

During the Reagan administration (1981–1989), it became popular to define terrorism in terms of national policy. Analysts pointed to terrorist states that used terrorism to attack American interests. Neil Livingstone (Livingstone & Arnold, 1986, pp. 1–10) lists five powers that served as the former Soviet Union's client states. Former Israeli Prime Minister Benjamin Netanyahu (1986, pp. 5–15) called the West to arms against the terrorist states. If you accept this logic, it solves the definitional dilemma. Terrorists were shadow warriors from Libya, Syria, Bulgaria, East Germany, and North Korea under the command of the former Soviet Union's Bureau of State Security (KGB).

However, the state-sponsored definition fell on hard times, even before the collapse of the Communist empire. James Adams (1986) thoroughly demonstrates that terrorist groups are not and never were controlled by sponsor states. Michael Stohl (1988, pp. 1–28) sounds another caveat. Some terrorist states did indeed offer logistical support and sympathy to terrorist groups, but their overall impact was insignificant. When the Soviet Union collapsed, the arguments of state sponsorship dwindled. Although some terrorists hiding in East Europe were arrested (the East Germans turned over names and addresses of the Red Army Faction to the new German federal police, for example), the nature of terrorism shifted in the last part of the twentieth century. Terrorism is too complex and too significant to be controlled by nation-states.

A different definition comes from Edward Herman (1983), who says terrorism should be defined in terms of state repression. Citing corrupt Latin American governments, Herman argues that repressive policies have resulted in more misery for more people than any other form of state-sponsored terror. In a separate publication, Michael Stohl (1988, pp. 20–28) sounds a sympathetic note, claiming terrorism is most frequently used by governments to maintain power. Walter Laqueur (1987, p. 6) says such conclusions are correct, and one would be foolish to deny that state repression has caused less suffering than modern terrorism. Yet, Laqueur argues, governmental repression is a long-term political problem, separate from modern terrorism. To include it in the discussion confuses the issue and does little to enhance our understanding of terrorism.

In an effort to solve the definitional dilemma, Alex Schmid (1983, pp. 70–111) tries to synthesize various positions. He concludes there is no true or correct definition because terrorism is an abstract concept with no real presence. A single definition cannot possibly account for all the potential uses of the term. Still, Schmid says, a number of elements are common to leading definitions, and most definitions have two characteristics: someone is terrorized, and the meaning of the term is derived from terrorists' targets and victims.

Schmid also offers a conglomerated definition of terrorism. His empirical analysis finds 22 elements common to most definitions, and he develops a definition containing 13 of those elements. Schmid sees terrorism as a method of combat in which the victims serve as symbolic targets. Violent actors are able to produce a chronic state of fear by using violence outside the realm of normative behavior. This produces an audience beyond the immediate victim and results in a change of public attitudes and actions.

Some scholars believe Schmid has solved the definitional dilemma by combining definitions. Others think he has refined the undefinable. While analysts wrestle with the problem, most end up doing one of three things. Some follow the lead of Crenshaw and Thomas Thorton (1964, p. 73) and look for illegitimate violence instead of political revolution. Others follow the lead of Schmid, either synthesizing definitions or using those of others. Finally, some people ignore the problem altogether. They talk about terrorism and assume everybody knows what they mean.

See Box 1.1 for a summary of the common definitions of terrorism and Box 1.2 for a list of some official definitions that are used.

TYPOLOGIES OF TERRORISM

A typology is a classification system, and there are as many typologies of terrorism as there are definitions. Models, classification systems, and typologies, however, offer an alternative to definitions, and they have several advantages. First, the broad scope of the problem can be presented. Terrorism is composed of a variety of activities, not a singly defined action. A typology captures the range of terrorist activities better than most definitions. Second, the scope of the problem allows the level of the problem to be introduced. Terrorism can be local, national, or international in occurrence. A typology helps identify what *kind* of terrorism is to be examined. Third, when the level of terrorism is identified, the level of response can be determined. Finally, by focusing on types of violence and the social meanings of tactics, typologies avoid the heated debates about the meaning of terrorism.

Typologies are not a panacea, and they do not solve all the definitional dilemmas. First, the process of terrorism is in a constant state of change. Models, taxonomies, and typologies only describe patterns among events. They are generalizations that describe extremely unstable environments. Typologies may increase our understanding of terrorism, but each terrorist incident must be understood in its specific social, historical, and political circumstances.

BOX 1.1   Definition of Terrorism

Jenkins and Laqueur: Illegitimate force used against innocents for political purposes

Livingstone: Warfare on the cheap

Crenshaw: Politically illegitimate attacks on innocent targets

Herman: Government repression

Schmid: Combat against symbolic targets

Another weakness of typologies involves the distortion of reality. After developing a model, some people, including scholars, try to fit particular forms of terrorism into it. They alter what they see so that it will blend with their typology. This has been especially true regarding Latin America. Governments, journalists, teachers, and revolutionaries have developed ideological typologies for Latin America and then bent reality to fit their political views. Changing events to fit a pattern can completely distort reality. When this happens, researchers only see what they want to see. In addition, typologies hide details. They produce patterns, not specifics, even when they are correctly applied.

Peter Fleming, Michael Stohl, and Alex Schmid (1988, pp. 153–195) criticize the use of typologies to describe terrorism, claiming they reflect the biases of the researchers. Typologies also tend to compare variables that should not be compared in different incidents. To be usable, these researchers believe, typologies must account for a group's political motivation, origin, scope of action, and the focus of its attention. Fleming, Stohl, and Schmid are critical of typologies because none of them has attempted to provide in-depth political analysis.

If you assume that Fleming, Stohl, and Schmid are correct, you may reject the use of typologies; however, they can have limited benefit. Although they do not solve the definitional problems or provide a method for examining deep-seated political and social issues, they can be useful in the more limited role of tactically identifying a security problem. Some noted authorities have approached terrorism in this manner.

TOWARD A TACTICAL TYPOLOGY
OF TERRORISM

Although this is not an optimistic thought, a simple assumption will help you understand terrorism. Humans live in a constant state of conflict. Indeed, it is impossible to have a human social organization without conflict. Even in the most peaceful community, social organization is maintained because the controlling group can force people to join the organization and force members to obey the organization's rules. The amount of force is subject to limitation, but

---

BOX 1.2   Official Definitions of Terrorism

Even governmental bodies have several definitions of terrorism.

State Department: Title 22 of the *United States Code* section 2656f(d) contains the following definitions: The term "terrorism" means premeditated, politically motivated violence perpetrated against noncombatant targets by sub-national groups or clandestine agents, usually intended to influence an audience. The term "international terrorism" means terrorism involving citizens or the territory of more than one country. The term "terrorist group" means any group practicing, or that has significant subgroups that practice, international terrorism.

SOURCE: *1999 Patterns of Terrorism.*

FBI: The FBI defines terrorism as "the unlawful use of force or violence against persons or property to intimidate or coerce a Government, the civilian population, or any segment thereof, in furtherance of political or social objectives." The FBI further describes terrorism as either domestic or international, depending on the origin, base, and objectives of the terrorist organization.

SOURCE: http://www.fbi.gov/publish/terror/terrusa.html.

Vice President's Task Force: Terrorism is the unlawful use or threat of violence against persons or property to further political or social objectives. It is usually intended to intimidate or coerce a government, individuals or groups, or to modify their behavior or politics.

SOURCE: Vice President's Task Force, 1986.

United Nations: A TERRORIST is any person who, acting independently of the specific recognition of a country, or as a single person, or as part of a group not recognized as an official part or division of a nation, acts to destroy or to injure civilians or destroy or damage property belonging to civilians or to governments in order to effect some political goal. TERRORISM is the act of destroying or injuring civilian lives or the act of destroying or damaging civilian or government property without the expressly chartered permission of a specific government, thus, by individuals or groups acting independently or governments on their own accord and belief, in the attempt to effect some political goal.

SOURCE: http://www.inlink.com/~civitas/mun/res9596/terror.html.

Defense Department: Terrorism is the unlawful use or threatened use of force or violence against individuals or property to coerce or intimidate governments or societies, often to achieve political, religious, or ideological objectives.

SOURCE: http://www.periscope.usni.com/demo/terms/t0000282.html.

Defense Intelligence Agency: Terrorism is premeditated, political violence perpetrated against noncombatant targets by subnational groups or clandestine state agents, usually to influence an audience.

SOURCE: http://www.periscope.usni.com/demo/terms/t0000282.html.

---

the ability to coerce is real. Therefore, social organizations are never truly "at peace"; they are always "at war." The amount and level of conflict varies, but conflict is normative.

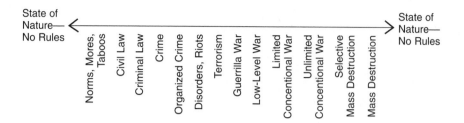

FIGURE 1.1 Spectrum of Conflict

If you accept this assumption, you will be able to understand terrorism. To illustrate this, consider a concept developed by the U.S. Army in the early 1970s. After the Vietnam War, the Army realized its mission was changing and it had to be prepared to fight any number of different styles of war. Conflict could range from low-level brushfire wars to nuclear devastation, and the meaning of war was nebulous at best. To clarify this situation, the U.S. Army spoke of a spectrum of conflict (see Figure 1.1). The spectrum was a continuum that ranged from low-intensity conflict to full-scale war. This scale probably more correctly reflects the human condition than the belief that we can either be at war or at peace. It also helps us understand terrorism.

Because humans live in a perpetual state of conflict and conflict management, civil coercive power has a place on the spectrum of conflict. Even before conflict rises to a military level, civil authorities routinely face challenges that must be met by implied or direct force. At the lowest level of organization, informal norms and mores enforce compliance, and if they fail, stronger coercive force is applied. In modern Western society, this may be civil or criminal law, whereas a more passive social group might use expulsion or shunning. Regardless, social groups always have the potential to exhibit coercive force to enforce behavior.

Terrorism is a form of violent civil disobedience, and it can be placed on a spectrum of conflict. At the most basic governmental level, the state faces low-level challenges with ordinary crime. This increases with group violence, then rioting and wider disorders, and finally terrorism. At this point, military options may be employed as the continuum moves to guerrilla war, low-level war, conventional war, technological war, wars of ecological destruction, and wars of oblivion.

Ethicists may correctly argue that we must always move to minimal conflict by using the least amount of force, but morality is not the issue here. What you should be able to see from the simple model is that terrorism is simply a form of conflict among social organizations that accept conflict as normal. There is nothing mystical about terrorism. It is simply a form of conflict between civil disorders and guerrilla warfare. If it is a form of conflict, its tactics can be modeled.

Over the past few years, I have used a typology to train military and police personnel in counterterrorism (Figure 1.2). It does not solve any definitional problems, but police and military officers have told me that it has helped them conceptualize their counterterrorist mission. This tactical typology may help you understand the issues involved in responding to terrorism.

The three parallel lines in the model symbolize three different measures that roughly correlate with each other. The first measure shows the level of activity. It is fairly simple to grasp: incidents on the low end equal low activity, whereas the high end represents increasing rates of violence. The second line represents the type of activity. The line itself indicates the size of the terrorist group. On the extreme left, directly correlated with low activity on the activity continuum, is a single individual. Size increases as you move to the right. This brings the first rule of thumb. In terrorism, the level of activity is generally correlated with the size of the group. Generally, *the larger the group, the greater its potential for terrorist violence.*

Notice that the second line is divided by a nebulous border separating criminal and political terrorism. This border is intentionally open because terrorists are free to move between the criminal and political boundaries. The openness is designed to illustrate the movement of political violence. Some criminal groups can become so large that they may act like terrorist groups. Small terrorist groups can become so focused on crime that they become nothing more than criminal gangs. Examples of these types of groups appear underneath the line.

The final continuum illustrates the type of response. Most criminal terrorism and a good share of political terrorism is a law enforcement responsibility. This means that when nonpolice units assist police agencies as part of a security force, they must think as the police do. For example, deadly force is always the last alternative in police operations. Additionally, legal procedures and an emphasis on individual rights guide each phase of a law enforcement response and investigation.

As you move across the continuum, however, response actions become more militaristic. Although deadly force remains the final option, law enforcement personnel must think of themselves as a team, much as the military does. The courts may allow certain amounts of latitude in procedures, such as internment in Northern Ireland, in the interest of public safety. Teamwork, however, does not imply an ability to operate outside legal norms. Despite the necessity to develop certain military tactics or employ the direct help of the military, extrajuridical activities cannot be tolerated. For example, police and military units of some countries have formed secret death squads, claiming terrorists have become too strong. If legal norms are violated, security forces can become little more than terrorists themselves.

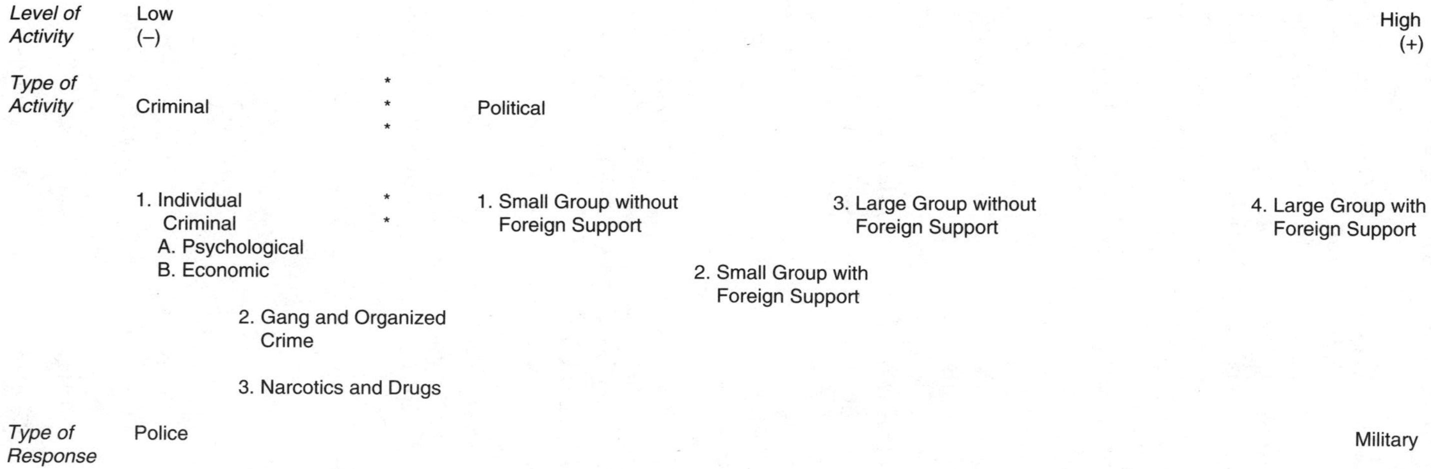

Level of Activity	Low (−)				High (+)
Type of Activity	Criminal		Political		
	*	*			
	*	*			
	*	*			

	1. Individual Criminal
	   A. Psychological
	   B. Economic
		*	1. Small Group without Foreign Support	3. Large Group without Foreign Support	4. Large Group with Foreign Support

		*			
	2. Gang and Organized Crime		2. Small Group with Foreign Support		
	3. Narcotics and Drugs				
Type of Response	Police				Military

FIGURE 1.2 Tactical Typology of Terrorism

THE TACTICS OF TERRORISM

The tactical typology is simply a verbal model to help in conceptualizing the state of terrorism. Yet, the practice of terrorism is not as stable as the loosely correlated model indicates. Brian Jenkins (1985) explains why. Traditionally, Jenkins says, there are six terrorist tactics: bombing, hijacking, arson, assault, kidnapping, and taking hostages. As religious fanaticism has grown in the past few years, the arsenal of terrorism has changed to include potential threats from weapons of mass destruction (Jenkins, 1996; Brackett, 1996, p. 45; White, 1986b, 2000). Yet, even religious terrorists use traditional terrorist tactics. The only addition to Jenkins's categories can be found in the realm of technology. In the age of information and electronics, disruption of services through electronic hacking has also become a tactic of terrorism.

Technology has another impact on terrorism. Jenkins calls this influence "force multipliers" (see Box 1.3). In military terms, a force multiplier increases striking power without increasing the strength of a unit. Terrorists routinely use force multipliers because it adds to their aura. All political terrorists and some criminal terrorists want to give the illusion that they can fight on another level. They want to move to guerrilla or conventional war, although they almost never do so.

Three force multipliers give the illusion that terrorists operate on a higher level. Christine Ketcham and Harvey McGeorge (1986, pp. 25–33) identify the first force multiplier as technology. The use of technological weapons or attacks on technological targets gives the illusion of a high level of activity. James Adams's (1986) analysis of finances in terrorism illustrates the second force multiplier: transnational support. Any group with the ability to cross national borders can operate on a higher level. Another force multiplier is the media. One incident can be converted into a "campaign" as live electronic media scramble to break the latest news. A frightening new force multiplier, according to Bruce Hoffman (1995), has been the introduction of religious fanaticism in terrorist activities. This has become so important that Chapter 4 will focus exclusively on violent religious behavior. Regardless of the source, force multipliers allow small groups or individuals to operate as if they were a larger group.

GUIDE TO THE KEY CONCEPTS

1. Terrorism is defined within social and political contexts. This is the primary reason that no single definition of terrorism will ever be successful.

2. In terms of contextual definitions, the meaning of terrorism is influenced by history, conflict, political power, political repression, mass media, crime, and the specific form that terrorism takes.

3. Since the meaning of terrorism fluctuates, a simple definition is probably the best course of action.

BOX 1.3 Force Multipliers in Terrorism

Rule of thumb: The larger the group, the larger its level of activity.

Exceptions—Force Multipliers
1. Technology
2. Transnational support
3. Media
4. Religion

Technology
Weapons enhancement allows a small group to operate on a higher level. Terrorists may use technology in their attack or attack a technological target. The two newest threats are cyberterrorism and weapons of mass destruction.

Transnational Support
Groups and individuals operating with foreign support bases may have a higher level of activity.

Media
Coverage can enhance the aura of the event. Many terrorist events are "made-for-TV" dramas. Twenty-four-hour news coverage leads to sensationalist fillers.

Religion
Religious fanaticism has changed the structure of modern terrorism. Religious terrorists are not constrained by social norms because they feel they answer to a higher power.

---

4. It is best to look at terrorism from a tactical standpoint, if you are focusing on security. Terrorism is simply a method of fighting. It terrorizes the public because violence is centered on places where people feel safe.

5. Tactically, terrorism has basic forms. These include: bombing, arson, hijacking, assault, kidnapping, taking hostages, and disruption of services.

6. Terrorists use force multipliers to increase their attacking power. Force multipliers include technology, transnational support, media coverage, and religious fanaticism.

FOOD FOR THOUGHT

Think about the last time you saw a television report on a terrorist event. What went through your mind? If the context of the event changed, would you have viewed it differently? If you had a definition of terrorism, would it have changed your view of the event? Does the event you recall fit only the tactical typology? If not, is there another system that would allow you to classify the act? What tactic did the terrorist(s) use? Did force multipliers play a role?

FURTHER READING

Walter Laqueur, *The New Terrorism*
Bruce Hoffman, *Inside Terrorism*

2

Individual and Group Behavior

This chapter focuses on some of the criminological aspects of terrorism. Terrorists have the same social and psychological motivations of all other people, and they tend to behave in predictable manners. Experienced hostage negotiators are keenly aware of the human needs and fears in even the most hardened terrorists. Yet, terrorists also behave differently than mainstream criminals. Terrorists place a greater emphasis on some of the factors that motivate normal behavior. For example, politics and religion are more important to many terrorists than they are to most people. In addition, the techniques that work against common criminality may not work against terrorists. Police officers cannot apprehend terrorists by using standard investigation and arrest procedures. Finally, terrorists must be able to justify their actions, at least to their own satisfaction. Since they have no legitimate social structure such as a nation-state or an official organization, the role of group support and the group's belief system become extremely important in understanding terrorist behavior.

After reading this chapter, you should be able to:

1. List the differences between the behavior of ordinary criminals and terrorists.
2. Discuss the importance of group reinforcement in terrorist behavior.
3. Summarize Cooper's "doctrine of necessity."
4. Describe a practical view of individual psychological profiles used in law enforcement.

5. Summarize Laqueur's argument against psychological profiles.
6. Explain Ross's structural and psychological model of terrorism.
7. Discuss the roles of youth, religion, and ideology in characterizing and justifying terrorism.
8. Describe the means-to-an-end argument and its relation to terrorism.
9. Explain the meaning of Gibson's American paramilitary culture.

TERRORISTS AND ORDINARY CRIMINALS

There are two "types" of criminology in the practical world of criminal justice. When using the word *criminology* in an academic setting, images of psychological and sociological theories appear in the minds of researchers and teachers. This is classic criminology, tracing its origins to Cesare Beccaria and working to the most modern theories of individual and group behavior. When the word is mentioned in a law enforcement agency, another image appears. Practical criminology focuses on the common actions of lawbreakers. Police officers are not as concerned with theories of criminality as they are with the practical aspects of criminal behavior. They want to know what criminals do so that they may deter them from a crime or catch them after the crime is committed.

The purpose here is to consider this second use of criminology, the applied actions in crime prevention and apprehension. This is important because terrorists commit crimes as they struggle for a cause, but they differ from ordinary street criminals. Law enforcement personnel must recognize the differences between typical criminal behavior and terrorist activity if they want to prevent crime and apprehend criminals. Terrorists have organizational structures, belief systems, and motivational values that separate them from ordinary criminals. Law enforcement officials are frequently the first government agents on the scene of a terrorist incident. If they fail to recognize that the scene may be something more than an ordinary crime, they may well miss the point of the investigation.

For example, a terrorist group bombed New York City's World Trade Center in 1993. Their purpose was to spread cyanide gas throughout the area and topple the skyscraper into other buildings, causing them to tumble like dominoes. Fortunately, the plot failed, and the bomb caused minimal damage and death. According to Steven Emerson (1994), when the police first began investigating the incident, they handled it like a typical crime. Even after they classified it as terrorism, they limited the scope of the investigation to a small group. Some months later, law enforcement officials and prosecutors were embarrassed to find they had stumbled on an international terrorist organization with an extensive religious ideology and a worldwide support network. They had the evidence shortly after the investigation began, but Emerson says they overlooked it. How could this happen? They handled the crime as an isolated incident.

In another example, ask yourself if malicious destruction of property is a simple misdemeanor or a felony? If someone breaks into a farm, destroys cages, and frees the animals, should this simply be reported as typical malicious destruction? Many law enforcement officers would answer yes, but you should consider the Animal Liberation Front (ALF) (www.nocompromise.org/alf/alf.html). In instructions to members and sympathizers, the ALF advocates the systematic destruction of farms that produce fur for clothing. Their Web page gives potential recruits tactics for the most effective destruction of mink farms. If a deputy sheriff or state trooper happens on such an attack, it will probably be classified as malicious destruction of property even though it may well be part of a larger operation.

To counter such tendencies in law enforcement, the Federal Bureau of Investigation has created localized terrorism task forces around the country. In theory, this allows the FBI to coordinate law enforcement resources in the face of domestic terrorism and to expand investigations. Internationally, the FBI also provides investigative resources when Americans are victimized by terrorism in other countries. Yet, the fact remains that individual patrol officers are usually the first people to arrive on the scene of a terrorist incident. They must recognize the traits of terrorism to begin the investigation. Terrorist investigations do not follow the pattern of most criminal investigations because terrorists seldom behave like normative street criminals.

Douglas Bodrero, the former Commissioner for the Department of Public Safety in Utah and former member of the International Association of Chiefs of Police Committee on Terrorism, offers a comparative analysis between terrorist behavior and that of ordinary criminals. Bodrero (2000) argues that typical criminals are opportunistic. This means that criminals tend to be impulsive. Most street criminals do not plan their crimes extensively, and they react to easy opportunities on the spur of the moment. Criminals are usually uncommitted. Even career criminals do not believe in crime as an ideology or religion. Crime is just a method for obtaining goods. Because of this lifestyle, criminals tend to be self-centered and undisciplined. Except for a small proportion of career criminals, ordinary street criminals are untrained. Their goal is to obtain cash or goods and get away.

Bodrero and most police officers base crime prevention and apprehension strategies on the assumptions about street criminals for one simple reason. They work. By hardening targets, denying opportunity, and conducting aggressive patrol, many ordinary street crimes like burglary can be suppressed (Harris, 1998). In addition, efforts to make the police an extension of the community can be utilized to reduce crimes that seem to defy suppression such as domestic violence (Trojanowicz et al., 1998). By using criminal intelligence files to keep track of known felons, criminal associations, and crime patterns, police suppress criminal activity. Police search for hangouts of local criminals, they know their friends and family, and they maintain sources of information about suspicious activity. These procedures not only serve as the basis of community policing, but they are also the essence of criminal investigation.

Bodrero (2000) says terrorist behavior differs from standard patterns of criminal behavior because terrorists are highly motivated and loyal to a particular cause. While ordinary criminals are opportunistic, terrorists are focused. They may select targets of opportunity, but the target has a symbolic value. Terrorists use crime to make a symbolic statement about a political cause.

For example, in August 1998, a group known as al-Qaeda or "The Base" destroyed two American embassies in Kenya and Tanzania. Osama bin Ladin, the leader of the group, chose the targets because they represented the best opportunity to strike America. Two items made the embassies attractive to bin Ladin. The compounds were close to his base of support, and he was able to control the terrorists more effectively by maintaining communication with his headquarters. Even though bin Ladin struck targets of opportunity, he did not behave like a typical criminal. He did not simply walk past the embassies and bomb them on the spur of the moment. He planned the attack in an area where he was relatively strong and America was correspondingly weak. This is not the way a criminal behaves.

If criminals are uncommitted and self-centered, terrorists find strength in a cause and the ideology or religion behind the cause. They are team-oriented, even when they act as individuals. For example, Taheri (1987) notes the preparation of suicide bombers. Suicide bombing has been employed by several Middle Eastern groups in their strikes against Israel. Tehari finds young people are systematically isolated and prepared for a suicide mission. Suicide bombers do not act alone. They are supported by an organization and sent on a mission. Being part of something greater than themselves becomes the basis for action. In another variation, some terrorists seem to be acting alone. More recent work (Schweitzer, 2000) indicates that this trend continues.

Ideology and religion are not limited to suicide bombers; they also influence individuals who will become terrorists for a single event. For example, Buford Furrow entered a Jewish day care center in August 1999 and began shooting people. He was a "lone wolf," or what is called a "berserker" (see Chapter 3). He had no extensive logistical network or support organization. Yet, Furrow was consumed by an ideology of hate and a religion that demonized Jews. He was not an uncommitted opportunistic criminal acting alone. He was an agent of an ideology on a divine mission. Again, as Bodrero (2000) indicates, this is not the pattern of typical criminals.

Bodrero says that criminals are undisciplined, untrained, and oriented toward escape. Terrorists are exactly the opposite. They have prepared for their mission, they are willing to take risks, and they are attack-oriented. Another example illustrates Bodrero's point. Sri Lanka has been plagued with a terrorist campaign since 1974. The Liberation Tigers of Tamil Elaam (LTTE), or the Tamil Tigers (see Chapter 3), are a fighting force of approximately 10,000 members. They run a training wing, ground force, and small navy. Their primary tactic is terrorism, and they are known for suicide bombings. In January 2000, a suicide bomber killed 13 people outside of the Sri Lankan prime minister's office. This was not an act of typical criminality. Like Osama bin Ladin's attacks in Africa, it involved training, discipline, and sacrifice. The suicide terrorism of the Tamil Tigers cannot be investigated as a typical suicide-murder. It results from preparation and training in a paramilitary organization.

The significance of Bodrero's (2000) argument can be measured in the investigative response to terrorism. When investigating a crime, police officers can take advantage of the behavioral characteristics of typical criminals. The most hardened criminals will usually act in their own self-interest, and they will make deals to receive a lesser sentence. When searching for a fleeing felon, law enforcement officers are usually successful when questioning known associates and keeping family and friends under surveillance. These tactics do not work in countering terrorism. (See Box 2.1.) Law enforcement, military, and security officials need to focus on ideology, group and individual behavior, and sharing information over broad geographical regions to successfully investigate terrorism.

GROUP REINFORCEMENT
AND THE JUSTIFICATION OF TERRORISM

Every person who uses force must seek to justify it. As the amount of force increases, the need to justify it becomes greater. Deadly force demands the greatest amount of justification. When a person threatens to kill or kills another person, he or she must feel it was right to do so. Executioners cannot cross-examine themselves if they want to do the job.

When a person engages in violent activity on the state's behalf, the government unveils its most sacred symbols and rituals to reward the person. Warriors need such rewards. Terrorists have the same need for social approval, but they rarely obtain it because their actions are not sanctioned by the governments they attack. They are routinely condemned by the population at large. Even when citizens approve of the cause associated with terrorism, they are reluctant to embrace and endorse the methods of mayhem. Terrorists must, therefore, look outside normative social channels to gain approval for their acts.

The terrorist group becomes the primary source of social reality for individual terrorists. It provides social recognition and reinforcement for its members. Like soldiers, who undergo a similar bonding process during basic training, potential terrorists join groups for varied reasons: they may be sympathetic to the cause, or they may simply be social misfits. The terrorist group reshapes identities and provides a ticket to social acceptance.

For social acceptance to work, however, the terrorist group must be isolated from mainstream society. Richard Cloward and Lloyd Ohlin's (1960) study of American urban youth gangs provides an analogy. The gang is a self-referential group in a world gone awry. By rejecting the norms of the urban environment, the gang is free to create its own norms. Israel's experience with Arab suicide bombers has shown that terrorists go through the same process. A terrorist must be isolated before beginning a mission, only interacting with

---

BOX 2.1   Differences in Typical Street Criminals and Terrorists

Typical Criminal	Terrorist
Crimes of opportunity	Fighting for political objective
Uncommitted	Motivated by ideology or religion
Self-centered	Group-focused—even berserkers or lone wolves
No cause	Consumed with purpose
Untrained	Trained and motivated for the mission
Escape-oriented	On the attack

SOURCE: Bodrero (2000).

---

others directly involved in the mission. During this period, the terrorist is constantly indoctrinated in the importance of the mission and reminded that the goal is more important than human life. Suicidal terrorists are often identified and housed together so that they can continue reinforcing each other. Like gang members, terrorists must enter a world of their own reality.

Paul Wilkinson (1974, pp. 23–25) says terrorist groups reinforce individual loyalty through the process of justification. They may argue that terrorism is a just revenge for social evils or that it is a lesser evil than the exercise of government power. Terrorism is also often justified as being the only course of action available. Regardless of the argument used, Wilkinson demonstrates, the terrorist group must develop its own parameters of ethical normalcy and go through a process of moral justification.

Jerrold Post (1987) compares the process of justification with group dynamics inside terrorist organizations. Post's research was designed to measure the effects of retaliation on terrorist groups. Some politicians have argued that terrorists can be stopped only when they know they will be repaid harshly for every act of violence. This is a politically popular deterrence argument, similar to one criminological school's insistence that swift and sure punishment deters crime. Post is not convinced such an argument is applicable to modern terrorism.

Post believes there is no single terrorist personality but that terrorists do follow similar behavioral patterns. The most important pattern has to do with group and individual acceptance. Terrorist groups are very much like criminal groups in having been rejected by mainstream society. The group becomes the only source of social reward because of its members' isolation. Terrorists reinforce one another. Post says this pattern holds true across cultures.

The individuals who are attracted to terrorist groups are as much outcasts as the organizations they seek to join. According to Post, terrorists are usually people who have been rejected by mainstream society and who fall in with like-minded individuals. This observation not only explains group reinforcement in terrorist organizations, but also demonstrates the reason terrorist groups remain isolated. Individual members only find rewards within the group, so the desire to remain isolated is reinforced. Post believes this results in an us–against–them mentality.

The constant reinforcement of antisocial behavior in terrorist groups produces conforming behavior inside the organizations, with the exception of strong leaders who may splinter the group. When mainstream society is rejected, the individual's only hope of social acceptance lies in the group that rewards behavior. If the group rewards antisocial behavior, the fanatic is further motivated to attack the norm. According to Post, the rejection of external authority results in the acceptance of internal authority because behavior must be reinforced somewhere.

This set of dynamics is applicable to any group rejecting social norms. For example, a young religious person who joins a fundamentalist denomination might well experience the same set of dynamics. The person will be encouraged to reject the norm and turn to the new way of life within the denomination. The initiate can spurn outside behavioral reinforcement and norms because the group provides its own set of incentives. Religious conversion in this sense is psychologically similar to accepting the values of any deviant group.

Yet religious conversion does not usually lead to terrorism. In fact, it almost never does. Post (1987) says the key point for conversion in terrorist organizations is when the group shifts from violent rhetoric to action. Once the group engages in criminal activity, a distinct split with society occurs. The crimes required by terrorism become the final gestures of social rebellion. Crime both reinforces group isolation and increases the risk of leaving the group. In Post's analysis, criminal activity marks the true beginning of a terrorist group.

THE "DOCTRINE OF NECESSITY"
JUSTIFICATION

H. H. A. Cooper (1977b, pp. 8–18) describes the process terrorists must undergo to justify their actions. He believes terrorists are motivated by the same things that motivate all human behavior. They have dreams and aspirations similar to those who receive socially acceptable rewards for their behavior, but terrorists have a problem. They cannot accept the world as it is, and though many people would join them in the rejection of current norms, terrorists also reject the possibility of peaceful means for social change. This is why they become terrorists.

Cooper argues terrorists may abhor violence, almost to the point of rejecting it completely. Most do not relish the thought of indiscriminate violence and murder. Still, Cooper says, terrorists are driven by their utter hatred of the social status quo. According to Cooper, the first step in becoming a terrorist is the violent rejection of normative society.

Although terrorists may not enjoy violence or wish to adopt terrorist methods, they are forced toward violence. Cooper says they cross the line into terrorism when they come to believe that continuance of the status quo is worse than the violence caused by acts of terrorism. He refers to this decision point as the acceptance of the "doctrine of necessity."

According to Cooper's analysis, terrorists must feel they are forced to turn to violence. Violence becomes necessary because there is no other alternative for correcting the injustices of contemporary society. This attitude engenders an ideology or doctrine of violence. Once potential terrorists accept the doctrine, they are free to engage in terrorism. The group reinforces individual decisions, and a campaign of terrorism can be undertaken. A doctrine of necessary violence justifies acts of terrorism, and once it is accepted, refraining from violence becomes immoral.

TERRORIST PROFILES—A PRACTICAL VIEW

The late Frederick J. Hacker (1976), a physician who developed expertise in terrorism and hostage negotiation, found that terrorists seek reinforcement based on their orientation to life. He refers to three types of terrorists: criminals, crazies, and crusaders. The categories are not mutually exclusive; any terrorist group could contain a variety of these personality types. Critics have maintained that Hacker's approach is too simplistic.

Street criminals comprise the first segment of Hacker's typology. Although almost all terrorists use criminal means, Hacker argues that criminal terrorism is rare. When it does exist, criminals who terrorize society do so frequently for monetary gain or to seek some sort of vengeance. Organized criminals frequently terrorize entire groups of citizens for economic gain, but this does not usually involve disruptive acts of political terrorism. Therefore, organized crime cannot be classified as terrorism because criminals have a vested interest in the status quo. Criminals rarely turn to terrorism because there is little economic payoff. For most street criminals, terrorism is generally a spur-of-the-moment idea involving taking hostages.

"Crazies," Hacker's term for mentally unstable violent people, are motivated by a variety of factors, but they are seeking some sort of psychological reward through terrorism. They are not political terrorists, although they may be used by political organizations. They are motivated by the thrill of violence or the feeling of power they get while engaging in violence. Psychological gratification justifies their actions. Mass murderers and serial killers fit into this category. Charles Manson's murders in California are an example of this type of terrorism.

According to Hacker, crusaders make up the bulk of political terrorists. Hacker describes the category as people who are using terrorism to change society. They are most likely to believe in Cooper's doctrine of necessity:

violence is accepted and justified in the name of the cause. Crusaders feel they must be violent for society to change for the better.

Updated practical classification systems have expanded Hacker's original view. Many law enforcement agencies attempt to determine whether terrorist actions are the result of criminal or political activity or whether the action has resulted from someone with mental illness. They employ a variety of techniques and have become more sophisticated in using behavioral science against many forms of criminality (Turvey et al., 1999). Agencies also attempt to assess the level of potential threats, and violent political extremists usually represent the most dangerous threat.

A practical example of such classification systems comes from the United Kingdom. Police officials in the U.K. make practical decisions based on profiles of terrorists and the classification of each incident. When faced with an act of terrorism, the local ranking police official makes an assessment of the event. If it is classified as a criminal activity or the result of a mentally deranged individual, the local police commander handles the incident. If the commander deems the action to be the result of political terrorism, the central government is informed, and the incident is handled on the prime minister's level. In addition, if the level of the threat is sufficiently high, the matter may also be referred to the national government.

Although such profiling has practical applications in law enforcement, the larger question remains: Is it possible to profile the terrorist personality? Some critics believe it is impossible to develop a meaningful terrorist profile.

TERRORIST PROFILES—

AN UNPROMISING VIEW

Walter Laqueur (1999, pp. 79–104) says that no one can develop a composite picture of a terrorist because no such picture exists. Terrorism fluctuates over time, Laqueur argues, and the profile of terrorism changes with circumstances. There can be no terrorist mosaic because there are different types of terrorism. Laqueur says we can be sure that most terrorists are young, but their actions and psychological makeup vary according to social and cultural conditions.

I argue (White, 2000) that it is possible to discern some of the characteristics of terrorist groups. Groups tend to be small and led by a charismatic individual. Weaker personalities gravitate toward the leader and express their inadequacies through the charismatic's leadership. Almost all groups are centered around religion or quasi-religion, and they express their beliefs in fanatical ways. However, my research suggests individual personalities vary so greatly that it seems impossible to produce a single behavioral profile.

Jerrold Post (1987), a well-known psychological expert in the field of terrorism, reinforces Laqueur's points. According to Post, terrorists are true believers in every sense of the word, and they tend to congregate only with other true believers. This fanaticism gives groups internal power and allows them to take fanatical actions.

Post says the extremist atmosphere of terrorist groups produces absolutist rhetoric. There is no room for compromise, and every aspect of life is painted in shades of black or white. The world is divided into two camps, and the process of labeling enemies draws terrorists closer to their fellow true believers. The group expresses its absolutism in idealistic terms and comes to accept it. Post thinks this is the crucial point in understanding how far terrorist groups will go with violence and destruction. They may detest violence, but they firmly believe they are justified in using terrorism to change a world that threatens them.

Laqueur (1999) believes other group characteristics can be discerned through the type of movement. Nationalistic and separatist groups are aggressive, and their actions are painted in horrible violence. Such violence may or may not be the result of psychological inadequacies. In democracies, Laqueur says, terrorists tend to be elitists. Nationalist movements produce terrorists from the lower classes, while religious terrorists come from all classes. Individual and group profiles are the result of political and social conditions.

In the final analysis, Laqueur believes it is impossible to profile a terrorist personality because terrorism is not the subject of criminology. In the past, he says, perfectly normal individuals have opted to engage in terrorism as a rational political statement. Terrorism is a political phenomenon different from ordinary crime or psychopathology.

TERRORIST PROFILES—
A PROMISING VIEW

Jeffrey Ian Ross (1999, pp. 169–192) offers an alternative view. Rather than attempting to delineate an individual profile, Ross says it may be possible to conceptualize terrorism in a model that combines social structure with group psychology. He believes such a model is necessary for policymakers to develop better counterterrorist responses.

Ross believes there are five interconnected processes involved in terrorism: joining the group, forming the activity, remaining in the campaign, leading the organization, and engaging in acts of terrorism. He says many analysts have attempted to explain terrorism based on these concepts, but they fall short because there is no model of terrorism. Rather than simply trying to profile the typical terrorist, Ross tries to explain how social and psychological processes produce terrorism. The model offers a great deal of promise.

There are two factors involved in the rise of terrorism at any point in history. The first centers around social structure. Structural factors include the way a society is organized, its political and economic systems, historical and cultural conditions, the number of grievances citizens have and their mechanisms for addressing grievances, the availability of weapons, and the effectiveness of counterterrorist forces. Ross says that modernization, democracy, and social unrest create the structural conditions that facilitate terrorism. In Ross's analysis, urban areas produce the greatest potential for unrest and the greatest availability of weapons. When governments fail to address social pressures in such areas, the likelihood of terrorism increases. When counterterrorist intervention fails, the amount of terrorism is likely to increase.

Ross believes structural factors interact with the psychological makeup of potentially violent people to produce terrorism. He says there are several schools of psychology that can be used to explain violence, but none is adequate to explain terrorism. As a result, he identifies five psychological factors involved in the development of terrorism.

Facilitating Traits

Unlike Post (1987), Laqueur (1999), and me (White, 2000), Ross (1999) believes terrorist research has identified a variety of prominent characteristics in individual terrorists. He calls these facilitating traits. Terrorists exhibit fear, anger, depression, guilt, antisocial behavior, a strong ego, the need for excitement, and a feeling of being lost. He says the more of these traits a person exhibits, the more likely that the person will engage in terrorism.

Frustration/Narcissism-Aggression

Narcissism-aggression means that a person has suffered a blow to the ego and reacts hostilely. Frustration refers to aggression channeled toward another person or symbol. Ross (1999) believes that high frustration may result in terrorist acts. This, in turn, interacts with structural factors to cause more violence.

Associational Drives

Most terrorist acts are committed by groups. Ross (1999) believes that when potential terrorists perceive benefits from particular groups, they tend to join those groups. Once inside, acts of terror are likely to increase because the group reinforces violent behavior.

Learning Opportunities

The existence of groups and engaging in acts of terrorism create an environment for teaching terrorism to others. As learning opportunities increase, Ross (1999) says, the amount of terrorism increases.

Cost-Benefit Calculations

The decision to engage in terrorism depends on the benefits of terrorist violence. If individuals feel they will realize gains from terrorist actions, terrorism will increase.

Although not a typical profile of a terrorist personality, Ross's (1999) ideas explain the transformation of terrorism across history and provide social and psychological indicators of terrorism. Ross believes certain psychological

factors interact with social factors to create a climate conducive to terrorism. Laqueur (1999) says a profile cannot be obtained because terrorism is a political activity, but Ross counters by demonstrating both political and psychological factors.

WARRIOR DREAMS

James William Gibson (1994) offers an interesting psychological analysis of violent rhetoric and political activity in the United States. He maintains the American extremist political right seeks an outlet for social frustration in a paramilitary culture. In *Warrior Dreams,* Gibson says extreme conservatives have suffered an identity crisis since the Vietnam War. Living in a culture that values guns, violent confrontation, and victory, Gibson says a number of extremists have submerged themselves in a paramilitary culture. This lifestyle involves an almost cultlike attraction to paramilitary activities, including paintball war games, paramilitary religions like Christian Identity, war films, war books, and a mercenary culture. He draws parallels to extremist movements in Nazi Germany to illustrate his thesis.

Gibson's assessments may be somewhat overstated. Very few individuals who are drawn to paintball games or shooting ranges commit their lives to militant extremism, but his theme is worth noting, especially as it applies to psychological justification. For example, Gibson notes a common thread in paramilitary literature. In the action–adventure genre, Gibson demonstrated, warriors are social outcasts whose only existence centers in violence. They can be close to no other person except other warriors. Family, sexuality, individual personality, and normative social relations are suppressed in a warrior environment.

The target of the warrior is also worth noting. Gibson says the dream warriors are in conflict with an enemy who totally lacks all standards of human decency. The enemy's name is interchangeable. He or she may be a communist, dope dealer, mafioso, criminal, academic, or liberal, but the enemy's mission is always the same: destroy American society and culture. The dream warrior responds, not by joining regular police or military forces, but by becoming a lone wolf, an eternal soldier in search of a war.

In terms of justifying terrorism, Gibson's thesis matches H. H. A. Cooper's (1977b) doctrine of necessity. The lone warrior has shunned the shackles of normative society. Even the rogue warrior cultures of SWAT teams and special commando units have no place in the dream warrior's life. These units reflect organized military values, and the dream warrior rejects them. He (and the dream warriors mean *he*) is at war with the status quo. In essence, the paramilitary culture of the extremist right justifies the actions of militias, groups like The Order, and neo-Nazis. It provides a formula for justifying terrorism.

KEY CONCEPTS

1. Terrorist behavior differs from that of ordinary criminals. Criminal investigation techniques must be modified to reflect these differences when examining terrorist cases.

2. Terrorists need to justify their actions. The terrorist group and its ideology serve as the primary means of justification.

3. Terrorists must believe that violence is necessary before they will resort to terrorism. Cooper says that they must believe maintaining the status quo creates more harm than the damage done by violence.

4. Law enforcement agencies typically separate terrorists into criminal, political, or mentally unstable categories.

5. Some analysts, such as Laqueur (1999), argue it is not possible to produce a terrorist profile.

6. Other analysts, such as Ross (1999), believe it is possible to profile terrorists. Ross combines social and psychological factors to do so.

7. Gibson (1994) believes there may be something about American paramilitary culture that helps produce violence.

FOOD FOR THOUGHT

List the factors you think contribute to criminal behavior. Divide those factors into individual motivators (psychological factors) and group motivators (social factors). Looking at these conditions, do you believe you can profile criminals? Now, do the same thing based on what you know about terrorism. Does your criminal logic apply to terrorists? Do you think you could use such a model to describe a person who committed an act of terrorism? Do you think it could help you to predict and prevent a terrorist event?

FURTHER READING

Walter Reich & Walter Laqueur, *Origins of Terrorism*

3

Changing Group
Structures and
the Metamorphosis
of Terrorism

I f psychopathic killers are excluded from the equation, modern terrorism tended to be a group activity until about 1990. Even today most terrorist groups are socially organized, managed, and maintained. Successful groups must be structured according to the same principles as any other organization. Labor must be divided in particular ways, and each subunit must complete its assigned specialty to complement the work of other units. Even though its goals are more difficult to accomplish because the work must be completed with extreme secrecy, a terrorist group must be organized and managed for success. Yet, an alarming trend has developed in the past few years. Individual terrorists have been taking action on their own or with the support of a very small group. This chapter discusses the more conventional organizations and the emerging solitary trend.

After reading this chapter, you should be able to:

1. Describe the relationship between group size and effectiveness.
2. Describe the basic organizational patterns common to terrorist groups.
3. Outline the management problems facing terrorist groups.
4. Summarize Adams's thesis on the importance of financing terrorist groups.
5. Describe the emergence of leaderless resistance, lone wolves, and berserkers.

TRYING TO WALK THE WALK

In 1970, a small group of radicals joined together in San Francisco to form the New World Liberation Front (NWLF). According to John Wolf (1981, pp. 63–64), the NWLF was responsible for 30 bombings over the course of the next 7 years. The NWLF claimed to be a "moral" revolutionary group, and it attacked only "legitimate" targets symbolized by corporate capitalism. Utility companies were a favorite, and the NWLF also bombed two sheriff's vehicles in the San Francisco area. They were at war with the establishment.

As the NWLF attempted to expand its operations, its leadership may have come to see the irony of its campaign. Even though the NWLF had hoped to be the vanguard of a revolutionary movement, few people were willing to join the revolution. In an attempt to compensate, the NWLF "expanded" its operations by forming a number of revolutionary brigades. In reality, these brigades represented nothing more than the same few radicals operating under a variety of new names (U.S. Marshals Service, 1988).

In frustration, the NWLF turned to a final ploy to obtain support. Linking up with another small band of militants, the group joined the prison reform movement and allied itself with a group of militant ex-convicts called the Tribal Thumb. This sealed the fate of the NWLF; whatever chance it had had to obtain even the slightest political support was lost through the alliance. Its association with violent felons cemented public opinion against the group. The NWLF was denounced and alienated. Aside from improving corporate security and law enforcement investigative techniques, the NWLF was a dismal failure.

The experience of the NWLF is an example of the failure of many modern terrorist groups. To make a major impact, a terrorist group must have the resources to launch and maintain a campaign of terrorism. Technological weapons and industrial sabotage are starting points, but they do not provide the basis for extended operations. Groups have to be large—at least larger than a few social misfits armed with bombs. To become large, the group has to generate popular political appeal with a cause acceptable to a large segment of the public.

Most terrorist groups do not have this appeal. They are organized like the NWLF, developing ornate organizational schemes and grandiose plots but lacking the ability to carry out a meaningful campaign. Small groups generally sponsor small amounts of violence. Individual acts may gain the public's attention through media exposure, but they lack the ability to maintain steady pressure on their opponents.

SIZE AND LENGTH OF CAMPAIGNS

Ted Robert Gurr (Stohl, 1988, pp. 23–50) conducted an empirical analysis of terrorist groups operating in the 1960s in an attempt to identify some of their operational characteristics. His work remains an important study of their organizational structure. In the past, many people assumed terrorism was the result of revolutionary activities, just as many today assume it is state-sponsored or a product of the right-wing. Gurr's data calls such simplistic conclusions into question.

Gurr's analysis produced some interesting conclusions. First, most actions involve only a few terrorists who generate more noise than injury. Second, although it is popularly believed that political revolutionaries dominate terrorist groups, the majority of successful groups embrace other doctrines, such as nationalism. Third, in most instances only large groups achieve results by mounting campaigns of terrorism; small groups cannot do so. Gurr concludes that there are diverse causes for terrorist violence and many remain to be identified. No matter what the cause, however, most terrorist campaigns end within 18 months of the initial outburst of violence.

Terrorism is short-lived because it seldom generates support. A terrorist campaign promises the greatest opportunity for success, but many terrorist activities remain isolated because they lack support structures. As a result, terrorists seldom challenge authority. Political revolutionary and radical groups do not generate the popular appeal needed to gain support for their activities. Gurr believes large groups become large because they embrace popular political issues. Only a few groups have been able to adopt popular positions since 1945.

A policy implication may be drawn from Gurr's study: If his conclusions are correct, they imply that most terrorist organizations are small, short-lived operations. Small groups are a law enforcement problem. Although terrorism is waged to gain political ends, the scope of most terrorist activities is too restricted to pose a serious threat to the state. The level of most terrorist activity would seem to dictate a police response. Small groups are not able to alter the political environment substantially. As in the case of the NWLF, standard investigative procedures can be used to stop small terrorist movements. Weapons of mass destruction may change these assumptions, but the analysis seems correct for conventional terrorism.

SIZE IS IMPORTANT

Vittorfranco Pisano (1987, pp. 24–31) illustrates the importance of group size with an analysis of terrorism in Italy from 1975 to 1985. There were a tremendous number of terrorist actions in Italy during the 10 years of Pisano's study, along with the relatively large number of groups responsible for the attacks. The reason for the plethora of groups, according to Pisano, was that most terrorist organizations were not capable of mounting a long-term campaign against the government. They could only strike a few times before their resources ran out or they were captured. Large Italian terrorist groups took advantage of this situation, using many different names in an attempt to confuse authorities. Yet, investigators came to realize only large groups were involved in sustained actions. Everyone else became "single-incident" terrorists; that is, they could mount only one operation.

Hizbollah serves as an example of a large successful group. In separate studies Hiro (1987) and Wright (1986, 1989) find that Hizbollah began as a political movement inside revolutionary Iran. In 1982, Hizbollah moved to the Bekka Valley in Lebanon in response to an Israeli invasion. The Israeli Foreign Ministry (1998) claims Hizbollah's movement to Lebanon allowed it to grow. Utilizing local support and continued financial backing from Iran, Hizbollah has emerged as a strong, semiautonomous structure. Its size allows Hizbollah to conduct extensive terrorist attacks against Arabs who disagree with its objectives, as well as against Israel. Hizbollah is large enough to maintain a campaign of terrorism.

The Liberation Tigers of Tamil Elaam (LTTE) is in a similar position. The LTTE began fighting the Sri Lankan government in 1976, claiming to represent the Tamil minority on the island nation of Sri Lanka. Because Sri Lanka has an extensive Tamil population, the LTTE has been able to recruit an extensive fighting force. O. N. Mehrota (2000), writing for the Institute of Defense Studies in India, estimates that it may number up to 10,000 members. Not only has the LTTE mounted an extensive terrorist campaign, including a track record of successful suicide bombings, but it also crossed the threshold into guerrilla warfare in 1983. Size is the crucial factor in LTTE operations.

As terrorist groups become larger, however, the level of response to the problem must be raised. Christopher Hewitt (1984) considered this issue when he began a study of the effectiveness of counterterrorist policies. Hewitt reflects Gurr's position by stating that small groups do not have the resources to damage an opponent over an extended length of time: They cannot launch a campaign. He believes terrorist campaigns are more important than isolated acts of terrorism, and terrorist campaigns demand expanded political responses.

Hewitt argues terrorist campaigns became important after World War II for two primary reasons. First, the campaigns of large terrorist organizations accounted for the majority of terrorism around the world. Small, isolated terrorist organizations failed to match their larger counterparts. Second, large terrorist organizations have prompted governments to employ macropolicies. Large terrorist organizations can actually bring about a change in government political response because they represent a problem far beyond the means of local law enforcement. Therefore, large groups represent political threats.

Yet, extremists rarely attract a political base—except among other extremists. In general, people do not readily flock to small terrorist organizations. Large groups like the Basque Nation and Liberty (ETA) and the Irish Republican Army (IRA) have gained support because their causes are so popular among their reference groups. Their methods may be extreme, but their political appeal has a broader base. Many small groups recognize this and attempt to follow the examples of the larger groups. By rhetorically abandoning their extremist positions and taking on a more popular political cause, small groups hope to broaden their appeal.

Extremists try to hide the most radical positions in nationalistic and religious messages. Murder and theft are disguised as patriotic acts. For example, in an anonymous tract titled "Wann alle Bruder Schweigen," a romanticized account of The Order, the writer claims the terrorists to be nothing more than American patriots fighting for their constitutional rights. Posse Comitatus reflected the same sentiments in "The Last Letter of Gordon Kahl," the story of a man who shot it out with police officers instead of paying taxes (Sapp, 1986). American militias maintain this tradition, and the left-wing German Red Army faction made similar claims from the opposite side of the political spectrum.

Despite attempts to expand and develop a broader political following, most terrorist groups fail miserably when they try to increase their size. Walter Laqueur (1987, p. 9) says this is because they are composed of fanatics. Such people do well to convert even other fanatics, and they have virtually no appeal in mainstream society. Terrorist groups remain small because they cannot see beyond their immediate agendas.

BASIC ORGANIZATIONAL STRUCTURES
OF TERRORIST GROUPS

James Fraser, a former counterterrorist specialist in the U.S. Army, discusses the organization of terrorist groups by analyzing two factors: the structure of the organization and its support. According to Fraser (Fraser & Fulton, 1984, pp. 7–9), terrorist groups are necessarily designed to hide their operations from security forces, and so analysis is difficult. Still, certain organizational principles are endemic to all terrorist groups. Organizations employ variations of command and control structures, but they are frequently organized along the same pattern no matter what causes they endorse.

The typical organization is arranged in a pyramid (see Figure 3.1). It takes many more people to support terrorist operations than to carry them out; therefore, the majority of people who work in terrorist organizations serve to keep terrorists in the field. The most common job in terrorist groups is support, not combat.

According to Fraser (Fraser & Fulton, 1984), the hierarchical structure of terrorist groups is divided into four levels. The smallest group is at the top and is responsible for command. As in military circles, leadership makes policy and plans while providing general direction. Other researchers have often pointed out that the command structure is not as effective as in legitimate organizations because of the demand for secrecy. The command structure in a terrorist organization is not free to communicate openly with its membership; therefore, it cannot exercise day-to-day operational control.

The second level in Fraser's hierarchy contains the active cadre. (Cadre is a military term; these are the same people most of us call "terrorists.") The active cadre is responsible for carrying out the mission of the terrorist organization. Depending on the organization's size, each terrorist in the cadre may have one or more specialties. Other terrorists support each specialty, but the active cadre is the striking arm of the terrorist group. After the command structure, the cadre of active terrorists is the smallest organization in most terrorist structures.

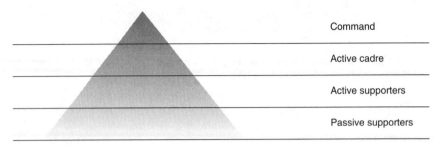

FIGURE 3.1 The Structure of Terrorist Groups

Source: James Fraser & Ian Fulton (1984), *Terrorism Counteraction*, FC–100–37 (Fort Leavenworth, KS: U.S. Army Command).

Under the active cadre is the second largest and the most important level of a terrorist organization. Active supporters are critical to terrorist campaigns. Any group can carry out a bombing or kidnapping, but to maintain a campaign of bombings and kidnappings takes support. Active supporters keep the terrorists in the field. They maintain communication channels, provide safe houses, gather intelligence, and ensure all other logistical needs are met. This is the largest internal group in the organization.

The last and largest category is the organization's passive supporters. This group is extremely difficult to identify and characterize because supporters do not readily join terrorist groups. Many times they are used without their knowledge; they simply represent a favorable element of the political climate. When a terrorist group can muster political support, it will have a relatively large number of passive supporters. When its cause alienates the mainstream, passive support dwindles. Passive support complements active support.

Most terrorist groups number fewer than 50 people and are incapable of mounting a long-term campaign. Under the command of only a few people, the group is divided according to specific tasks (see Figure 3.2). Intelligence sections are responsible for assessing targets and planning operations. Support sections provide the means necessary to carry out the assault, and the tactical units are responsible for the actual terrorist action.

Larger groups are guided by the same organizational principles, but they have major subunits capable of carrying out extensive operations. In particularly large groups, subunits have the ability to act autonomously. Large groups have the tactical units and the support sections to conduct terrorist campaigns.

Anthony Burton (1976, pp. 70–72) describes the basic structure of subunits. Terrorist organizations have two primary types of subunits: the cell and the column. The cell is the most basic type. Composed of four to six people, the cell usually has a specialty; it may be a tactical unit or an intelligence section. In some organizations, the duties of tactical cells vary with the assignment. Other cells are designed to support the operations.

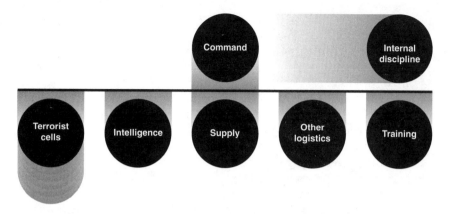

FIGURE 3.2 Terrorist Group Organization

Source: James Fraser & Ian Fulton (1984), *Terrorism Counteraction*, FC–100–37 (Fort Leavenworth, KS: U.S. Army Command).

Groups of cells form to create columns. Columns are semiautonomous conglomerations of cells with a variety of specialties and a single command structure. As combat units, columns have questionable effectiveness. They are too cumbersome to be used in major operations, and the secrecy demanded by terrorism prevents effective intercolumn cooperation. Their primary function is combat support because elements in a column can be arranged to support the tactical operations of cells.

While both Fraser's work and Burton's analyses appear to be dated, the structures they outlined are still applicable to groups. Patrick Seale (1992) finds the same type of structure when examining Abu Nidal. Reuven Paz (2000b) sees similarities with the organization of the Lebanese-based terrorist group Hamas. Religious terrorists such as the Japanese Aum Shinrikyo also copy the group model (Brackett, 1996). The only terrorists who do not follow typical organizational models are the emerging individualists. These are examined at the end of this chapter.

MANAGEMENT PROCESSES
AND PROBLEMS

It is easy to outline the organizational structure of terrorist groups. The reason is plain. Terrorists need to organize like any other group. You could probably make a fairly accurate diagram of most terrorist groups after taking an Introduction to Management class. Indeed, terrorist leaders face operational problems and seek to solve them with the same strategies you would learn in such a management class. Terrorist leaders also have special organizational problems (see Box 3.1).

The first problem is the need for secrecy. It dominates the operational aspects of terrorism and leads to a variety of problems not encountered in open organizations. Ironically, while secrecy is the greatest strength of the terrorist organization, it also reveals its greatest weakness. Sometimes a terrorist group's work is so secret that even the members do not know what they are doing. Terrorism demands secrecy, and secrecy prevents effective communication.

Because the necessity for secrecy is so great, each cell and each column is usually allowed a relatively high degree of autonomy. Terrorism is a decentralized affair, and the larger the group, the greater the degree of decentralization. This is not the most desirable kind of organization, but it is an operational necessity. Terrorists know a centralized structure is easily infiltrated and destroyed by security forces. One well-placed informant can destroy an entire organization.

Decentralization offers relative security: Very few people know many other members of the organization. This approach affords great protection but difficult administration. The organization of the Provisional Irish Republican Army can be used to illustrate the problem. The IRA is organized like most large terrorist groups. It is governed by a Supreme Council whose members are drawn from IRA battalion or column commanders. Column commanders are responsible for a number of cells, which in the IRA are frequently called by military names such as platoons, squadrons, and companies. The command of the IRA, however, has problems that emanate from secrecy and decentralization.

On paper, the organizational chart looks extremely logical. In practice, that logic is modified by the need for each unit to be protected from discovery. This means members of various cells and columns usually have no idea who the other members of the IRA are and what they are doing. They get their orders from one man, and that person supposedly represents the Supreme Council. This paves the way for potential splintering or, at the least, misunderstandings. It is easy to see why the IRA is difficult to manage.

To prevent factionalism and excessive autonomy, terrorist commanders turn to internal discipline for control. In essence, what the commanders continually threaten to do is to terrorize the terrorist organization. Factionalism and autonomy are controlled through fear of retribution.

Ironically, internal discipline can become a major stumbling block in the terrorist organization. There are two opposing dynamics at work, one pulling for cohesion and cooperation through fear and the other pulling for autonomy through decentralization and secrecy. Sometimes attempts at discipline backfire. For example, when leaders attempt to punish errant members by assassination, they may find themselves the target of disgruntled followers. As a result, large terrorist organizations frequently find themselves splitting.

Another problem of terrorist management is gaining immediate tactical support for operations. As Fraser (Fraser & Fulton, 1984) suggests, the most important element of a terrorist campaign is the amount and structure of active supporters. Without active supporters, launching a campaign is impossible.

BOX 3.1   Problems of Terrorist Management

Communicating within an infrastructure of secrecy	Avoiding fragmented ideologies
	Maintaining logistics
Coordinating activities despite decentralization	Training
	Financing
Maintaining internal discipline	

Though the press has frequently pictured terrorist leaders as secretive plotters controlling hidden armies of true believers, in reality terrorist leadership must exert itself to develop and maintain active support. The majority of time is spent creating networks of active supporters, not launching headline-grabbing operations.

Yoseff Bodansky (1986b) illustrates this point in his analysis of state-sponsored terrorism. According to Bodansky, the logistics of mounting a terrorist campaign are massive. To maintain political pressure on an established government through the use of terrorism, a vast infrastructure of active supporters must be created. Bodansky outlines the types of activities that accompany terrorist campaigns. At a minimum, terrorists need three basic operational supports. Intelligence is necessary to plan and carry out an attack. This includes everything from the selection and observation of the target to the forging of documents and travel papers. A direct logistical network must be established to supply terrorists with weapons, which is complicated by security procedures designed to detect them. Finally, a support network for safe houses, transportation, food sources, and medical supplies has to be arranged. Bodansky concludes that it takes 35 to 50 support people to keep a single terrorist in the field. Bodansky's (1999) subsequent work reinforces these initial findings.

Training is another need that complicates the business of terrorism. True believers may have the political motivation to engage the enemy, but they frequently lack the practical skills to do so. Terrorists must maintain bases to prepare for such tactical necessities as target practice and making bombs. True believers are easy to find, but trained fanatics are not. Terrorist groups must have both facilities and resources to support training activities.

Managing a terrorist campaign is also a complicated matter. It is conducted in secrecy, and yet the demands on the terrorist command structure are as great as the demands on the leaders of any organization. To compensate for the difficulty, some large international organizations have routinized their approach to terrorism by developing large bureaucratic organizations to manage their affairs. It is an alternative to allowing a state sponsor to dominate the internal affairs of the group.

Brian Jenkins (1987a) believes the bureaucratization of terrorist groups brings many complications to terrorism. Jenkins says some large terrorist organizations unintentionally developed into bureaucratic structures to meet the rigorous organizational demands of a terrorist campaign. Other organizations established such structures on purpose. Once the bureaucracies were in place, a new set of problems developed, essentially resulting from a standard bureaucratic problem: Once formalized, these structures must produce reasons to justify their existence.

All terrorists face management problems, and the issues involved in launching attacks are not simple. Terrorist attacks require political support, planning, organization, and resources. Every terrorist group, regardless of size, must take these factors into account. The resources must come from somewhere. Some analysts have argued that attempts should be made to uncover the resources behind the organizations. They believe too much time has been spent on examining the organizational structure of terrorist groups and not enough energy has been devoted to the support networks behind the structures. James Adams, defense correspondent for the *London Times,* raises this argument.

ADAMS'S ANALYSIS
OF THE FINANCING OF TERRORISM

In 1999 Harvey Kushner, a criminal justice professor from Long Island University, and I were discussing terrorist infrastructures with a doctoral candidate at an Academy of Criminal Justice Sciences conference. The student asked us where he could find the best analysis of the economics of terrorism. Without pausing, Kushner and I both blurted out, "James Adams." Although dated, Adams (1986) has produced the best analysis of financial infrastructures in terrorism. His work is, as Kushner aptly said to the student, a classic.

James Adams (1986) presents an excellent analysis of terrorist organizations in *The Financing of Terror.* His thesis is that terrorism changed between the 1960s and the 1980s and most Western defense policies failed to account for the change. Led by the United States, defense policy has been aimed at uncovering state-sponsored terrorism. Adams says this has resulted in a fundamental misunderstanding of the function and nature of terrorism. Major terrorist organizations are independent of states, and they have created independent financial support networks to stay in business. Adams concludes the best way to attack terrorism is to attack the financial structures that support independent terrorist organizations.

Adams (1986) believes modern terrorism grew from the revolutionary violence in the 1960s. As violence grew, he writes, the West developed two schools of thought to approach the problem. One school saw increased terrorism as a state-sponsored activity, used to support national military functions. The other school said terrorism could only be eliminated when the political causes of terrorism, such as injustices, were uncovered and eliminated. Adams believes both groups had a point but missed a central issue.

Modern terrorism is distinct from violence in the 1960s. It grew, was transformed, and came to possess a dynamic of its own. Nation-states became involved in sponsoring terrorism in both the West and East, but not in the manner envisioned by American defense policymakers: States do not play a major role in terrorism.

Terrorist groups tend to grow and function on their own. Just as Gurr (Stohl, 1988, pp. 23–50) and Hewitt (1984) point to the difficulties of maintaining a campaign, Adams (1986) is also perplexed by the ability of large terrorist groups to maintain their operations. If they do not enjoy overwhelming support from their client states, where do they get their resources? Adams found his answer in a variety of sources with a single common denominator: No matter how a terrorist group approaches its particular task, it has to have internal financial backing built into its infrastructure. Money is required to mount a terrorist campaign.

Adams examined a number of large terrorist groups to obtain his answer. To obtain autonomy in the struggle for Palestine, the PLO established an economic wing called Samed in 1970. Adams writes that Samed has developed into a rational business structure to support the PLO. It uses modern organizational theories providing economic benefits, salaries, and incentives to the fedayeen (holy warriors). Although Samed's headquarters were destroyed in the 1983 Israeli invasion of Lebanon, operations have moved to Tunisia, Algeria, and Syria. Samed runs farms and is rapidly building factories. It intends to become a strong economic force in the Middle East during the twenty-first century.

Adams also focuses his attention on the Provisional IRA. He states it is popular to believe the Provisional IRA gets most of its money from the United States. America, however, is not the prime source of its income. The Provisional IRA maintains its coffers by running an organized crime network in Northern Ireland. This transformation, from revolutionaries to underground gangsters, has proven to be the best method of financing terrorism.

In what Adams calls its "Capone discovery," the Provisional IRA found it could raise vast sums of money by frightening shopkeepers and business owners into paying protection money. The payment has two results for a typical shopkeeper. First, it guarantees Provisional IRA protection for the business in case of trouble (but this is not the prime motivation for the payment). The second and major purpose is to keep the Provisional IRA from attacking the owner's property or family. The Provisional IRA has taken in so much cash from its protection racket that it has been forced to launch a money-laundering scheme.

In 1972, the Provisional IRA found another way to finance terrorism when it entered the legitimate business world by purchasing a taxi company. The endeavor succeeded, and the Provisional IRA soon realized it could make even more money if it forced other companies out of business. Terrorism was used to dominate the market. The technique worked so well the Provisional IRA has set up other front businesses. Crime pays in Northern Ireland.

Adams (1986) believes tracing the financial resources of terrorism is important for a single reason. In its battle against terrorism, the West has been focusing on the wrong target. Adams says counterterrorism should concentrate on cutting off the source of terrorism. Terrorist campaigns are not waged in a vacuum; they require organization and resources. In the final analysis, this means they must be financed. Adams concludes that behind the structure of every large terrorist group lies a financial network. A terrorist campaign can be stopped by undermining a group's economic ability to wage a campaign.

Although terrorist organizations have transmogrified since Adams's analysis, their financial infrastructures follow the same principles. Harvey Kushner (1999) demonstrates this with the underground economic activities that support Middle Eastern terrorism in the United States. Bodansky's (1999) detailed analysis of the financial network that supports Osama bin Ladin shows the same type of infrastructure. On July 24, 2000, the *Washington Post* reported a number of Hamas supporters were arrested in North Carolina for allegedly using scams and illegal schemes to finance operations in the Middle East. Adams's thesis continues to be verified by terrorist actions.

LEADERLESS RESISTANCE, LONE WOLVES, AND BERSERKERS

As will be presented in Part II, modern terrorism reemerged after World War II (1939–1945) as a combination of anticolonial, nationalist, and left-wing political ideologies. When it first appeared, law enforcement agencies were surprised, and their tactics were ineffective. In Europe, terrorists seemed to move at will; and in the United States, local, state, and federal law enforcement agencies failed to solve almost all terrorist crimes. The Middle East seemed to be aflame with terrorism and regional wars. The situation in Northern Ireland was militarized as the British Army came to reinforce the Royal Ulster Constabulary, but Republican and Unionist terrorists ruled the day. Although terrorists did not topple any governments, they were in their first modern heyday.

By 1990, this situation had totally changed. The primary reason for this new state of affairs was that Western law enforcement became much better at dealing with terrorism. The police were quite successful at either infiltrating or monitoring groups, even in countries where restricted laws limited law enforcement's ability to collect information. Police officers in the United Kingdom developed informants in almost every segment of the Irish Republican Army. Left-wing and right-wing terrorism in the United States dwindled as police information increased. Left-wing terrorism in Europe seemed to disappear, although some ethnic groups remained effective. Just when it seemed as if law enforcement had triumphed, the terrorists changed their tactics.

The American Ku Klux Klan leader Louis Beam was one of the first to understand the situation. Group organization, infrastructure, and financing were the weakest links in the chain. Law enforcement officials had figured out methods for infiltrating extremist cells, and they placed informants and undercover officers inside violent organizations. When these methods failed, the police followed the money. These tactics threatened all but the most stable terrorist groups. Louis Beam proposed a solution. According to Mark Pitcavage (1999), Beam believed that a group, no matter how secret, simply could not evade law enforcement. As a result, Beam called for the elimination of the group.

Taking a page from Carlos Marighella (see Part II), Beam talked about "leaderless resistance" (White, 2000). Beam said extremist groups did not need to have extensive organizations; it was just necessary to do something. Resistance in any form was acceptable. There was no need to coordinate activities. Resistance was enough. Several movements followed the idea. Hans-Josef Horchem (1986) points to subversive Green extremists in Germany, doing everything from telephoning in bomb threats to placing glue in locked doors. The Animal Liberation Front (2000) advocates such tactics on its Web page. Timothy McVeigh's bombing of the Oklahoma City federal building in 1995 illustrates the extreme violent end of the trend. It is difficult to gather intelligence on a group when there is no group.

Another trend in Leaderless Resistance is the notion of the "Lone Wolf." This concept can be found in the right-wing fantasy novel *Hunter* (Pierce, 1989). The protagonist represents the ultimate small group, the individual, and the novel describes how an individual extremist can murder people of color and Jews in the name of white supremacy. Pierce, the extremist author of the novel, says the police cannot infiltrate a mind.

Eric Rudolph serves as an example of the Lone Wolf. Wanted in connection for four bombings from a 1996 attack that drew international attention at the Atlanta Olympics to a 1998 abortion clinic bombing that killed a police officer, Rudolph is almost a real-life parody of Pierce's Hunter. Unlike Hunter, however, Rudolph spends most of the time on the run. He has good reason to hide. Marlon Manuel (2000) of the *Atlanta Journal-Constitution* says local, state, and federal governments have spent millions of dollars trying to catch Rudolph to no avail. Most Lone Wolves tend to be single-event terrorists, but Eric Rudolph allegedly has been able to plot four incidents: the Olympic bombing, two abortion clinic bombings, and an attack at a gay nightclub that wounded 110 people. In addition, his antics have become the legends of right-wing folklore.

I have argued that another term, *Berserker,* can be used to describe some individual terrorists (White, 2000). The term Lone Wolf suggests that a person suddenly pops up out of nowhere, performs a sinister act, and vanishes. In reality, Mark Pitcavage (1999, 2000) says this does not usually happen. Eric Rudolph is an exception, and his notoriety is greater than his ability to strike. Most Lone Wolves are true believers who are well known for their associations in violent extremist circles. Some Lone Wolves are better viewed as true believing extremists who go off the deep end. The term glorifies their actions and should not be used. This is why I also use the term *Berserker.* It is more than an academic term. It has investigative consequences.

In old Norse and British warfare, a berserker was a warrior who went crazy in the midst of battle. Bernard Cornwell (1997), the gifted author of the *Sharpe's Rifles* series, provides a frightful description of such a warrior in a set of books about King Arthur. In a pericope from *The Winter King,* one of the young medieval heroes of the book, Dervel, is in a shield wall facing an army of Arthur's enemies. The shield wall is crucial. As long as the warriors have their shields locked together in front of them, the enemy will have a difficult time breaking through and winning. Young Dervel feels relatively safe behind this wall of shields.

Unfortunately, to Dervel's horror, two warriors step out of the enemy shield line and strip themselves. They dance naked, consumed by battle madness and mead, and are ready to charge Dervel's shield wall and accept certain death. They are drunk, they are naked, and they are removed from the world of common logic. They are also dangerous. Dervel's friends must lower their shields to strike the crazed Berserkers. In so doing, they will expose themselves to the enemy army. These naked madmen are not Lone Wolves. They are crazed true believers, though only temporarily insane. They are Berserkers.

The concept of the Berserker captures some individual extremist violence better than the term lone wolf. This is important for investigators. Berserkers can leave a trail of clues before they "charge a shield wall." For example, Buford Furrow, a right-wing extremist who attacked a Jewish center in Los Angeles, broadcasted his extremist involvement long before the attack. Benjamin Smith, another extremist who went on a murder spree in Chicago, was a public advocate of Creatorism (see Chapters 4 and 13). In practice, many lone wolves do not materialize from thin air. They are Berserkers who take violent, irrational actions. When extremists perpetually advocate violence and murder, they may produce a crazed individual who will go on a rampage.

KEY CONCEPTS

1. Terrorist organizations must be organized well enough to launch a campaign.

2. Only relatively large groups have the ability to maintain a campaign of terrorism; therefore, the goal of terrorist groups is first to appear large, then to become large.

3. Nonreligious terrorist groups employ propaganda and publicity in the hope of launching a campaign.

4. Groups must have a substantial support network to pose a threat—a network that is many times larger than the number of people employed in tactical operations.

5. Managing the operations of a terrorist group demands the same organizational skills that are needed to run any complicated social endeavor.

6. Successful terrorist groups develop financial independence.

7. Recently, some terrorists have taken individual single murderous actions to eliminate the need for group support.

FOOD FOR THOUGHT

Think about the way you would organize a group of 100 people to produce, distribute, sell, and service illegal computer software. Sketch your ideas in a make-believe organizational chart. Does your group look like a terrorist organization? What role does secrecy play in your organization? How would you manage 100 people? How could you keep such an organization from being discovered by the police? Could you accomplish something similar by abandoning your group and creating the software as a lone wolf?

FURTHER READING

David Rapoport, *Inside Terrorist Organizations*

James Adams, *The Financing of Terror*

4

Religion and Terror

The practice of religion is perplexing in human history. It is the most liberating experience humans can imagine, presenting ultimate mysteries and defining our relationship with the cosmos; but religion can also be used to justify violence, war, and repression. Some people would argue that for every good thing religion has created there exists an evil counterpart. The ultimate purpose of religion and its relationship to social violence are beyond our limited scope, but it is important to understand that religion and terrorism have become intertwined in the early years of the twenty-first century. In the years following World War II (1939–1945), ethnic issues, ideology, and nationalism dominated the world of terrorism. That changed in the 1990s. Today, the world of terrorism lies in the realm of violent theological expression.

After reading this chapter, you should be able to:

1. Explain how religion and terrorism become related.
2. Summarize Huntington's thesis about religion and international violence.
3. Describe Hoffman's analysis of religious terrorism.
4. Define the roles of apocalyptic and eschatological thinking in religious violence.
5. Describe the process of demonizing human beings.
6. Identify the issues involved in major contemporary religious conflicts.

THE LOGIC OF RELIGION AND TERRORISM

Anthropologist Marvin Harris (1990, pp. 437–453) believes human beings have experienced two types of religions, those based on killing and those espousing nonkilling. Killing religions developed during the food gathering cycles of preagrarian and early agricultural societies, and they were based on the premise that a deity would assist the community in times of crisis. Harris says these beliefs gave way to the nonkilling religions because the older religions did not protect early villages from the ravages of war and natural disasters. The nonkilling religions appeared in order to transcend everyday experience. Harris says the irony of the human experience is that that nonkilling transcendence is often transformed into a militant ideology designed to protect a state or some other social group. Why does this happen?

Several years ago, Mircea Eliade (1961), the late religious scholar from the University of Chicago, provided an answer. Eliade says the world of human experience is divided into two spheres, the ordinary and extraordinary. We use language and logical concepts to describe the ordinary or everyday world, but we use symbols and myths to talk about the extraordinary or spiritual world.

The ideas of famed mythological scholar Joseph Campbell (1949, 1985) complement Eliade's thesis. Campbell says we express our spiritual nature in symbols and myths, but we are limited when we try to talk about them. We have no spiritual language so we must talk about mystical experiences in everyday language. Since we have no words to describe the spiritual world in spiritual terms, we can only talk about these experiences the same way we talk about the common issues of life. The late Protestant theologian Paul Tillich (1957) says this can be dangerous because it can allow us to literalize symbols. This means the symbol no longer represents the sacred experience, but *becomes* the experience. When this occurs, the symbol displaces the myth and becomes an object of worship. Because of language, the symbol no longer points to the sacred. It has taken the place of the sacred.

Consider the following illustration of this process. Joseph Campbell (1985) argues that in the sacred stories of the Israelites, God promised the Hebrews a land flowing with milk and honey. In Campbell's analysis, God pledged "sacred space," a place where God and humanity could commune. Campbell says, however, that because the story is told in everyday language, the purpose of the sacred story is transformed. Rather than pointing to a sacred place of divine communication, the everyday language of the story makes it look as though God promised the Israelites a geographical location. In other words, the story is misinterpreted as "God promised Abraham the state of Israel." When the sacred story is interpreted in this manner, the liberating effect of the myth is subordinated to ethnic identity and nationalism.

Taking away abstract anthropological and theological concepts, let us look at two practical examples. Since 1991, parts of the Balkan peninsula—the area of Europe containing Serbia, Croatia, Slovenia, Bosnia, Yugoslavia, Kosovo,

Montenegro, Bulgaria, Albania, Romania, and Greece—has been devastated, first by a civil war, and then by seemingly endless fighting among several groups. A closer look at the issues surrounding the Balkans reveals the logic of religion and violence.

The renowned historian Ferdinand Schevill (1922) completed a definitive study of the Balkan peninsula about 80 years ago. Although much happened in the twentieth century, including the formation of the country Yugoslavia after World War I (1914–1918) and the partition of the entire region into several countries in the 1990s, the fundamental reason for conflict in the region did not change. It is based on three interpretations of religion.

Through the course of history, the Balkan peninsula became the area where Christendom violently encountered Islam in the eighth century. As Christian kingdoms began fighting Islamic kingdoms, the transcendent nature of both Christianity and Islam was subordinated to the political needs of each kingdom. The situation took another turn in 1054 when the Western Christian Roman Catholics and the Eastern Christian Orthodox church split over theological matters. Soon, Catholics and Orthodox Christians were slaughtering one another in the name of religion. Members of all three religions attacked one another with zeal, despite the fact that both Jesus and Mohammed preached a gospel of peace and both Christians and Muslims worshipped the same God.

This situation continued for the next 1,000 years with each side politically dominating the area at times in history and repressing the other two religions when gaining control. The symbols of nonkilling religions were transformed into deadly elements of political expression. When the country of Yugoslavia was created after World War I, ethnic and religious animosities did not disappear. Indeed, they surfaced again in World War II as each religious group fought the other two. Joseph Tito (1892–1980), a Communist leader, was able to create a coalition government that maintained a delicate peace after the war. After his death and the collapse of the Soviet Union, however, ethnic religious leaders reemerged, resulting in a religious bloodbath in the area at the end of the twentieth century.

Another practical example of this process comes from the American extremist right. In *The Turner Diaries,* a fictional work by white supremacist William Pierce, the main protagonist has a religious experience. Earl Turner, the novel's hero, has been committing small-time acts of violence against Jews and nonwhite races when he is invited to join a white terrorist group known as The Order. (An actual white terrorist group that operated in the American West in the 1980s took its name from this story; see Chapter 14.) As Turner is inducted into the terrorist group, he has the first religious experience of his life.

The fictional Turner describes himself as someone who is not religious, but an official of The Order gives Turner "The Book," a "holy" work describing God's plan to create a racially pure world in the face of Jews and people of color. Turner is taken aback. He admits to having a transcendent experience, but he says he does not know how to describe it. He can only respond by killing racial and ethnic "inferiors." (This accords with the theories of Eliade, Campbell, and Tillich.) Turner does not express his thoughts in theological terms, but he comes to realize he can only express his experience in everyday language. He does so by going on a streak of murder and mayhem. Terrorism and religion are fictionally united.

History is filled with stories of people who have literalized myths, taken sacred stories out of context, terrorized in the name of their deity, and expressed spirituality through violent actions. The process is constant. When people transform a nonkilling religious call for universal love into a mandate to love only those who look, act, and believe like them, they introduce a formula for religious violence. The process is completed when symbols and myths are literalized. Unfortunately, this is a part of terrorism.

HUNTINGTON'S CLASH OF CIVILIZATIONS

In 1993, Harvard Professor Samuel P. Huntington (1993, 1996) introduced a theory of conflict for the twenty-first century. Huntington maintains that past epochs were dominated by particular types of conflict. Medieval Europe from the Reformation (1517) to the Thirty Years' War (1618–1648) could be characterized by religious wars. After the Peace of Westphalia (1648), dynastic rights and territorial needs dominated international conflict. This gave way to nationalistic wars after the French Revolution (1789–1795). Nationalism dominated global wars until 1945, the end of World War II, when capitalism and communism threatened world peace in a nuclear standoff between the United States and the Soviet Union. When the Soviet Union collapsed in 1991, Huntington says, the world changed. The United States stands alone as the world's only superpower, and the struggles that threaten world peace will no longer focus on nationalism or ideology. Most wars will result from volatile regions where cultural confrontations threaten to spread violence. One of the major factors defining culture is religion.

Huntington (1993, 1996) argues there are eight primary cultural paradigms or civilizations dominating the modern world (see Box 4.1). They include: (1) Western, (2) Confucian, (3) Japanese, (4) Islamic, (5) Hindu, (6) Slavic-Orthodox, (7) Latin American, and (8) African. Each cultural region corresponds to a particular geographical area where people hold similar beliefs, values, and attitudes. The Western paradigm includes Western Europe, the United States, Canada, and Australia, while the Confucian culture contains China, parts of Siberia, and Southeast Asia. Although recently influenced by the West, Japanese culture is defined by Shintoism, Buddhism, and Confucianism. Islamic culture includes the Middle East, portions of the Indian subcontinent, Southwest Asia, and the Islamic portions of Southeast Asia. The Hindu paradigm dominates most of India, and the Slavic-Orthodox

---

BOX 4.1   Huntington's View of Civilizations

Western—United States, Canada,
Western Europe, Australia

Confucian—China, parts of Siberia,
Southeast Asia

Japanese—Japan

Islamic—Middle East, Turkey,
Southwest Asia, parts of Southeast
Asia, North Africa, Balkans

Hindu—India

Slavic-Orthodox—Russia and Eastern
Europe

Latin American—Mexico, Central and
South America

African—Africa

SOURCE: Huntington, *The Clash of Civilizations
and the Remaking of World Order*

---

civilization contains Russia and Eastern Europe. Huntington defines Africa and Latin America as emerging regions of many cultures.

Huntington (1993, 1996) believes international peace will be threatened in "torn countries." These are regions where more than one civilization exists within a single area. The Balkan peninsula, discussed previously, is a classic example of Huntington's thesis. Three civilizations, Western, Slavic-Orthodox, and Islamic, dominate the region. There is a tremendous amount of violence as these civilizations clash, and there is an ongoing potential for war. Huntington believes the United States must be careful to avoid intervening in these areas of cultural and religious conflict in the coming decades and believes hot spots will continue to produce violence.

Huntington's thesis has been widely debated in foreign policy circles, but his conclusions have much to do with the concept of religion and terrorism. Each cultural paradigm or civilization has religious zealots who seek to impose their views and will on everyone else. Each religion contains true believers who have literalized symbols and myths and subjugated them to ethnic and nationalistic aims. Regardless of one's evaluation of Huntington's thesis, one point is clear. Terrorism is emerging and will probably continue to appear from violent, true believers in these areas of conflict.

The implications for American law enforcement are twofold. First, America will be targeted by religious zealots from other cultural paradigms because these zealots believe the United States has intervened in their area in violation of a sacred norm. Western Europe and Japan will be targeted in the same manner. Second, since the United States routinely welcomes people from all other civilizations, it will have the potential for internal religious conflict. This hardly makes the United States a "torn country," but it does provide a battleground for zealots who want to violently change or punish America and for right-wing extremists who will violently oppose people who tolerate diversity and the government that encourages it. Religious terrorism and violent extremism will continue to be a problem for American police officers.

HOFFMAN'S ANALYSIS
OF RELIGIOUS TERRORISM

Bruce Hoffman of Saint Andrew's University in Scotland is one of the world's foremost experts on terrorism. Hoffman (1995) believes we are witnessing a resurgence and proliferation of terrorist groups motivated by religion. He says this phenomenon is changing the face of terrorism. Laqueur (1999) points out that religious terrorism is nothing new, but the appearance of apocalyptic groups is dangerous in a technological age. Why are experts like Hoffman and Laqueur concerned? The answer is that if terrorists behave differently from regular criminals, religious terrorists behave differently from ethnic or nationalistic terrorists. In short, religious terrorists are not constrained by the same factors that inhibit other types of terrorists.

Hoffman (1995) says terrorists motivated by religious imperatives differ from political terrorists in several ways. "Holy terror" contains a value system that stands in opposition to "secular terror." Hoffman says secular terrorists operate with the realm of a dominant political and cultural framework. They want to win, to beat the political system that is oppressing them. Their goal may be to destroy social structure, but they want to put something in its place. Secular terrorists would rather make allies than indiscriminately kill their enemies. Holy terrorists, however, are under no such constraints. They see the world as a battlefield between the forces of light and darkness. Winning is not described in political terms. The enemy must be totally destroyed.

For political terrorists, killing is the outcome of an operation. Again, religious terrorists differ. Hoffman (1995) says holy terrorists see killing as a sacramental act. The purpose of their operation is to kill. Pointing to Islamic terrorism as an example, Hoffman says the purpose of terrorism is to kill the enemies of God or convert them to Islam. Certainly, the vast majority of Islamic theologians would disagree with this and are offended by the use of the term *Islamic terror*, but keep in mind that we are talking about true believing, violent extremists. They convert a religion based on peace and justice into one of intolerant hatred. This is the nature of both religious violence and terrorism in any religion.

To illustrate Hoffman's point, refer to a Hebrew Bible or Christian Old Testament and turn to the book of Judges, Chapter 8, the story of the battle of Ai. In this story, God told Joshua to trap the warriors of the city, kill all of them, and then turn on the city. Nothing in Ai is to be spared, including unarmed civilian survivors. Today, no mainstream Jewish or Christian theologian argues that God would order such destruction. Most of them argue that these stories were written by people who conquered Canaan and then looked back to place a theological spin on their violent actions (Bright, 1981, pp. 144–161). Violent religious extremists in the United States, however, read such stories and believe they are directed to kill Jews and nonwhites because of them. This is what Hoffman is illustrating. Violent extremism can become

Islamic, Jewish, or Christian terrorism. Violent extremists take theological issues out of context.

Since they take actions out of context, religious terrorists have no social limitations on violence. As a result, they kill indiscriminately, doing so because they are killing the enemies of a deity. Religious belief is a ready-made source for justifying terrorism because it can sanctify the terrorist. When a person becomes a true believer and the religious doctrine sanctions the use of violence, terrorism is deified. To be "deified" means the act of terrorism itself is made sacred and holy. Religious terrorists are no longer working for mere mortals; they are on a mission from God.

Hoffman (1995) says religious terrorists believe they speak for the divine. Mark Juergensmeyer (1988) describes the condition that must be present for terrorists to come to this conclusion. Believers must identify with a deity and believe they are participating in a struggle to change history. They must also believe in cosmic consequences; that is, the outcome of the struggle will lead to a new relationship between good and evil. When they feel the struggle has reached the critical stage, violence may be endorsed and terrorism may result. According to Juergensmeyer, the proper combination of these beliefs can produce a fanatical terrorist.

Religion embodies a sacred ideology. When performing acts in the name of the deity, a religious person feels justified and righteous. This is true whether the cause is love or war, and it is not limited to socially illegitimate forms of violence. Governments frequently call on citizens to "praise the Lord and pass the ammunition." True-believing terrorists have done little more than mimic mainstream social patterns. They use the established social paths of religion and ideology to justify their actions.

Hoffman (1995) says that in political terrorism, terrorists attempt to create a theater. Their actions are symbolically designed to influence a wider audience. Religious terrorists again differ in this area. Because they are complete within themselves and define the realm of the deity, they have no wider audience. They are only playing to God and, thus, have no reason to constrain themselves.

There are two other dangerous trends in holy terror, according to Hoffman. First, religious terrorists are not utilitarian. (A utilitarian is someone who seeks the greatest amount of good for the greatest number of people.) Religious terrorists seek the greatest good for themselves. Second, they demonize their enemies. All terrorists degrade their opponents. This makes it easier to murder people, but religious terrorists take the process a step further. They equate their enemies with the ultimate source of evil. Enemies are devilish and demonic, in league with dark forces. It is not enough to beat them. The enemies must be eradicated from the cosmos.

Hoffman says these traits in religious terrorism create an environment conducive to the use of weapons of mass destruction. He extends this concern to Islamic terrorist groups, the Christian white supremacy movement, Jewish messianic terrorists in Israel, and the Sikh movements in India. As stated earlier, fringe elements of true believers substitute the concept of universal love with love for a selected group of believers. In this sense, the type of religion is almost immaterial, and this is the reason terrorist analysts use terms like Christian, Jewish, Islamic, Hindu, and Buddhist terrorism. (See Box 4.2.)

ROLE OF ESCHATOLOGY

In my own research (White, 2001), I argue that apocalyptic thinking and terrorism have become dangerous allies. When applied to terrorism, apocalyptic thinking invites terrorists to fight as holy warriors in a period of fanatic zeal when a deity is about to bring creation to an end. They believe God's reign is almost on us, and they are facing their last opportunity to purify creation before God's reign. The Greek-rooted word *apocalypse* means "revelation," but a better term to use is *eschatology.*

The term *eschatology* derives from the Greek word εσχατος, a concept dealing with the end of all material and purpose in time and space. In the Greek version of the Hebrew Bible, eschatology usually is interpreted as the "day of Yahweh," that is, a final judgment and the realization of God's purpose for creation. This Jewish idea influenced early Christian writers, but the meaning of God's final presence fluctuated in early Christian dogma (Kittel, 1964, Vol. II, p. 697).

Christians have expected God's final judgment for 2,000 years. Yet, they have not agreed on the form it will take. John Domonic Crossan (1999, pp. 257–287) describes four commonly held eschatological frameworks: ascetic, apocalyptic, ethical, and political. Ascetic eschatology refers to the process of self-denial, while the apocalyptic version envisions God's destruction of the existing order. According to Crossan, ethical eschatology is quite different. It calls for followers to embrace radically moral behavior in recognition of God's imminent reign. Crossan says political eschatology is frequently ignored today because it combines expectations of religious judgment with political action. People fear political eschatology.

Gunther Lewy (1974, p. 40) agrees, arguing that linking political beliefs with an end-of-time theology is a prescription for violence. Given the variety of meanings attached to eschatological expectations, it is not surprising to find that various terrorist groups have developed their own "end of the age" philosophy in apocalyptic theologies. As Lewy implies, some of these theologies are indeed quite dangerous. There are people who would like to violently usher in the new age, and an eschatological philosophy is tailor-made for individual terrorists who have rejected both the material world and the norms of social behavior. It provides a cosmic battlefield where forces for good are called to fight some unspeakable evil.

The consequences of eschatological terrorism are dramatic. Indeed, they are cosmic in proportion. All deterrents to violence are rendered meaningless by the promise of the new age. When violent eschatology is politicized on a

---

BOX 4.2   Hoffman's Analysis of Religious Terrorism–
Types of Terrorism

Criminal, Political, and Ethnic Terrorists	*Holy Warriors as Terrorists*
World is a political culture	World is separated into good and evil
Killing is a sad necessity	Killing is a sacramental act
Violence is limited by values	Violence is indiscriminate
Speak for the group	Speak for God
Influence the wider audience	Have no wider audience
Greatest good for greatest number	Greatest good for self
Enemies degraded	Enemies demonized

---

cosmic battlefield, Armageddon's warriors need no further justification to bear arms. They fight for a holy cause, and all actions are justified. As Bruce Hoffman (1995) says, there are no constraints for those in their final hours.

THE PROCESS OF DEMONIZATION

Hatred of an enemy is normal in conflict, and armies often dehumanize their enemies in order to attack them. The use of hate and hateful rhetoric in terrorism is equal to the use of inflammatory diatribes in the course of war. When religion becomes part of conflict, however, the situation changes. In religious wars, enemies do not simply represent people with opposing views. They represent the spawn of the devil. If religion enters any type of conflict, including terrorist actions, the situation becomes more volatile. It is difficult to kill other human beings regardless of the cause, but in a religious war, one does not destroy human beings. One destroys evil.

The process by which one group of people degrades its enemies to a point of equating them with some sort of cosmic evil is called demonization. It is a political process not limited to the practice of terrorism. Chip Berlet (1998) describes the road toward demonization as a three-step process. According to Berlet, the first step toward demonization is scapegoating. Many cultures use the idea of transferring sins from humans to something else as a way of making people pure. For example, Native Americans from the Ottawa tribe used to dig a hole in the ground, shout their sins into it, and cover it up. Scapegoating is part of this process.

The term *scapegoat* comes from the Hebrew Bible (Leviticus 16:20–22) where priests are told to place the sins of the people on a goat and send it into the wilderness. Human shortcomings are transferred to the goat, the scapegoat. Berlet refers to a similar type of transfer in his use of scapegoating, except that he means the causes of particular social problems are transferred to a group of people. Rather than seeing the scapegoat as a vehicle for removing sins, the scapegoat becomes a group of people that is blamed for a particular problem.

Everyone scapegoats to some extent. Professors may blame all collegiate problems on university bureaucrats. Police officers and soldiers are quick to blame organizational malfunctions on "the brass." Conservative commentators blame a perceived breakup of American families on feminism, while many feminists claim education is polluted because it emphasizes the study of dead white males. Scapegoating is inaccurate, and it represents gross simplifications of complex problems. Berlet (1998) argues that it is also a step toward demonization. When a particular group can be blamed as the cause of a social problem, it becomes easier to illogically simplify the problem and blame it on that group.

Berlet believes that if a group serves as a scapegoat, it is possible to believe the group operates in the realm of some type of conspiracy. This is the second step toward demonization. Conspiracy theories abound in religious terrorism. For example, in the Middle East, militant Muslims blame almost all problems on a conspiracy between the United States and Zionists in Israel. Although communist terrorist groups have shriveled since the demise of the former Soviet Union, die-hard Marxists use communism as a surrogate religion and contend that capitalists conspire to oppress the masses through manipulation of the economic system. Violent right-wing extremists in the United States believe social evils are caused by a conspiracy between Jews and bankers. Conspiracy theories imply that the scapegoats not only cause social problems, but they also have the ability to do so by conspiring together.

The question becomes: With whom do the scapegoats conspire? This is the final step in Berlet's analysis of demonization. The scapegoats become powerful because they have the ability to work in conjunction with the forces of ultimate evil. Not only do scapegoats cause problems by conspiring against their enemies, but they also obtain power by uniting with evil. When a group of people believes this has happened with the scapegoats, the process of demonization is complete.

Michael Barkun (1997), author of the best theological analysis of Christian Identity in print, illustrates Berlet's thesis in an examination of racist extremism in the United States. Barkun demonstrates that the white followers of Christian Identity believe all of America's social problems, indeed, all of the problems of history, are caused because Jews struggle against white people. Why do the followers believe this? Barkun says Christian Identity followers have ascribed satanic powers to the Jews. According to Christian Identity theologians, the Jews are powerful because they are children of the devil.

Barkun's findings are discussed in greater detail when examining domestic terrorism (see Chapter 14), but for now his work illustrates Berlet's (1998) thesis. Violent, intolerant extremists have dehumanized an entire religious group, linking them to ultimate evil. This is demonization, and it leads to violence because it is easier to terrorize demons than human beings. This is the nature of religious terrorism, and it is stronger than simple political terrorism. As Hoffman (1995) implies, killing demons is a sacramental act. The world of terrorism has become more dangerous because various groups of religious zealots have demonized members of other religions and cultures.

One word of warning is worthwhile, especially to those in criminal justice. Demonization is a neutral process. It works for religious terrorists, but it also works for any other group. When police officers dichotomize people into "us and them," it can be the first step toward demonization. Police officers regularly hear such expressions as Islamacists, Jewish militants, Christian extremists, and other derogatory phrases used to classify certain groups. Anytime governmental forces use degrading terms to describe groups or particular styles of behavior, they move toward demonization. This is dangerous. The language and the process of demonization have no place in American law enforcement.

A BRIEF OVERVIEW OF CONTEMPORARY RELIGIOUS CONFLICTS

The last segment of this chapter briefly outlines the major areas of conflict and religious extremism encountered at various points in the text: the Middle East, the Indian subcontinent, Ireland, and the United States. There are many areas of religious conflict in the world today, and these cases have been selected because they are included at various points in the text.

India

The historical driving force of religious conflict on the Indian subcontinent is the confrontation between Islam and Hinduism. While Hinduism and Buddhism enjoyed a comparatively tranquil coexistence, the clash between Hinduism and Islam is another matter. Muslim invaders began moving into India from Afghanistan around 1000 C.E. They were quite successful, subduing the local population of Hindus and establishing Muslim dynasties. The Hindus resisted the Muslim presence with violent secret terrorist groups.

About 1500, in northwestern India, a mystic claimed that God transcended localized religions. He founded a new religion called Sikhism that combined elements of Hinduism and Islam. While the Sikhs initially sought peace with Hindus and Muslims, their ideas were militantly rejected. Soon the Sikhs were arming themselves and defending their beliefs.

British and French imperialism dominated the subcontinent from 1600 to 1947. The British, who triumphed over the French in the region, took advantage of the religious differences in the subcontinent. They played Muslims and Hindus against each other and allowed both groups to distrust the Sikhs. This helped a small number of British soldiers and officials keep a large native population under control, but by 1900, the Hindus and Muslims formed a political alliance. Members of both religions worked together against Britain in the 1930s, when the Indian independence movement gained momentum.

Lord Louis Mountbatten, a member of the British royal family who would later be murdered by the Irish Republican Army, negotiated independence for India and created separate zones for Muslims and Hindus. This gave rise to the modern nations of Pakistan and India, but the peace was short-lived. After the British departed, Indians and Pakistanis battled over religion for half of a century. Religion has become part of terrorist violence in the region.

Essentially, there are four religious conflicts on the subcontinent. The most obvious is the Hindu-Muslim conflict as exemplified by India and Pakistan. The second involves disputed territory between the two countries, the area known as Kashmir. Not only have India and Pakistan fought over the region, but international terrorist groups have joined the fray on one side or the other. The third area of conflict involves struggles with the Sikhs. Militant Sikh terrorists have targeted Indians for the past few decades and have been responsible for the assassinations of several people, including a prime minister. Sikhs tend to side with Pakistan in the struggle over Kashmir. The final area of conflict is more ethnic than religious. It involves a struggle between the dominant Singhalese population with a minority group of Tamils on the Buddhist island nation of Sri Lanka.

Ireland

The main religious issue in Ireland is the struggle between ethnic Protestants and Catholics, but if you talk to mainstream Christian theologians and call Ireland a religious conflict, you will probably get a strong reaction. Christians, especially Irish Christians, are quick to point out that the conflict in Ireland has little to do with religion. They will most likely tell you that terrorism is the result of people misusing religion. You will probably hear that both Protestant and Catholic extremists are not religious at all. They simply use religion to identify people with politics. These arguments are essentially correct. Yet, they are at the base of religious conflict.

When religion is used to justify terrorist violence, the transcendent nature of theological expression must be replaced by an ethnocentric focus. God is replaced by some form of patriotism or ethnic identity. This process is called ethnocentric transformation. This is exactly what has happened in Ireland. It is not a fight about the nature of religion, it is a conflict about subordinating God to a political cause.

Bruce (1993, pp. 50–67) provides a description of ethnocentric transformation in Ireland. Bruce believes ethnicity takes precedence over religion in Ireland. This means it is more important to be identified with a particular group than it is to be a member of a church. Bruce says religious labels in Ireland are used to place people in distinct ethnic and political groups. If a person is Catholic, it does not necessarily mean that the person has committed to a life of faith. Terrorists use the Catholic label to describe nationalistic revolutionaries who want no part of Britain. Terrorist "Catholics" will kill British and Irish Catholics who disagree with their irreconcilable position.

Protestantism has the same connotation among violent extremists. Protestant terrorists do not embrace Presbyterianism or the Anglican church as an expression of religious zeal. Violent Protestant extremists use their religious label to define those who will use terrorism to keep Northern Ireland associated with the United Kingdom. Bruce concludes that religious labels in Ireland are synonymous with ethnic identification.

If a theologian argues that the conflict in Ireland is not religious, the argument is correct in the sense that both Catholics and Protestants have been seeking to end terrorism for quite some time. Many priests and pastors hold joint worship services and attempt to provide relief to anyone regardless of religious or ethnic identification. They do not commit terrorist acts over disputes concerning dogma. However, Catholic and Protestant terrorists make religious dogma subordinate to a political agenda.

The Middle East

There are three main sources of religious strife in the Middle East: militant Jewish fundamentalists who wish to expand Israel, Muslim militants wanting to eliminate Israel and restore Palestine, and Islamic fundamentalists who wish to purify their own states. Both sets of Islamic militants want to eliminate Israel. The sources of these views are presented in detail in Chapter 7. The theological positions are outlined as follows.

Hoffman (1995) says one of the Middle Eastern threats comes from Jewish extremists who have endorsed the use of mass terrorism to ensure the existence of Israel. Laurence Hanauer (1995) says these Jewish fundamentalists have endorsed violence as a means to establish "Eretz Israel," or the Greater Israel of biblical times. Three groups, Kach, Kahane Chai, and Gush Emunim, have identified Israel's traditional covenant with God as a mandate to reclaim the land of ancient Israel and make it exclusively Jewish. They are willing to use force against all non-Jews and Jews who "betray" the all-Jewish Israel. Their motivation is primarily religious. They wish to restore ancient Israel in preparation for the coming of a messiah.

Militant Islamic fundamentalists not only oppose the Jewish terrorists of Kach and Kahane Chai, but they also reverse the argument about the Palestinian homeland. Militant Muslims believe that Palestine is theirs. Clarence Bouchat (1996) cautions the West and the United States in particular not to view this radicalized position as the political goal of an Islamic bloc. Militant Muslims who want to eliminate all Jews from Palestine are extremists and no different from the militant Jews of the Greater Israel movement who seek to eliminate Muslims from the same area.

Militant Islam is not limited to questions about Israel. Fundamentalists in several Islamic countries are threatening to overturn established governments in the name of religion. David Kibble (1996) explains why. Kibble says everyone in the West needs to understand that there is no separation between church and state in Islamic countries. Governments claim to rule through the Qur'ran, the holy book of Islam. Terrorists who violently attack the establishment do so under the guise of theology. Therefore, unlike Ireland, much of the struggle in the Middle East is about theological dogma.

The United States

Douglas Bodrero (1999) identifies American theological extremism in four particular areas: apocalyptic cults, Black Hebrew Israelism, the Christian Identity movement, and other forms of white supremacy religions. According to Bodrero, apocalyptic cults believe that the world is coming to an end and that members of the cult will play some role in the eschatological event. An authoritarian leader gathers members in a cult and isolates them from the mainstream. Bodrero says this does not constitute a problem, unless the group becomes violent. When a leader uses rhetoric and violence to silence internal opposition, Bodrero believes the group may be on the path to violent extremist behavior. Doomsday cults emerge from such dynamics and believe they must take offensive action to bring about the end of the world.

Black Hebrew Israelism is a form of black supremacy. Its origins trace back to the Civil War and were relatively peaceful. Recently, Ben Ami Ben Israel, also known as Ben Carter, had a vision in Chicago telling him that African-Americans were the true Jews of old and the people who call themselves Jews are impostures. Whites are evil incarnate, descended from the devil. Bodrero (1999) says the most violent aspect of this movement formed in the Miami-based Nation of Yahweh.

My own research (White, 2001) summarizes white supremacy theology. Christian Identity is a theology that grew from a nineteenth century concept known as Anglo-Israelism. Its basic tenant is that the ancient tribes of Israel were Caucasians who migrated to Europe shortly after the death of Jesus. Whites are actually the descendants of the chosen tribes of Israel, and whites are asked to identify with the Israelites of old. Christian Identity is strongly anti-Semitic, claiming that humans originated from two seed lines. Whites are directly descended from God, while Jews originated from an illicit sexual union between the devil and the first white woman. Nonwhite races evolved from animals and are categorized as subhumans. Identity Christians believe that biblical covenants apply only to the white race and that Jesus of Nazareth was not a Jew, but the white Israelite son of God. Christian Identity views are championed by Aryan Nations, a variety of prominent Christian Identity pastors, Posse Comitatus, and the American Institute of Theology.

Nordic Christianity or Odinism is a hybrid form of Christianity and old Norse religions. It exists in two forms. Nordic Christianity combines a pantheon of Nordic gods under the triune deity of Christianity. Odin, Thor, and other Nordic gods serve Christ by militantly protecting the white Norse race. Pure Odinism, however, ignores Christian concepts. Enjoying a rebirth in nineteenth century Germany, Odinism simply involves the resurrection of old Nordic myths and worship of the Nordic pantheon. It migrated to the United States through the neo-Nazi movement. Both forms of Nordic religion call for the militant defense of race, bloodlines, and homeland.

Another form of militant right-wing Christianity can simply be called Freewheeling Fundamentalism. This form of religion rejects both the blatant racism of Christian Identity and the hybrid nature of Nordic religions. The "freewheelers" are fiercely patriotic and use religion to reinforce social beliefs, values, and behavior. They tend to believe the federal government is not mystically evil, but that it is opposed to the reign of God. They also believe agents of the government are in conspiracy to destroy America's monetary system and national sovereignty. Many of these groups oppose racism, and some claim they are not anti-Semitic. Freewheeling Fundamentalism is the religion of the Patriot movement.

The last form of religion is called "Creatorism," a religion originating with the World Church of the Creator (WCOTC). Founded by Ben Klassen, the WCOTC is secular, deistic, and racist. Klassen's purpose was to divorce white people from weak theistic religions, claiming such religions were ridiculous expressions of utopian ideals. Klassen said the creator placed things in motion and left people on their own. Klassen's slogan was, "Our race is our religion." Creating his own mythology in tracts on naturalistic health and *The White Man's Bible,* Klassen called on white people to fight Jews, nonwhite races, and whites who disagreed with racist philosophy. His successor, Matt Hale, who has taken the secular title *Pontifex Maximus* from Julius Caesar, calls for violence to protect the white race. The cry of Creatorists is RAHOWA, an acronym for Racial Holy War.

KEY CONCEPTS

1. Religion and terrorism become related when religious ideas are subordinated to political, ethnic, or ideological objectives.

2. Huntington believes nationalism and ideology have dominated international conflict for the past 200 years. Since there are no longer two competing ideologies dominating international affairs, he believes future conflicts may result from cultural paradigms clashing in certain parts of the world.

3. Hoffman states that religious terrorism is growing. Religious terrorists represent more of a threat than traditional terrorists because they are not limited by the same types of social restraints.

4. Eschatological thinking is dangerous when combined with terrorism because it produces an atmosphere where intolerant holy warriors engage in violence to usher in what they believe to be the final age.

5. Berlet describes the three processes of demonization as scapegoating, conspiracy, and forming an alliance with an ultimate evil force.

6. The major conflicts involving religious terrorism in the world today include: (1) the Indian subcontinent with struggles among Hindus, Muslims, and Sikhs, and ethnic fighting between the Singhalese and

Tamils; (2) Ireland, where militant Protestant and Catholic terrorists remain active; (3) the Middle East with militant Muslims and Jews; and (4) the United States with various cults and racial supremacy groups.

FOOD FOR THOUGHT

Bruce Hoffman believes religious terrorists differ from political terrorists of the recent past. Do you agree with this? What role do you think eschatology plays in terrorist behavior? Do such beliefs make religious terrorists more prone to use technological weapons? If you were in charge of a counterterrorist investigation against a religious group, what factors might you consider beyond a normal criminal investigation?

FURTHER READING

Mark Juergensmeyer, *Violence and the Sacred in the Modern World*

*

PART II

Essential
Background

5

The Origins
of Modern Terrorism

I t is virtually impossible to understand terrorism without examining the context of where and how it developed. Terrorism is as old as conflict, but modern terrorism has its roots in the Enlightenment. It developed throughout the nineteenth century, changing forms and ideology. Modern terrorism grew in Europe and migrated to the rest of the world. It provides the basis for today's experience with international terrorism. This chapter traces the origins of modern terrorism from the French and American revolutions to the Bolshevik Revolution in Russia in 1917.

After reading this chapter, you should be able to:

1. Briefly describe the impact of the American and French revolutions on terrorism.

2. Explain why the term *terrorism* came to be used to describe revolutionaries.

3. Summarize the role of nineteenth century anarchists and their influence on revolutionary, nationalistic, and right-wing terrorism.

4. Identify the proponents of violent revolutionary change among nineteenth century anarchists.

5. Describe how interpretations of the Russian Revolution and Trotsky's ideas have confused the central issues of Western extremism and terrorism.

6. Describe the debate about new and old terrorism.

ENLIGHTENMENT, REVOLUTION,
AND TERRORISM

Historians often call the eighteenth century the Age of Reason or the Enlightenment. This time period in Europe and America was characterized by a change in the way intellectuals approached social problems. Prior to the Enlightenment, common people were considered to be property of the state, and the state was the property of the noble classes who owned farmland. After the Enlightenment, forces of social revolution brought a new way of thinking about citizenship. Ordinary people came to believe the state existed to protect everybody, not just the nobles. The nobles and other people who held power were frightened by this type of thinking.

The thinkers of the Enlightenment began to question the logic of European social structure in the early 1700s. Another revolution in thinking, the Scientific Revolution, was responsible for creating the atmosphere that allowed the Enlightenment philosophers to raise social issues. The scientific discoveries of the 1600s had shaken the centuries-old notion that all creation was organized according to the medieval church's interpretation of Aristotle. If science could question the ability of the church to define the natural order, the social philosophers of the Enlightenment reasoned, then social science could question the economic and political order of society.

Just as Isaac Newton had isolated the principles of motion, social philosophers believed they could find the principles governing social actions and organizations. They divided themselves into many competing schools of philosophy. Yet, together they helped to create an environment where the old rules of social order no longer held true. From this platform, they began to question the authority of kings. Kings and other nobles were not enamored with this line of thinking.

The Enlightenment was an international intellectual movement. Although diverse in political opinions, the philosophers produced a common idea about government. They believed that governments should exist to protect individual rights and that the best form of government was democracy. The philosophers argued that citizens had rights, and governments were to be created to protect those rights. Common people were to control the government by a social contract or constitution that spelled out the rights of citizens and limited governmental power.

Americans living in British North America felt Great Britain was evolving toward a government that would protect rights and property. Yet, many American colonists also believed these basic rights were denied to Americans. By 1775, American talk of democracy moved from intellectual circles to the streets and eventually to the battlefields. The struggle ended in 1783, with the creation of the United States of America.

The American Revolution (1775–1783) was important in Europe, but it was viewed primarily as a "conservative" revolution. The locus of power moved from London to Philadelphia, and most American leaders (with notable exceptions, such as Thomas Jefferson) perceived the United States to be a British democracy without Britain. The birth of the United States was an evolutionary process. The Revolutionary War was seen within the context of traditional European power struggles, and its outcome was Britain without a king.

The French Revolution (1789–1795) was based on the same Enlightened principles of the American Revolution, but it took a very different and much more deadly tone. The American Revolution transferred power from the British upper classes to American upper classes. In France power was transferred *between* classes. The middle class wrestled power from the nobility and did so in an internal struggle dominated by ideological positions. It was extremely bloody and the first *revolution* in the modern sense of the word.

If America represented a long-term evolutionary process toward democracy, in 1795, France represented a radical shift in power structures. European governments not only took notice, but the nobles and their upper-class supporters were also frightened beyond their wildest dreams. They mobilized their armies to stop the French, and Europe was at war for 20 years.

The term *terrorism* appeared during this period. Edmond Burke, a noted British political philosopher of the eighteenth century, used the word to describe the situation in revolutionary Paris. He referred to the violence as the "reign of terror," and he used the word *terrorism* to describe the actions of the new government. Terrorism referred to the French government's slaughter of French nobles, their families, and sympathizers. Ironically, the meaning of terrorism would be changed within 50 years.

CLASS REVOLUTION
AND CHANGING MEANINGS

The reason the meaning of terrorism changed in Western minds was essentially because of the nature of European violence in the 1800s. The French Revolution did not bring democracy; it brought Napoleon. Under the surface, however, democratic ideas continued to grow. The ideas led to further political struggles and demands for freedom.

The democrats of the early 1800s were not united. Most of them believed in middle-class democracy, and they were reluctant to take to the streets, if the legislative process was available. They believed they could create constitutional monarchies and evolve into a system of democracy like the United States had done. The main objective of most European middle-class democrats from approximately 1815 to 1848 was to obtain a constitution ensuring liberty.

Other democrats were not so limited in their approach to democracy, and they based their views on economic developments. The entire Western world was in the throes of economic expansion and rapid industrial growth. (Historians refer to this period as the Industrial Revolution.) Looking at the pain caused by the Industrial Revolution and the growing power of capitalists (the economic owners of industry), radical democrats argued that democracy should be based not only on freedom, but also on social equality. This meant the class structure and distribution of wealth also had to be reorganized. These were radical ideas compared to the notion of middle-class democratic constitutions, but the radical democrats embraced class revolution.

The radical democrats working for the redistribution of wealth became known as socialists. They maintained that all institutions should be democratic, including the ownership and control of industrial production. Wealth was not a private matter; wealth belonged to everybody. The radical democrats believed political power should be held in common. Their concept of socialism was especially popular among some groups of displaced workers.

The chief spokesperson and intellectual for the socialists was Karl Marx. A German writing from London in the 1840s, Marx developed an international following. He claimed the key to democracy was found in the ability to control economic power, and he developed an elaborate argument to justify his position. Marx and his colleagues claimed the capitalist economic system exploited the lower classes for the benefit of others. He called for a change in the system.

The process of democratization was slow, however, and some of the radical democrats began to feel violent revolution was the only possible course of action. A small number of the radical democrats went underground, choosing subversive violence as a means to challenge authority. They became popularly known as "terrorists" because they hoped to achieve social revolution by terrorizing the capitalist class and its supporters.

Despite the many labels he received, Karl Marx was not a terrorist. Marx referred to "revolutionary" change, but he never clarified what he meant by revolution. Further, he did not advocate political bombing and assassination. In fact, on most occasions he publicly condemned it. He believed socialism was to be a reflection of democracy, not violence. A massive seizure of power by the general population might be justified, but individual acts of murder were not.

Upper-class fears of socialism increased in 1848. Early in the year, workers and middle-class merchants staged a revolution in Paris, declaring a new democratic republic. The radical democrats joined them. The idea of revolution spread like wildfire, and soon every major capital in Europe experienced some form of violent protest or revolution. It appeared democracy would carry the day. The democrats, however, did not effectively consolidate their revolutions. Another Bonaparte, Napoleon III, emerged in France, and military forces restored the royal families in central Europe. Only the United Kingdom, which had been slowly evolving into a democracy, weathered the storm.

When the revolutionaries of 1848 eventually failed, violent radical democrats took control of the revolutionary movement. They sought revolution through covert violence and assassination. Though they could not successfully confront armies and police forces in Paris, Vienna, or Berlin, they could plant bombs and set factories aflame. A campaign of subversive revolutionary violence followed. The term *terrorism* was increasingly used to describe this violence.

TERRORISM AND THE ROLE
OF THE ANARCHISTS

By the 1850s, the radical democrats divided into two streams. Militant socialists separated themselves from more peaceful socialists, and many of the people seeking peace referred to their movement as anarchism. The term *anarchy* was not new. It originated several hundred years earlier when Greek philosophers spoke of eliminating governments, but the nineteenth century gave it a new twist: These anarchists were socialists and, initially, attuned to the ideas of Karl Marx.

Pierre Joseph Proudhon (1809–1865) was at the source of modern anarchism. His political activities eventually landed him in a French prison, but Proudhon was not a man of violence. He called for the extension of democracy to all classes, to be accomplished through the elimination of property and government. Property was to be commonly held, and families living in extended communes were to replace centralized government.

Proudhon disagreed with Marx and other socialists about the role of government. Most socialists saw centralized government as a necessary evil. Like the democrats, the socialists believed government had to exist to protect the individual rights of citizens. Proudhon rejected all such notions, and he subsequently rejected the communists for their belief in government. He believed all government was an evil whose existence would always conflict with the rights of people to behave as they wished. Thus, small communes held the best hope for Western civilization.

Proudhon had revolutionary ideals, but his message was similar to Marx's call for revolution in that he believed in peaceful change. Despite many internal contradictions in his writings, Proudhon generally believed reason and logic would lead to the peaceful dissolution of Western society. Benign anarchy would develop through a natural evolution in human understanding.

Not all of Proudhon's disciples followed his call for this logical evolution; a number of them believed society had to be violently destroyed. They were called anarchist terrorists, and they changed the meaning of anarchism in Western civilization. There were several important terrorists among these anarchists, including Mikhail Bakunin, Sergey Nechaev, Peter Kropotkin, Johan Most, Emma Goldman, Nikolai Morozov, and Karl Heinzen.

Mikhail Bakunin (1814–1876) was a Russian revolutionary who fought the czar. He was joined in revolutionary activities by Sergey Nechaev. Later Russian terrorists formed an anarchist organization called the Narodnaya Volya (Peoples' Will), which operated from 1878 to 1881. The primary spokesperson of the Narodnaya Volya was Nikolai Morozov, and the organization's main tactic was to assassinate Russian government officials. Russian anarchists killed several officials, including Czar Alexander II.

Anarchists did not limit themselves to Russia. Karl Heinzen (1809–1880) was a radical German democratic who embraced anarchy. He came to the United States after the 1848 revolutions failed in Europe. Prince Peter

Kropotkin (1842–1921) was a displaced Russian who advocated revolution from exile in France. Johan Most was born in 1846 and emigrated to the United States. He advocated terrorism from a New Jersey–based newspaper and called for "propaganda by the deed" and the "philosophy of the bomb." Violent action was the best form of propaganda, according to Most. Most was joined by Emma Goldman (1869–1940).

Anarchism was an international movement, and leaders from several countries were assassinated by terrorist followers. This caused some opponents to believe an international anarchist conspiracy was threatening to topple world order. This was hardly the truth because anarchists were united only in spirit. Indeed, an international organization of anarchists would have been contradictory, as they inherently opposed large organizations. Regardless, fear of conspiracy grew, and many people came to believe anarchists were universally organized.

Ironically, nationalistic trends accompanied anarchist violence in the West. At the same time anarchists were calling for an end to government, a number of organizations were born which demanded a right to self-government. If the 1800s witnessed the growth of anarchism, it also saw the growth of nationalism. Many nationalists who found themselves under foreign control adopted the tactics of the anarchists in order to fight foreign powers occupying their lands. Nationalist groups throughout Europe turned to the philosophy of the bomb, and nationalistic terrorists began to follow the pattern set by the violent anarchists.

Nationalist groups did not view themselves as terrorists. They believed anarchists were fighting for ideas. Nationalists believed they were fighting for their countries. Anarchists were socially isolated, but nationalists could hope for the possibility of greater support. Governments labeled them as "terrorists," but nationalists saw themselves as unconventional soldiers in a national cause. Nationalists believed they were fighting patriotic wars. They only adopted the tactics of the anarchists.

The nationalist Irish Republican Army (IRA) grew from this period. Unlike anarchists, the IRA believed Ireland was entitled to self-government. They did not reject the notion of governmental control; the IRA wanted to nationalize it. Their weakness caused them to use the terrorist tactics fostered by the anarchists. In the twentieth century, other nationalist groups in Europe followed the example of the IRA. (See Chapter 6 for the development of terrorism in the IRA.)

Even though two distinct positions had emerged, it is not possible to completely separate nineteenth century anarchism and nationalism. Grant Wardlaw (1982, pp. 18–24) sees a historical continuation from anarchism to nationalist terrorism. Richard Rubenstein (1987, pp. 122–125) makes this point by looking at contemporary anarchist and nationalist groups. Rubenstein says the stages terrorists must go through to employ violence are similar for both types of terrorism. The moral justification for anarchist and nationalist terrorism is essentially the same.(See Box 5.1 for a partial list of leading anarchists.)

BOX 5.1 The Militant Anarchists	
Mikhail Bakunin	Johan Most
Sergey Nechaev	Emma Goldman
Peter Kropotkin	

J. Bowyer Bell (1976) gives an excellent example of the links between the anarchistic and nationalistic traditions by examining the IRA. Since 1916, the IRA has been inundated with socialist revolutionaries and nationalists who reject some aspects of socialism. Even though the two sides have frequently been at odds, both groups are heir to the same tradition. Modern nationalistic terrorism has its roots in anarchism. Both traditions formed the framework of modern European terrorism.

Terrorism in the modern sense came from violent anarchists in the late 1800s. The anarchists were based in Western Europe, but they carried their campaign to other parts of the world. The most successful actions took place in Russia prior to the 1905 and 1917 revolutions. Anarchist groups assassinated several Russian officials including the czar. Anarchism also spread to the United States. In America it took the form of labor violence, and American anarchists, usually immigrants from Europe, saw themselves linked to organized labor. The anarchist movement in America did not gain as much strength as the movement in Europe, and American anarchists were generally relegated to industrial areas. Right-wing extremism was not part of the anarchist movement, but by the mid-twentieth century, right-wing groups began to imitate tactics of violent anarchists. Much of this activity can be traced to unrest in Imperial Russia.

TERRORISM
AND THE RUSSIAN REVOLUTION

Late nineteenth century Russia differed significantly from the other great powers of Europe. Class distinctions between nobles and peasants were virtually the same as they had been prior to the French Revolution, and Russian peasants were beset by poverty. Industry had come to some of Russia's cities, but Russia's economic and governmental systems were not sufficiently geared to handle the changes. Czar Alexander II (who ruled from 1855 to 1881) vowed to make changes in the system. When he attempted to do so, he found himself in the midst of revolutionary terrorism.

The Narodnaya Voyla (Peoples' Will) represented violent socialist revolution. It was one of several political positions in Russia after 1850. Three groups felt they could reform and modernize the Russian state, but they disagreed about the ways to do it. One group, like Czar Alexander, wanted to modernize Russia from the top down. Another group, the intellectuals, wanted Russia to become a liberal Western democracy. Violent anarchists took another path. They believed Russian problems could be settled through revolution. The Peoples' Will was one such group. When it launched a campaign of revolutionary terrorism in the 1870s, it faced confrontation with conservative elements such as the church, police, and military. Members of the Peoples' Will came to believe it was necessary to terrorize these subversive organizations into submission.

The Peoples' Will evolved from Russian revolutionary thought. According to Laqueur (1999, pp. 15–16), the philosophy of anarchist terrorism in Russia was embodied by Mikhail Bakunin and Sergey Nechaev. Their revolutionary thought developed separately, and they met each other in the 1860s, forming an intellectual union. Both spoke of revolt against the czar, and both endorsed violence as the means to do it. Yet, even in the nation that would experience a violent anarchist campaign and eventually a communist revolution, Bakunin and Nechaev basically stuck to rhetoric.

Laqueur says their significance was their influence on later revolutionaries. They sparked violence and assassinations. Although they were ideologically linked to anarchism in Western Europe, they were distinct from their Western supporters. Russian anarchists were writing for a general population in the hope of sparking a democratic revolution. They were not radical revolutionaries in Laqueur's view.

Richard Rubenstein (1987, p. 103) disagrees with Laqueur. Rubenstein uses the examples of Russian revolutionaries to argue that there was no fundamental difference between nineteenth and twentieth century anarchism. Terrorists from both centuries wrote similar tracts and believed in the same ideals. When revolutionary terrorists of the twentieth and twenty-first centuries are considered, the only difference between the 1800s and today, according to Rubenstein, is time.

Regardless of the debate, the writings of the Russians were powerful. Nechaev (1987, pp. 68–71) laid down the principles of revolution in the "Catechism of the Revolutionary." His spirit has been reflected in writings of the late twentieth century. Rubenstein compared the "Catechism" to Carlos Marighella's *The Minimanual of the Urban Guerrilla* and found no essential differences. Both Laqueur and Rubenstein believe that Nechaev's influence lives on.

Bakunin (1987, pp. 65–68) believed the Russian government had been established on thievery. In "Revolution, Terrorism, Banditry," he argued that the only method of breaking state power was revolt. Such rhetoric did not endear Nechaev and Bakunin to the czar, but it did make them popular with later revolutionaries. Laqueur (1999) concludes such revolutionary pronouncements, however, correctly belong with Russian expressionist literature, not terrorist philosophy.

These philosophies guided the Peoples' Will. They murdered the police chief of Moscow and went on a campaign of bombing and murder. In May 1881, they succeeded in striking their ultimate target; they killed Czar

Alexander II. Ironically, this brought about their downfall. Alexander III (who ruled from 1881 to 1894) ended all attempts at reform. The Peoples' Will was eliminated, and revolutionaries went underground. Nicholas II (who ruled from 1894 to 1917) succeeded Alexander in 1894. Czar Nicholas was a man destined to be toppled by revolutionary forces.

Nicholas faced his first revolution in 1905, after his army lost a war to Japan. In addition to losing the war, Russia was consumed with economic problems and bureaucratic inefficiency. A group of unemployed workers began demonstrations in St. Petersburg, while some enlisted men in the Russian Navy mutinied. Their actions were brutally repressed, but the spirit of revolution burned below the surface. Russian revolutionaries needed another national disaster to create the atmosphere for victory. It came in 1914, when Russia entered World War I.

By 1917, the Russian people were tired of their economic woes and their czar. In February, a general strike in St. Petersburg turned into a revolution. Unlike 1905, the Russian Army joined the workers, and a new Russian government was formed. The Russians assured their allies that they would remain in the war, and they envisioned a period of capitalist economic expansion to save the beleaguered Russian economy. Workers Councils (Soviets) were established in major Russian cities.

The primary mistake of the February revolutionaries, called Mensheviks, was that they kept Russia in an unpopular war. This had two immediate ramifications. It created unrest at home, and it inspired the Germans to seek a way to remove Russia from World War I. The Germans found their answer in Vladimir Ilich Lenin. He promised to take Russia out of the war if the Germans would help him obtain power. After the German High Command assisted Lenin in returning to Russia and gaining control of the Bolsheviks (Communist revolutionaries who opposed the Mensheviks), Lenin orchestrated a second revolution in October 1917 and removed Russia from the war.

The Russian Revolution utilized terrorism in a new manner, and this had an impact on the way people viewed terrorism in the twentieth century. Lenin and one of his lieutenants, Leon Trotsky, believed terrorism should be used as an instrument for overthrowing middle-class, or bourgeois, governments. Once power was achieved, they advocated terrorism as a means of controlling internal enemies and a method for coping with international strife. Russia was very weak after the revolution. It faced foreign intervention, and it was torn by civil war. By threatening to export terrorism, Lenin and Trotsky hoped to keep their enemies, primarily Western Europe and the United States, at bay.

It is important to understand the connection between the Russian Revolution and terrorism for two reasons. First, by threatening to export terror, Lenin and Trotsky placed the fear of Communist revolution in the minds of many people in the West. To some, terrorism and Communism became synonymous. Though the Russians and later the Soviets were never very good at carrying insurrection to other lands, Western leaders began to fear that Communist terrorists were on the verge of toppling democratic governments. Despite the fact that Lenin and his successor Joseph Stalin (who ruled from

1922 to 1953) were most successful at another form of terror, murdering their own people, fear of Communist insurrection lasted well into the twentieth century, and some people still accept this belief as doctrine.

Some terrorist analysts accept it, too. For example, in 1986, Neil Livingstone described terrorism as a form of war sponsored ultimately by client states of the former Soviet Union. Adding the voice of journalism, Claire Sterling, in the same year, wrote that all terrorism was part of a Communist plot. Although there is no doubt the Soviets tried to support terrorist groups every time they got a chance, it is a gross simplification to assume a problem as complex as international terrorism could be blamed on a single source. To be fair to analysts like Livingstone, Soviet rhetoric did little to disprove his idea. In addition, Livingstone's analysis of state-supported terrorism is very good.

There is a valuable lesson to learn from ascribing too much power to terrorist conspiracies. Today, many respectable terrorist experts encourage American leaders to believe most terrorism is a result of militant Islam or the Islamacist movement. Salam Al-Marayati (1994) cites Yoseff Bodansky as an example. Al-Marayati says labeling Islam as a cause of terrorism misrepresents the principal tenets of the religion. Furthermore, it distorts the complex issues behind international terrorism. In the same way, the Russian Revolution was not the source of terrorism in the twentieth century, despite popular opinions. Modern terrorism is more complicated than this and cannot be blamed on a single demon.

A second reason for considering the Russian Revolution is that Lenin's victory and subsequent writings have inspired terrorists from 1917 to the present. While Communist terrorism was not part of an orchestrated conspiracy, it did influence behavior. Some terrorists scoured the works of Lenin and Trotsky, as well as other Russian revolutionaries, to formulate theories, tactics, and ideologies. Although not a simple conspiracy of evil, this influence was real and remains today.

OLD AND NEW TERRORISM

The Western tradition of terrorism is not new. Modern revolutionary terrorism evolved from anarchist violence of the late 1800s. Confusion about this point has resulted from misreadings of the Russian Revolution. Terror from the right, meanwhile, was hardly noticed, though after World War I, fascist gangs emerged in Europe and took over the governments of Spain, Italy, and Germany. Like the Soviets, fascists ruled by terror, but they were not terrorists in the modern sense. Contemporary terrorism was to emerge in the 1950s in anticolonial revolutions, and in the 1960s with political unrest in the West.

James Fraser and Ian Fulton (1984) maintain a distinction should be drawn between terrorism before World War II and modern-day terrorism. They refer to these phases as "old terrorism" and "new terrorism." Old terrorism was tied to the anarchist ideology. It was based on the radical philosophy of the bomb and, other than eliciting fear from established governments, was not very effective. They feel new terrorism is quite different, not in its philosophy but in its effectiveness.

Fraser and Fulton identify several factors that distinguish "new" terrorism from "old terrorism." The first is the news media. Terrorism reaches more people than it did in the past. This factor is closely related to a second, communications. News of terrorist incidents would not spread quickly were it not for instantaneous global communication links. Third, terrorist weapons are increasingly sophisticated and deadly. Old terrorism was linked to dynamite, but new terrorism employs a vast array of technological weapons. Finally, modern terrorists have increased their striking power through mobile command, support, and communications networks. New terrorists also enjoy increased mobility overall. According to Fraser and Fulton, all of these factors have changed terrorism.

Walter Laqueur (1987, p. 91) notes another difference, which can be summarized as improved targeting. Using experiences in Russia to support his contention, Laqueur argues that modern terrorists are more ruthless than their historical counterparts were. Not only does Laqueur believe the terrorism of historical terrorists was mainly rhetorical, but he also points out that Russian anarchists were extremely selective about their targets. He cites one case in which an anarchist refused to toss a bomb at a Russian official because he was afraid he would injure innocent bystanders.

Laqueur notes that this sensitivity is hardly typical of modern-day terrorists. He says modern terrorism has been typified by indiscriminate violence and the intentional targeting of the civilian population. Modern terrorists strike at governments by killing their citizens: They strike airliners, buses, and other targets containing innocent noncombatants with no vested interest in the outcome of a political struggle. Modern terrorists engage in the sensationalized murder of innocents.

Richard Rubenstein (1987, p. 103) wholeheartedly objects to such attempts to dichotomize violence into new and old phases. He claims there is no evidence that terrorists have become more violent, believing instead that conventional opinions are incorrect. Rubenstein believes terrorism today is the same as it was yesterday and there is little or no difference between old and new.

Setting aside the old-versus-new debate, it is clear that terrorism in the Western experience follows a certain tradition: In the West, terrorists are motivated by ideology or nationalism. This became clear after World War II. Terrorism was rejuvenated in the 1960s as a tool used by zealots across the political spectrum. Nationalist and revolutionary groups began to view themselves as protagonists in a struggle against Western authorities. According to David Rapoport (1988), the Vietnam War, anticolonial movement, and general questioning of social order provided cohesive links among terrorist groups.

An even greater difference emerged in the 1990s when terrorists focused on combining religious fanaticism with weapons of mass destruction. Bruce

Hoffman (1999), Ian Lesser (1999), and Walter Laqueur (1999) refer to this latter difference as "new" terrorism. However, perhaps it is more useful to view terrorism as a manifestation of violence in a particular time period. Terrorism evolves and manifests itself in differing ways. In a sense, this means terrorism is always new.

As terrorism evolved in the West from the French Revolution to the October Revolution in Russia, another form of terror appeared in the midst of World War I. Revolutionary leaders in Ireland were inspired by America's fight for freedom and the revolutionary writings of militant anarchists. Some espoused ideas from Lenin's book. Because of this, Ireland is the next stop in the story of the development of modern terrorism.

KEY CONCEPTS

1. The Scientific Revolution of the 1600s and the Enlightenment of the 1700s provided the political base for democratic government.
2. The American Revolution involved a conservative transfer of power between classes, but the French Revolution violently ripped power from the upper classes. Modern terrorism originated in this period.
3. By 1848, the term terrorism was used to describe the actions of violent radical democrats, socialists, and anarchists who revolted against established governments for the purpose of restructuring the economic order.
4. The tactics of Russian anarchists and eventually Russian Communists have served to inspire terrorists up to the present day.
5. Some people argue that the forms of terrorism described in this chapter are "old terrorism," but terrorism is always evolving and changing.

FOOD FOR THOUGHT

After a revolution, a new government will frequently order the execution of former government officials, if they fear a violent counterrevolution. In addition, when a new government is weak and threatened by enemies, it will frequently try to extend its revolutionary ideology into neighboring countries. Do you think this helps to explain terrorism? Are such courses of action moral? Are they logical? What do you know about modern revolutions in China, Cuba, or Iran? Do you see any link between revolutionary activities in these countries and the logic of terrorism?

FURTHER READING

For the American Revolution, see Kevin Phillips, *The Cousin's Wars: Religion, Politics, and the Triumph of Anglo America*

For France, see Christopher Hibbert, *The Days of the French Revolution*

For Russia, see Henry Christman's edited work *Essential Works of Lenin*

To compare revolutionary thought, see Dimitry Schlapentokh, *The Counter-Revolution in Revolution: Images of Thermidor and Napoleon at the Time of the Russian Revolution and Civil War*

6

The Origins
of the Irish Troubles

As terrorism grew in Russia from anarchists, the Peoples' Will, and the October Revolution, a similar type of terrorist campaign began to appear in the United Kingdom. Irish Republicans, long angered by the colonial rule of England, incorporated modern terrorist techniques in their campaign of revolution. The Irish developed nationalistic terrorism, and the Irish Republican Army set the stage for modern terrorism. In examining the development of modern terrorism, it is necessary to step back to consider the history, politics, and origins of modern terrorism in Ireland.

After reading this chapter, you should be able to do the following:

1. Sketch the origins and development of Anglo-Irish conflict.
2. Outline the early history of the Irish Republican Army.
3. Summarize the Easter Rebellion.
4. Describe the Tan War.
5. List the events that rejuvenated the IRA in the late 1960s and early 1970s.
6. Describe the origins, development, and logic of Orange terrorism.

THE ORIGINS AND DEVELOPMENT
OF THE ANGLO-IRISH CONFLICT

In August 1969, the British Army was ordered to increase its presence in Northern Ireland in an effort to quell a series of riots. (See map in Figure 6.1.) Although the British Army had maintained bases in Northern Ireland for a while, riotous situations in Londonderry and Belfast were suddenly far beyond the control of local police and the handful of British regular soldiers stationed in the area. On August 18, 1969, British Army reinforcements began arriving, hoping to avoid a long-term conflict. Their hopes were in vain. The British Army would soon become embroiled in a new outbreak of a war that had spanned centuries.

Ireland has not been completely ruled by the Irish since a series of Viking incursions in 800 C.E. Giovani Costigan (1980) writes that Irish culture originated with Celtic invasions three centuries before Christ. The Irish settled in tribal groups, and government was maintained through kinship and clans. No Celtic ruler or political authority ever united Ireland as a single entity.

In about 500 C.E., the Irish were introduced to Christianity and became some of the most fervent converts in the world. The medieval church played a large role in uniting Ireland, but the traditional Gaelic tribal groups still remained separate. They submitted to a central religion, not a central political system. The relations among Gaelic tribes became important when Viking raiders began to attack Ireland in about 800 C.E. The divided Irish were dominated by their Viking rulers, and the Norsemen used Ireland as a trading base and center of commerce. The Vikings built several Irish cities, including Dublin.

Viking rule of Ireland was challenged in 1014, when a tribal chieftain, Brian Boru, was declared High King of Ireland. He led a united tribal army against the Vikings and defeated them at Clontarf. Fate ruled against the Irish, however. At the end of the battle as King Brian knelt in prayer, he was assassinated. Dreams of a united Ireland crumbled with Brian Boru's death, and the clans and tribes soon divided leadership again.

Costigan (1980) believes this paved the way for a gradual Norman invasion of Ireland. The Normans were the descendants of William the Conqueror and had ambitions for extending their domains. With the Irish divided and the Viking influence limited, Normans began to stake out territorial claims on the island with the permission of the Norman king. The Normans were particularly successful in Ireland because they used new methods of warfare. By 1172, the Norman king of England had assumed the rule of Ireland.

The Normans and the Irish struggled in a way that was not reflective of modern fighting. The Normans could not maintain the field force necessary to control the Irish peasants, and the Irish did not have the technology that would allow them to attack smaller Norman forces barricaded in castles. Therefore, the Normans built castles to control Irish cities, and Irish peasants generally dominated rural areas. This situation continued until the sixteenth century.

FIGURE 6.1 Map of Ireland

The Protestant Reformation of the 1500s had a tremendous impact on Ireland. Wanting to free himself from the ecclesiastical shackles of Rome, the English king, Henry VIII, created an independent Church of England. He followed up by creating a similar church in Ireland, but the Irish Catholics could not stomach this move. They began to rebel against the English king, and the troubles created by the Reformation have literally continued into the twenty-first century in Ireland.

The problems of the early Reformation were magnified by Henry's daughter Elizabeth. Not content with merely ruling Ireland, Elizabeth I carved out the most prosperous agrarian section and gave it to her subjects to colonize: This resulted in the creation of the Plantation of Ulster. English and Scottish Protestants eventually settled there, displacing many of the original Irish inhabitants. This created an ethnic division in Ireland fueled by religious differences and animosities.

Costigan (1980) believes the 1600s in Ireland were dominated by three major issues. First, the Plantation of Ulster was expanded, and Irish peasants were systematically displaced. Many of them perished. Second, Oliver Cromwell came to Ireland to quell a revolt and stop Catholic attacks on

Protestants. He literally massacred thousands of Irish Catholics, thanking God for granting him the opportunity to kill such a large number of his enemies. Cromwell's name still stirs hatred as a result.

The third issue of the 1600s also involved Catholic and Protestant struggles, and the image of the conflict is still celebrated in ceremonies today. From 1689 to 1691, James II, the Catholic pretender to the British throne, used Ireland as a base from which to revolt against William of Orange, the English king. In August 1689, Irish Protestant skilled workers, called "Apprentice Boys," were relieved by the English after defending Derry through a long siege by the pretender. The following year William defeated James at the battle of the Boyne River.

The revolt was over, but the Protestants were now forever in the camp of the House of Orange. The Protestants have flaunted these victories in the face of the Catholics since 1690. Each year they gather to militantly celebrate the battle of the Boyne and the Apprentice Boys with parades and demonstrations. It fuels the fire of hatred in Northern Ireland and demonstrates the division between Protestants and Catholics. In fact, the current troubles started in 1969, when riots broke out in Londonderry and Belfast following the annual Apprentice Boys parade.

The 1700s and early 1800s were characterized by waves of revolt, starvation, and emigration. Irish nationalists rose to challenge English rule, but they were always soundly defeated. Each generation seemed to bring a new series of martyrs willing to give their lives in the struggle against the English.

Among the best-known revolutionaries was Thomas Wolfe Tone. From 1796 to 1798, Wolfe Tone led a revolt based on Irish nationalism. He tried to appeal to both Protestants and Catholics in an attempt to form a unified front against Great Britain. Wolfe Tone argued that Irish independence was more important than religious differences. In the end, his revolt failed, but he had created a basis for appealing to nationalism over religion.

Despite the efforts of people like Wolfe Tone, religious animosity did not die in Ireland. During the late 1700s, Protestants and Catholics began to form paramilitary organizations. Divided along religious lines, these defense organizations began violently to confront one another. The Orange Orders were born in this period. Taking their name from William of Orange, these Protestant organizations vowed to remain unified with Great Britain. The Orange Lodges soon grew to dominate the political and social life of the north of Ireland.

The early 1800s brought a new level of political struggle to Ireland. In 1801, the British Parliament passed the Act of Union, designed to incorporate Ireland into the United Kingdom. Struggle over the act began to dominate Irish politics. Unionists, primarily the Orange Protestants in the North, supported the act, whereas republicans, who became known as Greens, argued for a constitutional government and an independent Ireland. Daniel O'Connell led the republican movement in the early part of the century, and Charles Stewart Parnell, a Protestant, created a democratic Irish party to support the cause in the late 1800s.

The struggle for republicanism accompanied one of the saddest periods in Irish history. Displaced from the land, Irish peasants were poor and susceptible to economic and agricultural fluctuations. Historian Cecil Woodham-Smith (1962) documents that Ireland had undergone a series of famines in the 1840s, as peasants in the country began to rely on the potato as their main crop. In 1845, the crop failed, and agricultural production among the peasants came to a standstill until 1848. Even though thousands of Irish people began to starve, wealthy farms in the North exported other crops for cash.

The 1845–1848 famine devastated Ireland. Its effects were felt primarily among the poor, especially among the Irish Catholics. In an era in which other industrialized nations were experiencing a tremendous rise in population, Ireland's census dropped by 25 percent. As famine and disease took their toll, thousands of Irish people emigrated to other parts of the world. During this period, unionists in the North consolidated their hold on Ulster.

In the years following the famine, some members of the British Parliament sought to free Ireland from British control. They introduced a series of home rule acts designed to give Ireland independence. Charles Stewart Parnell and other republicans supported home rule, but they faced fierce opposition from unionists. The unionists were afraid home rule would shift the balance of economic power in the North. They believed continued union with Great Britain was their only option for economic success. Unionists were supported in British military circles.

Even though Parnell was a Protestant, most republicans were Catholics living in the southern portion of Ireland. Unionists tended to be Protestant skilled laborers, industrialists, and landlords in the North. The religious aspect of the conflict remained and was augmented by deep economic divisions.

Another aspect of the evolving conflict needs to be emphasized. By the nineteenth century, both the unionists and the republicans were fully Irish. This means neither side comprised transplanted settlers from another country, but the Catholics and the Protestants—despite all political differences—identified themselves as citizens of the Emerald Isle. Unionist Protestants in the North had lived in Ireland for generations, and they were as Irish as their Catholic counterparts. The unionists were able to call on Britain for help, but the struggle in Ireland began to take on the earmarks of an intra-Irish conflict. Irish unionists, usually Protestant, dominated the North, and Irish republicans, primarily Catholics, controlled the South.

THE EARLY HISTORY
OF THE IRISH REPUBLICAN ARMY

By the twentieth century, the struggle in Ireland had become a matter of the divisions between unionists and republicans. A host of other conflicts was associated with this confrontation, but the main one was the unionist-republican struggle. The unionists often had the upper hand because they could call on support from the British-sponsored police and military forces. The republicans had no such luxury, and they searched for an alternative.

Costigan (1980) believes that the republican military solution to the Irish conflict was born in New York City in 1857. Irish Catholics had emigrated from their homeland to America, Australia, Canada, and New Zealand, but they never forgot the people they left behind. Irish immigrants in New York City created the Irish Republican Brotherhood (IRB) as a financial relief organization for relatives in the old country. After the American Civil War, some Irish soldiers returning from the U.S. Army decided to take the struggle for emancipation back to Ireland. Rationalizing that they had fought for the North to free the slaves, they believed they should continue the struggle and free Ireland. The IRB gradually evolved into a revolutionary organization.

J. Bowyer Bell (1974) has written the definitive treatise on the origins and development of the Irish Republican Army (IRA). He states it began with a campaign of violence sponsored by the IRB in the late 1800s. Spurred on by increased Irish nationalist feeling in the homeland and the hope of home rule, the IRB waged a campaign of bombing and assassination from 1870 until 1916. Its primary targets were unionists and British forces supporting the unionist cause. Among their greatest adversaries was the British-backed police force in Ireland, the Royal Irish Constabulary (RIC).

The activities of the IRB frightened Irish citizens who wanted to remain united with Great Britain. For the most part, these Irish people were Protestant and middle-class, and they lived in the North. They gravitated toward their trade unions and social organizations, called Orange Lodges, to counter growing IRB sympathy and power. They enjoyed the sympathy of the British Army's officer corps. They also controlled the RIC.

The Fenians (named after a mythical Irish hero, Finn McCool) of the IRB remained undaunted by unionist sentiment. Although Irish unionists seemed in control, the IRB had two trumps. First, IRB leadership was dominated by men who believed each generation had to produce warriors who would fight for independence. Some of these leaders, as well as their followers, were quite willing to be martyred to keep republicanism alive. In addition, the IRB had an organization. It not only served as a threat to British power, but it also provided the basis for the resurgence of Irish culture.

At the turn of the century, no person embodied Irish culture more than Patrick Pearse. The headmaster of an Irish school, Pearse was an inspirational romantic. He could move crowds to patriotism and inspire resistance to British policies. He was a hero among Irish-Americans, and they sent hundreds of thousands of dollars to support his cause. He told young Irish boys and girls about their heritage, he taught them Gaelic, and he inspired them to be militantly proud of being Irish. He was also a member of the Supreme Council of the Irish Republican Brotherhood. When the concept of home rule was defeated in the British parliament, republican eyes turned to Pearse.

THE 1916 EASTER REBELLION

By 1916, the situation in Ireland had changed. The British had promised home rule to Ireland when World War I (1914–1918) came to an end. While most people in Ireland believed the British, unionists and republicans secretly armed for a civil war between the North and South. They believed a fight was inevitable if the British granted home rule, and each side was determined to dominate the government of a newly independent Ireland. Some forces were not willing to wait for home rule.

With British attention focused on Germany, leaders of the IRB believed it was time for a strike against the unionists and their British supporters. At Easter in 1916, Patrick Pearse and James Connolly led a revolt in Dublin. Pearse was a romantic idealist who felt the revolt was doomed from the start but believed it necessary to sacrifice his life to keep the republican spirit alive. Connolly was a more pragmatic socialist who fought because he believed a coming civil war was inevitable.

The 1916 Easter Rebellion enjoyed local success because it surprised everyone. Pearse and Connolly took over several key points in Dublin with a few thousand armed followers. From the halls of the General Post Office, Pearse announced that the revolutionaries had formed an Irish Republic and asked the Irish to follow him. The British, outraged by what they deemed to be treachery in the midst of a larger war, also came to Dublin. The city was engulfed in a week of heavy fighting.

Whereas Pearse and Connolly came to start a popular revolution, the British came to fight a war. In a few days, Dublin was devastated by British artillery. Pearse recognized the futility of the situation and asked for terms. J. Bowyer Bell (1974) points out the interesting way Pearse chose to approach the British: He sent a message using a new title, Commanding General of the Irish Republican Army, to the general in charge of British forces. The IRB had transformed itself into an army: the IRA.

Transformations continued in the political arena, and, ironically, what Pearse and Connolly could not achieve in life, they could achieve in death. Irish opinion was solidly against the IRA, and most Irish people held Pearse and Connolly responsible for the destruction of Dublin. The British, however, failed to capitalize on this sentiment. Rather than listen to public opinion, they cracked down on all expressions of republicanism. Dozens of republicans, including Pearse and the wounded Connolly, were executed, and thousands were sentenced to prison. The British promise of home rule seemed forgotten. Most Irish people were appalled by the harsh British reaction, and the ghosts of Pearse and Connolly rose in the IRA. Irish political opinion shifted to favor revolution.

THE INFLUENCE OF RUSSIAN REVOLUTION: DE VALERA, COLLINS, AND THE TAN WAR

Sinn Fein, the political party of republicanism, continued its activities in spite of the failure of the Easter Rebellion. When World War I ended, many of the republicans were released. Eamon De Valera, whose life had been spared because he was born in America, emerged as the leader of Sinn Fein. Michael Collins, who avoided extended imprisonment because he happened to walk over to one side of the room when other prisoners were singled out for punishment, came to the forefront of the IRA. Together De Valera and Collins began to fight for Irish independence in 1919.

Michael Collins studied the tactics of the Russian Peoples' Will and the writings of earlier anarchists and terrorists. He used these items as an inspiration for strategy and launched a guerrilla war against the British. After obtaining a list of British and loyalist Irish police and intelligence officers, Collins sent IRA terrorists to their homes and killed them. He attacked police stations and symbols of British authority. A master of terrorist strategy, Collins continued a campaign of terror against unionists and the RIC.

The British responded by sending a hastily recruited military force, called the Black and Tans because of their mismatched uniforms, and Ireland became the scene of a dreadful war. Both sides accused the other of atrocities, but murder and mayhem were the tactics of each party. The conflict became popularly known as the Tan War or the Black and Tan War.

Meanwhile, home rule had not been forgotten by more moderate groups. Politicians in Britain and Ireland sought to bring an end to the violence by formulating the steps to grant Irish independence. The main stumbling block was the North. Protestant unionists were afraid of being abandoned by the British. In 1921, the situation was temporarily solved by a treaty between Britain and Ireland. Under the terms of the treaty, Ireland would be granted independence while the northern section around Ulster would remain under British protection until it could peacefully be integrated into Ireland. Southern Ireland became the free state—the Republic of Ireland. The majority of people in Ireland accepted the treaty. Michael Collins also accepted the treaty, but the IRA did not.

When the treaty between Ireland and Britain was ratified in 1921, a civil war broke out in the newly formed Republic. Michael Collins led the Irish Army, while his former colleague Eamon De Valera took the helm of the IRA. The IRA fought Irish government forces, claiming that Irish independence had to extend to all Irish people. They rejected British control of the North. De Valera campaigned against his former colleagues and eventually orchestrated the murder of Michael Collins.

For their part, the British wanted nothing to do with the civil war in the southern areas. They tightened their hold on Northern Ireland and bolstered its strength with a new police force, the Royal Ulster Constabulary (RUC).

The northern unionists were delighted when the British established a semiautonomous government in Northern Ireland and gave it special powers to combat the IRA. The unionists used this power to gain control of Northern Ireland and lock themselves into the British orbit. Ireland became a divided country.

TRENDS IN THE IRA: 1930–1985

In 1927, De Valera was elected as Prime Minister. Although he passed several anti-British measures, he was soon at odds with the IRA. Two important trends emerged. J. Bowyer Bell (1974) records the first by pointing to the split in IRA ranks. By the 1930s, some members of the IRA wanted to follow the lead of their political party, Sinn Fein. They felt the IRA should express itself through peaceful political idealism. They believed they should begin working for a united socialist Ireland in the spirit of James Connolly.

Another group of IRA members rejected this philosophy. They believed the purpose of the IRA was to fight for republicanism. They would never be at peace with the British or the unionists until the North was united with the South. They vowed to carry on the fight. They broke with the De Valera government and formed a provisional wing of the IRA in the 1930s. The Provisional IRA vowed to keep up the fight, and De Valera turned on them. The Provisional IRA was silenced for a number of years. They launched an ineffective terrorist campaign in Northern Ireland from 1956 to 1962, and they fell out of favor with Irish republicans. Just when it seemed the Provisional IRA was defunct, a Catholic civil rights campaign engulfed Northern Ireland in 1969. The failure of the civil rights movement in Northern Ireland can be directly linked to modern Irish terrorism and the rebirth of the IRA.

Alfred McClung Lee (1983, pp. 59–97) records another trend in Ireland. Internally, the IRA split into a traditional official branch and a more militant provisional wing. He notes that externally the economic situation in Northern Ireland consolidated in favor of the Protestant unionists. From 1922 to 1966, the government in Northern Ireland systematically reduced the civil rights of Catholics living in the North. During the same period, the economic power of the unionists increased.

According to Lee, the political and economic conditions in Northern Ireland provided the rationale for a major civil rights movement among the Catholics. Although the movement had republican overtones, it was primarily aimed at achieving adequate housing and education among Ulster's Catholic population in an attempt to improve economic growth. The civil rights movement was supported by both Protestants and Catholics, but the actions of the Northern Irish government began to polarize the issue. Increasingly the confrontation became recognized as a unionist-republican one, and the old battlelines between Protestants and Catholics were redrawn. By 1969, the civil rights movement and the reaction to it had become violent.

The IRA had not been dormant throughout the civil rights movement, but it had failed to play a major role. For the most part, the leaders of the civil rights movement were peaceful republicans. The IRA could not entice the civil rights leaders into a guerrilla war, and it had virtually destroyed itself in an earlier campaign against the government of Northern Ireland. In 1969, the Provisional IRA was popular in song and legend, but it held little sway in day-to-day Irish politics. Some type of miracle would be needed to rejuvenate the IRA.

The reason for IRA impotence can be found in the second generation of Provisionals. Wanting to follow in the footsteps of their forebears, the Provisionals began to wage a campaign against the RUC in Northern Ireland in the late 1950s. They established support bases in the Republic and slipped across the border for terrorist activities.

Although they initially enjoyed support among republican enclaves in the North, most Irish people, unionists and republicans alike, were appalled by IRA violence. Even the Officials criticized the military attacks of the Provisionals. Faced with a lack of public support, the Provisional IRA called off its offensive in the North. By 1962, almost all of its activities had ceased. Some Provisionals joined the civil rights movement; others rejoined former colleagues in the Official wing. Most members, however, remained in a secret infrastructure and prayed for a miracle to restore their ranks and prestige. In 1969, their prayers were answered.

Repression on the part of the Northern government was the answer to IRA prayers. The government in Northern Ireland reacted with a heavy hand against the civil rights workers and demonstrators. Max Hastings (1970, pp. 40–56) writes that peaceful attempts to work for equal rights were stymied by Northern Irish militancy. Catholics were not allowed to demonstrate for better housing and education; if they attempted to do so, they were attacked by the RUC and its reserve force, known as B-Specials. At the same time no attempts were made to stop Protestant demonstrations. The Catholics believed the RUC and B-Specials were in league with the other anti-Catholic unionists in the North.

Issues intensified in the summer of 1969. Civil rights demonstrators planned a long, peaceful march from Londonderry to Belfast, but they were gassed and beaten by the RUC and B-Specials. On August 15, 1969, the Protestants assembled for their traditional Apprentice Boys celebration. Just a few days before, the RUC had enthusiastically attacked Catholic demonstrators, but on August 15, 1969, it welcomed the Protestant Apprentice Boys with open arms. The Catholics were not surprised: Many B-Specials had taken off their reservist uniforms to don orange sashes and march with the Protestants.

Protestant marchers in Londonderry and Belfast armed themselves with gasoline bombs, rocks, and sticks. They not only wished to celebrate the seventeenth-century victory in Derry, but they were also thrilled by the recent dispersal of the civil rights marchers and hoped to reinforce their political status by bombarding Catholic neighborhoods as they marched by. When the

Protestants began taunting Catholics, violence broke out. By nightfall, Belfast and Londonderry were in flames. Three days later, Britain sent the British Army in as a peacekeeping force. Ironically, the British Army became the miracle that the IRA so desperately needed.

According to most analysts and observers, the early policies and tactics of the British Army played an important role in the rebirth of the IRA. In an article on military policy, J. Bowyer Bell (1976, pp. 65–88) criticizes the British Army for its initial response. He says the British Army came to Ulster with little or no appreciation of the historical circumstances behind the conflict. According to Bell, when the Army arrived in 1969, its commanders believed they were in the midst of a colonial war. They evaluated the situation and concluded there were two "tribes." One tribe flew the Irish tricolor and spoke with deep-seated hatred of the British. The other tribe flew the Union Jack and claimed to be ultrapatriotic subjects of the British Empire. It seemed logical to ally with friends who identified themselves as subjects.

Bell believes this policy was a fatal flaw. Far from being a conflict to preserve British influence in a colony, the struggle in Northern Ireland was a fight between two groups of Irish citizens. Neither side was "British," no matter what their slogans and banners claimed. The British Army should have become the peaceful, neutral force, but it mistakenly allied itself with one of the extremist positions in the conflict. That mistake became the answer to IRA prayers.

Bell argues that the reaction of republican Catholics fully demonstrates the mistake the British Army made. The unionists greeted the British Army with open arms, but this was to be expected. Historically, the British Army had rallied to the unionist cause. Surprisingly, however, the republicans also welcomed the British Army. They believed that the RUC and B-Specials were the instruments of their repression and that the British Army would not continue those restrictive measures. It was not the British Army of the past. In republican eyes, it was a peacekeeping force. The republicans believed the British Army would protect them from the unionists and the police.

Such beliefs were short-lived. As the British Army made its presence felt in Ulster, republicans and Catholics were subjected to the increasing oppression of British Army measures. Catholic neighborhoods were surrounded and gassed by military forces searching for subversives, and the soldiers began working as a direct extension of the RUC. Londonderry and Belfast were military targets, and rebels fighting against the government were to be subdued. As confrontations became more deadly, republican support for the British Army vanished.

Feeling oppressed by all sides, Catholics and republicans looked for help. They found it, partly, in the form of the IRA. The Officials and Provisionals were still split during the 1969 riots, and the IRA was generally an impotent organization. According to Iain Hamilton (1971), the IRA pushed its internal squabbles aside, and the Officials and Provisionals focused on their new common enemy, the British Army. The new IRA policy emphasized the elimination of British soldiers from Irish soil and brushed aside internal political differences.

Robert Moss (1972, pp. 16–18) remarks that the British Army found itself in the middle of the conflict it had hoped to forestall. Alienated nationalists offered support for the growing ranks of the IRA. Each time the British Army overreacted, as it tended to do when faced with civil disobedience, the republican cause was strengthened.

Reporter Simon Winchester (1974, pp. 171–180) notes another outcome of the conflict: As IRA ranks grew, Orange extremist organizations also began to swell. While crackdowns by British Army patrols and incidents of alleged torture by intelligence services increased the ranks of the IRA, unionist paramilitary organizations grew in response. The British Army also began taking action against the unionist organizations and then truly found itself in the midst of a terrorist conflict.

In 1972, the British government issued a report on the violence in Northern Ireland. Headed by Leslie Scarman (1972), the investigation concluded that tensions inside the community were so great, once they had been unleashed, little could be done to stop them. The policies of the police and the British Army had done much to set those hostile forces in motion. The report concluded that normative democracy could not return until the people in Northern Ireland had faith in all government institutions, including the security forces. The report indicated that a legal method was needed to resolve the violence.

ORANGE TERROR

While most Irish terrorism is correctly associated with the IRA and its radical splinter groups, it is not proper to conclude that all Irish terrorism is the result of republican violence. Unionist organizations also have a long history of terrorism. They represent the Orange or Protestant side of terror.

Prior to the Easter Rebellion, there was little need for Orange militancy, since the Orange groups controlled the events in Ireland through the police and military. For example, the IRB began importing arms prior to World War I (1914–1918). Unionists, fearful of Catholic republican power, decided to arm themselves. Although the British government had forbidden importing arms, the police officers ignored this one night as thousands of illegal arms were smuggled into the Orange Lodges. The British Army also failed to act. Its officers had confined soldiers to their barracks while the arms were distributed.

The Orange position also enjoyed the backing of the military in other ways. Prior to World War I, it appeared home rule would be passed by the British parliament. In order to influence the vote, British officers began to resign their commissions en masse, forcing a crisis in government. The United Kingdom was on the verge of war with Germany; it could hardly fight without the leadership of its officer corps. Home rule was withdrawn, and Ireland remained under British control.

Things changed after the Tan War and the creation of the Republic of Ireland. Although De Valera waged war against his old colleagues, the IRA still brought terrorism to the North. At this point some unionist groups formed terrorist enclaves of their own. Their primary purpose was to terrorize the republicans.

Unionist terrorism has focused on retribution. When Green terrorists strike a target, Orange terrorists strike back. The Orange terrorists have also been involved in the assassination of Catholic leaders, especially outspoken leaders during the civil rights movement. Orange terrorism has never matched Green terrorism simply because unionists were able to use official organizations to repress Catholics in Northern Ireland.

Seamus Dunn and Valerie Morgan (1995) argue that this attitude may change. In 1985, the United Kingdom and the Republic of Ireland signed a peace accord regarding the governance of Northern Ireland. Known as the Anglo-Irish Peace Accord, the agreement seeks to bring an end to terrorism by establishing a joint system of government for the troubled area. Dunn and Morgan believe many Protestant groups feel betrayed by this agreement. They surmise such groups may resort to violence if they feel they have no voice in the political system. This may create a change in the style of Orange terrorism.

Orange terrorism did not follow a specific theory of revolution; it emerged as a reaction to republican terrorism. Orange terrorism has increased as a result of the loss of Protestant power in the North. The current status of this conflict will be reviewed when examining problems in contemporary terrorism later in this book.

In continuing the discussion of the development of modern terrorism, we now turn to the Middle East. Middle Eastern terrorists, both Jews and Arabs, studied the anarchists of Russia and the tactics of Michael Collins. Terrorism emerged in yet another form in the Middle East, the focus of the next chapter.

KEY CONCEPTS

1. The struggle for Irish independence lasted more than 1,000 years. It involved ethnic and religious struggle.

2. The Irish Republican Army (IRA) emerged from this struggle and staged a rebellion in Dublin in 1916.

3. Using tactics he learned by studying anarchists and revolutionaries in Russia, Michael Collins conducted a successful terrorist campaign after the failed 1916 revolution.

4. The failure to incorporate Northern Ireland in the Republic of Ireland forced a split in the IRA.

5. In 1969, renewed fighting rejuvenated the IRA.

FOOD FOR THOUGHT

The history of violence in Ireland brings three issues studied thus far in this book together. Religion has been part of the struggle since the Reformation. The distribution of wealth has been important because Ireland has been treated like a colony. Finally, revolutionary theories of the nineteenth century influenced Collins and his colleagues. Do you think a significant change in any one of these factors might have produced a more peaceful course for Ireland? Must politicians today consider all of these factors if they hope to bring peace to the region?

FURTHER READING

J. Bowyer Bell, *The Secret Army: A History of the IRA, 1916–1970.*

7

The Origins of Middle
Eastern Terrorism

The origins of modern terrorism have been reviewed in terms of its spread from Western European ideology to Russia, then back to the West by the incorporation of Russian revolutionary thought in the nationalist struggle in Ireland. Before discussing modern terrorism, it is necessary to look at the historical development of conflict in the Middle East. Several Middle Eastern groups took the concepts of modern terrorism and transformed them into a mode of conflict. This chapter introduces the development of religious and historical conflicts in the Middle East and the historical role of terrorism in the area.

After you read this chapter, you should be able to do the following:

1. Outline a religious, political, and historical introduction to the Middle East.

2. Provide a brief synopsis of the major problems in the Middle East.

3. Identify the three primary sources of terrorism in the Middle East.

4. Describe the Zionist movement in Palestine from the beginning of World War I to the Arab Revolt.

5. Describe the role of terrorism in the birth of modern Israel.

6. State the problems caused by intra-Arab power rivalries.

7. Explain the origins of Shiaism and its impact on revolutionary Iran.

AN INTRODUCTION TO THE REGION

The term *Middle East* refers to a section of the world that encompasses North Africa, Southwest Asia directly south of Turkey including the Arabian peninsula, Iran, and Afghanistan. (See map in Figure 7.1.) Some commentators also include Pakistan in their geographical definition of *Middle East* because it is dominated by Islamic culture. The term was coined by American naval strategist Alfred Thayer Mahan toward the end of the nineteenth century. Albert Hourani (1997) presents one of the most definitive histories of the area. According to Hourani, the area is dominated by two major concerns: the religion of Islam and the history of the Arab people.

The Prophet Mohammed, the founder of Islam, received a series of revelations from Gabriel, an angel known in Hebrew and Christian traditions, about 610 C.E. Mystified by his encounters with the angel and unable to write, Mohammed returned to his family after each event and related the angel's accounts of God's desires for humanity in a series of poems and verses. Dutiful family members recorded these revelations, and they were incorporated into a holy book called the Q'ran, or the Verses. Mohammed, elated by his angelic encounters with the Almighty, spread a message of universalism, love, and monotheism.

Although Mohammed's message was essentially based on love, discipline, and submission to God's will, merchants in his hometown of Mecca were incensed by his religious pronouncements. Mohammed spoke of a final judgment against evil. Such eschatology threatened the religious trade of Mecca, a trade center where various cultures crossed paths and many deities flourished in an atmosphere of polytheism. In short, there was a profit to be made in statues, charms, and relics, and Mohammed's talk of one universal power uniting humankind was bad for business. The merchants took the only logical step they could see. They tried to kill Mohammed.

Fleeing from Mecca, the Prophet's utterances did not stop. He gained a large following and in a few years returned to Mecca not only with a message of love, but also with a sword. Mohammed declared a holy war, a jihad, on all nonbelievers. Mecca became a holy city, and the Arab realm of Islam spread. At the time of his death about 632, Islam was a dominating and growing force in the Middle East.

Mohammed's followers spread Islam and Arabic culture through the Middle East in the years after his death. Two dynasties of leaders, the Umayyads (661–750) and the Abbasids (750–1258), ruled the area in the years following Mohammed. Hourani points out that these leaders, or caliphs, theologically divided the world into the Realm of Islam and the Realm of War. The purpose of Islam was to subject the world to God's will. Indeed, *Islam* means submission to the will of God, and a *Muslim* is one who submits.

About 1000 C.E. the Turks began to take the domains of the Abbasids. Struggles continued for the next 100 years until a Mongol advance from east

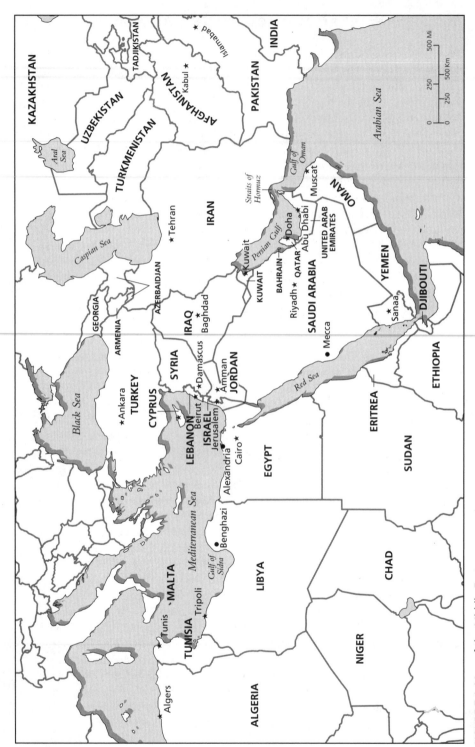

FIGURE 7.1 Map of the Middle East

Asia brought the Abbasid dynasty to an end. The Mongols were eventually stopped by an Egyptian army of slaves, and their descendants gave rise to a new group of Turks known as Ottomans. The Ottomans were aggressive, conquering most of the Middle East and large parts of Europe. The Ottomans fought the Iranians on one border and central Europeans on the other border for many years.

European relations with Islamic empires were not characterized by harmony. The West began its first violent encounters with the European attempts to conquer the Middle East known as the Crusades (1095 to about 1250). These affairs were bloody and instigated centuries of hatred and distrust between Muslims and Christians. European struggles with the Ottoman Empire reinforced years of military tensions between the two civilizations. Modern tensions in the area can be traced to the decline of Ottoman influence and the collapse of Iranian power in the eighteenth century. When these Islamic powers receded, Western Christian powers were quick to fill the void.

Yonah Alexander (1976) points out that issues of power shifts were complicated by a late nineteenth century concept called Zionism. Zionists began moving to Palestine in the 1890s for the purpose of establishing a Jewish homeland. This created some tension, as Syria and Egypt were vying for control of the area. The problem exploded in 1914, when World War I internationalized the political problems of the Middle East. Modern Middle Eastern terrorism can be traced to World War I's (1914–1918) political watershed.

A SYNOPSIS OF SOME MAJOR PROBLEMS

To understand terrorism in the Middle East, it is necessary to appreciate certain recent aspects of the region's history. To best understand the Middle East, keep the following assumptions in mind:

1. The current structure of Middle Eastern geography and political rule is a direct result of nineteenth century European imperial influence in the region and the outcomes of World War I.

2. Many of the Arab countries in the Middle East place more emphasis on the power of the family than on contemporary notions of government. However, Israel rules itself as a parliamentary democracy.

3. The modern state of Israel is not the nation mentioned in the Hebrew and Christian Bibles or the Islamic Q'ran. It is a secular power dominated by people of European descent.

4. Arabs, and Palestinians in particular, do not hold a monopoly on terrorism.

5. The religious differences in the region have developed over centuries, and fanaticism in any one of them can spawn violence. There are fanatical Jews, Christians, and Muslims in the Middle East who practice terrorism in the name of religion.

6. Although the Middle East has been volatile since 1948, the year Israel was recognized as a nation-state, modern terrorism grew after 1967. It increased after 1973 and became a standard method of military operations in the following two decades.

7. In 1993, however, the Palestine Liberation Organization (PLO) renounced terrorism. Ironically, this has created tremendous tension. On the Arab side, some groups have denounced the PLO's actions while others have embraced it. The same reaction has occurred in Israel, where one set of political parties endorses peace plans and another prepares for war. Middle Eastern peace is a very fragile process, and terrorism is a wild card. It can upset delicate negotiations at any time, even after a peace treaty has been signed and implemented (for an example, see Hoffman, 1995).

8. All of these issues are complicated by a shortage of water and vast differences in social structure. The area contains some of the world's richest and some of the world's poorest people. Most of them are far from water sources.

One can best begin to understand the Middle East by focusing on the world of the late 1800s. During that time period, three critical events took place that helped to shape the modern Middle East.

First, the Ottoman Empire, the Turk-based government that ruled much of the Middle East, was falling apart in the nineteenth century. This meant the Ottoman Turks encountered domestic challenges across their empire as various nationalistic, tribal, and familial groups revolted, and they faced foreign threats, too. The Iranian empire had collapsed earlier, but Great Britain, France, Germany, and Russia intervened in the area with military force. Each European country was willing to promise potential rebels many things, if they revolted against the Turks. Realistically, few of those promises could be kept.

The second critical event came from a political movement called Zionism. From 1896 to 1906, European Jews, separated from their ancient homeland for nearly 2,000 years, wanted to create their own nation. Some of them favored Palestine, whereas others wanted to move to Argentina. In 1906, those who backed Palestine won the argument, and European Jews increasingly moved to the area. They did not ask the Palestinian Arabs, the people who lived in Palestine, for permission.

Finally, European armies engulfed the Middle East from 1914 to 1918, as they fought World War I. They continued to make contradictory promises as they sought to gain spheres of influence in the region. When the war ended, the victorious nations felt they had won the area from the Turks. They divided the Middle East, not with respect to future political problems but to share the spoils of victory. This created long-term political problems.

THREE SOURCES
OF MIDDLE EASTERN TERRORISM

In the final analysis, the situation at the end of World War I set the stage for developments over the next 80 years. The political situation gave rise to three sources of terrorism in the Middle East: (1) questions about the political control of Palestine, (2) questions of who would rule the Arab world, and (3) questions concerning the relations between the two main branches of Islam: Sunnis and Shiites. Stated another way, these problems are:

1. The Palestinian question (control of Palestine)
2. Intra-Arab rivalries/struggles
3. The Iranian Revolution

These problems are all separate, but they are also interrelated. The sources of terrorism in the Middle East are symbiotic. That is, they are independent arenas of violence with a dynamic force of their own, but they are also related to and dependent on each other.

All forms of Middle Eastern terrorism exhibit certain common traits. Primarily, many Arab groups express dissatisfaction over the existence of Israel. They are not necessarily pro-Palestinian, but they find the notion of a European-created, non-Arab state in their lands offensive. Most Middle Eastern terrorist groups are anti-imperialist. The intensity of their passion wavers according to the type of group, but terrorism has largely been dominated by anti-Western feelings. Another symbiotic factor is the pan-Arabic or pan-Islamic orientation of terrorist groups. Although they fight for local control, most wish to revive a united Arab realm of Islam. Finally, Middle Eastern terrorism is united by kinship bonds. In terrorism, as in Middle Eastern politics in general, familial links are often more important than national identification.

When the Israelis practice terrorism, they usually claim their activities are conventional military actions. At times, however, the Israelis have used the same tactics the PLO used in the 1960s and 1970s. It is perhaps more accurate to argue that all Middle Eastern violence, Arabic and non-Arabic, is locked into symbiosis; it is interdependent. We will approach this problem with an examination of the world of the Middle East as it emerged from World War I.

ZIONISM IN PALESTINE: 1914–1936

The problems resulting from European imperialism became obvious in World War I. Because the Turks were allied with the Germans, the British encouraged the Arabs to revolt against the Turks. If the Arabs fought for the British, the British promised them freedom. But Britain had no intention of granting full autonomy to the Arabs; they wanted Arab help in destroying the Turks. In addition, they viewed the area as an important land link to India. The truth was that both Britain and France hoped to carve new imperial colonies from the Middle East when the war ended.

The British made other promises. (See Figure 7.2.) Partially in response to the Zionist movement and partially to keep the goodwill of American Jews, the British promised the Zionists a Jewish homeland in Palestine. On the other side of the region, in ancient Persia or modern Iran, the British approached the Russians with another deal. Iran would be divided into three parts, a northern area controlled by Russia, a southern zone under British rule, and a neutral area in between. When the war ended in 1918, the entire Middle East was controlled by the British, French, and Russians, but it was a powder keg.

In the years preceding the war, Zionism caused confusion in Palestine. Yonah Alexander (1976, pp. 211–257) argues that the early Zionist settlers hoped for peace, and there was every reason to think this would be possible. Even though most of the Jewish immigrants were European, the Arabs thought of them as Semitic people, and both groups identified with Palestine. Furthermore, the Zionists originally stated they had no desire to displace the Palestinians; they wanted to coexist with them. Others, however, had a hidden agenda. According to Alexander, the most ardent Zionists envisioned a state under Jewish rule, whereas the Palestinians had assumed Arabs would remain in control of Arab land.

Alexander also points to another prewar factor that became a source of Arab discontent. The Zionist movement took place at the same time the Ottoman Empire was breaking up. This encouraged several Arab groups to espouse nationalism for lands formerly dominated by the Turks. The Palestinians believed themselves to be part of Syria, and because the Turks had objected to Jewish settlement, the Palestinians were willing to consider Jewish immigration as an expression of Syrian nationalism. Alexander argues that it was a fatal mistake, for the Zionists held no such belief: The Jews had no intention of becoming part of Syria.

The contradictory British wartime promises, explicable in time of national threats but short-sighted in terms of foreign policy, did nothing to alleviate the tensions between the Palestinian Arabs and the newly arrived Palestinian Jews. On October 24, 1915, the British made an unclear promise to the Arabs. In return for a general Arab revolt against the Turks, the British agreed to support the creation of a united, independent Arab state at the close of the war. They refused to be specific about the boundaries because they did not know what the French would claim (Becker, 1984, p. 9). In 1916, however, they signed the Sykes-Picot agreement with France that divided the Middle East into spheres of influence.

The British believed this to be sound foreign policy. They had promised nothing because of the nebulous nature of their understanding with the Arabs. However, the Arabs felt they had been promised the ancient Arab realm of Islam. Although the British had gained an ally at little expense, the circumstances were

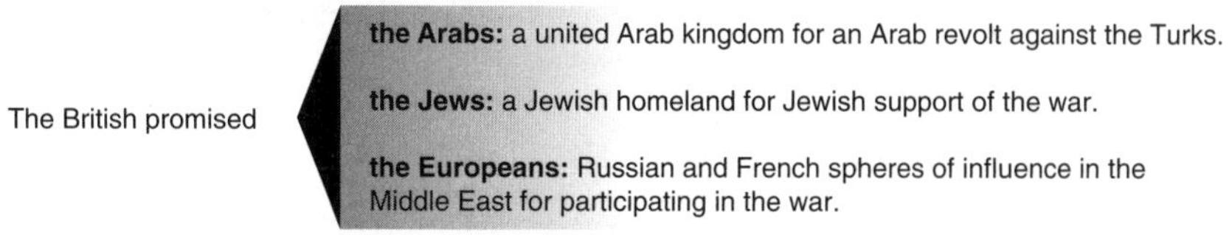

The British promised

the **Arabs:** a united Arab kingdom for an Arab revolt against the Turks.

the **Jews:** a Jewish homeland for Jewish support of the war.

the **Europeans:** Russian and French spheres of influence in the Middle East for participating in the war.

FIGURE 7.2 Britain's Contradictory Promises in World War I

ripe for resentments. While the British were courting the Arabs with meaningless promises, they also played to Jewish interests by promising British support for a national Jewish homeland in Palestine. Again, the British viewed this as good diplomacy. It would create Jewish support for the war, especially in America, and it would bring the Zionists into the war against the Turks. Western Zionist economic assistance might help to keep the French and Russians out of the area at the close of the war.

There was an added incentive: The Palestinian Jews had offered to raise troops to back the British cause, and this promised another army to fight the Turks. The British were delighted with such an offer of wartime help. On November 2, 1917, the British government, anxious to ensure Jewish support, issued the Balfour Declaration, promising a Jewish national homeland in Palestine.

At the end of the war, the British created a series of Arab countries dominated by strong, traditional family groups. Far from representing a united Arab realm of Islam, the British division was challenged internally by rival families and externally by other Arab states. Each family and each of the Arab leaders wished to unite Islam under their own banner. Major states eventually emerged from this scenario: Syria, Iraq, Saudi Arabia, Jordan, Egypt, Libya, and Iran. All the new nations dreamed of a pan-Islamic region, but none was willing to let another run it.

The Arabs also could not counter the continuing British influence, and neither a pan-Arabic realm nor a Jewish national state could develop under the watchful eyes of the British. In 1922, Great Britain received permission from the League of Nations to create the Protectorate of Transjordan. The mandate gave Britain control of Palestine and placed the British in the center of Middle Eastern affairs. But it came with a cost. It left neither Arab nor Jew satisfied. The Arabs believed they had received a false promise, and the Jews avidly demanded their right to a homeland.

While the British established the Protectorate, in Palestine feelings of nationalism and anger increased. Both Jews and Arabs resented the British, but neither side was willing to submit to the other if the British could be expelled. Sporadic violence began in the 1920s and spilled into open revolt before World War II (1939–1945).

An Arab revolt in Palestine began in 1936 and lasted until 1939. It was primarily aimed at the British, but the brewing hatred and distrust between the Arab and Jewish communities also came to the surface. Both Jews and Arabs fought the

British, but they fought each other at the same time. Animosity was overshadowed by the events of the early 1940s but resurfaced after the war. Both Jews and Arabs firmly believed the only possible solution to the problems in Palestine was to expel the British and eliminate political participation by one another.

THE BIRTH OF MODERN ISRAEL

In late 1945 and 1946, thousands of Jews displaced by the Nazi holocaust flocked to Palestine. Palestinian Arabs, seeing the danger presented by this massive influx of Jews, began to arm themselves. They had little assistance. The British empire was collapsing, and other Arabs were too concerned with their own political objectives to care about the Palestinians. Officially, the British had banned Jewish immigration, but there was little that could be done about the influx of immigrants. Jews continued to arrive, demanding an independent state.

In 1947, the situation was beyond British control. Exhausted by World War II, the British sought a United Nations (UN) solution to their quandary in Palestine. The UN suggested that one part of Palestine be given to the Arabs and another part be given to the Jews. The Zionists were elated; the Arabs were not. Caught in the middle, the British came to favor the UN solution, and they had reason to support it. The Jews were in revolt.

Modern terrorism resurfaced in Palestine just before the UN partition. A Jewish terrorist organization called the Irgun Zvai Leumi launched a series of attacks against British soldiers and Arab Palestinians. The purpose of the attacks was twofold. The Irgun believed individual bombings and murders of British soldiers would make the occupation of Palestine too costly. Second, the Irgun was concerned about the presence of Arabs in newly claimed Jewish areas. Threats, beatings, and bombings were used to frighten the Arabs away.

In a four-part series on terrorism, the History Channel (2000) pointed to one of the threads running through Jewish terrorism. Leaders of the Irgun studied the tactics of the Irish Republican Army's Michael Collins. They tried to incorporate Collins's methods in the Jewish campaign. Within 20 years, Palestinian Arabs would make the same discovery. (See the time line in Box 7.1.)

On May 15, 1948, the United Nations recognized the partition of Palestine and the modern nation-state of Israel. The Arabs attacked the new Jewish state immediately, and the Irgun's terrorism fell by the wayside. Both Arabs and Jews shifted to conventional warfare and would fight that way until 1967.

INTRA-ARAB RIVALRIES

Modern Middle Eastern terrorism is the result of continuing conflicts in the twentieth century. This section reviews the formation of some of the most important Arab states in North Africa and Southwest Asia. Instead of considering each story separately, the narrative blends Israel's development

---

BOX 7.1   Time Line of Critical Events to the Birth of Israel

1896–1906   Zionist Movement begins; the Zionists select Palestine as a homeland

1914–1918   World War I

1915   Promise of the Arab realm, dar al-Islam, to prominent Arab families

1916   Sykes-Picot Agreement—Britain and France agree to divide the Middle East into "spheres of influence"

1917   Balfour Declaration—Britain agrees to help create a Jewish homeland

1920–1922   Britain controls Palestine—the League of Nations officially recognizes the British Mandate of Transjordan

1936–1939   The Arab Revolt

1939–1945   World War II

1947–1948   Proposed partition—Israel becomes a nation on May 15, 1948

---

with the symbiotic nature of the conflict. This approach explains the relationship between intra-Arab rivalries and terrorism.

Although control of Palestine is always mentioned when dealing with contemporary Middle Eastern violence, the situation after World War I was not conducive to peace. Britain and France divided the ancient realm of Islam, known as dar al-Islam, and left the area ripe for confusion and bitterness. Aside from the Palestinian issue, other Arabs felt slighted by various peace settlements, and their dissatisfaction continued through the end of World War II. The French and British created a number of states that did not reflect the realistic divisions in the Middle East.

North Africa was completely dominated by Britain and France. Libya was divided into British and French sections, and it did not become independent until 1951. In 1969, Colonel Moamar Khadaffy seized power in a military coup, claiming Libya to be an anti-Western socialist state. Egypt achieved its independence before World War II but did not fully break with Britain until Gamal Nasser took power in 1954. Khadaffy sought to follow Nasser's footsteps, breaking with Egypt after Nasser's death in 1970.

Syria came under French rule from 1922 to 1946. After several military coups and a failed attempt to form a united republic with Egypt, a group of pan-Arabic socialists, the Ba'ath Party, seized power in 1963. They were purged by an internal Ba'ath revolution in 1966, and Ba'athist President Hafez Assad came to power in 1970 and ruled until his death in 2000. Aside from internal problems (especially problems involving a minority group of Alawites who practiced a number of Muslim, Christian, and pagan rituals), Assad believed that Lebanon and Palestine were rightly part of Greater Syria.

Lebanon has become one of the most violent regions in the area. Ruled by France until 1943, the government of Lebanon managed a delicate balance of people with many different national and religious loyalties. In 1948, when

Palestinians displaced by Israel began flocking to the country, the delicate balance was destroyed. Lebanon has suffered internal conflict ever since that time. Violence includes civil wars in 1958 and 1975–1976, continued fighting to 1978, an Israeli invasion in 1978, another Israeli invasion in 1982, Iranian revolutionary intervention from the 1982 Israeli invasion, a fragile peace in 1990, and the growth of a terrorist militia from 1983 to 1996. Several large militias still roam the countryside, although they agreed to be disarmed by the terms of the 1990 peace plan. Israel began abandoning Lebanon in the spring and summer of 2000. Militant Lebanese forces moved into the former occupied zones, seeking vengeance on militia members (known as the South Lebanese Army) who supported Israel.

The Persian Gulf region has another history. In an effort to secure the land route to India, the British established several states from the Mediterranean to the Persian Gulf in the nineteenth and early twentieth centuries. One branch of the Hashemite family received Jordan as a reward for assisting the British; another branch received Iraq. Jordan became a constitutional monarchy ruled by King Hussein from 1952 to 1999 and his son, King Abdullah, from 1999 to the present. Iraq's path was more turbulent. A 1958 coup eliminated the Iraqi Hashemites from power, and another coup in 1968 brought Ba'athist rule. Saddam Hussein, a Ba'athist, came to power in 1979.

Saudi Arabia and the Persian Gulf states fared somewhat better because of their immense wealth. Since 1902, the Saud family has been ruling Arabia, and the most sacred shrine in Islam, and many of the rich Persian Gulf states have been independent from Europe for centuries. Poorer states, such as Iraq, look at the Persian Gulf with envy, believing the whole area should benefit all of dar al-Islam, but not all has been peaceful in the Persian Gulf or Saudi Arabia. The Persian Gulf states were targeted by terrorist groups for their close connections to the United States before the 1991 Persian Gulf War. After the war, Saudi Arabia fell victim to the relationship. Although opposition is scrutinized, a small number of Saudis resent the continued American presence. Osama bin Ladin, the head of a terrorist organization known as The Base, bombed an American base in 1995 and killed 19 American soldiers in June 1996 in another blast.

From 1947 to 1967, the Middle East was dominated by a series of short conventional wars. Arab states failed to achieve unity, often seeming as willing to oppose each other as they were to oppose Israel. Rhetorically, all the Arab states maintained an anti-Israeli stance, but Jordan and Saudi Arabia began to pull closer to the West. They were enthusiastically led by the Shah of Iran.

In the meantime, the Israeli armed forces grew. Composed of highly mobile combined combat units, the Israeli Defense Force became capable of launching swift, deadly strikes at the Arabs. In 1967, the Israelis demonstrated their superiority over all their Arab neighbors. Although the combined Arab armies were equipped with excellent Soviet arms and outnumbered the Israeli forces, in six days Israel doubled its territory and soundly defeated its opponents.

After the 1967 Six Day War, the Palestine Liberation Organization (PLO) began a series of terrorist attacks against civilian Israeli positions. It was a turnaround from the old tactics of the Stern Gang and the Irgun, and it served to define Israeli relations with its Arab neighbors. The PLO soon split between moderates and radicals, but terrorism against Israel increased. Israel struck back against the PLO, wherever they were located. (The PLO is discussed in detail later in this book.)

In the meantime, the Arab states also split into several camps. One group, represented by King Hussein of Jordan, was anxious to find a way to coexist with Israel. A few nations, like Egypt, simply wanted to avenge the embarrassment of the Six Day War. Egypt would negotiate with Israel, but as an equal, not as a defeated nation. Other Arab views were more militant. Represented by the Ba'ath Party, groups of Arab socialists called for both Arab unity and the destruction of Israel. Along with several terrorist groups, they formed a Rejectionist Front, rejecting any peace with Israel. Finally, a group of wealthy oil states hoped for stability in the region. They publicly supported the struggle against Israel, while privately working for peace. Peace would ensure sound economic relations with their customers in the West.

Despite the myriad positions, the embarrassment of the Six Day War proved to be the strongest catalyst to action. The Egyptians and Israelis kept sniping at one another along the Suez Canal. Gamal Nasser, Egypt's president, vowed to drive the Israelis back and asked for Soviet help to do it. Breaking relations with the United States, Nasser moved closer to the Soviet camp. When he died in September 1969, Anwar Sadat, his successor, questioned the policy. By 1972, he threw the Soviets out, claiming they were not willing to support another war with Israel. Coordinating activities with Syria, Sadat launched his own war on October 6, 1973.

The Yom Kippur War, sadly named after a Hebrew festival celebrating God's atonement for all sin and reconciliation with humanity, reversed the defeat of the Six Day War. Catching the Israelis by surprise, the Egyptians drove Israeli forces back into the Sinai, while the Syrians drove on the Golan Heights. The Syrians almost captured Jerusalem before the Israeli Defense Forces managed to stabilize the front. Peace came three weeks later.

Satisfied with his victory, Sadat took a series of bold initiatives. Responding to an overture from the United States, Sadat renewed relations with Washington and stopped the minor skirmishes with Israeli troops by 1975. He visited Jerusalem in 1977 and publicly talked of peace.

In the same period, Menachim Begin became prime minister of Israel in September 1977. Begin was committed to maintaining control of the occupied territories, including Jerusalem, that Israel had won in the Six Day War. Begin's demand precluded peace with the Arab states because the Arabs demanded the return of the occupied territories. Despite the obvious differences, Anwar Sadat maintained a dialogue with Washington. Under the mediation of U.S. President Jimmy Carter, Sadat agreed to a separate peace with Israel, provided Israel would withdraw from the Sinai Peninsula. Begin agreed, and on May 26, 1979, Egypt and Israel signed the Camp David Peace Accord under Carter's watchful eyes. The decision cost Sadat his life. He was assassinated by Muslim fundamentalists in 1981 for agreeing to peace.

The Arabs rejecting peace with Israel fell into two camps. The radicals rejected any peace or recognition of Israel. The more moderate group was concerned about the fate of the Palestinians. Egypt's peace with Israel did not account for the Palestinian refugees in Israel or the occupied territories. At the same time, much of the West failed to pay any attention to legitimate claims of the Palestinians because radical Palestinians were involved in dozens of terrorist attacks. (See the time line in Box 7.2.)

In the symbiotic world of Middle Eastern terrorism, Palestine was frequently used as a cover-up for the intra-Arab struggle for power. In 1978, Israel launched a minor invasion of Lebanon followed by a full-scale attack in 1982. During this same time frame, Middle Eastern governments were consolidating internal power and looking at potential regional rivals. The Iranian government fell to revolutionary Shiites, and the American embassy was seized with all the inhabitants kidnapped by Iran's revolutionary government. As the United States eventually achieved the return of its embassy hostages, Saddam Hussein's Iraq and revolutionary Iran went to war. Terrorism increased as a horrible sideshow, while thousands died each month on conventional battlefields.

In the melee of the 1980s, Middle Eastern terrorism fell into several broad categories including: (1) suicide bombings and other attacks on Israeli and Western positions in Lebanon; (2) various militias fighting other militias in Lebanon; (3) state-sponsored terrorism from Libya, Syria, and Iran; (4) freelance terrorism to high-profile groups; (5) terrorism in support of Arab Palestinians; (6) attacks in Europe against Western targets; and (7) Israeli assassinations of alleged terrorists. Terrorists mounted dozens of operations for supporting governments, and several nations used terrorists as commandos. Airplanes were hijacked; airports were attacked; the United States responded with naval action, once accidentally shooting down an Iranian civilian airplane killing hundreds; and Europe became a low-intensity battleground.

Despite the appearance of terrorism, conventional war continued to dominate the Middle East, and Arabs struggled against Arabs. As the Iran-Iraq War neared its end, Saddam Hussein turned his attention to Kuwait. Feeling the British had unfairly removed Kuwait from Iraq before World War I, Saddam Hussein invaded the small country to gain control of its oil production. The result was disastrous for Iraq. Leading a coalition of Western governments and the Persian Gulf states, the United States struck with massive forces. Saddam Hussein's armies suffered greatly, and terrorism reemerged as a weapon to strike an overwhelming military power. As Iraq retreated in the Persian Gulf, terrorists began plotting new methods for striking the United States.

SHIA ISLAM AND REVOLUTIONARY IRAN

Americans found it convenient in the 1980s to speak of Iranian terrorism. After all, the Iranians had violated international law in the early stages of their revolution by taking the American embassy in Tehran. They were alleged to

---

BOX 7.2   Time Line of the Six Day War to the Persian Gulf War

1967 Six Day War—Israel defeats its Arab neighbors and occupies territories to the west bank of the Jordan River, the Golan Heights, the Sinai Peninsula, and Jerusalem

1968 Ba'athist coup in Iraq brings Ahmed Hassan al-Bakr to power

1969 Khadaffy takes power in Libya

1970 Nasser dies; Sadat becomes President of Egypt; Ba'athist reform in Syria; Hassad takes power

1973 Yom Kippur War

1975 Civil war breaks out in Lebanon—"War of the Camps"

1979 Camp David Peace Accord—Egypt and Israel sign a separate peace treaty

1979 Iranian Revolution

1979–1980 Iranian hostage crisis

1979 Saddam Hussein becomes leader of Iraq

1980–1988 Iran-Iraq War kills more than 1,000,000 people and ends in a stalemate

1981 U.S. Navy jets shoot down two Libyan planes in the Mediterranean

1982 Massive Israeli invasion of Lebanon

1985 Terrorist attacks throughout Europe; United States blames Libya

1986 U.S. Navy and Air Force aircraft strike Libya

1987 Terrorist attacks target Americans

1990 Iraq invades Kuwait

1991 Persian Gulf War—Iraq is driven from Kuwait

---

have staged several bombings in Lebanon, as well as attacks on other American interests in the Middle East. They had mined the Persian Gulf and were responsible for the deaths of U.S. troops. Finally, intelligence sources reported that the Iranians were allied with other terrorist states and supported a shadowy group known as Islamic Jihad. The media attributed this rise in terrorism to the rise of Islamic fundamentalism in Iran.

In some ways this popular conception is correct, but in other ways it is completely wrong. The 1979 revolution in Iran represented the flames from friction that started centuries earlier. Far from being a rebirth of fundamentalism, it was more indicative of a religious split in Islam.

At first glance, Iran fits in the category of an intra-Arab struggle. It uses terrorism against the West, but the tactic is also used against its Islamic neighbors. Iran waged a long, costly conventional war against Iraq. Certainly Iran's willingness to sponsor terrorism suggests the nature of warfare has changed. Yet, the issue runs deeper.

Iranians are not Arabs, and they practice a version of Islam somewhat distinct from orthodox practices. They maintained an empire in the face of the Ottoman Turks and struggled with them for years. This independence asserts itself in terrorism. The Iranians have been willing to export revolutionary ideals through terrorism, not for the sake of increasing Iran's grandeur but for liberating Islam in a holy war. Iran is in an ideological war with the world, and its recent actions make it a third source of terrorism in the Middle East.

To understand the Iranian Revolution and terrorism, one needs to focus on four major factors. First, it is necessary to consider the development and practice of Islam. Second, the recent imperial past of Iran should be reviewed; it helps to explain the Iranian hatred of both the West and the Soviet Union. Third, Iran's use of terrorism must be considered. Specifically, why is it attractive, and how is it used? Finally, the first three factors must be drawn together into the ideology that supports terrorism. The last two factors can be brought into focus rapidly once the first two factors are understood.

Islam is at the heart of the Iranian Revolution. When Mohammed died in 632, he left no one to watch over the new religion. Several followers joined to select a caliph, an earthly leader to replace the Prophet, but as in the case of Western Christianity, religion gave way to politics. Within 40 years after the Prophet's death, various caliphs had managed to assassinate their way to power, and Islam had divided into two primary groups. The Sunnis were orthodox followers who accepted the reign of temporal leaders. The Shias, on the other hand, believed their leaders to be descended from Mohammed; as such, they were divinely inspired and infallible.

Toward the end of the 600s, a group of Shias lead by the Imam (a religious leader) Hussein ibn-Ali marched on the Sunnis in what Hussein hoped would be a gesture of reconciliation. Hussein was warned in a dream that no reconciliation would take place and that he and his followers would be destroyed in a battle with the Sunnis. Dismissing all but his 72 most faithful followers, Hussein went to meet the Sunnis near the village of Karbala. They were massacred by 10,000 soldiers.

Since that time, the Shiites have attracted the poor and the hopeless. Karbala stands as the example of supreme willingness to submit to the will of God with the understanding that rewards will come after death. Karbala was the rallying cry of the Shiites for centuries as the religion moved to the eastern geographic realm of Islam. By the twentieth century, Shiites accounted for about 10 percent of all the Islamic peoples, but they constituted a majority in Iran. The message of Karbala and the martyrdom of Hussein became the rallying cries of the Iranian Revolution.

Dilip Hiro (1987, pp. 103–135) makes an important point about the relationship of Shiaism to fundamentalism in Iran. Although many Western observers believe the fanaticism of the revolution was due to a resurgence of fundamentalism, in reality it gained its intensity from the repressed lower classes of Iran emerging to practice their traditional religion. According to Hiro, Shiaism became the official religion of Iran around 1500, but Shiites were always oppressed, first by the dominant Sunni masters of the Ottoman Empire, then by the Westerners who controlled Iran through much of the past two centuries.

In an important way, religion is an expression of nationalism in Iran. A brief examination of Iran's colonial past explains why. Imperialism came to

Iran in the 1800s. According to Ramy Nima (1983, pp. 3–27), after 1850, the British began to view Iran as the northern gate to India. They were also very concerned about German imperialism and possible Russian expansion. For their part, the Russians saw a potential opportunity to gain a warm-water port and further their empire. They moved into northern Iran and prepared to move south. The British countered by occupying southern Iran. Both countries used the occupation for their own economic and military interests.

According to Nima, oil production had a tremendous impact on the way the British used Iran. The British established the Anglo-Persian Oil Company in 1909 and started taking oil profits out of Iran. Although direct economic imperialism has ended in Iran, Iranians still regard Western oil companies as an extension of the old British arrangement. They believe the Shah stayed in power by allowing Western corporations to exploit Iranian oil.

To some extent, this attitude reflects the history of Iran. Nima (1983) says the British became very concerned about Iran in the 1920s after the Communist revolution in Russia, believing Iran might be the next country the Communists would target. No longer in direct control of the south, the British searched for a leader to stem the potential Soviet threat, a leader whose Iranian nationalism would make him a Russian enemy. They did not believe such a man would be difficult to find because working-class Iranians hated the Russians as much as they hated the British. The British found their hero in one Reza Shah Pahlavi. In 1926, with British support, he became Shah of Iran.

Reza Shah was under no illusions about his dependency on British power. For Iran to gain full independence, he needed to develop an economic base that would support the country and consolidate his strength among the ethnic populations in Iran. Hiro (1987, pp. 22–30) says Reza Shah chose two methods for doing so. First, he encouraged Western investment, primarily British and American, in the oil and banking industries. Second, he courted various power groups inside Iran, including the Shia fundamentalists. At first, these policies were successful, but they created long-term problems.

Hiro points out that Reza Shah had to modernize Iran to create the economic base that would free his country from the West. He introduced massive educational and industrial reforms and embarked on a full-scale program of Westernization. This brought him into conflict with the Shiite holy leaders, who had a strong influence over the Iranian lower classes. Modernization threatened the traditional Shiite hold on the educational system and the Shiite power base. The Shiites, however, did not bring about the fall of Reza Shah; World War II brought about his fall.

Both Hiro (1987) and Nima (1983) explain Reza Shah's long-term failure as a result of his foreign policy. In the 1930s, Reza Shah had befriended Hitler, and he saw German relations as a way to balance British influence. He guessed that Iran would profit from having a powerful British rival as an ally, but his plan backfired. When World War II erupted, the British and Russians believed Reza Shah's friendship with the Nazis could result in German troops in Iran and Iranian oil in Germany. In 1941, the British overran southern Iran, while the Russians reentered the north.

Reza Shah was finished. He fled the country, leaving his son, Mohammed Reza Pahlavi, nominally in charge of the country. Mohammed Pahlavi became the modern Shah of Iran, but his ascent was traumatic. An Allied puppet in the beginning, the Shah had to fight for the same goals his father had failed to achieve. When he was on the verge of achieving power in the early 1950s, he found himself displaced by democratic and leftist forces. Like his father, the Shah fled the country.

In August 1953, Pahlavi returned to the office that had been denied him during Iran's brief fling with democracy. The Iranians had attempted to create a constitutional assembly, but the British believed they were moving too far to the left and would be swept into a Communist revolution. Using the fear of Communism, the British convinced the American Central Intelligence Agency (CIA) that the only hope for stability in Iran was to replace the deposed Shah. The CIA acted, and the Shah returned. America looked on the Shah as a friend, never realizing the Iranians viewed America's actions as part of a long tradition of imperialism.

Hiro (1987, pp. 30–100) provides a detailed account of the Shah's attempt to build his base and his eventual failure. In August 1953, the Shah formulated a plan to stay in power. Like his father, he believed that only modernization would lead to Iranian autonomy. Yet, he also feared his own people. He created a secret military police force, SAVAK, to locate and destroy his enemies. SAVAK was aggressive.

The Shah used a fairly effective strategy to employ SAVAK. Rather than taking on all his enemies at once, he became selective. He allied with one group to attack another group. SAVAK's enthusiasm for the torture and murder of political opponents complemented the policy. After 1953, the Shah found it convenient to ally with the Shiite holy men, who welcomed the Shah's support and turned a blind eye to SAVAK's activities.

According to Hiro, by 1960, the Shah's tenuous relationship with the fundamentalist clergy began to waver. The Shah no longer needed their support, and the Western reforms of Iranian society were popular with the middle class, the members of which profited from modernization. The Shiite clergy, however, felt the increasing power of the state as Shia influences and traditions were questioned or banned. From their seminary in the holy city of Qom, the clergy began to organize against the Shah, but it was too late. The Shah no longer needed the fundamentalists.

As the clergy organized demonstrations among theology students in Qom and marches of the faithful in Tehran, the Shah unleashed his forces. SAVAK infiltrated Shiite opposition groups in Tehran, and the army attacked Qom. There were thousands of arrests, and demonstrators were ruthlessly beaten or, in some cases, shot in the streets. By 1963, many potential opponents were murdered, and the Shah had many others in custody. One of his prisoners was the Hojatalislam Ruhollah Khomeini. In a gesture of mercy, the Shah ordered Khomeini deported to Iraq instead of executing him. That proved to be a mistake.

Nima (1983, pp. 41–77) describes Khomeini's rise to power among the fundamental Shiites. The Shah and his father had been very successful in limiting the power of the clergy because of the popularity of their reforms. The Shiite clergy began to make an impact on Iranian politics in the 1960s by wisely sidestepping the reforms and attacking the Shah where he was most vulnerable. Khomeini had spoken several times about the Shah's love affair with America. This raised the ire of common Iranians, to whom America seemed no different from their former Russian and British colonial masters.

Although Khomeini was arrested and deported in 1963, his influence actually increased. He was promoted to the rank of ayatollah and ran a campaign against the Shah from Iraq. Under his leadership, the mosque came to be perceived as the only opposition to the Shah and the hated SAVAK. According to Nima, Khomeini headed a network of 180,000 Islamic revolutionaries in addition to 90,000 mullas (low-ranking clergy), 5,000 hojatalislams (middle-ranking clergy), and 50 ayatollahs (leaders). The Shiite clergymen were able to paint the Shah in satanic terms owing to his relations with the United States; they called for a holy revolution and the restoration of Islam.

In his description of the revolution in Iran, Hiro (1987, pp. 66–96) sees the Shah's fall from power as a sequence of events beginning with Western criticism of the Shah's repressive policies. One of the most important factors was the election of Jimmy Carter as president of the United States. Carter pressured the Shah to end SAVAK's human rights abuses. Fearful of a loss of American aid, the Shah ordered SAVAK to ease off the opposition. Khomeini, who viewed Carter as a manifestation of satanic power, felt no gratitude toward the United States. He increased his revolutionary activities from Iraq.

The Shah pressured Saddam Hussein, the president of Iraq, to remove Khomeini. According to Hiro, this was one of the greatest ironies of the revolution. Khomeini was forced to flee Iraq in fear of his life and received asylum in Paris. Ironically, he was better able to control the revolution from Europe because Paris had a modern telephone system from which he could directly dial Tehran.

In 1977, Khomeini's revolutionary headquarters in Paris maintained an open telephone line to Tehran. Khomeini sent hundreds of revolutionary sermons to a multiple audiotape machine in Tehran, and his words were duplicated and delivered throughout the Iranian countryside. Khomeini's power increased dramatically.

Khomeini returned to Tehran in 1978. There was little the Shah could do. Although he had unleashed SAVAK and ordered his troops to fire on street demonstrators, the public had risen against him. Several groups were vying for power, but Khomeini seemed to be on top. In February 1979, the Shah fled from Iran. Khomeini, riding victoriously through the streets of Tehran, was still faced with problems. It was necessary to eliminate all opposition if the Islamic revolution was to succeed. The starting point was to attack all things Western. In his first victorious addresses, Khomeini pulled no punches. He said it was time to launch a holy war against the West and the traitors to Islam.

The Iranian Revolution of 1979 caused another form of terrorism to spread from the Middle East. Khomeini, filled with hatred for Saddam Hussein after being driven from Iraq, was content to wage a conventional war with his neighbor. However, such direct tactics would not work against a superpower. The United States and the Soviet Union, if they dared to intervene, would be subjected to a lower-level form of warfare. Because the superpowers could fight and win out in the open, the Ayatollah Khomeini chose to fight in the shadows.

Khomeini used a mixture of repressive tactics and political strategies to consolidate his power in Iran, and he is best understood within the Shiite tradition of Islam. Even after his death in 1989, Khomeini's call to Karbala and his message of martyrdom remain. The contemporary Iranian political experience can be approached from this context. It is also possible to approach terrorism from this perspective, since terrorism is a tactic in Iran's holy war.

Robin Wright (1986) makes this point in her examination of Shiite Islam titled *Sacred Rage*. According to Wright, the Ayatollah Khomeini was guided by the message of Karbala. Along with the Shiite clergy of Iran, he believed the Iranian Revolution was the first step in purifying the world. Israel must be eliminated and returned to Islamic rule. The West had become the handmaiden of the Jews, but the West was and remains the source of imperialism. Its influence is satanic and must be destroyed. Holy warriors are called to battle. Wright says Iran exports terrorism in this vein with revolutionary zeal.

To date, the primary target of Iran's external religious zeal has been Lebanon. Shiite fundamentalists began to flock to Lebanon in 1982 after the Israeli invasion, and Iran helped establish two terrorist organizations to support them, the Islamic Jihad (Islamic Holy War) and Hizbollah (Party of God). By 1996, both groups, though still supporting terrorism, were capable of acting as autonomous militias.

In another analysis of the impact of the Iranian Revolution, Wright (1989) argues that the future of the Islamic revolution is unclear. Comparing the Shiites with the 1917 Bolsheviks of Russia, Wright states the revolution could go in different directions. If the revolutionaries entrench themselves, they could spread the notion of an Islamic republic far beyond the bounds of Iran. However, they may fall victim to counterrevolutionaries. Currently, the issue is undecided, and questions about Iranian fundamentalism remain a source of terrorism in the Middle East.

KEY CONCEPTS

1. The Middle East was once the setting for one of the major empires of world history.

2. As the Ottoman Empire declined in the nineteenth century, European powers exerted imperial control over the Middle East.

3. With European support, the Zionist movement created the modern state of Israel in the midst of Arab lands.

4. The three major sources of terrorism in the Middle East are: (1) questions over who will rule Israel or Palestine, (2) struggles for power among Arab states, and (3) the future of revolutionary Islam. The three sources are symbiotic; this means that they depend on one another to stay alive.

5. Sunnis constitute the majority of Muslims, while Shiites make up most of the remaining 10 percent.

6. Since the resurgence of religious terrorism in the early 1990s, Islamic extremists have been trying to create a middle ground between Shiaism and Sunnism.

FOOD FOR THOUGHT

Ireland presented problems of religious violence within the same culture. The Middle East brings together differing cultures, ethnic groups, and religion. How does this change the problem? How do extremists make the problem worse? Do people tend to label all the people of a particular religious, ethnic, or political persuasion by the extremists in that group? If so, how does this complicate Middle Eastern violence?

FURTHER READING

Albert Hourani, *A History of the Arab Peoples*

8

Latin American
Influences on Terrorism

International terrorism is historically connected. Terrorism developed along specific lines in the last 50 years of the twentieth century, but the lines were interwoven. This means terrorism in one part of the world became related to other terrorist movements. Michael Collins studied Russian theories of revolution, and Middle Eastern terrorists began to follow the pattern of Collins. After a series of anticolonial revolts from 1945 to 1964, another set of ideas dominated the world of terrorism. The theories were spawned by Carlos Marighella and Ernesto (Che) Guevara. These theories were put into practice by a Uruguayan terrorist group called the Tupamaros. This Latin American influence has dominated the world of terrorism for the past 50 years.

After completing this chapter, you should be able to:

1. Discuss the theory of urban terrorism as described by Marighella.
2. Summarize the relationship between terrorism and guerrilla warfare.
3. Outline the campaign of the Tupamaros in Uruguay.
4. Describe the influence of the Tupamaros on terrorism in other parts of the world.
5. Describe the urban philosophy of the Tupamaros.
6. Summarize the Tupamaros's terrorist tactics.
7. Outline the organizational structure of the Tupamaros.

THE THEORY OF URBAN TERRORISM

The first wave of modern terrorism appeared in Africa and Asia after 1945. For the next 20 years, nationalistic rebellions broke out against Western colonial powers in struggles for independence. Some of the movements involved long guerrilla wars, while others involved terrorism. Some rebels, especially those in Latin America, equated economic revolution with national revolution, giving birth to ideological terrorism. Whether motivated by nationalism or ideology, the practice of modern terrorism began to gravitate toward one of two models: urban terrorism or guerrilla warfare.

The model for modern urban terrorism was intellectually championed by Frantz Fanon. Born on Martinique in 1925, Fanon studied medicine in France and became a psychiatrist. When Algeria revolted from French rule in 1954, Fanon was sent to Algiers, the capital of Algeria, to work in a mental hospital. His experiences there caused him to side with the rebels.

Fanon believed the pressures caused by exploitive imperialism were the primary causes for mental illness in Algeria. He produced two works, *The Wretched of the Earth* and *A Dying Colonialism,* as a result of his Algerian experiences. He died of cancer in 1961, a year before the Algerian War ended, unable to play a leading role in revolutions; his thought, however, was strongly imprinted on Africa, Asia, and Latin America.

In *The Wretched of the Earth,* Fanon indicts colonial powers and calls on all the colonized to practice terrorism. He writes that Western powers have dehumanized non-Western people by destroying their cultures and replacing them with Western values. Even when Westerners are not present, they are represented by a native middle class that embraces Western values and turns its back on the general population. Native culture is forgotten by the middle class as native intellectualism is replaced by Western traditions. The masses end up suffering a perpetual identity crisis: To succeed, they are forced to deny their heritage. Fanon argues the natives can only follow one course of action. He calls them to revolution.

To be sure, Fanon was no Gandhi. His only argument was for violent revolt, including guerrilla warfare and acts of terrorism. He claimed decolonization was destined to be a violent process because it involved replacing one group of powerful people with another group. No group would willingly surrender power. Therefore, according to Fanon, achieving freedom was inherently violent. Political action and peaceful efforts toward change were useless. Only when oppressed people recognized that violence was their only alternative would they be assured of victory. Fanon saw guerrilla warfare and individual acts of terrorism as tools of revolution. Guerrilla war was the initial method of revolt because Third World revolutionaries could not mount direct, conventional campaigns at the beginning of their struggles. Fanon's concept of guerrilla warfare was based in rural revolution, but urban terrorism would become the major weapon rendering colonial administration impotent.

Terrorism was to be limited to specific acts. Fanon argued that terrorism should not be used against the native population in general. Like Communist

Chinese revolutionary leader Mao Dze Dong, he believed it would alienate supporters. Instead, he proposed two targets for terrorism: white settlers and the native middle class. The purpose of terrorism was to terrorize Westerners and their lackeys into submission. Individual murders, bombings, and mutilations would force the white settlers to leave the country and frighten the native middle class away from their colonial masters. Brutality would be the example. It would bring on government repression, but this would only cause more natives to flock to the terrorist cause.

Popular throughout the Third World, Fanon's ideas flourished in Latin America (see Figures 8.1 and 8.2 for maps of Latin America). Beginning in Brazil, some revolutionaries believed the city would be the focus of Latin American revolution, and they embraced Fanon's idea of urban terrorism. They felt a revolutionary could create the context for an impromptu general uprising through the use of spontaneous violence. Directly reflecting Fanon, these revolutionaries believed terrorism could communicate with the people and infuse them with the spirit of revolt. The foremost proponent of this idea in Latin America was Carlos Marighella.

Marighella was a Brazilian legislator, a leader of the nationalist Communist party, and eventually a fiery revolutionary terrorist. He was killed by Brazilian police in an ambush in São Paulo in 1969. In two major works, *For the Liberation of Brazil* and *The Minimanual of the Urban Guerrilla,* Marighella designed practical guides for terrorism. These books have had more influence on recent revolutionary terrorism than any other set of theories.

Marighella wanted to move violence from the countryside to the city, and although his call to terrorism was politically motivated, his model was apolitical. He designed a method for organizing a campaign of terror that, for the past 40 years, has been employed by groups ranging across the political spectrum—from the Japanese Red Army to the Freemen of Montana.

Marighella believed the basis of revolution was violence. Violence need not be structured, and efforts among groups need not be coordinated. Violence created a situation in which revolution could flourish. Any type of violence was acceptable because it contributed a general feeling of panic and frustration among the ruling classes and their protectors. Marighella's most original concept was that all violence could be urban-based and controlled by a small group of "urban guerrillas." This concept of revolution spread from Brazil throughout the world.

Robert Moss (1972, pp. 70–72) provides an excellent synopsis of Marighella's writings in a four-stage model. Urban terrorism was to begin with two distinct phases, one designed to bring about actual violence, and the other designed to give that violence meaning. The violent portion of the revolution was to be a confederate campaign employing armed revolutionary cells to carry out the most deplorable acts of violence. Targets were to have symbolic significance, and although violence was designed to be frightening, its logic would remain clear with regard to the overall revolution. That is, those who supported the revolution need not fear terrorist violence.

FIGURE 8.1 Map of Latin America

The terror campaign was to be accompanied by a psychological offensive to provide peripheral support for terrorists. Not only would the psychological offensive join students and workers in low-level challenges to governmental authority, but it would also be used to create a network of safe houses, logistical stores, and medical units. In essence, the supporting activities would carry out standard military-support functions.

A campaign of revolutionary terrorism in an urban setting could be used to destabilize government power. A psychological assault would convince the government and the people that the status quo no longer held. They would come to feel that the terrorists were in control. When this situation developed,

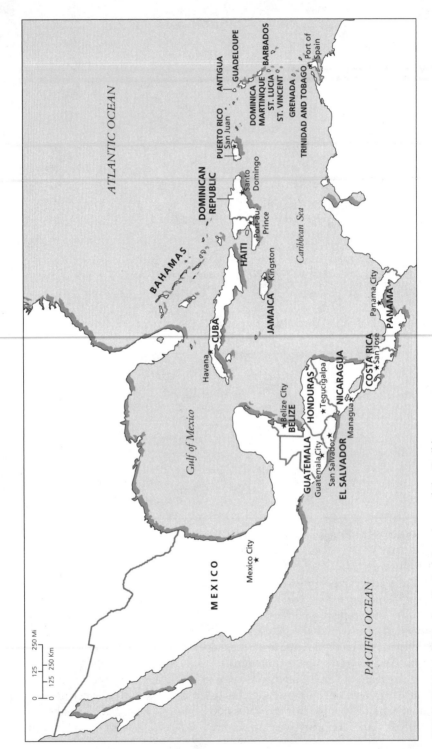

FIGURE 8.2 Map of Mexico, Central America, and the Caribbean

Marighella believed, the government would be forced to show its true colors. With its authority challenged and the economic stability of the elite eroded, the government would be forced to declare some form of martial law. This would not be a defeat for terrorism but rather exactly what the terrorists and their supporters wanted. Governmental repression was the goal of terrorism at this stage.

This view might appear to be contradictory at first glance, but there was a method to Marighella's madness. Marighella believed the public supported government policies because they did not realize the repressive nature of the state. The terrorist campaign would force the government to reveal itself, thereby alienating the public. With no place to turn, the public would turn to the terrorists, and the terrorists would be waiting with open arms. As the ranks of the urban guerrillas grew with the rush of public support, Marighella believed, the revolutionaries would gradually abandon their terrorist campaign. Their efforts would focus more and more on the construction of a general urban army, an army that could seize key government control points on cue. When the urban army had reached sufficient strength, all its forces would be launched in a general strike.

There is only one political weakness in Marighella's theory: It does not work. Unfortunately, however, it has helped several terrorist groups organize murder throughout the world. Marighella writes that the purpose of the urban guerrilla is to shoot. Any form of urban violence is desirable because a violent atmosphere creates the political environment needed for success. Terrorism could be utilized to create that environment, and terrorism could be employed with minimal organization. Therefore, terrorism is to be the primary strategy of the urban guerrilla.

Marighella outlines the basic structure needed for an urban terrorist group in the *Minimanual of the Urban Guerrilla.* The main operational group of a terrorist organization should be the firing group. Composed of four to five terrorists each, several firing groups are needed to construct a terrorist organization. They can join together as needed to concentrate their power, but their small size ensures both mobility and secrecy. For Marighella, the firing group is the basic weapon of the urban guerrilla.

In a single theory, Marighella provides the justification for violence and the organizational structure a small group needs to begin killing. Unlike Fanon, Marighella endorsed violence for the sake of violence. Another model of revolution emerged from Latin America that had a different structure. Emanating directly from the Cuban Revolution, this model calls for a more rational approach to violence.

TERRORISM AND GUERRILLA WAR

Guerrilla war is an age-old process. Several nationalistic rebellions were based on guerilla war after World War II, but the Cuban Revolution in 1956 captured the minds of left-wing ideologues. They came to view guerrilla war as a statement of revolution against capitalist powers. Like terrorism, guerrilla revolutionaries produced their own theories and models.

The Cuban Revolution did not create guerrilla warfare, but it popularized it throughout the world. Despite the fact that only one other guerrilla movement succeeded in overthrowing an established government, the Nicaraguan Sandinistas in 1979, guerrilla war is the preferred method of fighting among Latin American revolutionaries. Unlike the model for urban terrorism, the guerrilla model began with a successful structure then moved toward a theory.

The process began in the hills of Cuba. Fidel Castro tried to seize power in 1956, but he was soundly defeated. Retreating to the rural regions of Cuba, he surrounded himself with a ragtag group of revolutionaries, including a friend, Ernesto Guevara. "Che" Guevara was born in Argentina in 1928. After earning a medical degree at the University of Buenos Aires, he turned his attention from medicine to the plight of the poor. He believed poverty and repression were problems that transcended nationalism and revolution was the only means of challenging authority. He served the Communist regime of Guatemala in 1954 but fled to Mexico City when Communists were purged from the government. There he met the Cuban revolutionary leader named Fidel Castro, and Guevara's interests turned to Cuba.

Guevara immediately impressed Castro, and the two worked together to oust the Cuban military dictator Fulgencio Batista. After failing to seize power in 1956, Castro began to meet secretly with rural partisans. Organizing a command and support structure, the partisans grew to form regional guerrilla forces. As Castro's strength grew, he moved to more conventional methods of warfare and triumphantly entered Havana in 1959. Throughout the campaign, Guevara had been at Castro's side.

Inflamed with revolutionary passion, Guevara completed a work on guerrilla warfare shortly after Castro took power. Far from theoretical, it can be deemed a "how-we-did-it" guide. Translated copies of Guevara's *Revolutionary War* appeared in the United States as early as 1961, but the book did not enjoy mass distribution until the end of the decade. It describes both Guevara's evolution toward Marxism and the revolutionary process in Cuba, and it details the structure and strategy of Castro's forces, as well as the guiding philosophy of the Cuban guerrilla war. Guevara also outlines the revolutionaries' methods of operations and principles of engagement. With the advantages of hindsight, it makes a stirring description of how victory was achieved.

Anthony Burton (1976, p. 70) says Guevara did not provide a model for revolution, but such a model could be extrapolated from *Guerrilla Warfare*. Burton argues guerrilla revolutions based on the Cuban experience are typified by three progressive phases, each one designed to complement the previous ones. Guevara-style revolution begins with isolated groups. In phase two, the isolated groups merge into guerilla columns. The final phase brings columns together in a conventional army. The goal of the strategy is to develop a conventional fighting force, or at least a force that renders the conventional opponent impotent.

Terrorism plays a limited role in Guevara's guerrilla framework. Although Guevara's focus was on the countryside, he saw the need for small urban terrorist groups to wage a campaign of support. These actions, however, are to be extremely selective; their purpose is to keep government forces off-balance, terrorizing them in their "safe" areas, never letting them relax. The main purpose of terrorism is to strike at the government's logistical network; the secondary purpose is to demoralize the government. Terrorism is a commando-type tactic.

The theory of guerrilla war came after the appearance of Guevara's work, and it was popularized by a French socialist named Regis Debray. In *Revolution in the Revolution?*, Debray summarizes his concept of Latin American politics. He writes the region has one dominating issue: poverty. Poverty threads through the entire fabric of Latin American life and entwines divergent cultures and peoples in a common knot of misery. Poverty is responsible for the imbalance in the class structure, as the wealthy cannot be maintained without the poverty of the masses. Debray sees only one recourse: The class structure must be changed and wealth redistributed. Because the wealthy will never give up their power, revolution is the only method of change.

Debray's prime target was the United States. Although the United States does not maintain a direct colonial empire as did the countries of Fanon's focus, it does hold sway over Latin America. The United States dominates Latin America through economic imperialism. Behind every power in the south stands the United States. Debray holds the United States responsible for maintaining the inequitable class structure, and he holds the common Marxist belief that North American wealth caused Latin American poverty. It is quite logical, therefore, to target the United States.

Like Fanon, Debray continually talks of revolution. He sees little need for terrorism, however, and he minimizes the role of urban centers in a revolt. Debray believes revolution is essentially an affair for poor peasants and it can only begin in a rural setting with regional guerrilla forces. Terrorism has no payoff. At best, it is neutral, and at worst, it alienates peasants needed for guerrilla support. According to Debray, for a revolution to work, it must begin with guerrillas fighting for justice and end with a united conventional force. Terrorism will not accomplish this objective.

URBAN TERRORISM IN PRACTICE

In the early 1960s, a group of revolutionaries called the Tupamaros surfaced in Uruguay. Unlike their predecessors in the Cuban Revolution, the Tupamaros spurned the countryside to favor an urban environment. City sidewalks and asphalt became their battleground. A decade later, their tactics would inspire revolutionaries around the world, and terrorist groups would imitate the methods of the Uruguayan revolutionaries. The Tupamaros epitomized urban terrorism.

In the years immediately after World War II, Uruguay appeared to be a model Latin American government (see Figure 8.3 for a map of the country). Democratic principles and freedoms were the accepted basis of Uruguay's political structures. Democratic rule was complemented by a sound economy and an exemplary educational system. Although it could not be described as a land of wealth, by the early 1950s, Uruguay could be called a land of promise. All factors seemed to point to peace and prosperity.

Unfortunately, in 1954, Uruguay's promise started to fade. The export economy that had proven to be so prosperous for the country began to crumble. Falling prices on exported goods meant inflation and unemployment. Economic dissatisfaction grew, and by 1959, many workers and members of the middle class faced a bleak future. Uruguay had undergone a devastating economic reversal, and many workers grew restless.

In the northern section of Uruguay, sugar workers were particularly hard hit. Sugar exports had decreased in the 1950s, and sugar workers suffered all of Uruguay's economic woes. As a result, the workers took steps to form a national union, but several militant radicals interjected themselves in the union movement. When the sugar workers organized in 1959, the militants dominated the union and called for confrontation with the government.

By 1962, the union organizers believed they should move their organization from the rural north to Montevideo, to make its presence felt in the capital. Moderates joined militants in a united front and headed south. Even though their rhetoric was violent, union members felt an appearance in Montevideo would not only draw attention to their cause, but also help legitimize it.

Their logic seemed sound. Although Uruguay was predominantly rural geographically, most of the population lived in Montevideo, a metropolis of 1.25 million people. Demographically, the capital offered the promise of recognition. Unfortunately for the union, they did not achieve the type of recognition they were seeking. Far from viewing the marchers as a legitimate labor movement, the government considered them potential revolutionaries.

The sugar workers clashed with police, and several union members were arrested. One of those taken to jail was a young law student named Raul Sendic. Disillusioned with law school and his prospects for the future, Sendic joined the sugar workers. When police confronted the marchers in 1962, Sendic was arrested; he remained in jail until 1963. When he emerged, he had a plan for revolution.

Sendic had not seen the brighter side of Uruguayan life in prison. The stark realities of Uruguay's now-shaky political system were evident, as torture and mistreatment of prisoners were common experiences. If the population could not be kept contented by a sound economy, it had to be subdued by fear. Democracy and freedoms faded as Uruguay's economic woes increased. Sendic described the repression he saw in an article titled "Waiting for the Guerrilla," in which he called for revolt in Montevideo.

After Sendic was released from jail, several young radicals gravitated toward him. María Gilio (1972) painted a sympathetic picture of Sendic's early followers. According to Gilio, these young people were primarily interested in

FIGURE 8.3 Map of Uruguay

reforming the government and creating economic opportunities. Although they had once believed they could attain these goals through democratic action, the current repression in Uruguay ruled out any response except violence. Gilio believed the group of people who surrounded Sendic were humanist idealists who wanted to bring Uruguay under direct control of the people.

Others did not hold this opinion of Sendic and his compatriots. Arturo Porzecanski (1973) provided a more objective view of the group's next move. Sendic's group felt excluded from participation in the political system, and Sendic believed violence was the only appropriate tool to change the political order. In 1963, Sendic and his followers raided the Swiss Hunting Club outside Montevideo. The raid was the first step in arming the group, and the first step in revolution.

According to Porzecanski, the group was not willing to move outside Montevideo to begin a guerrilla war for several reasons. First, the group was not large enough to begin a guerrilla campaign because it represented radical middle-class students. Mainstream workers and labor activists had moved away from the militants before the march on Montevideo. Second, the countryside of Uruguay did not readily lend itself to a guerrilla war because unrest grew from the urban center of Uruguay. Third, the peasants were unwilling to provide popular support for guerrilla forces. Finally, Montevideo was the nerve center of Uruguay. All of these factors caused the small group to believe that it could better fight within the city.

In 1963, the group adopted its official name, the National Liberation Movement (MLN). But as they began to develop a revolutionary ideology and a structure for violent revolt, the group searched for a name that would identify them with the people, one with more popular appeal than the MLN acronym.

According to Christopher Dobson and Ronald Payne (1982b, p. 206), the MLN took its popular name from the heroic Inca Chieftain Tupac Amaru, killed in a revolt against the Spaniards 200 years earlier. Arturo Porzecanski notes this story but also suggests the group may have taken its name from a South American bird. In any case, Sendic's followers called themselves the Tupamaros.

By 1965, their ranks had grown to 50 followers, and they were building a network of sympathizers in the city. Instead of following the prescribed method of Latin American revolution based on a rural guerrilla operation, the Tupamaros organized to do battle inside the city, following the recent guidelines of Carlos Marighella. Terrorism would become the prime strategy for assaulting the enemy. The Tupamaros, unlike Castro, were not interested in building a conventional military force to strike at the government.

Porzecanski estimates the Tupamaros had expanded to nearly 3,000 members by 1970. Expansion brought an extremely decentralized command structure and the evolution of a grand strategy intended to result in national socialism. The Tupamaros claimed this program would allow the government to nationalize and distribute economic resources equitably. The Tupamaros were more interested in redistributing the wealth of Uruguay than establishing a socialist government. Rather than risk alienating the population with abstract Marxist rhetoric, they wanted to create an economy that would offer opportunities to Montevideo's working class. As they expanded, the Tupamaros constantly stressed that it was trying to foster a working-class revolution, in an effort to attract a following.

Despite their willingness to expound the national socialist propaganda, the Tupamaros never developed an elaborate philosophical base; they were more interested in action. Ross Butler (1976, pp. 53–59) describes the growth of the terrorist group by tracking their tactics. He says they engaged in rather inconsequential activities in the early stages of their development. From 1964 to 1968, they concentrated on gathering arms and financial backing. After 1968, however, their tactics changed, and according to Butler, the government found it necessary to take them seriously.

In 1968, the Tupamaros launched a massive campaign of decentralized terrorism. They were able to challenge government authority because their movement was growing, and a series of bank robberies had served to finance their operations. Armed with the power to strike, the Tupamaros sought to paralyze the government in Montevideo. They believed, as had Carlos Marighella in Brazil, that the government would increasingly turn to repression as a means of defense and the people would be forced to join the revolution.

The government was quick to respond, but found there was very little it could do. The Tupamaros held all the cards. They struck when and where they wanted, and generally made the government's security forces look foolish. They kidnapped high-ranking officials from the Uruguayan government, and the police could do little to find the victims.

Kidnapping became so successful that the Tupamaros took to kidnapping foreign diplomats. They seemed able to choose their victims and strike their targets at will. Frustrated, the police turned to an old Latin American tactic. They began torturing suspected Tupamaros.

Torturing prisoners served several purposes. First, it provided a ready source of information. In fact, when the Tupamaros were destroyed, it was primarily through massive arrests based on information gleaned from interrogations. Second, torture was believed to serve as a deterrent to other would-be revolutionaries. Although this torture was always unofficial, most potential government opponents knew what lay in store for them if they were caught.

The methods of torture were brutal. Gilio (1972, pp. 141–172) describes in detail the police and military torture of suspected Tupamaros. Even when prisoners finally provided information, they continued to be tortured routinely until they were either killed or released. Torture became a standard police tactic.

A. J. Langguth (1978) devotes most of his work to the torture commonplace in Uruguay and Brazil. The torturers viewed themselves as professionals who were simply carrying out a job for the government. Rapes, beatings, and murders were common, but the police refined the art of torture to keep victims in pain as long as possible. According to Langguth, some suspects were tortured over a period of months or even years.

In the midst of revolution and torture, the Tupamaros blamed the United States for supporting the brutal Uruguayan government. Their internal revolt thus adopted the rhetoric of an anti-imperialist revolution, which increased their popular support. The Tupamaros established several combat and support columns in Montevideo, and by 1970, they began to reach the zenith of their power. Porzecanski says they almost achieved a duality of power. That is, the Tupamaros were so strong that they seemed to share power equally with the government.

Their success was short-lived, however. Although they waged an effective campaign of terrorism, they were never able to capture the hearts of the working class. Most of Montevideo's workers viewed the Tupamaros as privileged students with no real interest in the working class. In addition, the level of their violence was truly appalling.

During terrorist operations, numerous people were routinely murdered. The eventual murder of a kidnapped American police official disgusted the workers, even though they had no great love for the United States. Tupamaro tactics alienated their potential supporters.

In the end, violence spelled doom for the Tupamaros. By bringing chaos to the capital, they had succeeded in unleashing the full wrath of the government. In addition, the Tupamaros had overestimated their strength. In 1971, they joined a left-wing coalition of parties and ran for office. According to Ronald MacDonald (1972, pp. 24–45), this was a fatal mistake. The Tupamaros had alienated potential electoral support through their terrorist campaign and caused the left-wing coalition to be soundly defeated in national elections.

The electoral defeat was not the only bad news for the Tupamaros. The election brought a right-wing government to power, and the new military government openly advocated and approved of repression. A brutal counter-terrorist campaign followed. Far from being alienated by this, the workers of Montevideo applauded the new government's actions, even when it declared martial law in 1972. Armed with expanded powers, the government began to round up all leftists in 1972. For all practical purposes, the Tupamaros were finished. Their violence helped bring about a revolution, but not the type they had intended.

THE INFLUENCE OF THE TUPAMAROS

Peter Waldmann (1986, p. 259) sums up the Tupamaros best by stating that they became the masters of urban terrorism. He believes that in terms of striking power, organization, and the ability to control a city, no group has ever surpassed the Tupamaros. They epitomized the terrorist role. As such, they served as a model for modern terrorist groups.

As the champions of revolutionary terrorism, the Tupamaros were copied around the world, especially by groups in the United States and Western Europe. Many American left-wing groups from 1967 on modeled themselves after the Tupamaros. In Western Europe, their structure and tactics were mimicked by such groups as the Red Army Faction and Direct Action. The Red Brigades split their activities among different cities, but they essentially copied the model of the Tupamaros.

The tactics and organization of the Tupamaros have also been copied by right-wing groups. In the United States, right-wing extremist organizations have advocated the use of Tupamaro-type tactics. Many revolutionary manuals and proposed terrorist organizations are based on Tupamaro experiences. In the right-wing novel *The Turner Diaries* (MacDonald, 1980), Earl Turner joins a terrorist group similar to the Tupamaros in Washington, D.C. The author describes the mythical right-wing revolution in terms of Carlos Marighella and the Tupamaros. The right does not give credit to the left, but it does follow its example.

The Tupamaros embodied the Marighella philosophy of revolution, initiating an urban campaign without much thought to structure, strategy, or organization. Although both Marighella and the Tupamaros believed the people would flock to the revolutionaries when government repression was employed, the opposite was true. The people endorsed repression.

When the Tupamaros roamed the streets, people were afraid. Banks were robbed, officials were kidnapped, and people were murdered. Daily fear was a reality, so much so that the government was provoked into action. Like the terrorist group, the government turned to murder and torture to eradicate the

Tupamaros. This may be the most frightening aspect of the experience: Revolutionary terrorism served to justify repressionist terrorism.

THE URBAN PHILOSOPHY

The fact that the Tupamaros created an urban movement is important in terms of the group's impact on violence in Latin America, but it also has a bearing on the way terrorist methods have developed in Europe and the United States. Historically, Latin American terrorism had been a product of rural peasant revolt. The Tupamaros offered an alternative to this tradition by making the city a battleground. They demonstrated to Western groups the impact that a few violent true believers could have on the rational routines of urban life. The urban setting provided the Tupamaros with endless opportunities.

Their revolutionary philosophy was also indicative of their pragmatism. Rather than accepting a standard line of Marxist dogma, the Tupamaros were willing to use national socialism as their political base; this demonstrated just how much they could compromise. According to one of their propaganda statements, they argued for a nationalized economy with guaranteed employment and social security. The export economy would remain intact, but profits would be shared among the people. Although this view hardly represents Marxism, the Tupamaros were willing to take such a stand to attract a working-class following. Socialism under national control was popular in Montevideo.

The tactics of the Tupamaros reflected the same pragmatism. Because the physical situation of Uruguay was not suitable for guerrilla war, the Tupamaros turned to the city. Just as they modified socialism to suit the political situation, they forged new, flexible, and pragmatic tactics for a new environment.

The Tupamaros used the concepts of Marighella in other ways as well. The basic unit of the revolution became Marighella's firing group. Tupamaros-style terrorism involved extremely small units engaging in individual acts of violence. Such action meshed well with Marighella's concept of a decentralized command structure, as well as his belief that any form of violence supported the revolution. Tupamaros violence did not need to be coordinated; it only needed to engender fear. In a war against social order, tactics and targets were modified to meet the circumstances.

The police replaced the army as the primary enemy, and financial institutions took the place of military targets. The urban war was a battle to gain resources and a psychological edge over security forces. The foliage and cover of the jungle countryside was replaced with the mass of humanity in the city. Guerrillas hid behind trees; the urban terrorists hid among people. They were protected by congestion, mobility, and the bureaucratic rigidity of the enemy. The Tupamaros were able to appear as average citizens until the moment they struck. When the battle was over, they simply melted back into the crowd (Waldmann, 1986, p. 260).

To accomplish these tactics successfully, the Tupamaros were forced to develop specific actions. Communication links inside the city assumed supreme importance, along with transportation. To assure these links, the terrorists had to master criminal activity. They communicated and traveled by means of an illegal network. They developed logistical support systems and safe houses to avoid confrontations with potential enemies. They traveled with false identification and collected their own intelligence from sympathizers. For all practical purposes, the Tupamaros became a secret army.

TUPAMAROS TACTICS

Although many observers note the Tupamaros spent little time discussing their grand strategy, the group did operate under some broad assumptions. Like other extremist groups, the Tupamaros knew their principles would have to be modified to win general support. The grand strategy centered on winning support from the middle and working classes. Because of the state of the economy and the lack of opportunity for educated people, the Tupamaros began their campaign with a good deal of sympathy in the middle class. Almost without exception, the Tupamaros's actions were taken in the name of the working class. See Box 8.1 for the Tupamaros's specific tactics.

The Tuparmaros realized they could not achieve popular support without the proper political circumstances. They believed they could only obtain power at a critical juncture when the political, social, and economic conditions were conducive to revolution. They called this juncture the *coyuntura,* and they aimed all revolutionary activities at this point.

John Wolf (1981, p. 82) says the Tupamaros saw violence as the only method to bring about social change. The coyuntura would never appear unless the people were incited to revolution. Terrorist violence was to be random and frequent, but it was only a prelude to a general attack. When the conditions were set, when the coyuntura was right, organized popular revolution would replace terrorism.

Arturo Porzecanski (1973, p. 21) says the coyuntura was to give rise to the *salto,* or the general strike for power. The purpose of urban terrorism was to keep the idea of the coyuntura alive. The salto, however, was a separate move. Urban terrorism would be replaced by an organized people's army during the salto. The stages of the coyuntura and the salto reflected the ideology of Marighella.

The coyuntura concept was maintained through terrorist tactics. Ross Butler (1976, p. 54) writes that the Tupamaros's tactics changed according to their ability to attract a following. Until 1968, Butler says, the Tupamaros focused on low-level activities: arson, propaganda, and exposing public corruption. As the ranks of the Tupamaros grew, they became more daring. In 1969, they shifted to bank robbery, and in 1970, they staged a $6,000,000

BOX 8.1 Tupamaros Tactics

Assassination	Internal discipline
Bank robbery	Infiltration of security forces
Kidnapping	Temporary control of urban areas
Propaganda	Redistribution of expropriated goods
Bombing	to the poor

---

robbery of a Montevideo bank. These activities were followed by a string of ambushes and kidnappings.

Porzecanski (1973, pp. 40–45) argues all of their tactics were designed to make the group self-sufficient. The tactics gave the Tupamaros logistical support and allowed them to operate without support from foreign countries. Their terrorist activities were complemented by a transportation and intelligence network provided by supporters.

Two of the most noted tactics were bank robbery and kidnapping. Bank robberies fell into the category of Marighella's concept of "expropriation." That is, the purpose of robbery was to finance the terrorist organization. The Tupamaros used bank robbery as their primary tactic of waging an urban guerrilla war. The banks became both symbolic and logistical targets, and the robberies upset Uruguayan society. Using a network of industrial, police, and military sympathizers, the Tupamaros mastered daring daylight robberies.

Kidnapping was also designed to produce both logistical support (through ransom) and propaganda value. There was as much drama in kidnapping as there was in robbery. The Tupamaros began by kidnapping local officials from Montevideo, but they found they could cause more disruption by taking foreigners.

On July 31, 1970, Dan Mitrione, an American police adviser assigned to assist the Uruguayan government, was kidnapped on his way to work. As he was being driven away, a gun pressed against his leg was accidentally discharged. The incident and the wound caused international headlines. Mitrione's case was especially newsworthy because he had a wife and a large number of children breathlessly awaiting his return in Indiana (Langguth, 1978).

Mitrione's story ended tragically. On August 10, 1970, his body was found on the streets of Montevideo. His hands had been bound, and two bullets had been sent through the back of his head. A Tupamaros message next to the body said he had been tried by a people's court, found guilty, and executed.

The Tupamaros kidnapped another foreign victim on January 8, 1971. Geoffrey Jackson, the British Ambassador to Uruguay, was taken and held for eight months. When it became apparent the British government would pay no ransom for Jackson, the Tupamaros discussed executing him. Instead, they released him in a gesture of goodwill, hoping to offset the working-class backlash that had followed Mitrione's murder. Jackson's account of the ordeal can be found in his book, *People's Prison* (also published as *Surviving the Long Night*).

Releasing Jackson was not out of character for the Tupamaros, even though they were known for their violence. They continually tried to maintain a Robin Hood image in their effort to win working-class support. One of their most noted actions in this role was the formation of the "hunger commandos." One Christmas Eve, this unit hijacked a shipment of groceries and distributed them among Montevideo's poor. These tactics were later copied by the Symbionese Liberation Army (SLA) in California when they demanded food distribution to the poor in return for the release of a kidnap victim.

Richard Clutterbuck (1975, p. 36) claims the Robin Hood tactics gained attention but failed to work. Food distribution and appeals to the working class could not neutralize violence and murder. Clutterbuck says that by 1972, the Robin Hood tactics had clearly backfired, helping form the backlash that led to the destruction of the Tupamaros. The working-class people of Montevideo saw the do-good activities as too little coming too late. Even Tupamaros humanitarian gestures were viewed with contempt because of the concurrent, violent terrorist campaign.

As Clutterbuck implies, the effectiveness of all Tupamaros tactics must ultimately be evaluated by the final result. In terms of increasing support, the tactics were initially successful, but they failed in the long run. From 1965 to 1970, the ranks of the Tupamaros increased dramatically. By 1970, however, the excessive violence of the Tupamaros had had a negative impact. It alienated the middle and working classes and eventually caused many leftists to return to a nonviolent Communist party. According to Waldmann (1986, pp. 275–276), the major mistake of the Tupamaros was that they alienated their supporters.

Tactics must also be evaluated according to the response of the enemy. Again, the Tupamaros enjoyed initial success, but failed to maintain momentum. At first, Uruguay's political authorities were completely confused in their dealings with the Tupamaros. They were frustrated at every turn, as the kidnapping problem illustrates. John Wolf (1981, p. 21) notes that from August 1968 until the execution of Dan Mitrione in August 1970, the police were unable to locate a single kidnap victim. The tactic appeared to work.

But although this tactic gained publicity, it also provoked a harsh police reaction. Torture increased, and police became more repressive. Ironically, the repression was greeted with public support. When forced to the brink, Uruguayan security forces turned to brutal repression, the one tactic they knew would work, and by 1972, it had become the legal norm.

In the final analysis, the Tupamaros's tactics failed. Ironically, their propensity toward violence changed the balance of public opinion in favor of the government. Yet, the tactics of the Tupamaros differ little from the tactics of most other terrorist groups. Even though the tactics ultimately failed, the organizational structure proved to be a model for others.

ORGANIZATIONAL CHARACTERISTICS

The Tupamaros were one of the most highly organized yet least structured terrorist groups in modern history. Only groups like the PLO and the IRA can rival the organization of the Tupamaros. Yet while both the PLO and the IRA enjoy a tremendous amount of external support, the Tupamaros existed almost entirely inside the borders of Uruguay. Because they were virtually self-sufficient, the growth, operations, and organization of the Tupamaros were amazing. If they failed to achieve success in the long run, at least their organizational structure kept them in the field as long as possible. The Tupamaros were nominally guided by a National Convention, which had authority in all matters of policy and operations. In reality, the National Convention seldom met more than once per year and was disbanded in the 1970s. Christopher Hewitt (1984, p. 8) notes the National Convention did not meet at all after September 1970. John Wolf (1981, p. 31) believes an Executive Committee controlled all activities in Montevideo. Arturo Porzecanski (1973), probably the most noted authority on the Tupamaros, makes several references to this same Executive Committee. For all practical purposes, it seems to have controlled the Tupamaros.

The Executive Committee was responsible for two major operations. It ran the columns that supervised the terrorist operations, and it also administered a special Committee for Revolutionary Justice. The power of the Executive Committee derived from internal enforcement. The job of the Revolutionary Justice Committee was to terrorize the terrorists into obedience. If an operative refused to obey an order or tried to leave the organization, a delegation from the revolutionary judiciary would usually deal with the matter. It was not uncommon to murder the family of the offending party, along with the errant member. The Tupamaros believed in strong internal discipline.

In day-to-day operations, however, the Executive Committee exercised very little authority. Robert Moss (1972, p. 222) states the Tupamaros lacked a unified command structure for routine functions. The reason can be found in the nature of the organization. Because secrecy dominated every facet of its operations, it could not afford open communications. Therefore, each subunit evolved into a highly autonomous operation. There was little the Executive Committee could do about this situation, and the command structure became highly decentralized. The Tupamaros existed as a confederacy.

Operational power in the Tupamaros was vested in the lower-echelon units. Columns were organized for both combatant (operational) and staff (logistical) functions. Wolf (1981, p. 35) writes that most of the full-time terrorists belonged to cells in the combatant columns. They lived a precarious day-to-day existence and were constantly in conflict with the authorities. According to Wolf, they were supported by larger noncombatant columns who served to keep the terrorists in the field.

The importance of the noncombatant columns cannot be overemphasized—the strength of the Tupamaros came from its logistical columns.

Without the elaborate support network of sympathizers and part-time helpers, the Tupamaros could not have remained in the field. Other groups that have copied their organizational model have not had the ability to launch a campaign because they lacked the same support.

Wolf's analysis of the support network includes peripheral support that was not directly linked to the Tupamaros organization. With Porzecanski, Wolf classifies supporters into two categories. One group operated in the open and provided intelligence and background information to the noncombatant sections. The other type of supporters worked on getting supplies to the operational sections. These sympathizers provided arms, ammunition, and legal aid. Both groups tried to generate popular support for the Tupamaros. When the government attacked the terrorists in 1972, its primary target was the support network. Police officials reasoned that if they destroyed the logistical network, they would destroy the Tupamaros.

In looking at the organizational chart of the Tupamaros, it is easy to envisage the entire operation (see Figure 8.4). The Executive Committee was in charge, but it ran a highly decentralized operation. Its main power came from the internal rule enforcement provided by the Committee for Revolutionary Justice. Columns were the major units, but they tended to be tactical formations. The real operational power came from the cells, which joined together for column-style operations on rare occasions. The combat striking power of the Tupamaros came from the four- to six-person groups in the cells. This organization epitomized Marighella's concept of the firing unit. Peter

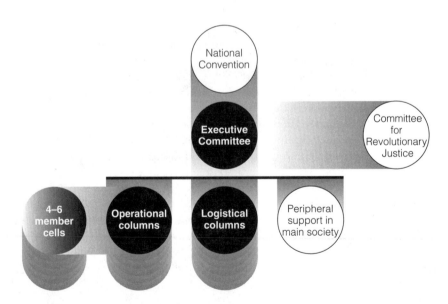

FIGURE 8.4 Tupamaros Organization

Source: John Wolf (1981), *Fear of Fear* (New York: Plenum).

Waldmann (1986, p. 259) sums up the Tupamaros best by stating that they became the masters of urban terrorism. He believes that in terms of striking power, organization, and the ability to control a city, no group has ever surpassed the Tupamaros. They epitomized the terrorist role.

The influence of the Tupamaros spread far beyond Latin America. When violence erupted in Western Europe and the Middle East in the 1960s and 1970s, terrorists cited Guevara and Marighella as their icons. The Tupamaros served as the model.

KEY CONCEPTS

1. Modern terrorism was influenced by theories from Latin America. The primary architects of modern terrorism were Carlos Marighella and Ernesto Guevara. The theoreticians behind the movements were Franz Fanon and Regis Debray.
2. Marighella developed a theory of urban terrorism. Guevara wrote a description of guerrilla war in the Cuban Revolution.
3. The nationalistic revolutions of the post–World War II period incorporated the theories of urban terrorism and guerrilla warfare.
4. Guerrillas use terrorist tactics selectively and do not engage in indiscriminate terrorism.
5. Terrorists lack the structural capabilities of guerrillas, and their tactical operations are limited to terrorism. They cannot wage a guerrilla war.
6. The Tupamaros of Uruguay embodied the concept of urban revolution. It is possible to gain an understanding of modern terrorism by studying the structure and tactical operations of the Tupamaros.

FOOD FOR THOUGHT

The Latin American urban philosophy dominated the concept of terrorism from about 1960 until the early 1990s, and it still influences many terrorist groups such as violent, right-wing North American extremists. Yet more recently, modern terrorism has been influenced by two other trends: violence lacking cohesive structure, and religious fundamentalism. How do you think these new factors will influence the urban model? What types of support structures must terrorists have regardless of their organizational philosophy?

FURTHER READING

Timothy Wickham-Crowley, *Guerrillas and Revolution in Latin America*

✳

PART III

Modern Terrorism

9

International Terrorism
and the Question
of Palestine

The anti-Western colonial revolutions from 1945 to 1964, as well as U.S. involvement in Vietnam from 1963 to 1975, spawned the growth of special warfare units in Europe and the United States. Western nations assumed they would be fighting counterguerrilla wars, but terrorists had other ideas. Utilizing an ideological framework imported from Latin America, international terrorists gathered under the banner of Marighella's "urban guerrilla war." This theme united divergent groups from Europe, Asia, and the Middle East. Some of them even trained together under Cuba's intelligence bureau, the DGI, and their instructors were none other than Uruguay's Tupamaros. By 1968, the world experienced a new campaign of violence that incorporated themes from nineteenth-century anarchism, the Russian Revolution, and Ireland. Subnational violence evolved into international terrorism, and began with questions about the future of the Palestinians.

After completing this chapter, you should be able to:

1. Explain the origins and importance of Palestinian terrorism.
2. Describe the importance of the PLO's battle at Karamah.
3. Outline the rise and purpose of Black September.
4. Describe how Palestinian terrorism influenced international terrorism.
5. Explain the impact of the 1982 Israeli invasion of Lebanon on the structure of Middle Eastern terrorism.
6. Summarize the development and operations of the Abu Nidal group.

THE GROWTH OF THE PLO
AND INTERNATIONAL TERRORISM

According to The History Channel (2000), Cuba hosted a number of revolutionary groups in a training session outside Havana in 1968. Several leftist and nationalist groups from around the world attended the event, including Yasser Arafat, leader of the Palestinian Liberation Organization (PLO). Arafat stated that revolution united all revolutionaries from the past to the present. He embraced the other revolutionaries in the Cuban training camps and promised to join them in international revolution. He believed Marighella's "urban guerrilla war" to be a theme uniting international revolution.

Arafat's organization, the PLO, was a conglomeration of several Palestinian nationalist groups that had been displaced by the formation of modern Israel (see Figure 9.1 for a map of the region). Beginning in 1957, Arafat gathered groups of disgruntled Palestinians in Jordan, and in 1964, he formed the PLO. His purpose was to create a political organization to help form a multinational alliance against Israel. He hoped Arab governments would jointly launch a war against the European-created state.

Arafat's dream came to fruition in 1967. Although Egypt and Syria played the dominant role in Arab politics, the nations surrounding Israel strengthened their military might and talked about the destruction of the country. Arafat played a very minor role in the alliance, but he hoped a war with Israel would serve the interests of the displaced Palestinians. The war came in June 1967, and it lasted six days. Unfortunately for the Palestinians, the war did not accomplish Arafat's objective. In what historians call the Six Day War, Israel destroyed the combined Arab armies in a matter of hours.

The Six Day War stunned the Arab world. Despite their abundance of military equipment and superior numbers of personnel, each Arab neighbor of Israel was soundly trounced by the Israeli military establishment (called the Israeli Defense Force or IDF). As James Bill and Carl Leiden (1984, p. 261) say, the Arabs had only looked strong; in reality, their armies had been relatively weak. They were torn with internal dissension and by officer corps more involved in internal politics than military proficiency. The end result was total defeat for Arab conventional forces. Their armies did not fight well against the Israelis in 1967. Clearly, the Arabs needed a new champion, and Yasser Arafat stepped forward to assume the role.

Janet Wallach and John Wallach (1992) point out that it is difficult to obtain an objective picture of Arafat in the West. He is viewed as a bloodthirsty terrorist by many, especially those whose sympathies are with Israel. On the other hand, he is perceived as a revolutionary hero and spokesperson of the Palestinians by others. Even in the Middle East, many view him with suspicion, and some view him with hatred. After several interviews with Arafat, his rivals, and his admirers, the Wallachs conclude that opinions about Arafat depend on the point of view. He is a chameleon, trying to be everything to everyone. Yet, the Wallachs reminded their readers that no one

FIGURE 9.1 Israel and its Neighbors

has accomplished more for the Palestinian Arabs than the self-made leader of the PLO.

In 1967, Arafat offered the defeated Arabs a new tactic. Instead of striking the IDF directly, he proposed terrorizing unfortified civilian targets. Using a group of warriors known as *fedayeen,* Yasser Arafat and Kahlil Wazir (also known as Abu Jihad, killed by Israeli intelligence in April 1988) began to attack Israel with the militant arm of the PLO, al Fatah. Fatah was created on October 10, 1959, for the purpose of waging war on Israel. When the PLO formed in 1964, Arafat became a leader in the movement and brought the philosophy of armed conflict with him. Fatah ran its first operation in 1965, blowing up an Israeli water pump. After the Six Day War, Arafat began launching hit-and-run strikes against Israel from Jordan. The actions made Arafat a hero in the eyes of the defeated Arabs.

The reality of Fatah's power was less glamorous than Arafat's growing reputation. Actually, Fatah was capable of doing little more than fighting with hit-and-run tactics. It was hardly a military power or much of a match for the IDF. Fatah could not fight soldiers, but its terrorists could murder civilians. After the Six Day War, Arab armies took little action. It was different for Fatah. Fedayeen, Fatah's holy warriors, began to attack schoolchildren, apartment complexes, farms, settlements, and other civilian targets.

Walter Laqueur (1987, p. 216) says Fatah was limited to three tactics: (1) sending small ambush teams from the Jordanian border, (2) planting bombs, and (3) shelling Israeli settlements from Jordan. Arafat called this guerrilla warfare; the Israelis called it terrorism.

Their initial successes caused the PLO's status to rise throughout the Arab world, and Arafat's fortunes rose along with it. With all the conventional Arab armies in disarray, only the PLO had the courage and will to strike. They were outnumbered and outgunned, and they did not even have a country. They had only the fedayeen. Their action was indirect, but the Arabs liked it. Furthermore, in terms of propaganda, the invincible Israeli Defense Force seemed to be incapable of combating the PLO's clandestine tactics.

KARAMAH

Edward Weisband and Damir Roguly (1976, pp. 261–262) say Fatah did not emerge as a significant fighting force until 1968, when it was forced to conventionally defend one of its base camps. On March 21, 1968, tired of raids from Jordanian-based PLO compounds, the Israelis launched a mechanized assault on the village of Karamah—one of Arafat's primary bases in Jordan. Weisband and Roguly say both sides distorted the facts, but the battle had an impact in the Arab world.

Jillian Becker's (1984, pp. 62–64) account of the raid on Karamah is extremely pro-Israeli, but it reflects the impact the raid had on the Arabs. According to Becker, the Israelis dropped leaflets two hours before the raid, telling Jordanians in the area to leave. The Jordanians dispatched a military force to resist the violation of their territory, and Fatah dug in at Karamah. The Israeli attack was ferocious, supported by armor and helicopter gunships. After heavy fighting, Karamah held firm despite the odds against the Palestinians.

To the Arab mind, it was a victory for the PLO, more specifically for Fatah and Arafat. Becker claims this was ironic because it was the Jordanian army that stopped the Israeli armor; Arafat had already fled the scene. Others maintain Arafat was present throughout the fighting. Yet, as Weisband and Roguly point out, Karamah became a PLO legend, and Yasser Arafat became a bona fide hero.

After Karamah, the PLO began a terrorist campaign in earnest against Israel. Terrorism became the only viable military tactic open to the PLO, and a whole set of other terrorist groups began to grow within the organization.

Like Fatah, they were not strong enough to strike the Israeli Defense Force directly, but they could strike civilians.

Terrorism represented the only method for a small group of relatively weak people to launch an offensive against a superior force. By attacking civilians, hijacking airplanes, and planning assassinations, terrorist groups within the PLO could attack the Israeli military indirectly. In Arafat's defense, terrorism was adopted by the PLO for the same reason the Irgun Zvai Leumi had used it two decades earlier: It was the only tactical option available. Terrorism was a military convenience.

In the meantime, Arafat became aware that terrorist targets were receiving considerable worldwide media attention. Under his tutelage, the PLO campaign became increasingly dramatic and public. Savage attacks resulted in television news features. Hijackings and hostage-taking incidents brought extended press coverage. They were made-for-TV dramas, and television used terrorists to keep viewers in front of the screen. In the media, it appeared the Palestinians were united in their struggle against Israel, and Arafat was willing to use the attraction of press coverage to bring attention to the plight of the Palestinian people.

The PLO came to symbolize much more than this in the realm of international terrorism. With publicity gained from a variety of airline hijackings, terrorists from other parts of the world came to train with the PLO. Nationalist terrorists from the Basque region of Spain and IRA terrorists trained in the Middle East. The ideological left turned to the PLO, and European left-wing terrorists flocked to PLO training centers. German leftists forged particularly strong links with the Palestinians.

In turn, terrorism became an expression of political unity for the PLO. But although all terrorism seemed to come from Arafat, the PLO splintered. When an organization uses terrorism, it must call on true-believing fanatics who do not readily make alliances or compromise with any form of leadership. Despite Arafat's attempt to coalesce the movement, various terrorist groups in the PLO started to go their own way as early as 1970. These groups included Naiaf Hawatmeh's Democratic Front for the Liberation of Palestine, George Habash and Wadi Hadad in the Popular Front for the Liberation of Palestine, and Walid Jabril's Popular Front for the Liberation of Palestine, General Command. Later notable defectors were Abul Abbas, Abu Ibrahim, and Abu Nidal. Walter Laqueur (1987) says that when the history of the PLO is written, it will be a chronology of continuous splits among splinter groups.

Arab leaders in Syria and Iraq had long been rivals of Jordan's King Hussein, and they saw potential benefits in the splintering PLO. The rival Ba'athists in Syria and Iraq began to view the PLO both as a potential instrument with which to achieve their foreign policy objectives, and as an ally against Jordan. The popularity of the PLO allowed it to act with more and more autonomy, and it joined with Syrian- and Iraqi-sponsored opposition parties in Jordan. This did not please the king of Jordan.

BLACK SEPTEMBER:
PLO TERRORISM SPREADS TO EUROPE

King Hussein of Jordan viewed the increasing strength of the PLO in his land with growing concern. He had entered the war against Israel with some reluctance and preferred to take a moderate stance in the pan-Arabic struggle. Closely identified with British culture and friendly with the West, Jordan did not endorse the radicalism of Syria and other militant Arab states. King Hussein was especially wary of Syrian and Iraqi expansionist dreams and was more concerned with the protection of Jordan than with a united Arab realm.

As the PLO grew, it identified more closely with militant Arab states, giving them a potential base in Jordan. Concerned with the growing influence of foreign nationals in his own land, King Hussein ordered the PLO to stop attacking Israel. He was not trying to protect Israel but to stop the spread of rival influences in Jordan.

But the PLO was on an all-time high and not about to quit. Radical elements in Iraq and Syria encouraged Arafat to defy Hussein's order. Members of the Ba'ath party, the pan-Arabic socialist movement with branches in Syria and Iraq, saw the PLO as a tool that could be used against the Israelis. More important, they came to view the organization as a weapon to help the cause of revolution and socialism among all the Arabs. Arafat defied Hussein's order and stepped up operations against Israel.

Arafat continued training in Jordanian PLO camps and invited revolutionaries throughout the Middle East to participate. His exiled Palestinian government took no orders from its Jordanian host. Raids against Israel were conducted by a variety of PLO and foreign terrorist groups, and Arafat's reputation as a revolutionary hero spread beyond the Middle East. This became too much for King Hussein. After Palestinian terrorists hijacked three airplanes and destroyed them in Jordan, the king decided to act. In September 1970, Hussein attacked the PLO.

Arafat and the PLO were taken completely by surprise. The PLO terrorist offensive against Israel had worked because the terrorists operated in base camps that, although subject to Israeli attack, were relatively immune from annihilation. This was not the case when King Hussein's Jordanian army struck; the PLO had nowhere to run. As Jordanian regulars bombarded PLO camps and launched an all-out assault, Arafat had no alternative. Too weak to stand and fight, he fled to southern Lebanon. It was his only option.

Arafat wanted to strike back at the Israelis. He could not control terrorists in the many PLO splinter groups, so he created a new group after King Hussein's September attack. He called the group Black September. Using German leftist allies, Black September began planning a strike against the Israelis. It came, with German terrorist help, in Munich at the 1972 Olympic Games. Black September struck the Olympic Village and took most of the Israeli Olympic team hostage, killing those who tried to escape. German police moved in, and the world watched a drawn out siege.

Black September terrorists negotiated transportation to Libya, but while moving to the aircraft designated to fly them from Germany, the German police launched a rescue operation. Plans immediately went awry. Reacting quickly, terrorists machine-gunned their hostages before the German police could take control. The Israelis and a German officer were killed. It was a terrorist victory, and European leftists and nationalists saw it as partially their triumph.

THE PLO AND THE CHANGING FACE OF MIDDLE EASTERN TERRORISM

In 1970, the expulsion of the PLO from Jordan marked a turning point in Middle Eastern terrorism. While Black September made ready for the attack on the 1972 Olympic Games in Munich, the Arabs had realized the potential of the PLO's tactics for other conflicts. As various terrorist groups split off from Arafat's control, a host of Arab states offered support and assistance. Strangely, their prime target was not Israel, and they were not overly interested in the Palestinian cause. In fact, the splintering PLO groups were often used as terrorist agents against rival Arab states. See Box 9.1 for a listing of these splinter groups.

Iraq first became a factor in the spread of internal Arab terrorism under President Bakr and later in 1979 under Saddam Hussein. Supported by the Ba'athist socialist party, leaders in Iraq envisioned a pan-Arabic state under socialist control. Of course, Israel had to be eliminated, but conservative Arab states were just as threatening. In addition, Syria posed a serious challenge to Iraqi leadership in the Arabic world. Bakr and Hussein were happy to use terrorism against Israel, fellow Arabs, fellow Ba'athists, and anybody else.

In the early 1970s, a Fatah recruiter came to Iraq to open a training center in Baghdad. The Iraqis began to recruit him and suggested he use his terrorists not only against Israel and its Western supporters, but also in the wider struggle for pan-Arabism. His name was Sabri al-Banna, better known in the West by the name Abu Nidal (Melman, 1986, pp. 69–75; Seale, 1992, pp. 111–113, 123–124). (Abu Nidal's exploits are covered in more detail later in this chapter.)

Partially as a response to Iraqi actions, Syria increased its presence in the shadowy world of terrorism. With designs on Lebanon and eventually Israel, Syria's territorial dreams, born after World War I, had not faded away. Syria followed a twofold policy with respect to terrorism. First, it actively encouraged the breakup of PLO terrorist organizations and promoted a situation of general anarchy in Lebanon. Second, it recruited radical splinter groups from the PLO and prepared them for a variety of missions. Although Israel was always deemed to be the main enemy in the Middle East, the Syrians attacked Arab targets as well. Terrorism would be used against Iraqi and Lebanese forces opposing Syrian influence. Most notably, anti-Syrian elements in the PLO would be subject to attack.

BOX 9.1   Splinter Terrorist Groups in the PLO

GROUP	PRIMARY LEADER
Black September	Yasser Arafat
Force 17	Hassan Salameh
PFLP (Popular Front for the Liberation of Palestine)	George Habash
DFLP (Democratic Front for the Liberation of Palestine)	Naiaf Hawatmeh
PFLP, GC (Popular Front for the Liberation of Palestine, General Command)	Walid Jabril
Black June or the Abu Nidal Group	Abu Nidal
Pro-Iraqi Groups	Abul Abbas, Abu Ibriham

Libya entered the fracas in 1969, when Colonel Moamar Khadaffy began to finance the PLO. Khadaffy supported the concept of a pan–Arabic socialist state, with Libya having supreme control. Although Libya enjoyed a fairly substantial income from its oil production, Khadaffy faced a problem similar to that of Syria and Iraq. His conventional military forces could not support his dreams. Terrorism seemed an interesting alternative. In 1974, Khadaffy introduced his own faction in the PLO and established base camps for terrorist training (Reese, 1986).

The new state-sponsored terrorists did not limit their attacks to traditional enemies. Although an international campaign of terrorism was being waged by a myriad of tiny terrorist groups in the 1970s, Syria, Iraq, and Libya fought each other. Terrorism was one of the weapons in their arsenals. As fighting spread, it spilled over into the Lebanese civil war. Lebanon's struggle for governmental stability became lost to the interests of several autonomous militias and various Arab terrorist groups.

THE INVASION OF LEBANON

In Lebanon, the mainstream PLO under Arafat became a fairly autonomous and potent force in the south. Further to the north, nationalistic Lebanese Christian and Islamic militias opposed each other, as well as the Palestinians and foreign interests. Syria backed its own militia in the hope of increasing its influence in Lebanon, and Iran joined the fighting after the Islamic revolution of 1979, establishing a new terrorist organization called Islamic Jihad. Endemic civil war raged in Lebanon as dozens of terrorists slipped across the border to attack Israel.

By 1982, the Israelis had had enough. On June 6, a massive three-pronged IDF force invaded Lebanon. The PLO and other militias moved forward to take a stand, but they were no match for the coordinated efforts of IDF tanks, aircraft, and infantry. The Israelis rolled through Lebanon. Soon they were knocking on the doors of Beirut, and Lebanon's civil war seemed to be over.

But Syria had other plans. Unable to tolerate Israel's presence in the area, the Syrians rallied all local militias, except the Christians, to their side and turned their own aircraft and tanks on the Israeli invaders. Israel found itself in a new war.

By the same token, Arafat was on the ropes. Surrounded and bombarded by the Israelis in Beirut, Arafat knew the Syrians had no love for him. If the Israelis won, Arafat would be doomed. If the Syrians won, they intended to install their own surrogates in place of the PLO. Even as the Syrian-backed forces fought the IDF, Arafat was out of options. In August 1982, he left Beirut for Tripoli with 14,000 fedayeen. Over 10,000 guerrillas stayed, but they joined the Syrians.

Although the PLO left Lebanon in defeat, the Israelis had little to cheer. They formed an alliance with the northern Christian militias and tried to find a way out of the murderous mess their invasion had created. For their part, the Christian militias went on a rampage. They massacred Palestinians in two Lebanese villages, Sabra and Shatila. When international television viewers saw pictures of a dead Palestinian toddler in a bloody diaper laying on top of a pile of bodies, people began to wonder what type of Christians the Israeli allies professed to be. Israel was in a morass, and the violence continued.

Ironically, the invasion created more terrorism. As the fedayeen retreated, new terrorists came to take their place. (The growth of such groups as Hamas and Islamic Jihad is described in Chapter 10.) It is necessary to explain the dilemma Israel faced in Lebanon. If the purpose of the Israeli militants in the Likud Party—the right-wing party that held power in Israel during the invasion—was to destroy terrorist bases in Lebanon, it failed miserably.

By 1983, the United Nations was heavily involved trying to negotiate a withdrawal of Israeli troops. Terrorist attacks against Israeli forces occurred almost daily, and the Syrians showed no sign that they were willing to negotiate. Despite this, the United Nations dispatched a large peacekeeping force to the area to separate the IDF from the Islamic militias. Thousands of Americans troops were involved in this deployment, and the Arabs believed these forces to be Israelis under another flag. American air and naval forces began selective attacks against the Lebanese militias. Islamic militias were quick to respond. The American embassy in Beirut was bombed twice, and the U.S. Marine barracks in Beirut were leveled by a suicide bomber. Hundreds of Marines were killed, and U.S. ground forces retreated from the area.

Eventually, the Israelis abandoned most of Lebanon after creating a "security zone" in the southern part of the country. They also created and supported the South Lebanese Army to deal with the Islamic militias and new terrorist groups. By 1991, the Israelis participated in bilateral peace talks under the sponsorship of the Soviet Union and the United States. Lebanon's endemic violence slowed in 1992, and it appeared that a newly elected government might bring peace to the northern region.

The south was another matter. New terrorist groups and militias attacked the South Lebanese Army as well as Israel. Suicide bombings increased as fundamentalist religion blended with the violence. In 1993 and 1996, the Israelis responded with two military operations against Lebanese militias, but once again they found themselves in a fight that seemed to have no end. Their merciless destruction of Lebanese lands caused hundreds of young Muslims to flock to the ranks of the militants. By 2000, Israel was ready to abandon Lebanon altogether. The South Lebanese Army was disbanded, and the Israelis withdrew. The new terrorist groups spawned by the invasion and subsequent war remained.

THE PLO IN EXILE AND RETURN

Yasser Arafat watched the situation from a distance. Although the charter of the PLO called for the elimination of Israel, he seemed to be virtually powerless. His rhetoric spoke of a holy war against Israel, but he did not have the power to back it up. While he played politics in exile, Abu Nidal and other terrorist organizations focused their attention on Israel. With Arafat in exile, Israeli commandos attacked and eliminated the PLO's mastermind of terrorism, Abu Jihad. Clearly, Arafat needed another tactic. He decided to negotiate with the Israelis.

In 1993, Arafat began secret talks with Israel in Oslo. Under pressure from the United States, a new Israeli government under Yitzhak Rabin slowly began to open a dialogue with the Palestinians. Rabin talked about giving the Palestinians a semiautonomous area in Israel, while Arafat formally abandoned terrorism and renounced the PLO clause that called for the elimination of Israel. In November 1993, Rabin and Arafat sign the Oslo Accords.

The path to peace was far from smooth. Arafat was elected President of the Palestinian National Council, but terrorists from Hamas, the Abu Nidal Group, and Islamic Jihad vowed to kill him for his cooperation with Israel. Ironically, Arafat promised the Israelis that he would crack down on terrorism. In Israel, the attempt to bring peace cost Rabin his life. In 1995, a Jewish religious extremist shot Prime Minister Rabin, hoping to derail the peace process.

In May 1996, another conservative Likud government under the direction of Benjamin Netanyahu took power and attempted to back away from the preliminary agreements with the Palestinians. By 1998, however, the Israelis and Palestinians signed the Wye Accords, and Arafat assumed power over the Palestinian National Authority. As of this writing, the future is still unclear. Israel and the Palestinians are still far apart on key issues that would bring peace between the two peoples. Arafat's internal enemies have branded him a traitor. In the mid-1980s, one of Fatah's splinter groups not only took the thunder from Arafat, it grew to dominate the world of international terrorism. Here is a timeline of the development of the PLO:

1948	Many Palestinian Arabs flee Israel.
1959	Fatah is created.
1964	The PLO is created in the Arab-occupied West Bank.
1965	Fatah launches its first attack.
1968	Battle of Karamah occurs.
1969–1970	The terrorist campaign increases.
1970	King Hussein drives the PLO to Lebanon.
1970	Differing PLO groups launch their own terrorist campaigns.
1972	Black September strikes the Munich Olympics.
1982	Israel invades Lebanon; Palestinians are massacred in the villages of Sabra and Shatila.
1987	The Intifada begins; Hamas forms.
1988	Jordan gives up its claim to the West Bank; Arafat renounces terrorism and recognizes Israel.
1990	Saddam Hussein embraces the PLO.
1992	Arafat and the Israelis begin dialogue.
1995	Arafat and the Israelis conduct elections in occupied territories.
1996	Hamas terrorism threatens peace; Arafat cracks down on terrorist groups.
1998	Palestinians and Israelis agree to the Wye Accords.
2000	Israel retreats from Lebanon; the PLO and Israel begin direct dialogues in Washington, D.C.

ABU NIDAL:

ORIGINS, STRUCTURE, AND OPERATIONS

Abu Nidal (Sabri al-Banna) serves as a perfect example of factionalism in the PLO. At one point, Abu Nidal and Yasser Arafat were comrades-in-arms in the struggle for Palestine, but as George Habash, Walid Jabril, and others broke from Arafat, so too moved a rebel organization called Black June. In the end, Abu Nidal and his organization became a mercenary group, not only abandoning Arafat, but also completely forsaking the Palestinian cause.

Patrick Seale (1992), a British veteran Middle Eastern correspondent who has extensive contacts among Palestinian leaders, provides the most comprehensive and objective account of Abu Nidal to date in *Abu Nidal: A Gun for Hire*. According to Seale, Abu Nidal joined Fatah in the hope of regaining a homeland for the Palestinians, but he soon became disillusioned with Fatah, especially with Yasser Arafat. When Arafat began the gradual shift away from terrorism in the early 1970s, Abu Nidal began to take action. In 1973, he authorized the murder of Palestinian moderates and went to Baghdad.

The Iraqis welcomed Abu Nidal with open arms and helped him build the infrastructure to support his own terrorist organization. At first, Abu Nidal's purpose was to purge Fatah, but the 1975 Lebanese civil war quickly drew his attention. He entered the war with his own agenda, also representing the interests of his Iraqi benefactors.

Seale states Abu Nidal's relations with the Iraqis started going bad after the rise of Saddam Hussein in 1979. Courting his former enemy, Hafez Assad of Syria, Abu Nidal moved his operations to Damascus in 1983. The Syrians, using their newfound terrorist allies through their air force's intelligence service, hoped to employ Abu Nidal in Lebanon. They soon found, however, that Abu Nidal was not easy to control. Once ensconced in Damascus, Abu Nidal's terrorists set up a command and control structure that defied Syrian intervention. He provided some services to his Syrian patrons (for example, he waged an assassination war against Jordan), but the Syrians gradually tired of Abu Nidal's insubordination. By 1987, he had worn out his welcome, and the Syrians were glad to be rid of him (Wege, 1991).

Seale says Moamar Khadaffy was happy to bring Abu Nidal to Libya. Khadaffy offered financial help and gave Abu Nidal space for recruiting and training terrorists. Most of the group continues to operate from secret bases in Libya today. Although they claim to represent the Palestinian cause, Abu Nidal works as a private contractor. Many of his hit teams have targeted other Arabs, including high-ranking officials of the PLO.

Ilan Peleg (1988, pp. 538–540) traces the origins of Abu Nidal to militant Iraqi rejectionism, an attitude that emerged in 1969. Rejectionism is a Middle Eastern political term meaning unilateral refusal of any peaceful settlement with Israel. Rejectionists rule out any settlement that acknowledges Israel's right to exist. This stance was the original basis of the Abu Nidal group.

Iraq was one of the more militant rejectionist countries. Like extremists in the PLO, they were appalled by Arafat's apparent softness toward Israel. The Iraqis also expressed a growing concern over Syrian influence in the PLO and Syrian designs on Lebanon. In 1969, the Iraqis established a PLO splinter group called the Arab Liberation Front to give themselves a voice in the PLO. Militant fedayeen began to gather in Baghdad under Iraqi protection. This attitude explains the warm reception Abu Nidal received in Baghdad in 1973.

Yossi Melman (1986) says the Baghdad mission was a recruiting trip for Arafat, but Abu Nidal turned on the PLO leader because of Arafat's moderation toward Israel. As a result, Peleg said, Abu Nidal raised and trained 150 to 200 terrorists before leaving for Assad's protection. David Schiller (1988, pp. 90–107) states that the growth of the Abu Nidal group should have come as no surprise to anyone familiar with the Palestinian struggle. Schiller believes the entire movement, from 1920 to the present, has been characterized by violent disagreements and terrorism. He views the factionalism that spawned Abu Nidal as nothing more than a reflection of the nature of Middle Eastern terrorism, and Abu Nidal as just another of the major characters trying to gain control of the PLO.

The birth of the Abu Nidal group may have mirrored standard Middle Eastern terrorism, but the group's exploits drew more attention than did those of its rival terrorist organizations. Abu Nidal operated on an international level, and he was particularly ruthless. Making no distinction among targets or the types of people in and around targets, Abu Nidal's terrorists became noted for the harsh brutality of their murderous attacks. His organization's international exploits gained attention: The world was a battleground for Abu Nidal (see Box 9.2 for a timeline of the development of his group).

Schiller points out that Abu Nidal first broke into the world of terrorism by striking an international target: In the mid-1970s, his group hijacked a British airplane en route from Dubai to Tunis. In a Western magazine interview, Abu Nidal said his first goal was to eliminate Zionism, but his second goal was to destroy the reactionary regimes in Syria, Jordan, and Lebanon. Carl Wege (1991) states that Abu Nidal had widened his war. Israelis, Arabs, and Westerners alike became his targets, and violence started to spiral. Abu Nidal dropped Syria from his list of enemies when Baghdad grew cold.

Both Schiller and Wege separately conclude that during the Syrian phase, Abu Nidal turned his wrath on Jordan and expanded operations to Europe. Seale reinforces this position. Schiller adds that German radicals, increasingly bored with their anti-American campaign because of the end of the Vietnam War, embraced the Palestinian struggle. In return, Abu Nidal embraced them and eventually the East European Communists. By the time of the 1982 Israeli invasion of Lebanon, Abu Nidal had a solid infrastructure in Europe. His group was truly an international terrorist organization.

Seale uses this period to describe Abu Nidal's fluctuating ideology. At the heart of his actions was a willingness to accept different dogmas. After the 1982 Israeli invasion of Lebanon, Abu Nidal established training centers and support camps in Lebanon. The group's activities increased, and Schiller says it increased further by the mid-1980s, when Libya was added to its list of supporters. In exchange for Libyan support, the organization was willing to do Khadaffy's bidding. When the Syrians rejected Abu Nidal, Libya had already prepared for his reception. Abu Nidal was a rejectionist, an Iraqi Ba'athist, a Syrian Ba'athist, and a Khadaffy socialist. Fighting was more important than ideology.

Seale has the best description of the move to Libya and its impact. As Abu Nidal's followers established bases in Libya, Abu Nidal himself went to Poland. Although his group prospered in Libya, it was less effective during his four-year absence. In addition, in 1991, Abu Nidal faced a revolt from some of his most loyal lieutenants. He purged the group with massacres in Lebanon and assassinations in Libya, while some of his leadership bolted. The internal executions—Seale documents several hundred killings—hurt the group's effectiveness but saved Abu Nidal's position.

Since the purge, Abu Nidal has been rebuilding the group through Libya. He runs the organization on fear, and Seale has an outstanding account of the

---

BOX 9.2   The Development of the Abu Nidal Group

1974	Abu Nidal goes to Baghdad.
1975	Infrastructure created in Iraq; assassinations begin.
1982	Bases established in Lebanon; after Arafat is forced from Beirut, Abu Nidal takes over Palestinian bases in Bekaa Valley.
1983	Gradually moves to Syria; new operations are undertaken against Gulf states, Jordan and Syria's enemies.
1984	Begins secret meetings with Khadaffy.
1985	Moves some bases to Libya; Rome and Vienna airport massacres.
1987	Evicted from Syria; concentrates forces in Libya; spends time in Poland.
1989	Leaders revolt; a trusted lieutenant forms the War Emergency Leadership.
1991	Allies with Saddam Hussein.
1992	Abu Iyad assassinated; purges begin; bases camps in Libya; Iraqi connections reestablished.
1992–1996	Murders in Lebanon.
1995	Attempted assassination of Arafat.

---

methods Abu Nidal uses to recruit and train terrorists. Abu Nidal's terrorists are controlled through torture, brainwashing, and individual terror. They are isolated and kept under the constant threat of torture and death for the slightest rule infractions. Many of his actions appear to be irrational, but they allow him to rule through fear and intimidation. Despite the purges and the defections, the group's infrastructure allows Abu Nidal to remain active in the world of murder and mayhem.

Seale gives a thorough picture of the group's organizational structure. Although the organization looks like many other terrorist groups, Abu Nidal has been successful because his group is so well-ordered. According to Seale, Abu Nidal rules by contempt and browbeating. His organization is managed by three groups: a small Political Bureau, a Central Committee, and a Revolutionary Council (see Figure 9.2). The Political Bureau is the most important, and Abu Nidal personally commands it from Tripoli.

The Secretariat is the staff organization of the Political Bureau, and in military terms, it would be considered the command-and-control structure. According to Seale, it is currently based in Lebanon and commanded by Abu Nidal's second, Dr. Ghana al-Ail. All operations, except those from the Committee for Revolutionary Justice, are centered in the Political Bureau and cleared through the Secretariat.

Several committees support overall operations. Terrorist operations are the mainstay of the organization, and they are controlled by the Military

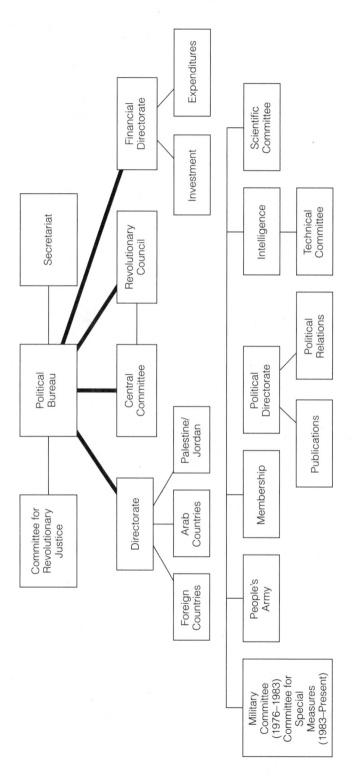

FIGURE 9.2 The Abu Nidal Organization

Source: Patrick Seale (1992). *Abu Nidal: A Gun for Hire* (New York: Random House), pp. 179–209.

Committee. Other committees support terrorist operations. The functions of these committees include intelligence, finance, technical support, a people's army in Lebanon, membership, and special missions. The most important internal group is the Committee for Revolutionary Justice. Its purpose is to terrorize the terrorists into proper behavior. This no small task. Over the years, Abu Nidal has killed over one-third of his followers for suspected breaches of discipline. Except for the Japanese Red Army, few terrorist groups have spent so much time murdering their own followers.

Organization differs little from other large terrorist groups. By changing the names of some of the various committees, one might think one was looking at the Provisional Irish Republican Army or Uruguay's Tupamaros. The unique aspect of Abu Nidal's organization is that it is based in several nations, and this presents a problem for security forces. Seale also points out that splintering has been minimized in the terrorist group by the constant purges. Except for the revolt in 1989, Abu Nidal's constant internal murders have minimized splintering.

KEY CONCEPTS

1. Modern international terrorism grew from events in the Middle East. Building on previous terrorist campaigns and utilizing Marighella's urban philosophy, the growth of the PLO was a dominant theme in international terrorism in the late twentieth century.

2. Terrorism came to the forefront in the Middle East after Arab conventional wars against Israel failed. Several organizations used terrorism to create an international audience.

3. The PLO's stand against an Israeli military strike at Karamah stood in contradistinction to the dismal performance of the Arab armies in the Six Day War. It made Arafat a hero, but King Hussein drove Arafat from Jordan in 1970.

4. Nearly a dozen splinter groups formed from the PLO. Arafat was unable to control these groups.

5. The 1982, Israeli invasion of Lebanon drove the PLO from the area, but it unintentionally spawned a variety of new terrorist organizations.

6. Arafat eventually abandoned terrorism and sought to make the PLO a source for protecting Palestinians and supporting their claim to a homeland.

7. PLO splinter groups embraced the Rejectionist position and abandoned Arafat. The deadliest and most successful former PLO group was under the control of Abu Nidal. He used both state sponsors and the war in Lebanon to enhance his position.

FOOD FOR THOUGHT

Terrorist groups tend to be small because they are dominated by charismatic individuals who lead dedicated bands of true believers. Do you think it was possible for Yasser Arafat to keep control of all militant Palestinian activity? What differences can you see between Black September and Black June? Can you find similar differences in the leadership styles of Arafat and Abu Nidal? Like Eamon De Valera in Ireland, Arafat has emerged as a popular political leader. Can someone like Abu Nidal follow the same course?

FURTHER READING

Graham Usher, *Palestine in Crisis: The Struggle for Peace and Political Independence after Oslo.*

Patrick Seale, *Abu Nidal: A Gun for Hire.*

10

Religion and Middle Eastern Terrorism

Middle Eastern terrorism is centered on the struggle for control of the area claimed by the Israelis and the Palestinians. Closely related to this issue is the spread of fundamentalist Islam beyond the Iranian Revolution. This struggle has appeared in three forms: struggle for control of the Palestinian movement, the directions of revolutionary Islam, and the spread of terrorism from the Afghan war. Since the mid-1990s, all three of these issues have been dominated by fervent religious fundamentalism. The Palestinian movement has been influenced by revolutionary Islam, especially from Hamas and Islamic Jihad. Other revolutionary groups are spreading in Egypt, Sudan, Pakistan, and Algeria. One of the main international threats comes from a group headed by Osama bin Ladin. Jewish fundamentalism has spawned its own anti–Arab terrorism. All of these violent extremist views threaten a very fragile peace process.

After reading this chapter, you should be able to:

1. Describe two different views of Islam and terrorism.
2. Describe the metamorphosis of Hizbollah and the Palestinian Islamic Jihad.
3. Summarize the philosophy and structure of Hamas.
4. Outline the history and structure of Osama bin Ladin's organization.
5. Explain bin Ladin's connections to fundamentalism and the links with terrorist violence in Egypt, Pakistan, and Algeria.

6. List and describe other religious terrorist groups in the Middle East.
7. Describe the problem of Jewish fundamentalism and violence.

TWO VIEWS OF ISLAM AND TERRORISM

The American view of Islam has been influenced by various presentations of Islamic extremism in the electronic media, and it has been influenced by popular misconceptions and stereotypes. Daniel Pipes (1983) wrote an outstanding theological and political analysis of Islam nearly 20 years ago. In an insightful summary of theological positions, Pipes demonstrates that many Western attitudes are incorrect. Islam is a legalistic religion more closely related to traditional Judaism than Pauline Christianity, even though all three religions worship the same God.

Unfortunately, Pipes's work did not receive the recognition and influence it deserved. If more policymakers had acted on Pipes's analysis, Americans may have found that many of their religious precepts match those found in Islam. Although most Muslims express religious concepts by combining theological and moral positions in political institutions, Islam is no more a religion of violent fanatics than Judaism or Christianity. Yet, many Americans have little knowledge of Islam. Today most Americans subscribe to one of two positions about Islam and terrorism.

Reuven Paz (1998) summarizes one particular position, but it can also be found in such journalistic examinations as Robin Wright (1986, 1989), Dilip Hiro (1987), and Amir Taheri (1987). This view states that Islamic fundamentalism is related to political violence in the Middle East. Paz pursues this further by asking the question: Is there an Islamic terrorism? His answer is yes.

Paz argues that Islam sees itself in a global war with the West. This is exacerbated by socioeconomic differences. Islamicists divide the world into the realm of Islam (dar al-Islam) and the realm of heresy (dar al-Harb). Islamic radicals have relegated the West to the realm of heresy. Paz says success against heresy is measured in the popular support of terrorist groups. Since Muslims in general see themselves in a struggle with the West for social and political reasons, Paz concludes that popular support of militant Islam indicates an "Islamic terrorism" exists. He says the West should not debate its existence, it should defend itself against Islamic terrorism.

Others are not so quick to accept such logic. David Kibble (1996) argues that Islamic fundamentalism seems to be a threat at face value. Radical groups of Islamics in Egypt, Saudi Arabia, Iran, and other areas appear to have declared war on the United States and its allies. Indeed, an American secretary of defense stated that Islamic fundamentalism is the greatest threat to American security since Communism. Kibble believes such fears are unfounded.

Kibble says there are pockets of Islamic extremism in the Middle East that sustain terrorism. He argues, however, that these segments are isolated and divided. There is a broad spectrum of religious and political beliefs in Islam that rejects violence. Kibble believes that when fundamentalists take power, it may be the first step toward democracy. He urges caution in labeling Middle Eastern violence as "Islamic terrorism."

Clarence Bouchat (1996) agrees. He says American fears and misunderstandings of Islam make it appear as if fundamentalists were united and threatening to gather the Middle East in a war against the West. This is not the case. Fundamentalists are a divided lot, just as religious fundamentalists in the United States are divided. The history of the West and the Middle East involves centuries of religious wars. Bouchat says more is to be gained by examining the religious similarities between the two regions than by using such terms as "Islamic terrorism."

It is quite clear that violent religious fanatics are playing key roles in Middle Eastern terrorism. This has resulted in a new type of terrorism in the region. In the 1990s, several international structures emerged in the name of religion. No longer relying on rogue states or the interests of competing nations, these groups have emerged as a cause unto themselves. Religion is the basis of their calling, and they attract followers throughout the region.

THE IRANIAN REVOLUTION
AND HIZBOLLAH'S METAMORPHOSIS

When Israel invaded Lebanon in 1982, the Iranians responded by sending their Revolutionary Guards, creating and supporting a new terrorist network. At first glance, the connection seems to be an illogical geographical link, but closer examination reveals the purpose. The Israeli invasion prompted responses throughout the Muslim world, and the Iranians, hard-pressed to deal with their young revolutionaries at home, found a perfect place to export their unruly zeal. Locked in a large war with Iraq, the Iranians found Lebanon a place to fan the fires of revolution.

The name Hizbollah literally means "the Party of God." According to Dilip Hiro (1987, pp. 113–181, 240–243), Hizbollah grew out of the Iranian Revolution as an extension of the Revolutionary Guards. The Revolutionary Guards were the military wing of the Ayatollah Khomeini's organization. Hizbollah assisted the Revolutionary Guards by attempting to purify the revolution. It attacked all forms of Western thought and sought to consolidate Khomeini's gains.

Hiro says the members of Hizbollah were not only interested in carrying out the goals of the revolution, but also concerned with the social conditions of Islam in general. This helped account for their loose organizational structure. The Party of God was more a meeting of similar minds than a group interested in a rigid, formal structure. Shiaism was the heart of Hizbollah, and Shiites throughout the Middle East were the concern of the group. The Shiites of Lebanon were no exception. Wege (1994) adequately demonstrates Hiro's argument. The term Party of God is taken from Islamic references and is directly related to the martyrdom of Hussein Ibn Ali. Failure to understand Hizbollah as an Islamic concept is a failure to understand the context of evangelical Islam.

According to Hiro, relations between Lebanese and Iranian Shiites had been close since the 1950s. When conflict broke out in Lebanon in 1975, Amal, a Shiite militia, was formed to protect Lebanese Shiites. Amal was trained by the PLO, but it developed and maintained strong Iranian contacts. In 1979, it grew in strength, and its members watched the Iranian Revolution with interest.

According to Anat Kurz (1994), Palestinian and Lebanese radicals found common ground in the 1980s. Nabih Berri was elected general secretary of Amal in 1980. This event caused concern among the more radical members of Amal, including those who supported the Iranian Revolution, because they believed Berri was a constitutionalist and too conservative. In 1982, the radicals left Amal for the Syrian-controlled Bekaa Valley, where they formed a new group, Islamic Amal, and awaited further developments. When the first Revolutionary Guards of Hizbollah arrived in the Bekaa Valley in 1982, they found willing allies in the Islamic Amal.

For the first few years of its involvement, Hizbollah acted more or less like a terrorist clearinghouse (Reuters, 1996a). Following orders from Iran, Hizbollah met as an independent organization, always willing to deny its Iranian connections. According to Israeli intelligence (Israeli Foreign Ministry, 1996), Hizbollah was directed by three central figures: Sheik Mohammed Hussein Fadlollah, Abus Musawi, and Hassan Nasrallah. Fadlollah, the target of an attempted American-sponsored assassination, was a charismatic spiritual leader. Nasrallah was a practical militarist, leaving the Islamic Amal militia to organize Hizbollah into a regional force. Musawi provided the loose connections to Iran.

From 1982 to 1985, Hizbollah formed a relationship with a shadowy terrorist group known as Islamic Jihad. According to Amir Tehari (1987), Hizbollah leaders met to give policy direction for Islamic Jihad. The council of leaders met in the city of Baalbek in Lebanon's Bekaa Valley and issued nebulous "suggestions" to Islamic Jihad. They also provided financial and logistical support for terrorist operations but kept themselves out of the day-to-day affairs of the terrorist group. By keeping their distance, Hizbollah's leaders were able to claim they had no direct knowledge of Islamic Jihad, and more importantly, they kept Iran from being directly linked to Islamic Jihad's terrorist campaign against Israel and the West.

During this same time frame, Hizbollah's role also began to change. As part of an organization designed to spread the Shiite revolution, Hizbollah was not content to act only as an umbrella group to support terrorism (Enteshami, 1995; Reuters, 1996a). Its leaders wanted to develop a revolutionary movement similar to the structure that gripped Iran in 1978 and 1979. Lebanon was inundated with several militias fighting for control of the government, and Nasrallah saw an opportunity. By following the pattern of the Amal militia, he began changing the structure of Hizbollah. In 1985, he established regional centers, transforming them to operational bases between 1987 and 1989. Taking over the organization after the death of Musawi, Nasrallah created a regional militia by 1990. In 1991, many of Lebanon's roving paramilitary groups signed a peace treaty, but Hizbollah retained its weapons and revolutionary philosophy. It became the primary paramilitary force in southern Lebanon (U.S. Department of State, 1996).

According to an analysis by Reuters (1996b), Hizbollah is currently fighting an undeclared war with Israel (see Box 10.1 for a sampling of its paramilitary activities). Vowing to disrupt the peace process and continue the revolution, members strike Israel in a style reminiscent of the early days of Fatah. The terrorist group it once commanded, the Islamic Jihad, has expanded and taken on a life of its own. Although Hizbollah conducts its own terrorist operations, it behaves more like a militia seeking control of Lebanon. Because most of the Lebanese militias were disarmed in 1991, Hizbollah's triumph in keeping its structure and weapons have placed it in a position of power. Like Abu Nidal, its structure allows it to act as a power broker in a world of shadow warfare.

By the same token, the paramilitary structure of Hizbollah has made it more of a conventional fighting force than a terrorist group since 1991. This results in a particular type of fighting. Unlike Islamic Jihad or the Abu Nidal group, Hizbollah's bases are in the open. When it strikes Israel, the Israeli Defense Force strikes back. Civilians caught in the crossfire are often at the mercy of opposing factions. In one tragic exchange, Israeli artillery shells hit a Palestinian village in April 1996, even though the shells were aimed at Hizbollah rocket launchers. Unfortunately, this type of exchange is nothing new to the area.

THE ISLAMIC JIHAD

Although Hizbollah found an ally in the Islamic Jihad when it came to the Bekaa Valley in 1982, the Iranian Revolution was not directly responsible for the birth of this terrorist group. Islamic Jihad began as a political movement inside the Muslim Brotherhood. Actually, there are several Islamic Jihads, and they are mostly nationalistic factions of the same movement. The group that receives greatest attention emerged after the 1982 Israeli invasion of Lebanon, and it came from the link with Hizbollah. This Islamic Jihad perfected three tactical innovations of terrorism: a dynamic "umbrella" organizational structure, the use of suicide bombers, and the shift away from hijackings and hostage-takings to individual kidnappings.

According to official Israeli reports (Israeli Foreign Ministry, 1996), Lebanon's Islamic Jihad was born in Israel and is currently commanded from Syria. Its leader, Dr. Fathi Shekaki, created the group in 1981. After the Israeli invasion of Lebanon, his fanatics flocked to Hizbollah and Hassan Fadlollah, the spiritual leader of Hizbollah. Shekaki and Fadlollah were immediately

BOX 10.1 A Sampling of Hizbollah's Paramilitary Activities	
December 1995	Hizbollah fires rockets from Lebanon into Israel.
February 1996	Terrorists try to infiltrate Israel in ultralight aircraft.
March 1996	Hizbollah plants several bombs around Israeli targets; militias ambush Israeli convoys and settlement; more rocket attacks on Israel.
April 1996	Rocket attacks on civilians in Galilee; Israel returns fire and hits innocent Palestinians.

SOURCE: Israeli Foreign Ministry, April 1996.

attracted to one another by similar visions, and Fadlollah brought Shekaki's organization under Hizbollah's umbrella.

The Israeli Foreign Ministry states that Shekaki participated in the "conference management" style of Hizbollah but took the organizational structure a step further. If Musawi and Nasrallah (the two leaders of Hizbollah) were looking for distance between terrorist activities and Iran, Shekaki saw the Hizbollah model as a new method for structuring terrorism. Rather than operating as a single entity, he broke Islamic Jihad into a multitude of smaller groups, creating distance between any terrorist act and the terrorist group. Each operation could literally have its own small terrorist group, and Islamic Jihad could hide in a flow of misinformation. In actuality, Shekaki's Islamic Jihad became an umbrella group, itself under the umbrella of Hizbollah.

Robin Wright (1986, pp. 84–86) writes that the structure of Islamic Jihad was different than anything the West had ever faced before. Most groups could be identified by an infrastructure and a support network. This was not the case with Islamic Jihad. It was a dynamic network distributing information from the secrecy of Baalbek. It contained a fluctuating number of secret organizations and cells. Although U.S. officials talked of state-sponsored terrorism, this group had no clear links to Iran. Islamic Jihad was a hidden army. As a result, its structure confused Western intelligence sources for nearly a decade.

To strike, Shekaki chose a new weapon: the suicide bomber. Amir Taheri (1987) states that after the first suicide bombing in 1983, Islamic Jihad launched a devastating suicide bombing campaign in Lebanon. In 1984, its activities spread to Kuwait and Tunisia, and it became clear that the struggle was not just for Lebanon but for the Islamic revolution. By 1986, in Taheri's estimation, fighting had moved to Europe. This brand of international terrorism is endorsed because it involves a holy war against all parties resisting the Islamic revolution. Taheri refers to it as the "holy terror."

The use of suicide bombers frightened and baffled the West, but it was logically explicable in terms of the conflict, according to Maxwell Taylor and Helen Ryan (1988). Taylor and Ryan examine the role of fanaticism in Shiite terrorism and conclude that the use of suicide bombers was particularly successful in Lebanon. A suicide bomber became an inexpensive guided missile ensuring the success of an attack.

After a series of bombings in 1983 and the retreat of the U.S. Marines from Beirut, the weakness of Western defensive systems was completely exposed. Military forces from France, Israel, and the United States had employed a fairly sophisticated security system appropriate to peacekeeping situations in Western diplomacy. In several instances, suicide bombers penetrated these defensive perimeters and struck targets with relative ease. Taylor and Ryan suggest this demonstrates a fundamental weakness of technologically based defense: None of the defenders had predicted the role of suicide in the Lebanese conflict.

Taylor and Ryan argue it is necessary to define terrorism in Middle Eastern terms rather than to extrapolate from Western norms. From the Western perspective, suicide attacks seem rooted in illogical fanaticism. Yet, this interpretation does not fit the Shiites fighting in Lebanon. Bombing was a logical policy—in fact, one of the few policies that worked against established military power. Because delivery of the bombs had to be guaranteed if the policy was to work, it was also logical to employ sacrificial warriors as delivery sources.

Shekaki also used another tactic, kidnapping. The development of specialized hostage rescue teams in the United States, Great Britain, and Germany forced Islamic Jihad to search for new hostage-taking tactics. Airplanes were hijacked, but hostages had to be dispersed. New Western rescue units, such as the British Special Air Service, the German GSG-9, and the American Delta Force, made traditional methods of taking hostages too risky. Kidnapping developed as an attractive alternative to massive hostage taking. Counterterrorist forces might be able to free hostages in a single incident, but dispersed kidnapping victims were another issue.

Islamic Jihad toyed with the idea of kidnapping in 1983, and by the next year, they launched a wholesale kidnapping campaign. At one point, they held more than 40 Western hostages. Hizbollah and Islamic Jihad saw they could not only gain the attention of the West with kidnappings, but also influence the behavior of Western governments.

The kidnapping policy of Islamic Jihad had several practical functions. It could be used to punish a country for acting against the Shiites. Hostages could be released for propaganda value, or, when an enemy took action against Islamic Jihad or its supporters, hostages could be executed. Finally, threats of harm to hostages or additional kidnappings could be used to influence another government's actions.

Tactical innovation came as a surprise to the West. In a special article prepared for the *New York Times,* Philip Taubman (1984) writes that the United States had few solid leads on the Islamic Jihad, despite enhanced intelligence efforts. In a related article, Eric Pace (1984) describes the innovative use of car bombs in the Middle East. The West seemed at a tactical loss when dealing with Islamic Jihad. The Israelis took a different approach. Instead of mapping the hierarchy and flow of money, Israel identified the group's leaders and went after them.

The Israeli Foreign Ministry (1996) says Shekaki was captured and deported in 1988, but he resurfaced in Damascus in 1989. In the aftermath of the Persian Gulf War, Islamic Jihad moved its activities to Israel. Directing operations from Syria, Shekaki continued the struggle against Israel. When Arafat accepted the Israeli olive branch and elections in the occupied territories, Shekaki abandoned support for the Intifada (a general uprising) and returned to terrorism.

Shekaki addressed the issue in an interview with *Time* magazine (1995). He spoke of no peace until Israel was destroyed. He also reiterated his willingness to employ human-guided missiles, the suicide bombers. Unlike Hamas, he stated that Islamic Jihad was willing to accept a liberated Palestine devoid of a united Arab realm. The U.S. Department of State (1996) took such statements at face value, pointing to threats for an expanded suicide bombing campaign in 1995. Shekaki was killed in Malta in 1995.

Shekaki's successor, Dr. Ramadan Abdallah Sallah, has maintained the Shekaki philosophy. The Israeli Foreign Ministry (1996) says that as of 1992, Islamic Jihad is no longer able to hide as easily as it could in its early stages. Israeli and Western intelligence agencies have developed internal profiles of the group, and some of its leaders are known. More importantly, the growth and emergence of Hizbollah removed the umbrella covering of Islamic Jihad. The Shekaki faction was forced to operate like most other terrorist groups.

Following elections in the occupied territories, Islamic Jihad, like Hamas and Hizbollah, began a no-holds-barred campaign to disrupt the peace process. Israeli soldiers were kidnapped and executed, and bombings increased. The Israelis responded with controversial measures. Specialized squadrons of selected soldiers would raid suspected terrorist hideouts. Under this policy, suspects were interned while all their resources, including their homes, and the resources of their supporters were destroyed. Several suspected terrorists had been killed during these operations, and hundreds of homes were bulldozed into the ground.

The U.S. Department of State (1996) sums up Islamic Jihad's threat well. The State Department says it is a loose affiliation of several fanatical groups. It still probably receives aid from Iran, but the convoluted nature of the group makes it difficult to expose. Islamic Jihad does not have a hierarchy or infrastructure similar to other groups. Because it is so loosely bound, any one of the many groups may act autonomously.

HAMAS

One of the most volatile militant organizations in the Middle East is the Islamic Resistance Movement, better known as Hamas. Unlike Hizbollah and Islamic Jihad, it grew from the Palestinian movement. Mirroring the philosophy of the Rejectionists, Hamas's position is that the state of Israel should not exist. The only acceptable solution to the Palestinian problem is to eliminate

Israel and create a united Arab realm. According to Hamas, the state of Israel and anyone who supports it are abominations to Islam.

To understand Hamas, it is necessary to go back to the events right after World War I. Because of the British promises, many Arabs felt that the entire Middle East, from North Africa to the Iranian border, would be united under one great Arabic banner, dar al-Islam. When European powers divided the area, taking control of some regions and placing their Arab allies in control of others, many Arabs were infuriated. One group of frustrated Muslims took action. Founded in Egypt about 1925, the Muslim Brotherhood rejected the new territorial lines. They called for unification of the entire Arab realm under the law and control of Islam.

In 1967, the Muslim Brotherhood began to grow in the occupied territories. Unlike the Ba'athists who expressed unity through modern socialism, followers of the Muslim Brotherhood wanted to purify Islam and unite with other Arabs under religious law. In some ways, the philosophy of the Muslim Brotherhood was a combination of the religious intensity of the Iranian Revolution and the unification principles of the Ba'athists, but the Muslim Brotherhood primarily represented ethnicity more than politics or religion. Their call for unity was as old as the Q'ran.

The group registered as a religious organization with the Israeli government in 1978, and its stated purpose was to be evangelical. Members attempted to convert followers into a more pristine version of Islam. They worked through universities, schools, and mosques. In the 1980s, however, as Arafat gravitated toward moderation, the Muslim Brotherhood maintained its rigid views on the unification of the realm of Arabs and the necessity to rule through Islamic law. When the demand for Palestinian self-government began to dominate the Palestinian movement, the Muslim Brotherhood rejected the call.

Self-government was abhorrent to the Muslim Brotherhood because no nation should exist outside dar al-Islam. If the fedayeen of Fatah were to betray their people by talk of compromise, the Muslim Brotherhood would take a different path. As a result of their disagreement with the goals of the Intifada, members of the Muslim Brotherhood formed Hamas, an Arabic acronym for the Islamic Resistance Movement, in 1987. The group has been active ever since.

Following the tactics of the old Irgun, Hamas has attempted to outdo former Palestinian terrorists. In its own literature, Hamas says that it is in a war with the Jewish people, as well as the state of Israel. The purpose of every operation is to kill Jews, and by killing Jews, all the Zionist settlers and their allies will be driven from the area. It is not enough to kill only the Jews, however. "Good" Muslims will kill anyone who accepts peace with the Jews or who speaks of an independent Palestine. The only acceptable outcome for Hamas is the united realm of Islam.

Hamas is well-financed and organized. As any large terrorist organization, it is composed of strike units, as well as logistical support columns. Its tentacles reach far outside the Middle East, including support bases in the United

States. Ironically, its size has caused a moderate group to emerge from the ranks of the fanatics. Arafat has tried desperately to work with the moderates to stop the spread of terrorism. The goal of Hamas terrorists is to disrupt the peace process. They may succeed. Since 1989, they have been responsible for several hundred terrorist attacks.

Being a large organization, tens of thousands strong according to a 1996 State Department estimate, Hamas has a centralized structure with many branches. According to Ahmad Rashad (1996), an apologist for the group, Hamas's strength comes from Palestinian dissatisfaction with the PLO. Rashad states Arafat's softened attitude toward Israel prompted the rise of Hamas in 1987. As enthusiasm grew, Hamas's goal was to become the sole representative of the Palestinian people. Accordingly, it divided its operations into four main spheres: administration, charity, politics, and military affairs.

Rashad states that the most successful military actions have been taken by the Izz el-Din al-Qassam Brigades. Emerging from the military wing of Hamas, the al-Qassam Brigades swelled with recruits after Arafat's renunciation of terrorism in 1993. The brigades are divided into two factions: an intelligence wing and a commando wing.

Ironically, according to Rashad, the intelligence wing does not gather military intelligence. If Rashad is to be believed, the intelligence wing serves as an internal police force. It has three primary duties. First, it enforces Islamic law among the Palestinians, including the execution of offenders. Second, it serves as the main instrument for distributing propaganda throughout the occupied territories. Finally and very interestingly, it is the logistical support network for military operations. Reading through Rashad's propaganda, it is safe to assume the intelligence wing is designed for internal discipline and to supply and hide active terrorists.

The commando wing is designed for terrorist attacks, and it has three primary sections: training, operations, and intelligence. Rashad did not mention bombing or ambushes, two al-Qassam Brigade specialties, but he pointed with pride to "the abduction of enemy soldiers." This admission is quite appropriate. Taking a page from lessons in Lebanon, Hamas has kidnapped and executed individual Israeli soldiers. Although he refuses to identify the total number of commando units, Rashad identifies two groups that operated in the occupied territories and states the remaining groups functioned at-large. In essence, the military wing is organized in the manner of any large terrorist group.

Hamas represents the continuing struggle for control of the Palestinian voice. Whereas the PLO has rejected terrorism, Hamas has embraced it, and it has become a rallying point for those wishing to continue the struggle with Israel. If anything, Hamas represents the issue so aptly identified by Ahmad Khalidi (1995). There can been no end to terrorism, Khalidi says, until the rights of Palestinians are guaranteed. Hamas will certainly maintain its appeal to disenfranchised Palestinians until that time.

THE RISE OF OSAMA BIN LADIN

To understand the rise of Osama bin Ladin, it is necessary to keep two things in mind. First, there is a trend among Islamic fundamentalists to attempt to bridge the theological gap between Sunnis and Shiites. This trend began to develop in Iran about 1988. According to Dov Waxman (1998), Iran has moved from a postrevolutionary, nationalist phase to the real politics of pan-Islam. That is, Iranian leaders slowly moved away from their blind allegiance to Shiaism and began supporting militant Sunnis. Revolutionary Iranians began sending money and support to Sunni terrorist groups in Lebanon, believing Iranian Shiites and Lebanese Sunnis were working for the same cause. Militant Sunnis followed suit, calling for peace between Sunnis and Shiites. Osama bin Ladin, a Saudi Arabian, was one such Sunni.

The second important factor in the rise of bin Ladin was the Soviet-Afghan War (1979–1989). In 1979, the Soviet Union invaded Afghanistan. Seven major guerrilla groups formed to resist the Soviets, and the United States enthusiastically joined the fray with arms and economic support. The resistance fighters called themselves the Holy Warriors, the mujahadeen. Embraced by the U.S. government, they traveled the United States calling the Soviets "foreign devils" and "infidels." Few of Ronald Reagan's political leaders noticed that the mujahadeen leaders used the same terms to describe Americans.

In 1989, the Soviets retreated from Afghanistan in complete disarray. Not only had they lost the war, but the Soviet Union also soon found itself in a state of collapse. Yael Shahar (1998) says the mujahadeen saw the fall of the Soviet Union as a sign of total victory. The Soviet Union had not collapsed under the weight of political, economic, and military factors, but in the minds of the mujahadeen, it fell by the hand of God. The Soviet retreat was a sign of God's power over Satan, and if God could bring down the Soviet Union through the work of the mujahadeen, other evil nations were doomed to destruction. The primary targets of the mujahadeen were Israel and the United States. One of the mujahadeen leaders who fervently believes in this view is Osama bin Ladin.

Yosseff Bodansky (1999) writes the most detailed biography of bin Ladin, although the work is polemical and does not seek objectivity. Bodansky says bin Ladin was one of 51 children born to a rich Saudi Arabian construction magnate in 1957. Bin Ladin received a university education and joined the family business, but he soon left Saudi Arabia to join the Afghan fight against the Soviet Union. At first, he lent support to the mujahadeen, later forming his own unit of guerrilla fighters.

While in Afghanistan, he fell under the influence of Sheik Abdullah Azzam, a doctor of Sharia (Islamic law). Azzam had been working for the Palestinians in the mid-1970s, but he became disillusioned with their nationalism and emphasis of politics over religion. Azzam believed Islam should rule over all forms of conflict. He left the Palestinians for a Saudi university to teach Islamic law.

Azzam was the answer to bin Ladin's prayers. As the rich Saudi construction engineer sought a path to holy war, he found the theology of Azzam to his liking. According to Azzam, the realm of Islam had been dominated by foreign powers for too long. It was time for all Muslims to rise up and strike Satan. The Soviet-Afghan War was just the beginning. The mujahadeen were in a holy war against all things foreign to Islam.

Bodansky points out the United States would hardly have been excited about funding such a group of rebels, but the Pakistani Intelligence Service (ISI) intervened. The ISI was concerned with the growing threat of the Soviet Union, but it had its own agenda for national security. Pakistan offered to act as the surrogate for the United States, training the mujahadeen and providing their base camps. According to Bodansky, all money, weapons, and other logistics would be funneled through the ISI. The American Central Intelligence Agency took the bait, and the ISI prepared for war against America's enemy. It also prepared for a larger war without telling the CIA.

Osama bin Ladin was in the midst of these activities. Training in Pakistan and Afghanistan, he financed mujahadeen operations and taught the guerrillas how to build field fortifications. By 1986, he left the training field for the battlefield. Enraged with the Soviets for their wholesale slaughter of Afghan villagers and use of poison gas, bin Ladin joined the front ranks of the mujahadeen. Allied with hundreds of radical militants throughout the world, Osama bin Ladin became a battlefield hero. When interviewed for *ABC News* by John Miller (1998), bin Ladin would not discuss these exploits. He simply stated that all Muslims are required to fight in the jihad.

The ISI was spreading the jihad. Bodansky argues that while watching the disputed Kashmir province (an area claimed by both India and Pakistan), leaders from the ISI were not content to limit their war to the Soviet Union. In 1986, the ISI began filtering some of the arms intended for the mujahadeen to Sikh terrorists in India. When this diversion was successful, the ISI began filtering arms and logistics to Muslim militants in Kashmir. Bodanksy says Shiite militants in Iran noticed the ISI actions and began to view the Afghan war as an expression of Islamic unity. In the meantime, Pakistan began to see itself as a leader in the pan-Arabic movement.

Things did not go as well for Azzam. When the Soviets were preparing to withdraw, the ISI created its own Afghan guerrilla force and used it to take control of major areas of Afghanistan. Azzam believed the United States was behind this action. Before he could take action on his own, he was killed in a terrorist attack by unknown assailants. Bin Ladin accepted the status quo and enjoyed warm relations with the ISI. He returned to Saudi Arabia after the war to resume his construction business.

The Saudi Arabian government was not to happy to see bin Ladin return. Not attractive to the Saudi royal family, bin Ladin was immensely popular with the people. Saudi Arabia is not an open democracy that tolerates diverse opinions and dissension, so bin Ladin's political activities were limited. He brought several mujahadeen—his "Afghans"—to Saudi Arabia with him and put them to work on construction projects. The Afghans had job security, and bin Ladin became independently wealthy.

The situation changed in 1990. Saudi Arabia houses two of the most holy shrines in Islam, the cities of Mecca and Medina. To millions of Muslims, including bin Ladin, these are sacred areas that must be protected by Muslims. This is considered holy ground. In 1990, Saddam Hussein, leader of Iraq, invaded Kuwait. The Saudi royal family appealed for help, and thousands of non-Muslim troops arrived in the holy land to fight Saddam Hussein. The American-led coalition called this military buildup "Desert Shield." When "Desert Shield" became "Desert Storm" in February 1991, radical Muslims were appalled to find Muslims fighting Muslims under American leadership. After the war, the Saudi government allowed American troops to be stationed in Saudi Arabia. This was too much for bin Ladin. He thought of declaring his own war.

Bodansky says bin Ladin was influenced by the pan-Islamic movement and the role of Iran. Putting aside differences between Shiites and Sunnis, radical Muslims found Satan arrayed against Islam; Satan came in the form of the United States. Bin Ladin worked with the Iranians to bring eschatological Sunnis and Shiites together in an organization called the International Muslim Brotherhood, but he wanted to go further. By April, he was training and financing terrorist groups and calling for the overthrow of unsympathetic Muslim governments.

PBS *Front Line* (1998) says these actions brought a Saudi crackdown, and bin Ladin was forced to flee. He first went to Afghanistan and then to Sudan. Bodansky states bin Ladin found friends in the radical government of Sudan, and he expanded his operations. By the end of 1992, bin Ladin had nearly 500 Afghans working for businesses that he established in Sudan. He also saw internationalism as the best means for striking the United States, and he refused to base his operations in any single country. In December 1992, a bomb exploded in a hotel in Yemen, a hotel that had been housing American troops. *Front Line* says U.S. intelligence linked the attack to bin Ladin.

DECLARING WAR ON THE UNITED STATES

Osama bin Ladin redefined the meaning of terrorism in the modern world. To understand this, it is helpful to compare his movement to the Palestinian movement. The PLO tried to become a state military organization, and it failed. It first operated in Jordan, then Lebanon, then Tunisia, and finally it renounced terrorism. Violence could only be carried out by splinter criminal groups on a subnational level, and these groups could not be controlled by the PLO. Abu Nidal's version of terrorism, on the other hand, used multiple support bases for Palestinian radicals. Instead of becoming a state, he moved within many states with many different types of organizations, eventually hiring out his terrorists to state supporters. Osama bin Ladin differs in his approach from both forms of violence. With the wealth of his construction empire as backing, bin Ladin transcended the state and operated on his own.

Yael Shahar (1998) argues bin Ladin's entrepreneurial efforts give him the freedom to finance and command his own terror network. His connections with his Afghans and his reputation as a warrior give him legitimacy. Bin Ladin does not need a government to support his operations. He has the money, personnel, material, and infrastructure necessary to maintain a campaign of terrorism. He only needs a place to hide.

According to *Front Line,* bin Ladin went on the offensive in 1993. Using his contacts in Sudan, he began searching for weapons of mass destruction. His Afghans sought to purchase nuclear weapons from underground sources in the Russian Federation, and he began work on a chemical munitions plant in Sudan. Bodansky says he also sent terrorists to fight in other parts of the world. Bin Ladin's Afghans went to Algeria, Egypt, Bosnia, Pakistan, Somalia, Kashmir, and Chechnya. U.S. intelligence sources also believe they came to the United States, and they linked him to the 1993 World Trade Center bombing.

Bin Ladin was active in Somalia when American troops joined an endemic civil war to bring food to the area. In October 1993, a U.S. Army Black Hawk helicopter was downed while on patrol in Mogadishu. U.S. Army Rangers went to the rescue, and a two-day battle ensued in which 18 Americans lost their lives. In an interview with *ABC News*'s John Miller, bin Ladin claimed he trained and supported the troops that struck the Americans.

Bin Ladin was also involved in assassination attempts. In 1993, his Afghans tried to murder Prince Abdullah of Jordan. In 1995, U.S. intelligence sources believe he was behind the attempted assassination of Egyptian President Hosni Mubarak. According to *Front Line,* bin Ladin called for a guerrilla campaign against Americans in Saudi Arabia in 1995.

Bombing also entered bin Ladin's arsenal of mayhem. In 1995, his Afghans killed five American service personnel and two Indian soldiers with a truck bombing in Riyadh, Saudi Arabia. In 1996, he struck in Dharan, killing 19 Americans with another truck bomb. Bin Ladin called his group of Afghans, al-Qaeda or The Base.

Bin Ladin followed these actions by calling for a holy war against the United States and its allies. In 1996, Osama bin Ladin officially "declared war" on the United States. He followed this by two religious rulings, called *fatwas,* in 1998. Magnus Ranstorp (1998) argues these writings reveal quite a bit about the nature of al-Qaeda and bin Ladin. First, bin Ladin represents a new phase in Middle Eastern terrorism. He is intent on spreading the realm of Islam with a transnational group. Second, he uses Islam to call for religious violence. Bin Ladin is a self-trained religious fanatic ready to kill in the name of God. Finally, bin Ladin wants to bring death. Whether with conventional weapons or weapons of mass destruction, bin Ladin's purpose is to kill. In his fatwa of February 1998, he calls for the killing of any American anywhere in the world.

In August 1998, bin Ladin's terrorists were behind two horrendous attacks in Africa, bombing the American embassies in Nairobi, Kenya, and Dar es

Salaam, Tanzania. The Nairobi bomb killed 213 people and injured 4,500. The Dar es Salaam explosion killed 12 and wounded 85. An FBI investigative report gives an indication of bin Ladin's methods.

BIN LADIN'S BOMBINGS

Bombing has been one of Osama bin Ladin's primary terrorist tactics. He has been linked to the 1993 New York City World Trade Center bombing, a bombing in Kuwait, and three bombings targeting American military personnel. Despite his involvement in murder, no one was prepared for the attacks he launched on August 7, 1998. Bin Ladin's attacks in Nairobi and Dar es Salaam drew the attention of the world.

According to the FBI (2000), Osama bin Ladin and Mohammed Atef began planning an East African operation against the United States after American intervention in Somalia in 1992 and 1993. Atef, who runs the military and training wing of al-Qaeda, began building an infrastructure for a terrorist bombing in Kenya about 1994, with the assistance of Wadih El-Hage, an American citizen from Texas. Another group under the leadership of Abu Ubaida, one of bin Ladin's associates, established a base in Tanzania. Both groups purchased houses with a large garage and a high fence surrounding the property. Both of these bases served to hide the activities of the terrorists.

In Nairobi, the terrorists assembled a team, including a military leader, bomb technicians, truck drivers, and weapons specialists. The initial plan was to attack the embassy with a truck and two terrorists. One terrorist was to frighten Kenyans away from the perimeter of the embassy building, while the other was to drive the bomb-laden truck inside. The primary explosive agent was TNT. When the truck approached, the driver and his assistant found the driveway blocked. The assistant fled the scene, while the driver committed suicide by detonating the bomb. The terrorist succeeded in creating much property damage, but the human carnage was horrific. Although bin Ladin's terrorists wanted to murder Americans, they managed to kill or maim most of the Kenyans who happened to be passing by the embassy, only killing a few Americans.

A similar team was assembled in Tanzania, except the plan called for a single suicide bomber. Once again, the team used a house surrounded by a privacy fence to plan the attack. The terrorists made no attempt to warn Tanzanians in the area. Shortly after the attack in Nairobi, a single terrorist drove a truck loaded with explosives to the U.S. embassy in Dar es Salaam and detonated the bomb. This time bin Ladin's group only murdered Tanzanians. No Americans were killed.

The ambiguity of American counterterrorist policy emerged in the wake of the bombing. Was this a military matter, or should it be handled as a breach of international law? The United States responded in two ways. First, FBI antiterrorist task forces composed of federal agents, state, and local police officers went to both scenes. In the subsequent investigation, two arrests were made and a fuller picture of al-Qaeda began to emerge. Task force investigators testified before a federal grand jury and arrest warrants were issued for bin Ladin, Atef, and other members of al-Qaeda.

President Clinton, however, had another response as well. Armed with intelligence of possible locations of bin Ladin's bases, and with possible evidence of chemical weapons production in Sudan, Clinton ordered a cruise missile attack against selected targets. The missiles destroyed a factory in Sudan, although subsequent reports questioned the material being produced there, and missiles also landed on six bases in Afghanistan. Bin Ladin escaped. Critics claimed these actions were designed to divert attention from Clinton's impending impeachment trial. Regardless, the cruise missiles symbolized a substantial departure from the antiterrorism task force's legalistic approach to the bombings.

Bin Ladin remains popular among Muslim radicals. He has established links with Egyptian terrorist groups and has sent his Afghans to many different countries. In June 2000, his followers began launching suicide bombings against Russian soldiers in Chechnya. Ranstorp (1998) argues bin Ladin will eventually tumble because his theological tirades do not reflect the basis of Islam. He is theologically untrained and does not enjoy the support of Muslim clerics. However, he will continue terrorist operations, and American planners need to ask the question: Do we handle bin Ladin as a military or law enforcement problem?

OTHER GROUPS COMBINING RELIGION
AND VIOLENCE

Osama bin Ladin does not hold a monopoly on religion and violence in the Middle East. Egypt has become the center for two such terrorist organizations, the Islamic Group (IG) and the Egyptian Islamic Jihad. The Islamic Group is a loose confederation of militants who follow the teachings of Sayyid Qutb, a militant who was executed in 1966. According to the Institute for Counter-Terrorism (ICT) (2000), the IG grew after many Islamic radicals were released from Egyptian prisons in 1971. They created cells with many names throughout the country and bound themselves in a theological confederation. Fanatics from the IG assassinated Egyptian President Anwar Sadat in October 1981.

IG terrorists have been active since that time. ICT experts estimate IG terrorists may number in the thousands. They have been the culprits behind bombings and assassination attempts in the 1990s. In 1997, they murdered 58 people who were touring Egypt to view the pyramids. In 1999, the IG declared a cease-fire in the wake of over 1,000 victims since 1992. Since the group is so loosely bound, only some of the militants may abandon attempts to eliminate violence.

The Egyptian Islamic Jihad, or al-Jihad, has no plan to turn from violence. According to the U.S. Department of State (1999), the Egyptian Islamic Jihad is an international group with operatives in the United Kingdom, Afghanistan, and Pakistan, as well as Egypt. The ICT (2000) believes the group also operates in Sudan, Albania, and Azerbaijan. The U.S. Department of State says Islamic Jihad is divided into two segments. One segment works primarily in Egypt, focusing on individual assassinations. It is particularly known for its attacks on Coptic Christians. The other segment operates under Osama bin Ladin in Afghanistan.

Another militant group originating in North Africa is Algeria's Armed Islamic Group (GIA). The GIA formed in 1992 after military forces in Algeria overturned the election of Islamic fundamentalists. They have been most known for massacring their fellow citizens in attacks on Algerian villages. The U.S. Department of State (1999) also notes the GIA has been involved in the murders of several Western visitors in Algeria, and in 1995, GIA terrorists began to carry their operations into France.

Two other major religious groups also operate in the Middle East. The Harakat ul-Mujahdeen (HUM) is an anti-Western terrorist organization based in Pakistan. It has been linked to Osama bin Ladin and has also engaged in anti-Indian violence in Kashmir. The Jamaat ul-Fuqra is another Pakistani group seeking to purify Islam. Like HUM, it has sanctioned violence against Hindus in Kashmir. Unlike HUM, it has operated in the United States. Its members have been convicted of fire bombings, murder, and fraud in the United States.

JEWISH FUNDAMENTALISM
AND VIOLENCE

Religious violence in the Middle East is not limited to militant Islam. Jewish groups have also been involved in terrorist violence, and some of them have direct links to the United States. Militant Judaism is based on the biblical notion that the Hebrew God has promised to restore the state of Israel. The theology is racist, eschatological, and linked to the conquest and possession of territory. No other groups are permitted to control sacred territory, according to militant Judaism, and the Messiah can only appear when the state of Israel has been restored. Such thinking has produced deadly results.

One militant group is called Kach (Thus!). It was created by Rabbi Meir Kahane, an American Jewish cleric who immigrated to Israel in 1971. Serving pulpits in New York City in the early 1960s, Kahane's descriptions of religion and the superiority of Jews began to grow more militant. In 1968, he created the Jewish Defense League (JDL), a group that was involved in several terrorist incidents in the United States. Moving to Israel in 1971, Kahane combined politics and biblical literalism to demand that all Arabs be expelled from territories occupied by Israel. He called for the militant creation of Greater Israel, the ancient Israel of King David. He was assassinated in 1990 in the United States.

Kahane's son, Benjamin, created a new group, Kahane Chai (Kahane Lives), shortly after Kahane's assassination. According to the U.S. Department of State (1999), both groups have been involved in harassing and threatening Palestinians, and they have threatened to attack Arabs and Israeli officials who seek peace. Baruch Goldstein, a member of Kach, killed nearly two dozen Muslims as they worshipped in a mosque in 1994. When both groups issued statements in support of Goldstein's terrorism, the Israeli government declared Kach and Kahane Chai to be terrorist organizations. President Clinton signed an executive order prohibiting Americans from involvement in the groups in 1995. Kach and Kahane Chai are committed to stopping any peace proposal that recognizes the territorial rights of Palestinians.

Laurence Hanauer (1995) states that Kach and Kahane Chai have defined God's biblical promises in terms of territory. In the Hebrew Bible, God makes a covenant with Abraham and his descendents. (Muslims have the same story in the Q'ran and believe they are also Abraham's children.) Hanauer argues that militant Judaism takes the focus away from a covenant with people and focuses it on conquering new lands. This creates a climate for increased terrorism.

The leaders of these ethnocentric movements are sophisticated and socially connected. While Kach and Kahane Chai alienate most Israelis due to their violent rhetoric, other movements with the same views have grown. Hanauer says the Gush Emunim, a fundamentalist Israeli settlement in Palestinian territory, is one movement. Gush Emunim has the same set of beliefs as the violent fundamentalists, but they appear to be normative due to the violent rhetoric of the other groups. This has generated political support for Gush Emunim inside Israel.

Hanauer sees several problems with fundamentalism and the prospects for peace. First, the fundamentalists denounce the existing social order because it is not racially pure. All social, economic, and political problems are blamed on the failure to ascend to the moral high ground of Jewish biblical literalism. Second, the fundamentalists claim the exclusive right to determine the truth. Third, they advocate an ideal order, and Gush Eumunim and Kach claim the Messiah can only return once the existing order is purified. Fourth, the national identity of Israel and its political legitimacy can only be determined through religion. Finally, all current events are defined within a narrow fundamentalist framework.

Hanauer believes such fundamentalism may result in increased terrorist violence. Fundamentalists do not answer to democratic ideals; they answer directly to their concept of God. The land of Israel is deified in their theology, so any attempt to achieve a land settlement is demonized. Jewish fundamentalism leads to violence. Hanauer concludes that Baruch Goldstein, the terrorist who murdered the Muslim worshippers in 1994, was not a loner who simply snapped. He was the product of a Jewish fundamentalism rooted in territorialism. Hanauer believes this structure will produce more religious terrorism.

KEY CONCEPTS

1. Islam is not a militant religion. Although it is legalistic, it shares many concepts with Judaism and Christianity. All three religions worship the same deity.

2. Hizbollah grew from the 1979 Iranian Revolution. Moving to Lebanon in 1982, the group evolved into a militia capable of supporting terrorist activities.

3. The Palestinian Islamic Jihad grew from an earlier Iranian-sponsored umbrella terrorist group. It is most known for suicide attacks in Israel.

4. Hamas grew from the Muslim Brotherhood. It also conducts suicide bombings and other attacks against Israel.

5. Osama bin Ladin is a Saudi millionaire who joined the mujahadeen in the Soviet-Afghan War. He created a self-financed international terrorist network after the Persian Gulf War in 1991, and he has been behind several attacks on the United States.

6. Other religious terrorists in Islamic countries include: Egypt's Islamic Group, the Egyptian Islamic Jihad, the Armed Islamic Group in Algeria, and Pakistan's Harakat ul-Mujahdeen and Jammat ul-Fuqua.

7. Jewish fundamentalist groups also create the climate for terrorism. They refuse to recognize the right of any Palestinian homeland within the borders of a "Greater Israel."

FOOD FOR THOUGHT

Imagine a group of Islamic, Jewish, and Christian leaders generates a massive international following and demands that the world's governments gather to create a peaceful solution to Middle Eastern violence. Leaders in Jordan, Syria, Egypt, Libya, Israel, Saudi Arabia, and Lebanon agree. With great fanfare, the Algerian president joins the delegation and leads it to Cairo where all the leaders sign a treaty of peace. What do you think will happen? Will religious terrorists accept this treaty?

FURTHER READING

James Turner Johnson, *The Holy War Idea in Western and Islamic Traditions*

Simon Reeve, *The New Jackals: Ramzi Yousef, Osama bin Ladin, and the Future of Terrorism*

Andrea Nusse, *Muslim Palestine: The Ideology of Hamas*

11

International Terrorism: The Rise and Fall of the Left and Right

Many of the questions about international terrorism have been centered in the Middle East for the last 30 years, but the rest of the world also experienced a wave of terrorism, even as the Palestinian issues dominated headlines. It began with left-wing violence in Europe. As this ideological violence spread, groups soon identified with the struggles around the Palestinian question. Influenced by Uruguay's Tupamaros, left-wing terrorists followed the organizational model of Carlos Marighella. Most saw themselves as the enlightened vanguard of some type of socialist revolution. International right-wing groups began to appear to contest what they believed to be a leftist revolution. Such ideological terrorism dominated much of Europe until 1994.

After reading this chapter, you should be able to:

1. Give an overview of Western Europe's experience with left-wing terrorism.
2. Outline the story of Germany's Red Army Faction.
3. Describe the demise of other European left-wing terrorist movements.
4. Summarize the history of the Japanese Red Army and its links to international terrorism.
5. Discuss the resurgence of the extremist right outside the United States.

LEFT-WING TERRORISM IN EUROPE

Middle Eastern violence did not grow in a vacuum. In the late 1960s, Irish terrorism flourished in the wake of a failed civil rights campaign in the North, and Basque terror grew as the Basque Nation and Liberty sought independence from Spain. Accompanying this surge of nationalist terror was a campaign of ideological terrorism. It began in Germany with anti-Vietnam War protests, and spilled into France, Belgium, and Italy (see Figure 11.1 for a map of the continent). The terrorist groups modeled themselves after the Tupamaros and allied with the Palestinian cause.

Some authors like Claire Sterling (1986) and Benjamin Netanyahu (1986, 1997) have argued this represented an organized international campaign of terrorism against the West. A closer scholarly analysis suggests this is not the case. Some terrorist groups did cooperate, especially the German Red Army Faction and the PLO, but there was no general conspiracy of terrorist groups (see Box 11.1 for a list of prominent left-wing terrorist organizations). For the most part, they learned from each other and copied tactics, much in the same way that Manachem Begin studied and copied Michael Collins.

Before the fall of Communism, Raymond Corrado and Rebecca Evans (1988, pp. 373–444) examined Western European terrorism, and concluded it has developed into a variety of forms with few common threads. Modern indigenous terrorism, however, developed from two bases: left-wing and right-wing ideology and nationalism. Dormant after World War II, indigenous terrorism began to reemerge in the 1960s. Corrado and Evans believed this renewed growth was a response to Western European modernization and industrialization. The ideological terrorists of the 1960s, both on the left and the right, were expressing their frustration with the social structures imposed by a modern industrial society.

Corrado and Evans argued that the fundamental difference between ideological and nationalist terrorists can be found in their goals. Ideological terrorists in Europe reject the economic and social structure of industrial capitalism; they want a new order. Despite ideological division, both the left and the right fight for this goal. The line between left-wing and right-wing terrorism is growing blurry. Nationalists, on the other hand, frequently embrace capitalism and fight for ethnic self-determination. They desire economic opportunity within the context of a strong national identity.

By 1988, Corrado and Evans concluded, the popularity of nationalistic and left-wing terrorism was changing. They suggested that pluralism of Western democracies opened the door to peaceful participation in the political system and offered opportunities for change. Violence no longer seemed an attractive method for expressing grievances. As pluralistic governments worked to relieve frustration, the attractiveness of terrorism waned, and terrorists lost their support base. Corrado and Evans assumed terrorist violence would fade away, only reappearing in a few sporadic incidents. Had the political structure of Europe remained constant since their writing, they would have been correct: Left-wing terrorism was out of vogue, and nationalist terrorism was on the decline.

FIGURE 11.1 Europe

Few terrorist analysts—indeed, few scholars, politicians, soothsayers, or prophets—predicted three key events that changed the political destiny of Europe. In 1989, the Berlin Wall came down, and Germany eventually reunited. To the south, new nations emerging from the former Yugoslavia took up arms and resumed a centuries-old struggle. But the greatest change of all came in the east. The Soviet Union dissolved, along with the authoritarian rule of the Communist party in the former Soviet Union republics and Eastern Europe. These three changes occurred at a time when Western Europeans were

---

BOX 11.1   Fighting Communist Organizations: Europe 1967–1992

GROUP	LOCATION
Red Army Faction	Germany
Red Brigades	Italy
Communist Combat Cells	Belgium
Direct Action	France
First of October Anti-Facist Organization (GRAPO)	Spain
17 November (17 N)	Greece
Dev Sol	Turkey

SOURCES: RAP-issued "Peace Communiqué," April 10, 1992; Dennis A. Pluchinsky (1993), "Germany's Red Army Faction: An Obituary," *Studies in Conflict and Terrorism* 16: 135–157.

---

taking bold steps toward economic and political unity. By 1992, Europe and the world had changed.

Although not trying to predict the dramatic political changes in Europe, Dennis Pluchinsky (1982, pp. 40–78) did not share Corrado and Evans's optimistic views about declining terrorism, and he proved to be right. Pluchinsky saw Europe as a major terrorist battleground due to external factors and indigenous support for terrorism. Pluchinsky also believed international and state-sponsored terrorism would grow in Europe, and a greater threat was posed by "supraindigenous" terrorism. By this, Pluchinsky meant that local terrorist activities would extend beyond local boundaries, a step beyond indigenous terrorism. Pluchinsky's primary concern for Europe was its potential role as a battleground. Each time a government brings one variety of terrorism into check, Pluchinsky argued, a new strain appears. Unfortunately, no analyst of terrorism was more correct.

As the structure of Europe and the world changed from 1989 to 1992, the structure of European terrorism also changed. Just as Pluchinsky predicted, terrorism went through a metamorphosis. Ideological terrorism swung from left to right, changing its structure as it moved. Nationalistic terrorism remained, but conflict rose in the form of ethnic violence. Ethnic violence grew into open warfare in the Balkans. New criminal organizations appeared, and old ones were revitalized. In the end, modern European terrorism grew beyond the bounds of limited terrorist attacks.

After an unprecedented growth since 1968, left-wing terrorism began to decline by 1986. Whereas Corrado and Evans saw the decline as evidence of eroding political support for terrorism, other analysts believed it would be a prelude to a new leftist campaign. Pointing to the unification of left-wing terrorist groups, these analysts feared conspiracy was at its zenith around 1985. They believed all the radical groups in Europe were forming to create a single superterrorist network. They warned a new terror campaign would be worse than anything the West had experienced.

Stephen Segaller (1987, pp. 36–40) had another suggestion. Direct Action in France, the Communist Combat Cells of Belgium, the Red Army Faction of Germany, the Red Brigades in Italy, and other groups were all uniting, but the reason for unification was exactly the opposite of what many analysts thought. The leftists were seeking unity out of weakness, not strength. The political assumptions made by Corrado and Evans were correct. Left-wing extremism had run its course. The very societies the terrorists were trying to undermine had won the struggle. How had this happened?

Segaller had the answer, and it matched the Corrado-Evans thesis. Modern European terrorism emerged in the 1960s as an extreme reflection of left-wing activism. Fueled by the Vietnam War, European leftists were influenced by events in Latin America, as well as revolutionary leaders such as Carlos Marighella. The Red Army Faction (also known as the Baader-Meinhof Gang in its early days) began a campaign in Germany, followed by copycat groups and more long-term terrorist organizations in other countries.

By 1970, most left-wing groups and the resurgent nationalist groups modeled themselves after Uruguay's Tupamaros. Segaller said that although European terrorists longed for a Marighella-style revolution, they never achieved it because they were too weak. In 1985, they faced up to their own weakness, trying to form a confederation to gain momentum.

The left-wing coalition was an effort to pool dwindling resources and support. Members of the Communist Combat Cells of Belgium went to Paris searching for the French terrorist group Direct Action. Shortly afterward, the leadership of Italy's Red Brigades also made overtures to Direct Action. West Germany's Red Army Faction (RAF) expressed an ideological union with these groups, and Direct Action responded by publishing several communiqués, claiming a new left-wing unified terrorist movement had formed. In reality, the left-wing terrorist groups were sounding a retreat, possibly even a death knell.

THE RED ARMY FACTION

The experience of Germany's Red Army Faction serves as a good example of what had happened. Schura Cook (1982, pp. 154–178) argues modern German terrorism evolved through several stages. In the early stages, young Germans imported American culture and the youthful rebellion of the 1960s. This was followed by a period of hypersensitivity to U.S. injustices and corresponding naïveté about the real pain caused by political terrorism. Finally, a campaign of terrorism emerged when militant radicals became willing to sacrifice individual victims to an idealistic cause.

The Baader-Meinhof Gang (BMG) has commonly been described according to the stages outlined by Cook. As the forerunner of the RAF, the BMG originated among a group of militant extremists at the Free University of Berlin. On April 3, 1968, Andreas Baader and his girlfriend, Gudrun Ensslin, decided to move beyond student protests and confrontations. They set fire to two department stores with incendiary bombs. The BMG was born of this action.

Jillian Becker (1977) documents the history of the BMG from 1968 to 1976. Although she gives the BMG credit for too many aspects of German terrorism, Becker paints an entertaining picture of the German revolutionaries. According to Becker, the group was made up of chic radicals in Berlin's university circles. Leftist students were content to challenge the system with propaganda, demonstrations, and other tolerable social dissent until they gathered around a militant core: Andreas Baader and Gudrun Ensslin. The core expanded to include a few dozen others, including Ulricke Meinhof.

In Becker's analysis, the revolutionary purity of Baader was questionable. He was motivated by the antisocial behavior of his radical clique and their loose attitudes toward group sex. In addition, he enjoyed the thrill of robberies and criminal life. In Becker's estimation, he was more of a criminal than a revolutionary. Ulricke Meinhof, in contrast, was dedicated to an idealistic revolutionary cause. Before meeting Baader, she was active among leftist students and helped publish an underground newspaper combining revolutionary ideology with soft pornography. In the late 1960s, Meinhof became acquainted with Baader, and the two gravitated toward one another as they moved through radical circles. Horst Mahler, a lawyer who joined the student movement, helped provide the catalyst for violence. When Baader and Ensslin suggested a campaign of direct action, Meinhof joined the cause.

After beginning a low-level campaign of action, Becker states, the BMG moved to bigger and better concepts. Inspired by the writings of Carlos Marighella, the group turned to bank robbery as a means of expropriation. The group financed itself through a series of robberies, and whereas Meinhof remained dedicated to the revolutionary cause, Baader seemed to enjoy the high-profile life of a major criminal.

Baader did little to change this image. He not only wanted to wage a terrorist campaign, but he also wanted to wage it in style. For example, before bank robberies, he urged the group to steal automobiles to use as getaway cars. As he only wished to travel in style, he insisted his compatriots steal BMWs. This became the trademark of BMG bank robberies—so much so that the BMW was popularly dubbed the "Baader-Meinhof Wagen."

Such exploits necessarily drew the attention of law enforcement authorities. After initial failures, the German police slowly began to close in on the gang. By 1972, the leading members of the group, including Baader and Meinhof, were in jail. The German government increased its security to contain the terrorists, and the campaign of bombings, robberies, and murders seemed to be at an end. According to a *New York Times Magazine* special report, Baader and Meinhof were doomed to failure because they could generate no public support (Lasky, 1975).

Despite the arrests, the group began to exhibit a resilient quality. Hans-Josef Horchem (1985, pp. 63–68) points to this phoenix-like quality in an article on German terrorism. Following the arrests of the key leaders in 1972, the group launched a series of bombing attacks. In 1973, they established a new infrastructure and fought to release their jailed comrades. The Baader-Meinhof Gang would begin a cycle of collapse and resurrection lasting until the end of the twentieth century.

Before their arrests, Baader and Meinhof had changed the name of their group to the Red Army Faction. Although they continued to be known popularly as the Baader-Meinhof Gang, the new name was accepted by their followers. While the West Germans built a special prison for Baader and Meinhof, free members of the RAF refused to sit by idly. They selected new leaders and prepared for a new terrorist campaign.

Even when jailed, RAF leadership seemed to work. Subsequent investigation revealed several attorneys were in league with the terrorists and involved in supplying jailed members with contraband and maintaining a network between them and the outside organization. Over the next 20 years, leading members of the RAF were continually apprehended, but the organization perpetually rose from its ashes—at least, it rose without its original leaders. Meinhof eventually committed suicide by hanging herself, and Baader and other leaders shot themselves in 1977, after an attempt to rescue them failed. (Some critics claimed they were murdered by German authorities.)

The RAF reached a turning point in 1977. Until that time, members were painted as misunderstood romantics of the revolutionary left. They were glamorized, and their criminal exploits were sensationalized. In October 1977, their image was exploded when allies of the group hijacked an airplane and brutally murdered Jurgen Schumann, the pilot. Several subsequent murders turned public opinion against the RAF.

Horchem (1986) relates the experiences of the RAF to the broader problem of German terrorism. His analysis helps place the development of the RAF in perspective. The Baader-Meinhof Gang was one of three modern expressions of German left-wing terrorism. The RAF was eventually joined by two other groups called the June 2 Movement and the Red Cells. Each group operated independently of the other, although the June 2 Movement was absorbed by the RAF in 1980.

Horchem stresses the RAF's unique ability to regenerate itself. The original leadership of the RAF was jailed in 1972. By 1973, a new infrastructure had been created, but its leaders were jailed in 1974. Yet, in 1976, the group was active again, and its activities peaked in 1977. Although it lost favor in 1977 because of a series of murders, the group was resurrected in 1981, 1983, and 1985. In the late 1980s, it focused almost exclusively on an anti-NATO campaign, with a new generation of terrorists.

By 1985, the RAF faced possible extinction. Many members fled to the safety of East Germany; others sought to continue the revolution. In their search, however, they found support for neither targets nor activities. Dennis Pluchinsky (1993) gives the reason. As with other fighting Communist terrorist groups, the RAF had lost its base of support and its reason for existence. The attempt to unite with other terrorist groups was nothing more than an attempt to replace a dissolving infrastructure. It did not work. In 1992, the RAF issued a peace proclamation.

Since 1992, all has not been well. The RAF set off sporadic bombs in 1993, 1994, and 1995, but the actions were not indicative of its early ability to wage a terrorist campaign. They still may rise from the ashes as they have done in the past, but they will need a new infrastructure to do so.

Other incidents went sour for the state. Grenzschutzgruppe-9 (GSG-9) is an elite German counterterrorist unit with some of the best troops in the world. In 1994, GSG-9 troopers were arresting former RAF members based on information they had received from Stasi (the former East German political police). Two terrorists resisted arrest in a train station, killing a GSG-9 trooper. Rather than completing the arrest, one of the troopers executed the wounded terrorist who had just killed the police officer. Ironically, the RAF's greatest impact in the 1990s has been the resulting martyrdom of its slain terrorist.

On May 28, 1998, the RAF issued a communiqué stating that it was ceasing operations. Christoph Rojahn (1998) says the announcement was surprising. The RAF was the product of three successive generations of terrorists. Rojahn believes their impact was quite ironic. They did little to influence the political agenda of the left, the position they were trying to influence, but they succeeded in changing the political order of Germany in two ways: They were responsible for the massive internal security apparatus that dominates Germany today, and they managed to keep the extreme left from being effective on the political spectrum.

Rojahn says the RAF is a dismal failure in the final analysis. They mistook the rantings of a vocal minority of Germans to be a statement from the general population. Although they maintained a campaign of violence for decades, they were never able to link with a mainstream issue. They could not attract the support of the radical left, with the exception of the following in their own narrow group. Rajahn concludes that the 1998 declaration of peace was a recognition of failure.

The RAF has simply become ineffective and outmoded. When interviewed for the History Channel (2000), a former RAF terrorist who has finished his prison sentence stated remorsefully that the RAF failed to understand the process of political change. He concluded it was wrong to practice terrorism. The RAF members simply did not comprehend the magnitude and ineffectiveness of their crimes (History Channel, 2000).

THE DEMISE OF OTHER
WEST EUROPEAN TERRORIST MOVEMENTS

Southern Europe has experienced a similar decline in left-wing terrorism. Xavier Raufer (1993) demonstrates that Italy's Red Brigades (BR) serve as another example of the weaknesses in the left. When the Red Brigades approached Direct Action in 1985, they were already rapidly fading from their glory days of headline-grabbing murders. Raufer believed the Red Brigades would soon follow the unilateral peace declaration of the RAF.

Vittorfranco Pisano (1987) provides one of the best descriptions of the Red Brigades. Pisano identifies nearly 300 left-wing groups in Italy that appeared between 1967 and 1985, and he states most of them had a Marxist-Leninist orientation. The best known group was the Red Brigades. Formed in Milan when Renato Curio broke away from a left-wing working-class political organization, leaders gathered more militant followers and announced plans for a terrorist campaign in 1970. Margherita Cago joined Curio and later became his wife. The future militants called their organization the Red Brigades, and Curio's 1970 group of militants became known as the Historical Nucleus, which was part of the Red Brigades.

Pisano states the BR's violent Communist ideology made no mystery of its strategy for revolution. Curio and Cago sought to make the cities unsafe for any government official or sympathizer. They believed a climate of violence would help bring about a revolution in Italy and eventually in all of Europe. Members of the BR saw themselves as the vanguard of a worldwide Communist revolution. They believed sensational violence would be their key to the future.

The organization of the Red Brigades was unique in European terrorism. They came closer to matching the Tupamaros model than did any other group in Europe. They were bound in a loose confederation, with a central committee meeting periodically to devise a grand strategy. A key difference, however, was that whereas the Tupamaros operated only in Montevideo, the BR had a variety of urban centers. Each unit, therefore, became a fairly autonomous organization within its own area. The BR managed to establish independent headquarters in several major Italian cities.

The structure of the BR made it extremely difficult to penetrate. Police might have penetrated a group in one city but have had little effect on units in other towns. Because each unit was autonomous, there was no single command structure for the authorities to combat. Decentralization was the key to the Red Brigades. They killed, kidnapped, took foreign hostages (including an American general), and even kidnapped and killed the Italian prime minister. They were responsible for hundreds of terrorist incidents.

Despite their decentralization, Pisano notes a tactical innovation common to divergent BR units. The BR used standard terrorist tactics but developed a twist to their delivery. Instead of launching a series of seemingly unrelated crimes, the BR would attack in clusters. Several attacks were designed to occur simultaneously or in sequence. This intensified their effect, and cluster assaults added to the aura of BR attacks.

Pisano divides the evolution of the BR into three stages. From 1970 to 1974, the group learned terrorism. Pisano describes this as a demonstration phase. The heyday of the BR ran from 1975 to 1981, when it launched a massive terrorist campaign. In 1982, it went into a downward spiral because of a number of factors, including a police crackdown and the loss of public sympathy among the left. From 1983 to 1986, Pisano credits the BR with only five attacks. When the

BR went to Paris in 1985, it did so out of weakness. Little had been heard from the organization in the last decade of the twentieth century.

Currently, left-wing terrorism in Europe is out of vogue. Dennis Pluchinsky (1993) demonstrates that only three groups remained active in the mid-1990s—Dev Sol in Turkey, GRAPO in Spain, and 17 N in Greece. Raymond Corrado and Rebecca Evans were correct; the ideological basis for left-wing terrorism has been eliminated. The left followed a similar pattern in the United States, and will be covered in the chapters on domestic terrorism.

THE JAPANESE RED ARMY

International terrorism also developed in the Far East and intertwined leftist ideology with Japanese nationalism. It came in the form of the Japanese Red Army (JRA), and before the JRA's campaign was ended, the terrorists would forge links with other international terrorists. Ironically, its most active cell would operate in Lebanon.

The Japanese Red Army was one of the most unique terrorist groups to emerge from the 1960s. It can be classified as a left-wing group in the Western tradition (that is, in the Western economic tradition), but it exhibited some cultic characteristics. The most definitive work to date on the group is *Blood and Rage: The Story of the Japanese Red Army* by terrorism specialist William Farrell (1990). According to Farrell's analysis, the Japanese Red Army emerged from the second generation of post–World War II dissatisfaction in Japan. After World War II, Japanese youth suffered an identity crisis. This transformed into growing university unrest in 1955 and the beginning of academic radicalism by 1959.

In 1962, Farrell says, university violence increased. The Communist party was behind much of the unrest, but the student movement reflected the concerns of other students in Western Europe and the United States. As protests against the Vietnam War brought mass demonstrations, student activities turned to rioting in 1968. In addition to the issues that bonded Western and Japanese students together, the Japanese were also concerned about the U.S. military presence in Japan, growing tuition costs, and the strict hierarchy of university admissions procedures. They were expressive. Violence was so great that universities did not admit a freshmen class in 1969.

Farrell writes the Japanese Red Army was spawned in the turmoil of 1969. During the protest movements of the late 1960s, young Communists formed the Red Army Faction, modeled after West Germany's group of the same name. Other ethnocentric students gathered in a more nationalistic group, the Kerhin Ampo Kyoto, not only to attack the structure of capitalism, but also to protest the military partnership between Japan and the United States. The most militant students left both groups to form the United Red Army, which eventually gave birth to the Japanese Red Army. The Japanese Red Army conducted its first operation in 1970, hijacking an airplane to North Korea. The

North Korean Intelligence Service accepted the young Communists with open arms and offered support for the movement.

Farrell believes the hijacking was a metamorphosis for the Japanese Red Army. Members soon drew away from the student movement (although they still encouraged rioting and violent confrontations) to engage in violent revolution. Solidifying their relationship with the North Korean Intelligence Service, Farrell states the group followed the path of urban revolutionaries. They engaged in confrontational street violence, armed robberies, bombings, and assassinations. Yet, just as the group was in the process of initiating a low-level campaign, it did a very strange thing. The Japanese Red Army split into two different orientations.

Splitting is not unusual for true-believing terrorists, but the Japanese Red Army split was unique. Farrell demonstrates that the more conventional faction of the Japanese Red Army internationalized itself. Establishing a branch in the Middle East, Shigenobu Fusako began building an infrastructure in Beirut. She brought her lover to Beirut and lured other Japanese radicals there, despite the fact that Japanese Red Army leadership did not want to expand into the Middle East.

Forming a union with George Habash's Popular Front for the Liberation of Palestine, the Japanese Red Army terrorists sought to fight capitalism by attacking Israel. In 1972, they were tragically successful. Japanese Red Army terrorists shot a group of passengers waiting in line at the Lod Airport in Israel, and tossed hand grenades at the survivors. Instead of attacking the Jewish allies of the United States, however, they had inadvertently struck Puerto Rican Christian pilgrims on a tour of Israel.

Shigenobu was elated with the "success" of the Lod Airport operation and began to expand Japanese Red Army activities. Continuing training with Habash, she moved into Asia, targeting American interests and governments that were friendly to the United States. She made contacts with radical groups in Western Europe and brought Japanese into other Middle Eastern operations. Shigenobu had truly formed an international terrorist ring.

Shigenobu had reason to be disenfranchised with domestic leadership. Mori Tsuneo, the Japanese Red Army's leader in Japan, continued the terrorist campaign in 1972 with a murder spree—an action where he murdered his own followers. In a bizarre, cultlike action, Mori took the Japanese Red Army into the wilderness and began killing several members one at a time. Some victims were beaten to death by other terrorists; some were tied up and left to die out in the elements. The purpose of the operation was to purge and purify the Japanese Red Army. Mori was arrested, and the surviving members of the Japanese Red Army were taken into custody after a police siege.

The group was eventually able to reemerge and conduct operations in Japan. They attacked a Japanese police station, and in 1974, they murdered the wife of a police commander during an attack on the commander's home.

The real thrust of the Red Army, however, came from Shigenobu's internationalism. She sponsored a hijacking in 1977 and attacks in Europe and Asia throughout the late 1970s. Things seemed to come to an end in 1982, when the PLO was forced to evacuate Beirut. Shigenobu fled to the Bekaa Valley and Syrian protection.

Many analysts of terrorism believed the Japanese Red Army was defunct, but Farrell says Shigenobu brought the group back to the forefront. Enraged by the 1985 U.S. bombing of Libya, Shigenobu renewed the Japanese Red Army's international operations. By 1986, Japanese Red Army terrorists were active in several Asian countries, and they began to attack U.S. interests in the region. In the same year, the Japanese Red Army launched an operation in Madrid. These activities were followed in 1988 by bombings and attempted bombings of U.S. Navy installations. A Japanese Red Army terrorist managed to bomb American naval personnel in Italy, and if not for an alert New Jersey state trooper, the Japanese Red Army would have conducted an attack in the United States. The trooper, following his suspicions during a routine traffic stop, uncovered the Japanese Red Army's plot to attack the United States.

Farrell believes Shigenobu will keep the Japanese Red Army active well into the 1990s. Farrell thinks its international posture, links to Palestinian radicals, and organizational structure made the Japanese Red Army a viable international terrorist organization, and he also believes links with the North Korean Intelligence Service, strengthened in 1987, will keep the group active in Asia.

By 1993, however, reports of Japanese Red Army activity had declined. The U.S. Department of State (1994) claims Shigenobu had formed contacts with leftist groups in Europe and might be receiving funding from Libya. The Japanese Red Army was also strengthening its infrastructure in Asia. Is the Japanese Red Army, however, following the lead of fighting European Communist groups? In the last U.S. Department of State analysis of the group, the Japanese Red Army numbered no more than 30, and its activities have been limited since 1988. Farrell shows the Japanese Red Army has had phoenix-like qualities, and it may indeed rise from the ashes again. However, it may be seeking alliances out of weakness.

Regardless, Shigenobu remains in charge, and she is a murderous leader. The lastest U.S. Department of State (1999) assessment suggests the Japanese Red Army is attempting to establish an infrastructure in Manila and Singapore, and it believes the remnants of the group are based in Syrian-controlled Lebanon. Several members of the Japanese Red Army are in jail, and a number of new arrests were made in 1995 and 1996. Shigenobu remains at large.

NEOFASCISM REJUVENATES

Right-wing extremists were active in Europe during the heyday of left-wing terrorism, and they assumed new roles in the 1990s. From 1967 to 1986, the favorite tactic of right-wing individuals and groups was anonymous bombing. Around 1982, however, an internal shift of emphasis occurred, and by the end of the decade, many right-wing terrorists moved into the open.

The 1990s witnessed rapid growth of neofascist movements in Germany and Austria, as right-wing militants in Austria and Germany began to respond to left-wing violence. *Der Spiegel,* a German news magazine, estimated the total number of right-wing activists to be approximately 1,400 in 1980. Two years later, Dobson and Payne (1982b, p. 183) placed the figure at approximately 20,000 in more than 70 groups. Right-wing groups, however, probably inflated their numbers, just as right-wing groups did in the United States. Horchem's (1986) analysis suggested the number of right-wing extremists who were actually violent was quite small. Regardless, a clear trend emerged from 1970 to 1990. Membership in right-wing groups was increasing.

The Middle East has become an important training ground for small right-wing terrorist groups. Horchem believes a number of fascist groups trained in various locations in the Middle East between 1970 and 1981. In addition, right-wing groups acted as European agents for such organizations as Black September. The right-wing groups were intrigued by the anti-Israeli and anti-American positions of many Middle Eastern terrorist groups. Ironically, fascist terrorists were trained by the same organizations that trained the RAF.

German right-wing terrorism has been more limited than terrorism from the left. Peter Merkl (1986, pp. 241–245) believes neofascists were generally more selective about their targets. Rather than engaging in indiscriminate violence, they targeted individuals. Jews, Russians, and Americans were selected for attack. There were exceptions and occasional public bombings, but in general, terrorism on the right was limited.

Merkl examines the activities of the Military Sports Group Hoffman to demonstrate his point. The group was started by Karl Heinz Hoffman in the late 1970s and soon achieved a reputation for intensive military training. This drew the attention of German law enforcement authorities, who began to monitor the group. It followed the pattern of other neo-Nazi groups, and the police watched it with interest.

Horchem (1986) says Hoffman went to Beirut in 1979 to receive training from the former leader of Black September. He took 15 colleagues with him, and they underwent extremely rigorous training in PLO camps. Hoffman severely beat one of his compatriots for a breach of discipline, and the offender subsequently disappeared. Four members of the group deserted after Hoffman's disciplinary tantrum, but the remaining members returned to Germany in the summer of 1980.

According to Horchem, two Germans were murdered on Hoffman's orders in 1980. Merkl states this provoked a crackdown from the German police. When they went into action, almost all the Military Sports Group's members were arrested; Hoffman was among those taken into custody. In 1982, two other members were arrested in Rome. The group became defunct through arrest and conviction.

Merkl believes the first small right-wing groups fit into categories similar to that of the Military Sports Group. They resembled 1930s-style Nazi SS action groups, and they alienated a large portion of German society. Their fight was intended to purify Germany, expel all foreigners, and reunite the country.

Some fascists set off bombs in public places, but most analysts and law enforcement authorities believe these actions were the work of individuals. Neo-Nazi groups selected their targets with greater care than that.

In 1989, neo-Nazi violence began taking a new direction. Ingo Hasselbach (1996; Hasselbach & Reiss, 1996) details the experience by explaining his days as a Nazi leader. As Germany moved toward reunification, some extreme nationalists took solace in Nazism. Hasselbach, who claims to have become drawn into the movement as an expression of rebellion, watched the neo-Nazi movement grow as Germany reunited. Its common themes were nationalism, racial purity, anti-Semitism, and hatred of non-Germans. Hasselbach stated that, at the time, he felt kinship with Nazis throughout the world, especially those in the United States.

As the fascist movement grew in the 1990s, the nature of violence changed. From a group perspective, the Nazis were fragmented in much the same way as any terrorist group. In Hasselbach's unit, for example, violent confrontation occurred between those who favored the SS (the black shirts) and those who favored the SA (the brown shirts). It is interesting to note these same differences plagued Hitler in the 1930s until he finally ordered the murder of the brown shirts. Although the new Nazis practiced terrorism, most of their efforts were aimed at street confrontations. However, in 1991, the Nazis sought mainstream political status.

Aside from traditional terrorism, Nazis routinely engage in mass street attacks. Swarms of hooligans overwhelm the intended target, usually foreigners or political opponents, and beat them senseless. In October 1992, Nazis attacked members of the U.S. Olympic team in this manner. Such tactics were common in Germany and Austria through 1995. In addition, the Nazis introduced an old American terrorist technique: the letter bomb. Several people were targeted with such bombs in Austria and Germany in 1994 and 1995.

Hasselbach claims Nazi bombings, murders, and group attacks are molding the attitudes of many young people in Germany. In addition, Nazi street fighting spills over into higher forms of violence. Attacks on foreigners, for example, grew into group murders, and street fighting escalated to urban rioting. Hasselbach came to believe those actions would tear Germany apart, and he left the Nazis. Neo-Nazism, however, has enjoyed a resurgence throughout Europe, South Africa, and the United States.

KEY CONCEPTS

1. Left-wing terrorism in Western Europe grew out of social and political frustrations about 1965. By 1970, several groups were operating in Western Europe.

2. Left-wing terrorists saw themselves as the vanguard of some type of socialist revolution. The democratic nature of Western governments

provided mechanisms to redress many inequities, and potential supporters of extremist measures found they had legitimate political outlets.

3. Politically bankrupt, European leftists linked themselves closely to the
   Palestinian cause.

4. By 1995, most left-wing violence had disappeared.

5. The Red Army Faction serves as an example of the experience of
   Europe's left-wing ideological terrorists.

6. Other left-wing groups followed the basic pattern of the RAF.

7. The Japanese Red Army grew from the same political factors that
   spawned European left-wing violence, but it reflected the social structure of Japan. It was unable to function inside its own country and
   migrated to the Middle East as a result.

8. Right-wing terrorism developed as a reaction to left-wing violence. In
   1989, Nazi violence in Germany and Austria took the form of street
   fights, riots, selected murders, and bombings.

FOOD FOR THOUGHT

In November 1999, Seattle, Washington, virtually came to a standstill, as several anarchists, left-wing extremists, labor activists, environmentalists, and
unemployed people demonstrated and eventually rioted, protesting a meeting
of the World Trade Organization. Many of the protestors were mainstream
laborers. Although the protest turned violent, most of the demonstrators were
concerned about the increased globalization of the economy and its impact on
workers and the environment. Does this concern indicate the political agenda
is shifting from the right to the left? If people feel they can have no impact on
multinational companies, what responses might we see? Do you think the
activities in Seattle indicate left-wing extremism may reappear? If so, do private corporations and democratic states have mechanisms to address such concerns in a peaceful manner? If not, what do you think will happen?

FURTHER READING

Idris Sharif, *The Success of Political Terrorist Events: An Analysis of Terrorist Tactics
and Victim Characteristics 1968 to 1977*

Richard Clutterbuck, *Guerrillas and Terrorists*

12

Nationalistic
and Ethnic Terrorism

For many years, analysts of terrorism examined European, nationalist terrorist groups within the same framework of left-wing terrorist groups.
Robert Trundle, Jr. (1996) questions this assumption. Trundle says the
structure of ethnic violence is changing, but analysts of terrorism have tried to
squeeze emerging ethnic violence into the older left-wing model. At one time,
this process may have worked, but it is currently obscuring understanding of
ethnic violence. Trundle has a point. Ethnic terrorism has become more dominant than ideological violence in the first part of the twenty-first century.

After reading this chapter, you should be able to:

1. Summarize Byman's argument about the logic of ethnic terrorism.
2. Describe the development of terrorism in the Basque region of Spain.
3. Outline the operations and status of the PKK.
4. List the changes that have occurred in Irish terrorism as a result of the
   1985 Anglo-Irish Peace Accord and the other peace initiatives that followed the agreement.
5. Describe the attempts to outlaw terrorism in Ireland.
6. Summarize the evolution of security force tactics in Ireland.
7. Offer a criminological analysis of Irish terrorism.
8. Summarize the issues involved in the terrorist campaign of the LTTE in
   Sri Lanka.

BYMAN'S LOGIC OF ETHNIC TERRORISM

Daniel Byman (1998) of the RAND Corporation advances a thesis on the structure and logic of ethnic terrorism. Byman says ethnic terrorism differs from terrorism carried out in the name of ideology, religion, or economic gain. He acknowledges the growing influence of religion on terrorism, but he believes ethnic terrorism is a unique entity, even though the line between ethnic and religious violence is blurred. Ethnic terrorists are usually more nationalistic than their religious counterparts. He uses evidence from the Liberation Tigers of Tamil Eelam (LTTE), the Kurdish Workers Party (PKK), the Provisional Irish Republican Army (PIRA), and the Basque National and Liberty (ETA) as evidence for his thesis.

Ethnic terrorists attempt to forge national identity. Their primary purpose is to mobilize a community, and they do so by appealing to the nationalistic background of a particular ethnic group. Byman says terrorist activity is used to make a statement about the group's identity. When the inevitable government persecution follows terrorist actions, it draws attention to the group and allows the terrorists to present themselves as victims. This increases public awareness and sometimes finances and support. Terrorism also polarizes other ethnic groups and forces them to either ally with the terrorists or oppose them.

Violence plays a special role in ethnic terrorism. Whereas political terrorists use violence in a symbolic manner and religious extremists use it to make a theological statement, violence is the *raison d'étre* of ethnic terrorism. It keeps an idea alive. As long as a bomb goes off or a police officer is murdered, the identity and existence of ethnic differences cannot be denied. Violence sustains the conflict, even when political objectives are far out of reach. The fear created by violence serves ethnic interests. Violence also serves to undermine moderates who seek peaceful solutions.

Fear is a special tool of ethnic terrorists. Political terrorists direct fear toward an external audience in the hopes of creating an illusion that the government's sociopolitical structure cannot work. Violent ethnic terrorists use fear to polarize various constituencies. The government, for example, is told that it is not welcomed in the ethnic enclave. Violence declares the government illegitimate. Other ethnic groups are told to avoid the terrorists' areas. Fear polarizes cultural differences, forcing greater identification with one's own group. Fear also keeps a group from developing alternative identities.

Byman argues governments are limited in their response to such fear. They can enter the game and try to promote rival identities. They can also engage in group punishment, but this usually backfires, and only drives moderates to the terrorist camp. They can try to gain the cooperation of moderates, but moderates usually lack the strength to control the terrorists. Finally, they can open the doors to political participation. Many governments are reluctant to do this, however, because it seems as though they are rewarding political violence. In essence, fear is a powerful weapon for ethnic terrorists.

Ethnic terrorists have a built-in audience. Ideological terrorists must focus on the whole political spectrum, while violent religious extremists must address a broad theological audience. Ethnic terrorists simply tell their constituency that they are part of the group. Byman says there is no room for converts, nor is there a place for mass appeal. Either you are in, or you are out.

Most analysts focus on the outcomes of a terrorist campaign. They ask: What do the terrorists hope to achieve? They measure the success of the campaign and the response of security forces to assess the effectiveness of counterterrorist actions. Byman argues this technique is not applicable to ethnic terrorism. Violence is the form of terrorist communication, and success is measured in the continuing threat of violence. Any target outside the ethnic enclave will suffice because there is no such thing as an innocent bystander. Anyone not in the group is an enemy, and violent action against the enemy is the measure of success.

Unlike ideological terrorists, ethnic terrorist organizations tend to be long-lasting. They can build logistical structures much easier than ideological terrorists, and they can hide in a ready-made population. Some groups suffer as an ideological entity, but become stronger when they abandon political beliefs for their ethnic core. For example, Byman argues Hizbollah is much stronger as a Palestinian group than it was as the "Party of God." What this implies is that ethnic terrorists need to be handled differently by security forces. In Byman's words, the tried-and-true methods of counterterrorism do not work against ethnic violence.

What does he suggest as an alternative? When faced with a campaign of ethnic terrorism, Byman says new methods must be invoked. Moral outrage has no place in countering ethnic terrorism, because it will only lead to group cohesion. A government must convince the leaders of the ethnic group in question that it has a vested interest in maintaining the social structure and it can achieve its goals by working within the current system. Byman suggests three methods for government policy: Empowering the ethnic community, winning over moderates to the political system, and encouraging self-policing.

When examining nationalistic and ethnic terrorism, Byman's suggestions seem to work. Governments that have employed these strategies have been successful in reducing violence in areas such as Ireland, Turkey, Spain, and Sri Lanka. Yet the situation is always volatile. Just when it appears security forces are making strides, terrorist violence can frequently be used to derail attempts to bring peace. Some of the prominent ethnic terrorist movements are examined with Byman's thesis in mind.

THE ETA IN SPAIN

The Basque region of France and Spain has long been a source for major nationalist terrorism in Europe. Primarily located in Spain, the Basque region extends over the Pyrenees into France. Basque separatists believe they should be allowed to develop a homeland in Spain, and since the 1950s, Basque separatism has been an important issue in Spanish politics. Many Americans are not aware of the Basque lands, because they are unaware of the evolutionary nature of many European nations. Robert Clark (1979) explains that the Basque region of Spain has always had its own language and culture. It has not existed as an independent kingdom since 1035, but it has maintained its own culture separate from Spain. This changed when Francisco Franco, the fascist Spanish dictator, forcibly campaigned against Basque national identity. A 1950s resurgence of Basque nationalism reflected a centuries-old tradition of unique language and culture.

Edward Moxon-Browne (1987) examines the Basque separatist movement and its relation to terrorism. Moxon-Browne maintains that current problems are the result of a gradual loss of national identity that began in the nineteenth century when Madrid assumed greater control of the region, and accelerated in the early twentieth century because of industrialization. After the Spanish Civil War (1936–1939), Generalissimo Francisco Franco completely incorporated the Basque region into Spain, banning its language and expressions of national culture. Regaining them became the focus of the modern struggle.

Terrorism grew out of the nationalist movement. Moxon-Browne says the Basque Nation and Liberty (ETA) formed as an offshoot of a nationalist political party in the 1950s. Composed of young, frustrated nationalists who wanted regional autonomy, the ETA was not originally violent, but its members turned to violence when Franco tried to repress the movement. In 1966, the ETA voted to follow the example of the Third World and engage in armed revolution. In 1968, they started a terrorist campaign. A more militant group, the ETA-M, broke away from the ETA in 1974. ETA-M described itself as the military wing of the ETA and, according to Moxon-Browne, was responsible for the worst atrocities of the 1970s and 1980s. Both groups have waged a campaign under the name ETA. The campaign reached its zenith between 1977 and 1980 and declined steadily throughout the 1980s. The ETA was responsible for more than 600 deaths between 1968 and 1996.

Robert Clark (1984) has studied the characteristics of Basque terrorists, and Moxon-Browne uses this as a basis to describe the characteristics of the ETA. Membership matches the composition of the local population, although most terrorists are males. The ETA is primarily a working-class movement, as are many nationalist terrorist groups. Its members were not necessarily raised in a Basque family, but they were raised in Basque enclaves and feel a strong ethnic identity. The overwhelming majority feel they are fighting for all the members of their community.

One of the most interesting characteristics of the ETA is that its members did not view terrorism as a full-time activity. According to Moxon-Browne's research, they kept some type of employment while serving in the ETA. In addition, most members only engaged in terrorism for about three years. After this, they returned to their full-time occupations.

Clark (1984) says the eventual goal of Basque terrorism is regional independence. In this sense, the ETA is very similar to the IRA. Another parallel is that the majority of Basques do not support the terrorist campaign, even though most support nationalism and some form of independence. In these circumstances, one of the prime tasks of the Spanish government has been opening the political system to the Basques, while allowing them to maintain their cultural heritage. This strategy has served to delegitimize terrorism.

In the late 1980s, the Spanish government began to further delegitimize the ETA by fostering democracy in the Basque region. Although this did not limit nationalistic desire, it gave nationalists a peaceful outlet for their views. They became participants in the control of their destiny. Steven Greer (1995) points to the national police force as evidence of the effects of democratization. It turned the tables on the ETA. By opening peaceful avenues, such as self-policing, both the Spanish and the Basques were able to denounce violence. The ETA found it harder to operate.

Francisco Llora, Joseph Mata, and Cynthia Irvin (1993) point to another change in the ETA. As Spanish authorities opened opportunities for democracy and national expression, the ETA transformed itself into a social movement. Only hard-core militants were left to preach violence, and faced with a growing lack of support in Spain, they began seeking sanctuary in France. The French government, however, began taking actions of its own; although the government has been traditionally sympathetic to Basque nationalism, French prosecutors reversed their position charging over 70 ETA members with terrorism in 1994, and convicting over 60 ETA members by 1995. The base of ETA support appears to be eroding.

The ETA has almost become a terrorist group in exile. The French, Spanish, and Basques do not want them. Michel Wieviorka (1993) states that opening the political system has made it impossible for the ETA to maintain the myth that it represents the Basque people. In the end, Wieviorka says the struggle was twofold: cultural and political. When the political system opened, ethnic cultural identity was not strong enough to support violence. Repressive policies created the tension, and when they were removed, the support for fighting eroded. If Wieviorka's thesis is correct, ETA capabilities will eventually be limited to sporadic violence, or it may even disappear. At this time, however, the ETA still engages in terrorist violence.

Siamik Khatami (1997) summarizes the situation well, and his thesis reflects Byman's conclusions about the logic of ethnic terror. Khatami says that since the fall of the Soviet Union, the ETA and its political wing have become more entrenched in a working-class ideology. They believe the economic structure of the Basque region provides its ethnic identity. Khatami says the ETA will not compromise on ethnic identity. This gives Spanish authorities a solid opportunity to open the doors of political participation to middle-class Basque moderates. If the government does this, Khatami believes, it will become the best weapon against ETA violence.

THE PKK IN TURKEY

The Kurdish Workers Party (PKK) is a Marxist-Leninist terrorist organization composed of Turkish Kurds. It operates in Turkey and Europe, targeting Europeans, Turks, rival Kurds, and supporters of the Turkish government. It represents the same ruthless brand of Maoism as the Shining Path, murdering entire villages who fail to follow its dictates. On the other hand, it fits perfectly Robert Trundle's warning about placing nationalist movements in left-wing revolutionary models. The PKK has developed chameleonlike characteristics. Although it started as a revolutionary Marxist group, since 1990, it has employed the language of nationalism. It is even more startling that since 1995, it has also used the verbiage of religion.

Nur Bilge Criss (1995) offers one of the better descriptions of the PKK. The organization was created in 1974 to support the notion of an independent Kurdistan, a highland region spanning southeast Turkey, northeast Iraq, and northwest Iran. Unlike other Kurdish groups, the PKK wanted to establish a Marxist-Leninist state. Taking advantage of Kurdish nationalism, the PKK began operation in 1978, hoping to launch a guerrilla war.

Criss states that the plans for revolution proved too grandiose. There was sentiment for fighting the Iraqis, Iranians, and Turks, but not enough support for the Communists. Most Kurds wanted autonomy, not Communism. Stymied by the failure of the guerrilla movement, the PKK settled for a terrorist campaign. This matched both their infrastructure and ability to fight.

PKK leaders took further steps in September 1980, moving operations to the Bekaa Valley of Lebanon. While training there, they met some of the most accomplished terrorists in the world, and after the 1982 Israeli invasion, they quickly found allies in the Syrian camp. For the next two years, the group trained and purged its internal leadership. When it emerged in 1984, the PKK was ready to wage a terrorist campaign.

Once in Turkey, the PKK turned its attention to rural guerrilla war. Because it had an indigenous support base, terrorists were able to launch a fairly large campaign against Turkey. Money and arms also came from Syria, enhancing the PKK's effectiveness. They were particularly ruthless. Within the next few years, the PKK had murdered more than 10,000 people. Criss says the majority of these murders came as a result of village massacres. Turkey responded by isolating the PKK from their support bases and counterattacking PKK groups.

Criss states the tactics had a negative effect on the Kurds. Although they were ready to fight for independence, they were not willing to condone massacres and terrorist attacks. The PKK responded in 1990 by redirecting offensive operations. Rather than focusing on the civilian population, the PKK began limiting its attacks to security forces and economic targets. The PKK also modified its Marxist-Leninist rhetoric and began to speak of nationalism.

In a 1995 interview (Korn, 1995), PKK leader Abdullah Ocalan reiterated the new PKK position. When asked if he was a Marxist, Ocalan stated that he believed in scientific socialism. Ocalan said it would become a new path because the Muslim population and the Kurds in particular had suffered at the hands of Marxist-Leninists. He cast his statements in anti-imperialist format, stating that Kurdistan was only resisting imperialist powers.

In October 1995, Ocalan asked for the United States to mediate between the PKK and Turkey. Ocalan said the PKK was willing to settle for a federation instead of complete autonomy. Although U.S. officials immediately rejected the terrorist's rhetoric, it was nothing new. Criss points out that the PKK started speaking of federal status in 1990. Irrespective of the form of government, Ocalan wanted semiautonomy. In the October 1995 letter to the United States, Ocalan asked for federal status "like the United States." Earlier that year, he asked for the same thing, "like the Russian Federation" (Korn, 1995). The most dramatic announcement came later. By December, the PKK was using the rhetoric of Islam.

It is not surprising to hear a Muslim use Islam and socialism in the same context (Moamar Khadaffy has done it for years), but it was surprising to hear it from the PKK. Yet upon further examination, it was completely understandable. Ocalan had been moving in an anti-Western direction for many years. His terrorists attacked a NATO base in 1986, and they kidnapped 19 Western tourists in 1993. His newfound religious aspirations were probably an expression of old-style, anti-Western actions. Additionally, there was something more. In June 1996, an Islamic fundamentalist government came to power in Turkey. Ocalan wanted to show he was not the ogre who massacred civilians in their villages, but that he was simply a good Muslim.

The leftist Dev Sol organization has been shaky, but the PKK has managed to survive. Declaring a unilateral cease-fire in December 1995, it has placed Turkey in an awkward position. According to Criss, Ocalan's religious rhetoric plays well not only among Kurds, but also throughout the Middle East. Writing before the 1996 election, Criss predicted Turkey would move closer to the Islamic world to counter this threat. He also said the supreme irony is that Turkey may be drawn away from NATO to an Iraqi or Iranian alliance in an effort to counterbalance the Kurds and the Syrians.

The PKK also represents the pejorative nature of terrorism. When the terrorist label is applied to a group like the PKK, the whole movement falls into question. Kurds have long suffered at the hands of their neighbors. The Iranians have slaughtered them, and Saddam Hussein used rockets and poison gas to destroy entire Kurdish villages. The PKK is a terrorist organization, but expressing Kurdish nationalism is not a terrorist act. Many thousands of Kurds were victimized by state terrorism long before the PKK unsheathed its sword.

Turkish authorities captured Abdullah Ocalan in Kenya in 1999, and a security court sentenced him to death in June. In the fall of 2000, Turks began operations against the Kurds. The question of ethnic violence remains open. The PKK has thousands of supporters in Turkey and in Europe.

IRELAND AND THE MUTATING IRA

J. Bowyer Bell (1998), an expert on Irish terrorism, describes the problem of peace in Ireland as a long ending to a lengthy process. The IRA declared a cease-fire in 1994, but broke it in 1996. Trying to bring life into the 1985 Anglo-Irish Peace Accord, British Prime Minister Tony Blair invited the most militant Irish nationalists to the peace table in 1998 and continued negotiations. This brought the ethnic Irish party, Sinn Fein, to the table, but more militant Irish republicans broke ranks. This led to the birth of the Real IRA (RIRA) or the True IRA, as well as several other Orange and Green terrorist organizations. These groups renewed a campaign of violence in 1998, hoping to destroy the Anglo-Irish peace initiatives.

J. Bowyer Bell is not optimistic about any political entity's—government or otherwise—ability to bring peace to the island nation by avoiding every avenue of conflict. Bell says there are too many agendas and too many people served by ethnic violence. Seamus Dunn and Valerie Morgan (1995) point out that Protestant violence may also increase because many Protestants believe the British government has abandoned them. The growth of Orange organizations like Red Hand Defenders and Orange Volunteers, two new terrorist groups that have disavowed the peace accords, serve to reinforce these conclusions.

Chapter 6 presented the origins of modern Irish troubles. Today, even when two governments are trying to bring an end to the violence by acknowledging historical issues, the fighting continues. Why is this so? What has been done? Will peace policies work? To answer these questions, one needs to examine the attempts to outlaw Irish terrorism, the evolution of security force tactics, and the criminology of Irish terrorism.

OUTLAWING TERRORISM
AND INTERNMENT

In 1972, the United Kingdom's Lord Chief Justice Diplock was dispatched to Northern Ireland to examine the possibility of using criminal law to combat terrorism. Diplock's committee issued a report, and it became the basis of one of the most controversial policies in Northern Ireland. Under Diplock's recommendations, security forces were given the power to arrest and intern without warrant or trial. Courts were given the power of secret trial and testimony.

The style of enforcement changed over the next two decades, but a special form of martial law developed in conjunction with the Diplock courts. The policy was based on a longstanding tradition of martial law in Ireland. The Special Powers Act, first enacted during the Irish Civil War in 1922, granted expanded powers to police officers and allowed courts to operate on a secret basis. The act was renewed each year until 1933, when it became a permanent part of Northern Ireland's legal code. Diplock's recommendations kept with past practices, and they resulted in a series of Emergency Powers Acts (EPA) from 1973 to 1995. These laws united military units, the constabulary, prisons, and courts in a single executive governmental justice system.

Finn (1987) argues Diplock's committee proceeded on the assumption that the Northern Irish criminal justice system could not deal with the problem of terrorism. Terrorism had resulted in three legal problems. First, common-law rules of evidence tended to protect terrorists. Second, under normal criminal procedure, witnesses and victims could be threatened by members of Protestant or Catholic terrorist organizations. Finally, the Diplock committee feared favoritism in juror selection and trial verdicts.

The EPA gave the government key powers: The powers of police search and seizure were expanded, and the police were enabled to stop and question citizens without reasonable suspicion. Although they were not given arrest authority, military forces operating in support of the police were allowed to stop and question civilians, and detain suspected terrorists for the police. Far more controversial were the practices of internment—arresting a suspect without formal charges—and trial without a jury. Protection against such governmental powers is generally assumed by citizens of most Western nations.

In effect, outlawing terrorism made the criminal justice system in Ireland nothing more than an administrative process. Officials responsible for the security of Northern Ireland could issue an administrative order to detain a suspected terrorist. No criminal charges had to be filed because the suspect was not under arrest. The suspect could be held for 28 days unless a police official decided there was a reason for further detention.

As the United Kingdom and Ireland attempt to bring peace to the North, extrajudicial courts have been removed. The Diplock courts served a purpose in preventing terrorism, but the goal of the 1985 Anglo-Irish Peace Accord was to return criminal infractions in Ireland to the realm of peacetime law. In 1998, the British and Irish governments developed a new program for outlawing terrorism (Baer & Wood, 1998). Under the provisions of this agreement, most former suspects would be released from prison in a general amnesty with the understanding that they avoid associations with terrorist organizations. On the list of traditional terrorist groups were the new organizations, including the Continuing Irish Republican Army, Loyalist Volunteer Force, Irish Nationalist Liberation Army, and Real Irish Republican Army.

The British government has moved in the direction suggested by Byman. They have appealed to moderates, hoping to empower the republican community. Oonagh Gay (1998) demonstrates that terrorism will remain outlawed under the new government, and both Irish and British forces will be charged with preventing terrorism. The British Parliament (House of Commons, 1998) has agreed to restructure and train the Royal Ulster Constabulary (RUC) for this new mission.

The Evolution of Security Force Tactics
in Northern Ireland

Selecting a new role for the RUC is no easy task, but it is something the police are interested in doing. Indeed, it is something they must do, if peace is to succeed. Aside from the historical issues surrounding the constabulary, the problem of violent extremism remains. Militant republican and unionist organizations threaten the peace accord. While this will be the "long end game," as Bell indicates, it can be managed if the political process can withstand a limited amount of factional violence. To understand the issues facing the RUC, a brief look at the development of the security tactics follows.

From a criminal justice standpoint, one important factor has dominated the experiences of security forces in Northern Ireland from 1969 until 1985: The police and military were used in combined operations. After 1985, military units were still used to support police operations, and commandos from the Special Air Services mounted independent attacks on the IRA. This meant that security in Northern Ireland fell into the exclusive domain of neither the police nor the military. Both organizational structures were forced to learn a variety of nontraditional roles. The learning process was painful, and often developed through trial and error. Although the conflict was demilitarized after 1994, any law enforcement or military commander charged with counterterrorism can learn much from the RUC-British Army experience.

When the first troops arrived in Belfast and Londonderry in August 1969, they were hardly prepared for the tasks that faced them. Aside from the political misunderstanding reported by Bell, the troops were thrown into an urban peacekeeping role with little or no preparation. Combat troops were utilized essentially as an extension of police power. These troops had limited knowledge of police functions; therefore, they tended to approach hostile situations as if they were engaging an enemy. The young troops who patrolled Northern Ireland from 1969 to 1970 came from the British Army of the Rhine. Trained to destroy any potential invading Soviet forces in Germany, these young soldiers took it upon themselves to destroy their new Irish enemies. Most accounts recorded that overreaction was not uncommon.

Robert Moss (1972, p. 24) writes that the British government quickly began to realize the gravity of this situation. As rioting and demonstration gave way to a campaign of terrorism, it appeared the presence of the British Army would be needed for quite some time. This meant preparing troops for a different type of duty. Units assigned to Northern Ireland began to receive special training in peacekeeping duties.

It is best to examine the military response in a series of phases. These are rough outlines that obscure details, but they can illustrate the evolution of the military's tactics. In 1969, the British Army simply responded to riots; then it attempted to isolate Republican neighborhoods. From 1970 to 1973, Peter Janke (1974) reports, the British Army was employed to create a more neutral peacekeeping force. Despite this goal, the British Army engaged in massive roundup operations against IRA suspects, and still approached Northern Ireland as if it were a military target. Policies and actions during those periods isolated Catholic communities, and increased the strength of the IRA.

From 1973 to 1978, British Army policy changed drastically. According to retired British Colonel James Deerin (1978, pp. 670–675), the British Army learned from its previous mistakes. Rather than approaching Ulster as a war zone, the British Army conceived of its role as one of police support. Deerin says troops were not soldiers; they were an extension of police security. He adds that this role was learned by trial and error from overreaction during the early years of military involvement.

In 1978, British Army policy changed again, not so much through internal evaluation as through a change in British attitudes toward Northern Ireland. The British government increasingly viewed Ireland as an Irish problem, but it would not abandon Ulster for fear of a civil war (Kelley, 1982, p. 227). Prime Minister Margaret Thatcher followed this policy of "Ulsterization" by reducing the number of British troops and increasing the number of Irish citizens in security forces throughout 1985. The signing of the Anglo-Irish Peace Accord temporarily solidified this process.

In the latest phase, military policy has followed three patterns. First, when military forces are used, they are generally employed to augment civilian police power. Second, specialized operations units (such as the Special Air Service, air surveillance, and intelligence) were employed for limited operations, but British Army activity declined significantly after 1985. Third, on August 31, 1994, the IRA called for its members to join the peace process. Some groups inside the IRA have tried to sabotage this order, but the IRA's position further reduced the role of British military forces. Even when the cease-fire failed, the RUC handled the situation on its own.

Based on the recommendations of several official inquiries, the British government took a series of steps to restore faith in the RUC and make it a neutral civil power. It was a long-term process that began in the early 1970s and has continued to date. Two general strategies were used to accomplish the objective. First, the B-Specials and other overtly Protestant aspects of the RUC were officially dissolved. Second, the RUC and other organizations in the justice system began to recruit Catholics for enforcement, judicial, and security roles.

According to Deerin, the RUC became the mainstay of security forces in Northern Ireland. Although it was armed with emergency powers, its primary job was to respond to terrorism as a violation of criminal law. When the British Army modified its role to one of police support in 1973, the RUC became completely responsible for counterterrorist operations. Military force was only called on for support during hazardous calls and additional security patrols during emergencies. Military personnel were constrained by strict rules of engagement very similar to the police guidelines.

In the area of investigation, the police and military began to cooperate fully. The RUC used standard criminal investigation techniques and began building files on known and potential terrorists. The British Army gathered information through military intelligence sources. Military procedures became controversial, however, when abuses of interned suspects were reported. Some international observers concluded the British Army tortured several IRA suspects to gain information in the early 1970s.

The 1980s saw a more subtle and effective form of persuasion. Security forces began to use known terrorists as their sources of information. Finn mentions the technique: Informants have been used to infiltrate extremist factions among both Republicans and Unionists. Known as "supergrasses," they are allowed to give secret testimony in Diplock courts. Many people have been convicted without other corroborative evidence. The use of supergrasses has been extremely controversial, but it has been effective.

During their early employment, both police and military forces were plagued by misunderstanding and overreaction. There is no doubt that many human rights abuses occurred. However, security force policy evolved and eventually helped calm a tremendously complex, violent situation. Additionally, the increased competence of security forces seemed to result in a less confrontational attitude, according to analysts like Deerin. In the long run, police and military policies to preserve peace were more effective than the murders of terrorists. Only the most extreme Orange and Green terrorists are attempting to thwart the peace agreement, and most of them have lost public support. Albeit by trial and error, the British Army and the RUC learned how to fight a counterterrorist war.

Steve Bruce (1995) reiterates Bell's point through an examination of Protestant groups. Bruce says two unionist terrorist groups, the Ulster Defense Association and Ulster Volunteer Force, will not let IRA violence go unanswered. Seamus Dunn and Valerie Morgan (1995) agree. In the early 1990s, Dunn and Morgan argue, the Protestant community began to grow leery of progress made with the Anglo-Irish Peace Accord. If the Protestants feel they are being socially and economically abandoned, the analysts conclude, they may not abandon violence.

Regardless, the level of violence dropped in the last years of the twentieth century. Extremists on both sides will never be satisfied, and they will probably resort to sporadic terrorism. The greatest challenge to those willing to continue with the peace accord will be to manage the conflict through criminal justice forces and the rule of law. The next generation may experience peace, if the conflict continues to follow the path of demilitarization.

A CRIMINOLOGICAL ANALYSIS
OF IRISH TERRORISM

Robert Pockrass conducted in 1987 an in-depth study into the nature of terrorism in Northern Ireland. He examined the patterns of violence from 1969 to 1984 by relating the motivations of the killers to the selection of their victims. Specifically, he asked what types of people became victims and why they were killed.

Pockrass believes Irish violence is cultural. Other revolutionary countries have experienced more violence, he argues, but Irish violence is a kind of national expression. It is glorified in poetry, literature, and song. It is the celebrated event of the past, and the expected outcome of the future. The sad reality of such a cultural expression is seen in the number of people killed by terrorist violence.

Pockrass argues Irish violence can best be understood by focusing on the motivation behind it. Feeling that too often terrorists are dismissed as abnormal, he suggests their actions be evaluated in terms of outcome. Pockrass believes terrorists operate with a goal in mind. When analysts focus on the goal, they may not be able to decipher all of the motives behind terrorist activity, but they can often determine the primary motive.

This approach could lead to better predictive models of terrorism. Pockrass identifies four categories of terrorism in Northern Ireland. Sectarian violence involves interreligious conflicts—that is, fighting between Protestants and Catholics. Interorganizational violence includes the internal struggles of Unionist and Republican terrorist organizations. The final categories are terrorist attacks on noncombatants and similar attacks on security forces. Pockrass relates each type of violence to the motivation behind it.

Sectarian violence went through an evolutionary development. In 1969, it was primarily mob action. In the riots that engulfed Northern Ireland that August, mobs of Catholics confronted mobs of Protestants. Violence was random and dominated by the psychology of the mob. This was not terrorism.

According to Pockrass, terrorism entered sectarian conflicts when individuals abandoned mob rioting around 1971, and started hunting for selected targets. Random mob violence had not been extremely deadly; terrorism changed that situation. As attacks became individualized, the amount of violence increased along with its effectiveness.

The initial purpose of rioting and terrorism was to convey an illusion of power. By participating in a mob or selecting an individual victim from the other side, Catholics and Protestants sought to intimidate each other by fear. As individual terrorist murders increased, Pockrass says, the motivation began to change. In some cases, murders were committed to force a change in policy. Others were committed for revenge. In analyzing sectarian murder, pure hatred and a desire to kill also played a leading role.

Interorganizational violence was motivated by other factors. Both Republican and Unionist terrorist groups used murder as a means of enforcing internal discipline. It was also used to take revenge against informants and set examples for potential informants. The use of supergrasses by security forces has resulted in a number of deadly internal killings.

Attacks on noncombatants seem to have three motives. First, killing public officials increases the aura of power around terrorists. Second, the sophistication of many of the attacks also brings attention to the cause. Finally, revenge has become an important motive. Pockrass notes that a number of off-duty correctional and judicial personnel have been targeted. Corrections officers have been murdered for alleged cruelty toward inmates, and judges have been murdered for their sentencing. The IRA and the more militant republican Irish National Liberation Army (INLA) even assassinate Catholic judges because they view them as national traitors.

In the 1980s, the increasing trend in Northern Ireland was to attack members of the security forces. Pockrass maintains this has been a tactic primarily favored by republican terrorists because they see themselves as fighting a war for national liberation. Unionist terrorists have also attacked security forces, but generally these have been responses to being attacked. Republican terrorists have rechanneled most of their efforts since 1976 into attacks on the security forces.

Given the motivation of political conflict, there are other reasons for attacking security forces. Indiscriminate attacks against civilians threatened a potential backlash from the population. As random violence declined, the lines of terrorism became more clearly demarcated. The RUC and its supporters were defined as the enemy by Republican terrorists. Republican organizations hoped to force a withdrawal of RUC forces and support similar to the British withdrawal in 1921.

Pockrass says this analogy breaks down when tested. The RUC and Ulster Defense Regiment are not British forces. They are Irish, and they have nowhere to retreat. The terrorists can only hope they will become demoralized or emigrate from Northern Ireland to join the British. Neither possibility seems likely to Pockrass and, indeed, did not occur before the peace movement.

THE LIBERATION TIGERS
OF TAMIL EELAM

The Tamil Tigers (Liberation Tigers of Tamil Eelam, or LTTE) are fighting for an independent homeland for nearly 3,000,000 Tamils in northern and eastern Sri Lanka. The Tamil Tigers have waged a guerrilla campaign using terrorism as both a prelude to guerrilla warfare, and a way to support uniformed guerrillas in the field. They have killed thousands and assassinated prominent political figures such as Indian Prime Minister Rajiv Ghandi and President Ransinghe Premdasa of Sri Lanka. They also continue to attack moderate Tamils who oppose their cause. The basis of ethnic conflict is exacerbated by struggles between Hindus and Muslims. The struggle for Sri Lanka has been a long, dirty, and terrible war.

Manoj Joshi (1996) summarizes the conflict in Sri Lanka for *Studies in Conflict and Terrorism*. Joshi traces the struggle's origins to the autonomy India gained at the end of World War II. As India sought to bring internal peace among Hindus and Muslims, the island of Sri Lanka (formerly known as Ceylon) faced a similar problem. In addition to religious differences, the Tamil minority in Sri Lanka was concerned about maintaining its ethnic identity. Tamils along the southeastern coast of India supported the Sri Lankan Tamils in this quest. As the Sri Lankan government was formed, the Tamils found themselves in positions of authority. Although they accounted for only 17 percent of Sri Lanka's population (the Sihalas account for the majority), the Tamils were well-represented in the bureaucracy. This changed in 1955.

Claiming that Tamils dominated the Sri Lankan government, the Sihala majority forced the government to adopt a "Sihala-only" policy. Tamils began to grumble, and some spoke of violence. A Tamil assassin killed the Sihala leader in 1959, setting the stage for violence. Seeking sanctuary in the Tamil region of India, militant Tamils filtered across the short expanse of ocean to wage a low-level terrorist campaign through 1975. Spurred by their successes, they began larger operations.

The Tamil experience was similar to the situation in Ireland. Buoyed by religious differences and ethnic support, Tamil separatists could begin a guerrilla campaign by waging terrorist war. Their ethnic support base gave them the opportunity to do so. In 1975, Veluppillai Pirabhakaran, a young Tamil militant, took advantage of the situation and formed the LTTE, the Liberation Tigers of Tamil Eelam. (Eelam means "homeland.") Joshi says Pirabhakaran faced problems similar to other terrorists. Although he raised money through bank robberies, and conducted assassinations, Pirabhakaran needed to eliminate rival terrorists to claim leadership of the movement.

The Tamil Tigers eventually emerged as the leading revolutionary group and launched Sri Lanka into a full-blown terrorist campaign. The Tamil Tigers were not satisfied with this, however, wanting to build a guerrilla force and eventually a conventional army. The Sihala majority reacted violently in 1983. Ignoring the government, Sihala protesters flocked to the streets of Colombo, Sri Lanka's capital, in a series of anti-Tamil riots. Many Tamils fled to India, and the Tamil Tigers returned to terrorism.

Joshi says reactions to the riots were a turning point for the Tamil Tigers. Unable to ferment the revolution from above, they established contacts with the Popular Front for the Liberation of Palestine. Since that time, the Tamil Tigers have mounted three on-again, off-again terrorist campaigns. At first, India responded by forming a joint peacekeeping force with Sri Lanka. India's primary purpose was to keep violence from spilling over into the mainland. Joshi says India reevaluated its policy after a number of assassinations and violent encounters, and the government has vowed never to send troops to Sri Lanka again.

The Tamil Tigers have incorporated a variety of tactics since 1984. Their ability to operate is directly correlated to the amount of political support they enjoy during any particular period. In 1988 and 1992, they sought to control geographic areas, and they moved using standard guerrilla tactics, forming uniformed units. They even created an ad-hoc navy. In weaker times, they relied on bank robberies, bombings, and murder. In the weakest times, they have also employed suicide bombers. They used suicide attacks in 1995 on land and sea.

The situation in Sri Lanka has parallels to the political situation in Ireland, but the pattern of growth in the Tamil Tigers reflects Uruguay's Tupamaros. Before 1983, Joshi estimates the Tamil Tigers had only 40 followers. The anti-Tamil riots were a catalyst to growth, as links were formed in the Middle East.

Terrorist training camps appeared in the Tamil region of India in 1984 and 1985, and the training cadre included foreign terrorists. India responded by signing a joint peace agreement with Sri Lanka, and soon found itself under attack from a highly organized terrorist group.

When not attacking India, the Tamil Tigers launched operations in Sri Lanka. Although they had once struggled to be recognized as the leaders of the independence movement, Joshi says the Tamil Tigers ruthlessly wiped out their opponents and terrorized their own ethnic group into providing support. Yet security forces enjoyed several successes, and by 1987, the Tamil Tigers were in retreat.

According to Joshi, this was a very dangerous period for the Tamil Tigers. In fact, they were almost wiped out. Retreating to the jungle, the Tamil Tigers abandoned the new-found position of power and practiced terrorism from jungle hideaways. They increased contact with Tamil bases in India, using India for their logistical support. Politically adept, the Tamil Tigers asked for a cease-fire in 1989, giving India a chance to withdraw from the joint security force. No sooner had the Indians left than the Tamil Tigers renewed their attack on the Sri Lankans.

In 1990, the Tamil Tigers expanded their operations by incorporating a fishing fleet between Sri Lanka and India. By 1991, the Indian Navy was forced to respond to the growing threat, and India was once again targeted by Tamil terrorists. Not only did the Tamil Tigers fight small-scale sea battles with the Indians, but Tamil Tiger terrorists also succeeded in assassinating Prime Minister Rajiv Ghandi on May 21, 1991. When Indian authorities cracked down on Tamil bases, the Tamil Tigers increased their terrorist attacks against India.

From 1994 to 1995, the Tamil Tigers waged another bombing and assassination campaign, and although their bases in India were limited, they held geographic strong points on Sri Lanka. They did what no other terrorist group has been able to do. Supported by guerrilla strongholds, Tamil Tigers appeared in uniforms in 1994 and fought pitched battles with the Sri Lankan security forces. Suicide bombings increased during the same timeframe. Faced with open revolution, the Sri Lankan government signed a peace agreement in January 1995.

Joshi's research ended in the summer of 1995. The peace accord broke down, and the Sri Lankan Army went on the offensive. The Tamil Tigers suffered several setbacks, but they made headlines in 1996 with suicide bombings in Colombo. In the spring of 1996, Sri Lankan security forces launched an all-out assault on Tamil strongholds on the northern portion of the island. Some commentators (de Silva, 1996; Berthelsen, 1996) believed this would be the end of the Tamil Tigers. They were wrong.

Rohan Gunaratna (1998) argues the LTTE is in a unique position because it has such a large guerrilla base. The guerrillas are perfectly capable of fighting a protracted war against security forces, and if defeated, the LTTE can revert to terrorism. Indeed, this has been the LTTE's tactic. In the wake of new fighting, the LTTE has followed the path of suicide bombing. While the guerrilla campaign subsided a bit in 1999, suicide bombings increased in 2000. The hardcore LTTE is a long way from any negotiated settlement. The hope of the Sri Lankan government is to attract moderate Tamils into a coalition government and deprive the Tamil Tigers of their ethnic and guerrilla support. Regardless, suicide bombings keep the campaign alive.

KEY CONCEPTS

1. Byman believes ethnic terrorism differs from other forms of terrorism and must be countered with different tactics.

2. The Basque region of Spain has been subjected to a campaign of ethnic terrorism since the 1950s. Today, hardcore ETA militants have retreated into their ethnic identity and target all those who oppose them, even middle-class Basques.

3. The PKK is a Kurdish terrorist group. Its leader has been arrested, but supporters in Europe and Turkey number in the thousands.

4. The Anglo-Irish peace process has spawned more radical groups from both the Unionist and Republican camps.

5. After the initial encounters in Ireland, the United Kingdom attempted to outlaw terrorism by circumventing the legal system. Both Ireland and the United Kingdom have abandoned this policy, although terrorism is legally defined and remains outlawed.

6. Security force tactics in Ireland began with police operations, and shifted to combined police and military operations. Under the peace discussions, counterterrorism has been demilitarized. Both Ireland and the United Kingdom hope to create a constabulary in Northern Ireland that reflects the ethnic composition of the population.

7. The LTTE emerged from the Tamil population in Sri Lanka. It became so strong that it was able to move from terrorism to guerrilla war. In 1995, the LTTE began a campaign of suicide bombing. Even if the Sri Lankan government can peacefully incorporate the majority of Tamils, suicide bombings keep the idea of Tamil liberation alive.

FOOD FOR THOUGHT

Byman argues that ethnic counterterrorist measures should include attempts to win moderate nationalists into the governmental camp. The Spanish have tried to do this by creating a Basque national police force, and the United Kingdom is seeking to do the same with changes in the Royal Ulster Constabulary. Yet violence continues. Why? If the Sri Lankans created a Tamil police force, what impact would this have on the LTTE? Do you think suicide bombings send a different message to potential ethnic supporters than a nonsuicide attack?

When an ethnic group creates martyrs, what impact does this have on moderate members of the same ethnic group who want to seek a peaceful solution to social injustice?

FURTHER READING

David Carment, Patrick James, & Donald Puchala (Eds.), *Peace in the Midst of Wars: Preventing and Managing International Ethnic Conflicts*

13

Terrorism
in the United States

When compared to the rest of the world, terrorism is neither unique nor new in the United States. Although this chapter focuses on more recent events, domestic terrorism is older than the United States. Nationalistic terrorism began during frontier wars in the seventeenth century and has continued to the present day. Violent ideological extremism dominated many issues in the 1800s, leading to many terrorist acts. As militant labor movements grew in the post–Civil War (1861–1865) era, revolutionary terrorism and repressionist terrorism made appearances in the United States. Only recently charged as the lead agency for domestic terrorism, the Federal Bureau of Investigation has been tracking potential foreign terrorists since 1935. This chapter introduces the varieties of terrorism that have recently evolved in the United States, while Chapter 14 focuses exclusively on emerging ideological terrorism.

After reading this chapter, you should be able to:

1. Summarize approaches to domestic terrorism as analyzed by Gurr, Bell, and Cooper.

2. Discuss the problems surrounding the conceptualization of domestic terrorism.

3. Define three methods for defining domestic terrorism, and explain the relationship between them.

4. Summarize Brent Smith's analysis of American terrorism.

5. Summarize Steven Emerson's analysis of Middle Eastern terrorist groups in the United States.

DOMESTIC TERRORISM: EARLY WORKS OF COOPER, BELL, AND GURR

The United States has a long history of political violence, but until recently, few scholars characterized this experience as "terrorism." Two exceptions to this rule were H. H. A. Cooper and Ted Robert Gurr. Cooper directed the preparation of the report on terrorism by the National Advisory Committee on Criminal Justice Standards and Goals. Gurr is one of the nation's leading political scientists and an expert on domestic political violence. Cooper and the National Advisory Committee provided the conceptual framework for domestic terrorism, and Gurr placed terrorist violence within the perspective of the American political experience. Both scholars initiated their work before it was popular to speak of domestic terrorism.

Cooper and coauthors produced an outstanding report in 1976 on the political context of domestic terrorism. Combining the examination with work on civil disorders, Cooper demonstrated the need to prepare law enforcement and other supporting agencies for emergencies. His colleagues presented a series of recommendations for emergency response. Although the Report of the Task Force on Disorders and Terrorism is 20 years old, the standards of performance it suggests remain valid.

If Cooper's team developed a pragmatic emergency response planning model, Gurr placed terrorism within its historical context. In the article written with J. Bowyer Bell (1979), Gurr argues that terrorism is a tactic used by the weak to intimidate the strong and, in turn, by the strong to repress the weak. In this sense, America has a history overflowing with terrorist activities. Various political movements have used forms of terrorism to seek political gains. At the same time, industrial giants and those holding power have historically used terrorism to maintain control over workers and unions.

Bell and Gurr begin their review by looking at the late 1800s. Despite the American paranoia about radicals, terrorism in the nineteenth century was primarily aimed at protecting the status quo and the economic environment. The actions of company security police and private corporations were often terroristic in nature. They were designed to keep workers from disrupting production. Labor radicals, however, also behaved violently; the labor movement of the late nineteenth century was replete with violence. Bell and Gurr label this a manifestation of terrorism.

Labor violence was not the only source of early U.S. terrorism. The frontier had its own special form of violence. As the frontier expanded, the laws of the United States trailed far behind. Settlers developed their own brand of makeshift justice. At times, this type of justice spilled over into vigilante activities. Bell and

Gurr refer to some aspects of the vigilante movement as terrorism. The Ku Klux Klan after the Civil War is an example.

Although there is a long history of American political violence, Bell and Gurr separate modern American terrorism from its historical predecessors. In the 1960s, they argue, the character of American terrorism began to change. Domestic terrorism became rooted in radical politics, nationalism, and the international community's experience with terrorism. The use of terrorism to maintain social order was forgotten in the modern setting, and domestic terrorism was defined as a radical phenomenon.

Bell and Gurr believe modern domestic terrorism has been entirely derived from foreign models. Both political revolutionary groups and nationalistic groups in the United States took their ideas from terrorists in the Middle East and Asia. In this sense, both types of groups saw themselves as being involved in a broader struggle of international proportions.

Their logic had a catch, however. Bell and Gurr note that American terrorist groups did not have the same impact as their foreign counterparts. The American public totally rejected the violence of the revolutionary groups, and popularity was never fully achieved, even among their most sympathetic audiences. United States revolutionary terrorists ended up as small bands of social misfits who had very little impact on the political system. As a result, the United States has been spared the excesses of revolutionary terrorism.

Bell and Gurr issue two caveats along with their conclusion. First, even though United States has avoided significant domestic terrorism, both criminals and political activists have used terrorist tactics on a local level, particularly the tactic of taking hostages. Second, nationalistic terrorists have been far more successful than revolutionaries at launching campaigns, because they have an indigenous base of support. As an example, Bell and Gurr cite Puerto Rican terrorists. Although they have not had a major impact, Puerto Rican terrorists have enjoyed more success than revolutionary terrorists because of this support.

In a later work, Gurr (1988a) updates some of these ideas about domestic terrorism. He offers a typology, outlining three types of terrorism: (1) vigilante, (2) insurgent, and (3) transnational.

Vigilante Terrorism

Gurr indicates that the growth of right-wing extremists is indicative of vigilante terrorism. The purpose of vigilantes is to defend the status quo or return to the status quo of an earlier period. Gurr believes the Ku Klux Klan, Christian Identity Movement, and other white supremacy organizations are examples of vigilante terrorism that rely on right-wing rhetorical traditions.

Insurgent Terrorism

Gurr describes insurgent terrorists in revolutionary terms. Black militants, white revolutionaries, and Puerto Rican nationalists fall into this category. Insurgent terrorism aims to change political policies by direct threats or action against the government. It is the political antithesis of vigilante terrorism because it attacks the status quo.

Transnational Terrorism

Transnational terrorism occurs when nonindigenous terrorists cross national borders. Gurr identifies several sources of transnational terror in the United States. Some foreign nationals have carried their fights onto U.S. soil, and some domestic groups have been inspired by foreign events. In other cases, foreign countries may have begun to target Americans at home. However, Gurr does not believe the threat of transnational terrorism has been as great as has been popularly believed. Of course, he was writing before the bombing of the World Trade Center.

PROBLEMS OF CONCEPTUALIZING
DOMESTIC TERRORISM

If scholars like Gurr, Bell, and Cooper were examining domestic terrorism decades ago, why was it so difficult for those charged with security today to prepare for it? There are probably several reasons. American law enforcement is focused on local issues, and is dominated by anti-intellectual feelings. Most police managers do not think abstractly, and they pride themselves on pragmatism. When critical thought is applied in law enforcement, it is inevitably focused on local issues. Terrorism is simply too exotic for most agencies, even after a bombing in Oklahoma City.

Another problem is that American law enforcement officers routinely deal with terrorism, while referring to incidents in question as routine crimes. Even the FBI, which has performed well when countering and capturing domestic terrorists, labels the majority of domestic terrorist activities under nonterrorist headings in the Uniform Crime Report. In addition, the FBI's reports on domestic terrorism do not classify many terrorists' acts as "terrorism." By the same token, in the 1980s, the FBI's practical methods for countering terrorism were recognized throughout the world, and they became the only agency that could coordinate thousands of local American police departments in a counterterrorist direction. The irony of their efforts was that the FBI simply did not call much of their work counterterrorism.

Closely related to this problem is the simple fact that most American terrorism is little more than criminal activity. Bombing serves as an excellent example. According to a *New York Times News Service* (1996) analysis, domestic bombings tripled between 1985 and 1994, from 1,103 to 3,163. Whereas cases like the 1993 World Trade Center bombing and the 1995 destruction of the federal building in Oklahoma City gain notoriety, the overwhelming number of American bombings deal with individual criminal vendettas. In other words, most American terrorism is criminal, not political.

Finally, the United States was not routinely targeted by terrorists until 1982. Before then, most American terrorist movements died for lack of support. Since 1982, however, terrorists have produced an increasing number of American victims. Beginning with attacks overseas, the attacks finally crossed American borders. Even though the majority of incidents still involve low-level criminal activity, Americans have sadly learned that they cannot automatically dismiss terrorism.

Before classifying the types of activities in the United States, it is necessary to mention that criminologists classify crime for the analysis of social phenomena. From a tactical perspective, however, an immediate response to terrorism does not depend on a label appropriate for criminology. It is much more important to realize that American police officers routinely handle terrorism, even though they call it by a variety of names.

Tactically, police and security forces should keep two issues in mind. First, a beat police officer is usually the first responder to domestic terrorism. Second, the investigation techniques used in large, sensationalized terrorist incidents are the same techniques a local agency would use to investigate a stink bomb placed in the locker room of a high school football team. Therefore, the FBI is somewhat justified in the use of its reporting system. From a practical perspective, counterterrorism depends on the fundamentals. Good investigative skills, such as the collection and preservation of evidence and good interviewing techniques, are far more important than the appropriateness of the label.

The opposite is true from a criminological perspective. Using a label can define the political response to an incident, and when the term "terrorism" is applied to a crime, public fears increase. Terrorism has a political meaning beyond the immediate crime, even though the terrorist incident may be nothing more than a localized crime (Cooper et al., 1976; Smith, 1994). Most governments allow security forces greater latitude when dealing with terrorism and terrorists, and the American police cannot be content to focus on the immediate application of counterterrorist tactics, if they want to maintain the democratic basis of policing. Therefore, we need to briefly examine some typologies of domestic terrorism to see how they might enhance our understanding.

One of the early attempts to classify domestic terrorism came from the National Advisory Committee on Criminal Justice Standards and Goals (Cooper et al., 1976, pp. 3–7). The report cites several types of terrorism. Political terrorism is described as violent criminal behavior designed to produce fear for political outcomes. Nonpolitical terrorism is simply designed to produce fear, whereas quasiterrorism involves nonpolitical terrorist activities during the commission of crimes. The report also describes limited terrorism violence aimed at changing government policy, and it talks about state repression. In essence, the report provides a typology similar to those discussed in Chapter 1.

The FBI provides a de facto typology simply by the categories it uses in its reports on domestic terrorism. John Harris (1987, pp. 5–13) summarizes these in the FBI Law Enforcement Bulletin. According to Harris, five types of groups were responsible for domestic terrorism in the 1980s. These groups included: (1) white leftists, (2) Puerto Rican leftists, (3) black militants, (4) right-wing extremists, and (5) Jewish extremists. Like the FBI reports on domestic terrorism, Harris's article does not include criminal incidents involving terrorist tactics. He limits his topic to the problem of political terrorism.

According to Harris, all domestic terrorist groups, with the exception of Puerto Rican nationalists, lack an indigenous base, and they tend to have localized ideological bases. Types of groups are generally defined by location. For example, white supremacy groups tend to be rural, whereas revolutionary groups are generally urban. Because it tends to be geographically confined, American terrorism does not affect all local police agencies in the same manner.

Closely related to this type of summary is a classification system developed by Brent Smith (1994). Using FBI data, Smith places terrorist groups into three broad categories: (1) right-wing extremists, (2) left-wing and single-issue terrorists, and (3) international terrorists. (Note how closely this resembles Gurr's typology.) Smith believes that right-wing groups form a category by themselves, but that left-wing groups are different. Single-issue groups, criminal gangs, ecologists, and old-style leftists fit neatly into the left-wing extremist category. International terrorists form the remaining group. Smith's system is examined more closely in the next section because he has probably written the best criminological analysis of terrorism in the United States.

In the mid-1980s, I developed a classification system in a work for the International Association of Chiefs of Police (White, 1986). I suggested that domestic terrorism comes from the following sources: (1) foreign groups operating on American soil, (2) revolutionary nationalists, (3) the ideological right, (4) the ideological left, and (5) criminal groups using terrorist tactics.

Foreign groups operating on American soil fall into two categories. There are nationalist groups that carry their struggles onto American soil, and there are foreign groups targeting the United States on American soil. Both the potential and the realization of this type of terrorism increased in the 1990s. Nationalist terrorism in the United States mainly stems from Puerto Rican separatists, and the ideological right reemerged in the early 1990s as an active source of domestic terrorism.

The remaining groups have been less effective. Unlike extremists on the right, left-wing terrorists have not fared well in recent times. According to James Stinson (1984), left-wing groups were forced to merge into a loosely bound confederation of terrorist groups. Perhaps the most frequent, yet least effective, form of domestic terrorism has emanated from criminal groups.

There are other classification systems that not only serve to sort existing data, but also label certain actors as terrorists. Harris's view presents the official government response. Cooper's summary, and my fivefold typology, serve as practical guides to investigation. Smith's typology is the best for criminological analysis, but it is surprisingly close to the other typologies.

Despite their pejorative nature, typologies of domestic terrorism are inevitably related. They must account for a variety of ideologically motivated actors, revolutionaries, and zealots with a host of different causes. No matter how you decide to arrange the categories, you still cover the same ground.

Therefore, it is probably best to consider a typology that helps provide a long-term criminological analysis.

SMITH'S ANALYSIS OF TERRORISM
IN THE UNITED STATES

Using data from official sources, Brent Smith (1994) presents one of the best factual summaries of recent terrorism in the United States, and probably the single best criminological analysis of domestic terrorism. The factor separating the average criminal from the average terrorist is motivation. According to Smith, terrorists remain criminals, but they are motivated by ideology, religion, or a political cause. Like Paul Wilkinson, Smith does not examine criminal terrorism as a tactical typology. (It would have been difficult to do this because he uses FBI data, and the FBI does not measure criminal terrorism.) Smith's analysis of terrorism includes three primary motivating factors: (1) right-wing extremism; (2) left-wing extremism, nationalistic terrorism, and single-issue violence; and (3) international terrorism.

Smith's research reveals several important findings. American terrorism grew increasingly to a high level about 1985, just at the time the government was improving its counterterrorist tactics. Better government efficiency led to a series of arrests that decimated terrorist groups by the late 1980s. Right-wing groups attempted to reemerge, but the left-wing groups did not. Left-wing terrorism remained a viable entity, however, because left-wing extremists were typically more loyal to their cause than were their right-wing counterparts. The left-wing groups also remained supported by Puerto Rican nationalists and single-issue groups such as ecological terrorists. In fact, Smith believes ecological terrorists have a great potential for violence in the future.

Although many analysts have tried to profile terrorists, Smith takes two methodological steps that give a better picture of American terrorists. He does this by listing the characteristics of domestic terrorists, and comparing left-wing and right-wing extremists. His findings indicate that American terrorists differ from their international counterparts. Native-born terrorists tend to be older than international terrorists, and foreign operatives working in the United States follow that trend. Many domestic terrorists are over thirty, whereas international terrorists in the United States tend to be older than the young extremists in other parts of the world. Terrorism is a fairly infrequent crime and most often handled as a normative violation of criminal law. Smith says it is difficult to conduct research on domestic terrorism because the database is so small. Although ideological groups differ in their beliefs, Smith notes that both those on the left and the right tend to fund themselves through armed robberies.

Although both extremes seem to be committed to armed robbery, the left and right actually differ quite a bit. Smith compares left- and right-wing terrorists in five categories: (1) ideology and beliefs about human nature,

(2) economic views, (3) geographic bases of support, (4) tactics, and (5) selection of targets. Left-wing terrorists favor Marxism, target the economic status quo, base themselves in urban environments, and select symbolic targets of capitalism. Right-wing terrorists are vehemently anti-Marxist and very religious. In addition, they support the economic system without supporting the distribution of wealth, base themselves in rural areas, and focus attacks on symbols of governmental authority. Although their ideology differs, both groups use similar terrorist tactics.

Smith offers several ideas for further examination. For example, he says left-wing terrorists were more active in the 1980s than right-wing terrorists. Official data demonstrate this is true, but possibly this is due to the way official data are reported. For example, many right-wing terrorist activities are simply reported as regular crimes. Would the levels of activity be the same if the FBI counted all possible terrorist incidents as terrorist activities?

In another comparison, Smith says left-wing groups tend to follow the Marighella model of revolution, whereas right-wing groups stay in fortresses in rural areas. Again, the data demonstrate this is correct. Is this a difference in philosophy or geography? Right-wing groups frequently barricade themselves, but other activities like Louis Beam's "leaderless resistance" (discussed in the last section of this chapter) are straight from Carlos Marighella. Perhaps the fortress mentality of right-wing groups is primarily due to geographic factors, particularly their favoring of rural locations.

Asking such questions does not detract from Smith's work or the validity of his conclusions. The data he used, and his historical analysis, demonstrate his conclusions time and time again. His internal logic gives his criminological conclusions validity. If you teach yourself to question the way data are reported, however, you will begin to approach the study of terrorism on a critical level. When reading a criminological study, always ask, how did the data affect the findings?

In terms of the extremist right, Smith traces the resurgence of right-wing terrorism in the 1980s. He believes the right-wing groups began the decade on a high note, but they fell apart by 1984. They formed several organizations to try to rejuvenate the movement. Smith believes they failed. Some of their more recent activities are discussed fully in the last segment of this chapter.

Smith says left-wing terrorists have undergone no major transformation, remaining essentially the same from the 1960s to the present. Several protest groups began conglomerating around the Students for a Democratic Society (SDS) in 1967, and by the end of the decade, some of them had become violent revolutionaries. By 1970, left-wing groups began acting in concert and frequently joined with Puerto Rican nationalists. When the Macheteros, a violent Puerto Rican nationalist group, emerged in 1979, they soon found allies among violent leftists. Smith says left-wing groups tended to act in a coordinated fashion, and evidence indicated they were linked internally. He also says Puerto Rican terrorists were supported by Cuba. Smith's research confirms earlier findings of analysts such as James Stinson (1984).

According to Smith, the May 19 Communist Organization (M19CO) was one of the more recent successful left-wing terrorist groups. Emerging from elements of the SDS, Black Panther Party, and Student Non-Violent Coordinating Committee, the M19CO united several violent leftists under a common umbrella. The group formed in 1977, taking its name from the birthdays of Ho Chi Minh (a North Vietnamese Communist leader) and American Muslim leader Malcolm X. The M19CO was racially mixed, and approximately half of the terrorists were women. A few months after its formation, members of the group launched a campaign to free "political" prisoners and attack capitalism.

The M19CO was most active from 1980 to 1984. They conducted several robberies, planted bombs at military installations and private businesses, and murdered some of their victims. They attracted members of many other left-wing groups, and Smith found that they spawned temporary splinter groups under a variety of names. Their most infamous activity occurred in 1981, when M19CO members robbed an armored car, killing a guard and wounding another, and then murdered two New York police officers who were deployed at a road block.

In 1984, the group's luck began to run out. Several members were indicted for a myriad of crimes, while others were on the run. Smith points out that some members were incarcerated on simple charges to give the government time to investigate more serious offenses. He does not mention the success of the Joint Terrorism Task Force managed by the FBI, the New York City Police Department, and the New York State Police, since this was beyond the scope of his analysis. (The Task Force not only proved successful against the M19CO, but also demonstrated its worth again in the successful investigation and prosecution of the World Trade Center bombing.) By 1989, all members of the M19CO were either in prison or hiding.

Another left-wing group operating in the recent past was the United Freedom Front (UFF). Like the M19CO, the UFF was composed mainly of anti-Vietnam War activists and protesters. Although not as active as the M19CO, the UFF became infamous for its ability to bomb American businesses. Members of the UFF and its clone group, the Armed Resistance Unit, were captured and jailed after the murder of a New Jersey state trooper. Despite their attempted activities, left-wing terrorists virtually disappeared after 1990.

Puerto Rican nationalist terrorism emerged from a different context, despite its links with left-wing revolutionaries from 1972 to 1980. Smith demonstrates that Puerto Rican groups were able to continue operating, despite the decline in left-wing terrorism. The Armed Forces of National Liberation (FALN) began operating in the United States after 1945, and they were joined by other Puerto Rican terrorists in following decades. One of the most notorious groups is the Macheteros. Other groups include the Volunteers for the Puerto Rican Revolution (OVRP), the Armed Forces of Liberation (FARP), the Guerrilla Forces of Liberation (GEL), and the Pedro Albizu

Campos Revolutionary Forces (PACRF). Before the decline of the left, Puerto Rican terrorists routinely joined left-wing operations.

Smith states the Puerto Rican groups were the only domestic terrorists with strong international links in the 1980s. (Data in the next section suggest that Middle Eastern groups developed the same links in the next decade.) Smith believes Puerto Rican revolutionary support comes primarily from Cuba, and many members are in hiding there. Aside from carrying out the largest armored car robbery in the United States, Puerto Rican groups have conducted several bombings, assassinations, and even a rocket attack against FBI headquarters in San Juan. They have selectively murdered U.S. citizens, especially targeting U.S. military personnel stationed in Puerto Rico.

Since the fall of the Soviet Union, Puerto Rican terrorists have been less active, but their infrastructure remains intact. Ronald Fernandez (1987) explicates the reasons for Puerto Rican nationalist terrorism in the United States. Puerto Rico was colonized by the Spanish shortly after the European discovery of America, and the Spanish ruled the island for nearly three centuries. This changed in 1898, when the United States captured Puerto Rico in the Spanish-American War.

At first, the Puerto Ricans welcomed the United States as liberators, believing they were going to be granted independence, but they were disappointed. Instead of freeing the island, the United States granted Puerto Rico commonwealth status. Its special relationship to the United States grew with the increasing military importance of the island. Currently, the population is divided by three opinions. Some desire Puerto Rican statehood. Others want to create an independent country, and some of these people favor a Marxist government. A third constituency wants to maintain commonwealth status. This leaves the United States with a paradox: No matter which group is satisfied, two other groups will be disappointed.

According to Fernandez, terrorism has become one means of revolution. To return to Smith's analysis, although it is safe to assume that left-wing groups have fallen from the limelight, the problem of Puerto Rican violence will not simply evaporate. Law enforcement officers must continue to respond to Puerto Rican terrorism, but at some point, American policymakers need to resolve the status of Puerto Rico to the satisfaction of its people. This task will not be easy.

In Smith's analysis, ecological terrorists represent a similar problem. In the past few years, ecological terrorists have manifested their movement in two areas. First, some groups have focused on land-use issues, attacking developers and loggers. Smith points to one such group, the Evan Mecham Eco-Terrorist International Conspiracy (EMETIC), tracing their campaign of violence in the name of the environment. A second type of group, illustrated by the Animal Liberation Front, protests the use of animals in human experiments. Both ecological groups mirror the characteristics of left-wing terrorists, and members are fanatically dedicated to their cause. Smith believes they may lead domestic terrorist activities in the twenty-first century.

Smith also focuses on international terrorism in the United States, arguing that since 1985, the United States has experienced foreign terrorism as surrogate warfare. Although this issue is fully discussed in the next section, Smith raises an interesting point about American policy. When terrorists attack the United States, law enforcement agencies frequently need the help of the military and intelligence communities. This creates the possibility that military forces will be used to fight political crimes by using American law, raising serious questions of Constitutional authority.

In addition, in response to international terrorism, the United States has given its law enforcement agents the power to arrest terrorists on foreign soil. Smith believes this met with measured success, but its weakness was uncovered in 1993 when the World Trade Center was bombed. Although we have carried the war to foreign soil with the criminal justice system, Smith concludes, the war has been carried back to us. This exemplifies the policy question discussed in the previous paragraph. Critics ask: If international terrorism is a form of war, why is the United States fighting it with the criminal justice system? This issue is discussed in Chapter 17.

Smith's work concludes with a criminological analysis of domestic terrorism. Laws on American terrorism are exceptionally vague, and international terrorists tend to plead guilty more frequently than right-wing and left-wing terrorists. Left-wing terrorists fare the best in court, whereas few right-wing cases are dismissed. Smith says there are insufficient data to determine whether sentences differ. Although the public may perceive terrorists are not punished harshly enough, limited data indicate terrorists receive substantially longer sentences than traditional criminals. Finally, terrorism is a matter of attitude. Smith believes a person is not a terrorist until the government applies the label. That label can have long-term effects.

EMERSON: JIHAD
IN THE UNITED STATES

Brent Smith's research covers foreign terrorism in the United States, but another controversial report on terrorist infrastructures in the United States needs to be examined. Steven Emerson, a network news correspondent who has spent several years covering the Middle East, produced a PBS program entitled *Jihad in America* in 1994. Previously, he also analyzed Iraqi attempts to target the United States with terrorist actions (Emerson & Del Sesto, 1991).

Although domestic terrorism has been an eclectic conglomeration of criminals and ideologues, the situation may change if Steven Emerson is correct. In the Middle East, the United States has been closely identified with Israel and former European imperial policies. This link has prompted attacks on Americans throughout the world, but radical Muslims have longed to carry their attacks to American soil. They have been unable to do so, however, because of the tremendous amount of logistical support required to strike across the Atlantic Ocean from the Middle East. Emerson suggests this may no longer be a problem. According to his research, Middle Eastern terrorist groups have established infrastructures in the United States, infrastructures that allow them to support terrorism on American soil.

Emerson outlines the beginning of the process in a work with Cristina Del Sesto. According to their research, Saddam Hussein backed a terrorist organization in Baghdad that existed primarily to attack American and European interests. The organization developed in 1984, when Abu Ibrahim broke with Abu Nidal and began working directly for Saddam Hussein. Abu Ibrahim's trademark was a unique luggage bomb. Produced in a special assembly plant in Baghdad, the bombs were composed of plastic explosive shaped within the liner of carry-on luggage. Abu Ibrahim sent agents out with the purpose of downing American passenger airplanes.

Eventually named the Hawari Association, Abu Ibrahim's organization folded under pressure from the U.S. Department of State. In 1986, American officials forced Saddam Hussein to officially end his association with Abu Ibrahim after several bombings and attempted bombings. Saddam Hussein agreed, but he maintained contact through the Hawari Association's new commander, Abdullah Labin. The U.S. Department of State was under orders not to object, because the United States favored Iraq in the Iran-Iraq War. When Saddam Hussein became the official enemy of the United States in the Persian Gulf War, Emerson says he did so with a terrorist infrastructure designed to attack the United States.

Still, the Hawari Association was based in the Middle East. Like other terrorist groups in the area, it lacked the ability to strike the American mainland—until 1988. Emerson believes groups of Islamic terrorists began building networks within the United States in the late 1980s, and they did so, indirectly, with American help. To understand this irony, we need to briefly recall events in 1979.

American President Jimmy Carter faced serious Middle Eastern problems in the last year of his presidency. American hostages were being held in Tehran, the capital of Iran, after the Ayatollah Khomeini had taken power. There were strong American sentiments favoring some form of military action. In addition, the Soviet Union invaded Afghanistan during the same year, attempting to install a puppet government in Kabul, the capital of Afghanistan. Resistance fighters flocked to an Afghan guerrilla movement, and President Carter—and later President Ronald Reagan—offered American support to the guerrillas. They were known as the Afghan Mujahadin, and very few Americans knew for what they stood. Most Americans simply assumed they were anti-Soviet guerrillas.

The Central Intelligence Agency, with the endorsement of most Americans and both political parties, sent millions of dollars to the Mujahadin through Pakistan. The CIA trained and outfitted guerrilla units, taught them how to use weapons (including handheld Stinger antiaircraft missiles), and in some cases even planned operations with them. As one CIA analyst says in Emerson's television program, "it was done because they were fighting the Soviet Union."

When the Soviets left in 1989, the Mujahadin felt they were victorious. They believed pure Islam had triumphed over the godless infidel. In the thrill of victory, the Mujahadin began searching for more infidels. Unfortunately, the United States, a country that had supplied, trained, and welcomed Mujahadin leaders and supporters in its homeland, found itself as the primary target.

Emerson claims the Mujahadin's Holy War against the former Soviet Union turned into an international campaign against Israel, its supporters, and moderate Muslims. For the first time, Islamic radicals had bases in the United States, and Emerson linked the 1993 World Trade Center bombing to the domestic terrorist networks. This infrastructure developed late in the Afghan rebellion, when Mujahadin leaders traveled the United States to gather support against the Soviet invaders. When the Soviets retreated in 1989, those American support networks remained intact. All the American weapons in the hands of the Mujahadin, including Stinger missiles, could be turned on new enemies. Ironically, as we helped the Mujahadin in the 1980s, the United States did not realize that Americans would become the next target.

Former Associate Deputy FBI Director Oliver B. (Buck) Revell, interviewed on Emerson's PBS program, agrees with Emerson's assessment. Revell states that once the Mujahadin and their associates came to the United States, they found a hospitable environment. They could raise money, film videos, run printing presses, and eventually attack the very country whose freedom they enjoyed. Revell says that for the first time in American history, the United States housed a terrorist infrastructure that stretched from the American heartland all the way through the Middle East to Southeast Asia. Revell states it is the most global network of terrorists the United States has ever faced.

Emerson credits Abdullah Azzam for completing the most important infrastructure. Born in Palestine, Azzam left his homeland to join the Mujahadin in the early 1980s. Centering his activities in Pakistan, Azzam soon came to understand the vast amount of support the United States was funneling through the area. Leaving Pakistan, he helped establish the Alkifah Refugee Center in New York. According to Emerson, American officials did not realize the Alkifah Refugee Center was the front for another organization, an organization calling for jihad. In fact, the Alkifah Refugee Center's Arabic letterhead called for holy war.

In 1989, with the Soviets in disarray and their political system on the verge of collapse, Azzam turned his attention to the United States. According to Emerson, Azzam spread his jihad network through 38 states, with multiple bases in Pennsylvania, Michigan, California, Texas, and the New England states. Azzam returned to Pakistan in 1989, only to be killed by an assassin, but his work was completed by several supporters, including his cousin Fayiz Azzam.

Emerson names several prominent officials working in various radical groups in the domestic jihad. Tamim al-Adnani is the most vigorous recruiter and successful fundraiser among all the leaders. Emerson says Tamin al-Adnani has assisted in domestic terrorist incidents, including the World Trade Center bombing. Fayiz Azzam, Abdullah Azzam's cousin, gives rhetorical speeches calling for blood and holy war. Elsayyid Nossair, who was charged with the murder of militant Rabbi Kahane and convicted of lesser offenses, maintained a clearinghouse for terrorist literature before his arrest. Even in prison, Emerson says, Nossair helped plan the World Trade Center bombing.

Emerson says, the most important holy warrior operating in the United States was Sheik Omar Abdul Rahman. Before being charged with acts of terrorism in the United States, Rahman had been expelled from Egypt for conspiracy in the 1981 assassination of Egyptian President Anwar Sadat. Moving to New York City, members of Rahman's group helped plan the assassination of Rabbi Kahane, while recruiting terrorists for a holy war against the United States. Emerson's PBS program caught Rahman in Detroit in 1991 calling for conquest of the infidel's land. Rahman has since been indicted for acts of terrorism, including complicity in the World Trade Center bombing. Emerson states that Sheik Abdul Wali Zindani has taken Rahman's place, and Zindani has been involved in assassinations and bombings around the world.

Emerson also says well-known terrorist groups have established bases in the United States. He claims the Islamic Association for Palestine (IAP) is Hamas's chief propaganda arm in the United States. Under the name Asqa Vision, the IAP produces many films, including military training videos. Based in Richardson, Texas, the IAP is one of several organizations with links to Hamas. Islamic Jihad has a base in Tampa, Florida. Hizbollah also has a network in the United States.

Emerson claims to have found over 30 radical Middle Eastern groups in the United States, adding that the FBI has confirmed that terrorist groups have command centers in California, Nevada, Texas, Florida, Illinois, and New Jersey. Buck Revell says the intention of these groups is to harm the United States and keep it from being able to take international action.

Emerson's critics claim he has overemphasized the threat and has unfairly targeted Muslims. Brent Smith's research reveals most foreign terrorism in the United States only represents potential violence, and very little has come to fruition. Yet, Emerson feels future acts of domestic terrorism are inevitable. He sees the growth of Middle Eastern terrorist group infrastructures as one of the greatest challenges to the American criminal justice system.

ABORTION CLINIC BOMBINGS
AND TERRORISM

During the 1980s, the United States witnessed almost 40 bombings of abortion clinics in various states, and the 1990s brought new trends. Individual workers were attacked, arsons and bombings increased, and in a few incidents, militant religious fanatics murdered abortion clinic workers.

There is no easy resolution to the abortion debate, as proponents of each side believe they are morally correct. The side favoring the right to choose an abortion feels it is defending Constitutional rights. Those against abortion often believe they are following God's will. No matter which side dominates, the other side may react violently. The abortion debate represents a political issue in which the positions have been identified by militant extremes. As such, it is a perfect example of terrorism.

David Nice (1988) attempts to produce a theory of violence by examining trends in abortion clinic bombings. He states the literature reveals several explanations for violent political behavior. One theory suggests social controls break down under stress and urbanization. Another theory says violence increases when people are not satisfied with political outcomes. Violence can also be reinforced by social and cultural values. Finally, violence can stem from a group's strength or weakness, its lack of faith in the political system, or its frustration with economic conditions.

Nice matches trends in abortion clinic bombings against these theories of violence. By examining 30 bombings from 1982 to 1985, he finds some patterns. First, bombings tended to be regionalized. Along with two in Washington, D.C., the bombings occurred in eight states, only three of which had more than four bombings. Nice compares the social factors in the detonation areas with the theories about violence.

Nice concludes that abortion clinic bombings are related to several social factors. Most of the bombings occurred in areas of rapidly expanding population and declining social controls. This means bombings tended to occur in urban areas. The slowest-growing states in the United States did not experience bombings, whereas half of the fastest-growing states did.

Bombings also reflected a method of communicating frustration with political processes and outcomes. Bombing is a means of taking direct action. Nice notes most bombings took place where the rate of abortions to live deliveries is relatively high. Abortion bombers feel compelled to action by social and political circumstances. They believe they are making a positive impact on the political situation. Nice also notes bombings predictably occur more frequently in states that have a highly active militant antiabortion constituency.

States that experience bombings also exhibit a greater toleration for crimes against women. Clinic bombings are highest in areas where cultural and social violence against women is more acceptable. States that have passed laws against domestic violence experience fewer bombings than states with no such laws.

Bombings are also a sign of weakness. Although seemingly paradoxical, areas that have strong concentrations of antiabortion sentiment do not experience as much bombing when such sentiment is not accompanied by activism. In addition, Nice says that when high populations of Roman Catholics, Baptists, or Mormons are present, bombings decline. When potential bombers feel outnumbered, however, they may take action because they feel weak.

In summary, Nice found abortion clinic bombings were positively correlated with every theory of violence, except the theory of economic deprivation. There was no relation between abortion clinic bombings and economic conditions. Nice concludes antiabortion violence appears in areas of rapid population growth where the abortion rate is high. As social controls decrease and desires to substitute political controls increase, bombings develop into a form of political action.

KEY CONCEPTS

1. Domestic terrorism has been hard to conceptualize, because the United States has had limited exposure to modern terrorism.

2. Works by Bell, Gurr, and Cooper indicate that the United States has had a violent past, but the experience has not been described as terrorism. Gurr's classification system includes vigilante, insurgent, and transnational terrorism.

3. Brent Smith's work demonstrates that American terrorism followed the pattern of international terrorism on a smaller scale. It is probably the single best criminological analysis of domestic terrorism.

4. Steven Emerson argues that the United States is plagued by an infrastructure of Middle Eastern terrorist groups, including Hamas, Islamic Jihad, and Hizbollah.

5. Antiabortion clinic terrorism is increasing. It appears in the form of bombings, arson, threatened biological attacks, and murders of doctors, nurses, and caseworkers.

FOOD FOR THOUGHT

Terrorism is changing. Groups and infrastructures are disappearing, and violent religious zealots and ideological fanatics are replacing them. Theodore Kaczynski, the so-called Unabomber, conducted a campaign of individual political murders and attacks from 1978 to his arrest in 1996. In June 1993, he voiced ecological and anarchist views, and in September 1995, the *New York Times* and *Washington Post* jointly published his political manifesto. Was Kaczynski a terrorist or a serial killer? Do you think there is a difference between the two? If you were part of the investigative team, would you handle the Unabomber investigation differently than any other bombing or arson? If you defined the Unabomber as a terrorist, what impact does that have on the investigation?

FURTHER READING

Brent Smith, *Terrorism in America: Pipe Bombs and Pipe Dreams*

14

Violent Extremism
in the United States

When international terrorism resurfaced in the antigovernment and anticolonial movements of the post–World War II era, most Americans believed terrorism was something that happened in other places. Even when left-wing terrorists bombed college campuses and murdered police officers, both the American public and law enforcement agencies handled such events as regular crimes. This attitude gradually began to shift in the late 1980s, as homegrown extremists copied the tactics of foreign terrorist groups. At the dawn of the new century, American law enforcement also came to the realization that violent criminal extremism is a form of terrorism.

After reading this chapter, you should be able to:

1. Outline the history of right-wing extremism in the United States.
2. Describe the philosophy of current right-wing extremist thought.
3. Describe the importance of *The Turner Diaries* and *Hunter.*
4. Summarize the tactics used in right-wing extremist crime.
5. Describe the ideology of radical ecologists and animal rights extremists.
6. Summarize the theology of Black Hebrew Israelism.

A BRIEF HISTORY OF RIGHT-WING
EXTREMISM IN THE UNITED STATES

On the morning of April 19, 1995, television and radio special-news reports indicated there had been some type of explosion in Oklahoma City. Within minutes, reports claimed an explosion had occurred in or near the federal building. These reports were quickly amended, and finally, the news told of a large bomb. Reports of the size and capacity of damage increased with each passing moment, and by noon it was apparent that the United States had suffered a devastating terrorist attack.

As scenes of crippled children, dead bodies, and smoldering wreckage dominated the nation's television screens, attention turned toward the Middle East. Conventional wisdom placed blame for the incident on some militant Islamic sect. Many Arab Americans were harassed, and some were openly attacked. The country was shocked when a crew-cut, young white male was arrested for the bombing. It was hard to believe that the United States had produced terrorists from its own heartland.

Although many people were shocked, even a cursory history of right-wing extremism in the United States reveals that extremist ideology and violent political behavior is nothing new (White, 2001). The first incident of antifederal behavior came shortly after the Revolutionary War (1775–1784). In 1791, the federal government levied an excise tax on the production of whiskey. Farmers in western Pennsylvania, a top whiskey-producing area in the country, were incensed. The unpopular tax provoked riots and created general disorder. In October 1794, President George Washington mobilized the National Guard of several states and sent the troops to Pennsylvania. The "rebellion" quickly ended, but not the resentment against the federal government.

Antifederal attitudes were common in some circles in the early 1800s. The so-called "Know-Nothings" operated in the eastern United States prior to the Civil War (1861–1865). Organizing under such names as the Order of the Sons of America and the Sons of the Star Spangled Banner, these groups were anti-Catholic, anti-Irish, and anti-immigration. They felt Catholic immigrants were destroying American democracy. When confronted by authority, party members would claim to "know nothing." Their name evolved from this response.

Although the American Civil War had many causes—slavery, farming versus industry, and sectionalism—one of the greatest causes for war was the power of the federal government. Southerners questioned the legitimacy of the federal government, and they believed Congress was taking the powers reserved for the states. Most Southerners were not fighting to preserve slavery; they were fighting to keep the power of local governments. When the Confederacy was defeated in 1865, the issue did not die.

Agrarian failures and depressions spawned radical economic theories and responses in the 1870s and 1880s. These rural movements were complemented by labor violence and the introduction of anarchism from the left (see Chapter 5). Businesses and local and state governments frequently repressed both left-wing and right-wing versions of extremism. After the turn of the century, though, mainstream Americans came to believe that the left posed a greater threat to democracy. This attitude increased after 1919, when a wave of left-wing terrorism swept the country. As a result, right-wing extremist organizations grew. They not only popularized extremist views, but they also claimed judges, elected officials, and police officers in their ranks. Right-wing extremists also turned to an organization that had been created in the wake of the Civil War, the Ku Klux Klan (KKK).

The Ku Klux Klan had been the brainchild of Confederate cavalry genius General Nathan Bedford Forrest. Bedford Forrest had intended to create an antiunionist organization that would preserve Southern culture and traditions. When the newly formed KKK began terrorizing freed slaves, Forrest attempted to disband the organization. It was too late, and the KKK began a campaign of hate. It had nearly died out by the early twentieth century, but it revived in the extremist atmosphere following World War I (1914–1918).

It is best to think of the Klan in terms of history. The KKK has operated in three distinct phases. Shortly after the Civil War, "knight riders," hooded night riders, terrorized African-Americans to frighten them into political and social submission. This aspect of the Klan faded by the end of the century, and the second phase of the Klan came in the 1920s, as it sought political legitimacy. During this period, the KKK became popular, political, and respectable. It collapsed in the wake of a criminal scandal. The modern KKK grew after World War II (1939–1945), becoming, up to the present day, fragmented, decentralized, and dominated by hate-filled rhetoric.

The development of the modern Klan parallels the growth of right-wing extremism from the 1930s to the present. After the popularized Klan was rocked by political scandal, right-wing extremism emerged in the midst of the Depression (1929–1939). It was characterized by fundamentalist interpretations of religion, radical patriotism, and a belief that economic woes were the result of a worldwide conspiracy of international bankers. The right-wing believed banking was controlled by Jews.

Michael Barkun (1997) describes the growth of extremism from a religious view. Barkun says that a new religion, Christian Identity, grew from the extremist perspective. Starting with a concept called Anglo-Israelism or British Israelism, American right-wing extremists saw white Americans as the representatives of the lost tribes of Israel. Wesley Swift preached this message in a radio ministry from California beginning in the late 1940s. Two of his disciples were William Potter Gale and Richard Butler. Gale went on to form several right-wing associations, including Posse Comitatus. Butler retired from an engineering career, moved to Idaho, and formed the Aryan Nations. Gale and Butler preached Swift's message of Christian Identity.

Barkun points out that Christian Identity helped to provide the basis for violence among the extremists. Prior to the Christian Identity movement, American extremism was characterized by ethnocentrism and localized violence. Christian Identity gave a new twist to the extremist movement. Barkun says that it was used to demonize the Jews (see Chapter 4). Christian Identity provided a theological base for stating that white people originated with God and Jews came from the Devil. Such eschatological presumptions are deadly.

MODERN RIGHT-WING RESURGENCE

The appearance of modern right-wing extremism came to fruition around 1984, and has remained active since that time. According to my research (White, 2000), several issues hold the movement together. First, the right-wing tends to follow one of the forms of extremist religions. The name of God is universally invoked, even by leaders who disavow theism (a belief in God). Second, the movement is dominated by a belief in conspiracy. Followers feel they are losing economic status because sinister forces are conspiring to swindle them out of the American dream. The primary conspiratorial force was Communism, but after the fall of the Soviet Union, it became the United Nations. The extremist right believes a conspiracy of Jewish bankers works with the United Nations to create a New World Order. Finally, right-wing extremism continues to embrace patriotism and guns. They want to arm themselves for a holy war.

In his popular historical work *Dreadnought: Britain, Germany and the Coming of the Great War,* Robert K. Massie (1991) points to the hysteria in Great Britain and Germany during the naval race before World War I. Both the British and the Germans demonized one another, and their national rivalries often gave way to irrational fears. In one of the more notable British reactions, the fear of German naval power gave rise to a particular genre (or style) of popular literature. Massie states these stories had a similar theme. Secret German agents would always land in the United Kingdom and destroy the British Empire through some type of subversive plot. Whether poisoning the water supply, destroying the schools, or infiltrating the economic system, the fictional Germans never attacked directly. They were mystically secretive, and they were everywhere.

The actions of right-wing extremists fit Massie's description of the hysterical fears in Britain. Extremists believe alien forces are conspiring to destroy the United States. Bill Stanton (1991) says that in 1978, the Ku Klux Klan led the way into the modern era when it emerged in Georgia and North Carolina as a paramilitary organization. Within a decade, many members of the extremist right had followed suit. Not only were they willing to accept conspiracy theories, but they were also ready to fight the hordes who would destroy the American way of life.

Brent Smith (1994) paints a realistic picture of right-wing extremism, arguing that terrorism from the right wing is fairly limited. Groups are rural and tend to emerge from farm-based compounds. For example, Posse Comitatus formed as a tax protest group and engaged in violent resistance to local law enforcement. The most celebrated case dealt with Gordon Kahl, who killed three law enforcement officers in North Dakota and Arkansas before being killed in a shoot-out. Another group, the Order, was a militant offshoot of the white supremacy movement. By 1987, however, the Order was defunct, and the right wing was fading.

Even while this was happening, most right-wing criminal activities were not labeled as terrorism, and even though the celebrated cases of violent right-wing extremism faded in 1987, the ideology that spawned them did not. So-called "hate crimes" increased, creating concern among criminal justice researchers (Hamm, 1994). Membership in extremist groups grew after their apparent collapse in 1987, and by 1994, the extremists were back in business. A look at the structure of the right-wing movement explains why.

According to Allan Sapp (1985), the right-wing movement had evolved into three distinctive trends by 1984. The first trend involved the white supremacy movement. The groups involved the four main branches of the Ku Klux Klan, neo-Nazis, and a relatively new group called the Aryan Nations. Sapp and other researchers (Holden, 1985; Wiggins, 1985; Coates, 1987) believe the Idaho-based Aryan Nations hold the key to the unification of the white supremacy movement. Richard Butler, leader of the Aryan Nations, interacts with the leaders of several white supremacy movements and holds an Aryan Congress each year to draw the white supremacists together. White supremacy did not disappear with the elimination of the Order.

Sapp says the second trend in extremism is survivalism. Survivalists withdraw from society, forming compounds in rural areas. Irwin Suall and David Lowe (1987) describe these groups as hybrids, combinations of old supremacy groups and more sophisticated modern hate groups. These groups typically establish themselves on a communal basis, rallying around a strong leader. Secluding themselves in armed compounds, they wait for the eventual collapse of government. The existence and philosophy of these groups are critically important to the change in right-wing extremism in the 1990s.

The final category in Sapp's typology deals with religion. Many right-wing extremists follow a religion called Christian Identity. Deriving their ideas from a nineteenth century concept called Anglo-Israelism, Christian Identity followers believe that white Europe is composed of the lost tribes of Israel. The Hebrew Bible is nothing more than the story of the struggle between white Israelites and Satanic Jews. (Jews are said to have come from an illicit sexual union between Eve and the Devil.) White Europeans were chosen by God to lead the Aryan Nations. Denying the basic tenets of Christian love, Christian Identity is an ideal religion for the extremist right.

Although such theories make sense to the extremists, they are so radical that few thinking people would follow them. As a result, Brent Smith demonstrates that extremist right-wing groups were waning by 1987. Richard Butler tried to compensate for declining numbers by inviting Skinhead youths to the Aryan Nations Congress in Hayden Lake, to little avail. True believers remained loyal to the cause, but they were few and far between.

Things changed about 1991. Three issues rejuvenated the extremist right (Stern, 1996). First, the Brady Bill (named for President Reagan's Press Secretary James Brady, who was disabled in an assassination attempt) caused many conservatives to fear federal-gun control legislation. The extremist right played to those fears, toning down issues like white supremacy and Christian Identity, and claiming the intrusive federal government was out to destroy gun ownership. Extremists felt they had an issue that appealed to mainstream conservatives. By stressing the fear of gun control, right-wing extremists hoped to appear to be mainstream.

The second issue dealt with a botched U.S. Marshal's attempt to arrest Randy Weaver on a bench warrant in the mountains of Idaho. A white supremacist and adherent of Christian Identity, Weaver was charged with selling illegal firearms to undercover agents from the Bureau of Alcohol, Tobacco, and Firearms (ATF). Weaver was arrested and released on bail. He refused to appear for the assigned court date, and U.S. Marshals attempted to bring him in. Tragically, United States Marshal William Degan and Weaver's young son, Sammy, were killed in the ensuing shoot-out. The FBI responded by laying siege to Weaver's Ruby Ridge mountain cabin. In the following days, an FBI sniper shot and killed Weaver's pregnant wife before his surrender (Walter, 1995).

The Ruby Ridge incident had a strong symbolic impact on the extremist right. According to Stern, Bo Gritz, a leading extremist figure, drew national attention to the siege when he came to negotiate a surrender. Gritz is an articulate, charismatic individual who retired as a colonel from the U.S. Army Special Forces, and his voice and opinions carry far beyond the extremist right. He left Ruby Ridge saluting Skinhead demonstrators and calling for the formation of special resistance forces (SPIKE groups) to prevent further standoffs (Walter, 1995).

Closely related to Ruby Ridge, in the minds of the extremist right, was a third event: the federal siege of the Branch Davidian compound near Waco, Texas. In 1993, ATF agents attempted to serve a search warrant on the compound, but they were met with a hail of gunfire. Four agents were killed, and several were wounded. After a three-month siege, FBI agents moved in with tear gas. Unknown to the agents, the compound was laced with gasoline. When the FBI moved in, the Branch Davidians burned their fortress, killing over 70 people, including several young children held inside the compound.

Stern says the Waco siege also became a symbol for the extremist right, even though it had very little to do with the right-wing movement. An ATF report (1994) said that in reality, the Waco siege involved a group of people led by a demitted Seventh Day Adventist, Vernon Wayne Howell. Taking advantage of the weak and distraught, Howell changed his name to David Koresh and established the Branch Davidian compound outside Waco. According to the ATF, Howell gathered illegal weapons and committed a variety of unlawful activities. Howell ruled his flock with messianic illusions, claiming that the end was near and he would save the world. In the end, he simply murdered his followers rather than admit his messianic failings, but he set the stage to be embraced by the extremist right. Although he had nothing to do with right-wing extremists per se, he had the right formula: guns, a survivalist compound, and a belief in a Warrior God.

If Stern is correct, the Brady Bill, Ruby Ridge, and Waco gave new life to the fading right-wing movement, and a shift in the religious orientation of the extremist right helped to rejuvenate their ranks (see Figure 14.1). Although many American Protestants would agree that the United States was the new chosen land, perhaps even a new Israel, few could stomach the blasphemy and hatred of Christian Identity. In the 1990s, however, the religious message changed.

Christianity underwent strange transformations in the hate movement (White, 1996, 2001). Some extremists adopted Norse mythology. Following Erich Luddendorff, a German general from World War I, extremists began preaching Nordic Christianity. Using ancient Norse rites, they claimed to worship the Triune Christian Deity, but they added Odin (Wotan) and Thor. Odin, the chief of the Norse gods, called Nordic warriors to racial purification from Valhalla, Viking heaven. Thor, the god of thunder, sounded the call with a hammer that shook the heavens. Popular with German Nazis before World War II, Nordic Christianity surfaced in Michigan, Wisconsin, Montana, and Idaho in the 1990s.

In another religious derivation, Creatorism rejects Judaism and Christianity altogether. Creatorists claim the Creator left humanity on its own, and each race must fend for itself. Embracing the urban Skinheads, Creatorists call for RAHOWA (Racial Holy War). They produce racially oriented comic books designed to appeal to alienated white youth. They also publish *The White Man's Bible.* Creatorists argue that an intervening, loving God is nothing more than an idle lie. White people have been left on their own by a deistic Creator, and they are expected to fight for their survival. Essentially, Creatorism is a Skinhead religion with more violent tendencies than Christian Identity.

If extremists were trying to achieve the mainstream political acceptance through issues like gun control, taxation, and the New World Order, however, they could not appeal to Odin. The majority of right-wing extremists retreated to more conservative churches and relied on individual interpretations of frontier theology to justify antigovernment actions. This group can loosely be described as "Free Wheeling Fundamentalists."

Unlike the hate religions, the free wheeling fundamentalists do not believe the American government is part of a Satanic conspiracy. They do believe, however, that the federal government and local governments are their enemies and that God will assist them in their confrontation with evil. Employing antifederalist rhetoric, they boost their call to revolution with appeals to frontier-style Christianity. They call on a personal God—a self-defined concept of divinity usually not recognizable in the Hebrew, Muslim, or Christian scriptures. By 1995, this movement became very popular in the rural West and Midwest, and it has set the stage for right-wing extremism into this century.

Militias thrive on conspiracy theories. Stern says they believe the United States government is leading the country into a single world government controlled by the United Nations. Stern claims the militias believe the New World Order is a continuation of a conspiracy outlined in *The Protocols of Zion,* a book written after World War I, claiming that Jews are out to control the world. The militias play on conspiracy, fear of government, racism, antiabortion rhetoric, and anti-Semitic fears. In Stern's analysis, Bo Gritz, John Trochmann, and the

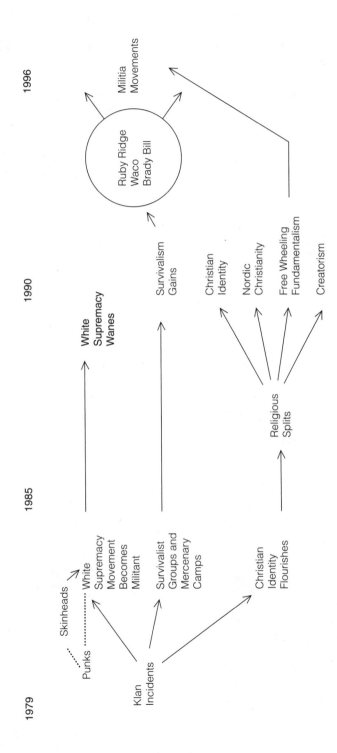

FIGURE 14.1 American Right-wing Terrorism, 1979–1996

white supremacy leaders are one and the same. Stern links the militia movement to Christian Identity.

Research conducted by the Strategic Intelligence Division of the Bureau of Alcohol, Tobacco, and Firearms (1995) suggests the militia movement is far from monolithic. ATF analysts believe militias tend to be issue oriented. Groups gather around taxes, abortion, gun control, and/or Christian Identity. My own research (White, 1995, 1996) reflects the ATF findings. Militias are almost always religious, but few embrace Christian Identity, Nordic Christianity, or Creatorism. For justification, they rely on Free Wheeling Fundamentalism and violent passages of Christian scripture quoted out of context. Most simply interlace their antitax, antigun control rhetoric with out-of-context biblical quotations. One militia group in Detroit is even composed mainly of African Americans.

There is one more thing to say about the militia movement. Simply joining a militia group does not make a person a terrorist. Incidental observations have indicated that several people have joined the militias out of a sense of powerlessness. As a reporter from the *Toledo Blade* quipped to the author, these are folks who never quite made it. The reporter says the militia makes them feel important, and he is probably correct. Many militia members are frustrated, overwhelmed, and socially unable to cope with the rapid pace of change in the modern world. They may be extremists, but they are not terrorists.

This is not to say that the militia movement is not related to domestic violence—far from it. Many militia groups provide the rhetoric for violence. For example, according to my research (White, 1996), there are five major militia groups in Michigan that gather to discuss paramilitary affairs: the Michigan Wolverine Corps, the Michigan Constitutional Militia, the Detroit Constitutional Militia, the Michigan Theater Command, and the Northern Michigan Militia. Their talk is almost always centered in religion and violence. Such a combination is dangerous, but people do not leave their local meetings to commit terrorism. The danger comes when a few true-believing individuals leave the main group and decide to take direct action.

This process may be demonstrated by the 1995 bombing of the federal building in Oklahoma City. If the government's case is correct, prosecutors have not found a militia group ready to destroy the federal government. What they found were people influenced by paramilitary rhetoric. The aged, out-of-shape members of Michigan's various militia groups would be hard-pressed to conduct a bombing like the destruction in Oklahoma City. In addition, most members of the militia were appalled by the carnage. They did not support it. But true believers who hear the call to violence may take direct action. The primary danger of paramilitary rhetoric is that it can inspire true believers to murder.

Paramilitary groups operate on different levels. For example, the Arizona Vipers allegedly planned to blow up a number of federal installations in 1996, and many of them eventually pled guilty to possessing illegal explosives. Interviews of several prominent militia members indicate, however, that they had never heard of the Arizona Vipers. The Freemen of Montana represent another variation. In this case, the Freemen of Montana allegedly terrorized a small town by flaunting laws like an urban gang. When the federal government took action, creating another siege, militia members across the country expressed support but took steps to increase their ideological distance from the Freemen of Montana. Paramilitary groups come in a variety of shapes and sizes, and most of their action is rhetorical. The Arizona Vipers and the Freemen of Montana are exceptions. Rhetoric turns to violence when small detached groups emerge from larger extremist groups.

A brief case study of Michigan can be used to illustrate the point. The militia groups based there center their focus on tax protests, fighting gun control, common law, and complaints about government. Only one of the groups embraces Christian Identity. Despite watchdog group estimates and their own inflated numbers, I believe the estimate of membership is 6,000, and this number is very generous. Several high-ranking law enforcement officers share this conclusion. It includes families, friends, and casual supporters. The primary activities of the groups are weekend feasts of "beanie weenies" and antigovernment religious meetings.

WILLIAM PIERCE'S BLUEPRINT
FOR REVOLUTION

William Pierce is a white supremacist with headquarters in rural West Virginia. He leads an organization called the National Alliance, and his organization recently purchased Resistance Records, a recording label for Skinhead hate music. Pierce holds a Ph.D. and worked as a college professor. He has long drawn the attention of watchdog groups, scholars, and law enforcement officers (Pitcavage, 2000). Why does he create so much interest? He has written two novels which idealize a white American revolution, and anyone concerned with counterterrorism should read these works.

Pierce's most noted novel is *The Turner Diaries*. Written under the pseudonym of Andrew MacDonald (1985), *The Turner Diaries* is a fictionalized account of an international white revolution. The work begins as a scholarly flashback from "New Baltimore" in the year 100, and it purports to introduce the diary of the protagonist, Earl Turner, during the "Great Revolution," a race war that mythically took place in the 1990s.

For the most part, *The Turner Diaries* is a diatribe against minorities and Jews. It is well-written and easy to read. The danger of the work is that it is correct from a technical standpoint. *The Turner Diaries* is a how-to manual for low-level terrorism. Using a narrative or storytelling format, Pierce describes the proper methods for making bombs, constructing mortars, attacking targets, and launching other acts of terrorism. Anyone of average intelligence who reads *The Turner Diaries* will leave the book with an elementary idea of how to become a terrorist.

The second offshoot of *The Turner Diaries* is more subtle. The book could serve as a psychological inspiration for violence; that is, it could inspire copycat crimes. The frequent diatribes and the philosophy behind the book justify murder and mayhem. Pierce presents the destruction of nonwhite races, minorities, and Jews as the only logical solution to social problems. Although he is not religious, he uses a general cosmic theology, presented in a "holy" work called *The Book,* to place Earl Turner on the side of an unknown deity.

Some extremists who read this book have taken action. Robert Matthews, for example, founded a terrorist group called the Bruder Schweigen (the Silent Brotherhood) or the Order based on Turner's fictional terrorist group. The Oklahoma City bomber Timothy McVeigh was arrested with a worn copy of *The Turner Diaries.*

Written in 1989, *Hunter* is another Pierce novel written under the pen name Andrew MacDonald. Although not as popular as *The Turner Diaries, Hunter* tells the story of a "lone wolf" who decides to launch a one-person revolution. Hunter stalks the streets to kill African Americans, interracial couples, and Jews. The book is dedicated to a real-life killer, and like *The Turner Diaries,* it could psychologically inspire copycat crimes. In 1999, two right-wing extremists went on killing sprees in Chicago and Los Angeles in a style reminiscent of *Hunter.*

Extremist literature is full of hate, instructions, and suggestions. Pierce has introduced nothing new in the literature of intolerance. However, he has popularized terrorism in two well-written novels. Unfortunately, they could also serve as a blueprint for violence.

CRIMINAL BEHAVIOR AMONG RIGHT-WING EXTREMISTS

True Believers + Violence + Political Eschatology = Law Enforcement Problems

The past 10 years of right-wing extremist behavior has produced a pattern of criminal behavior (White, 2000). Right-wing extremists fall into three categories: Nonviolent offenders, violent defenders, and violent attackers. This section elaborates on each type of activity.

As with most other forms of terrorism, nonviolence dominates extremist behavior. Right-wing extremists tend to be more vocal than violent, and more prone to rhetorical writing than activity. Such expressions are not criminal in nature, unless they can be directly linked as the cause of a specific crime. Nonviolent offenses deserve the attention of law enforcement not only as potential violations of the law, but also as indicators of potential violence.

Many of the nonviolent right-wing extremists simply drop out. In essence, they declare their independence from the United States. They cite all types of bizarre cases and obscure laws (mostly nonexistent) that give them the "constitutional" right to renounce their citizenship. As a result, they frequently declare that they are sovereign citizens and U.S. laws do not apply to them. They will frequently drive with "constitutional drivers' licenses" and "registration permits." Some of these homemade documents look very official. When they are taken to court, they will often claim that U.S. courts are unconstitutional and they have no authority over sovereign citizens.

More vocal nonviolent offenders tend to engage in disorderly behavior. These types of offenders will frequently interrupt local government meetings. They also disrupt court proceedings, frequently lecturing judges, attorneys, and juries on the "true" meaning of the law. Aside from disrupting duly elected officials, the primary danger from these types of offenders is escalation. They may become violent when approached by law enforcement officers or other government officials.

The last class of nonviolent offenders is more problematic. These people are "paperhangers," people who utilize false documents. One of the most common tactics is passing bogus cite drafts, phony checks drawn on nonexistent accounts. Utilizing nonexistent laws or ridiculous interpretations of history, they frequently claim that the Constitution has given them the power to unencumber funds from the government, banks, or businesses. These offenders then write checks or cite drafts against these bogus claims. Another tactic is to file bogus liens against individuals and then write checks against these nonexistent funds.

Right-wing paperhangers also produced a variety of "common law court" documents. They claim the Constitution allows them to establish their own jurisdictions, governmental units, and courts. Utilizing these bogus documents, they issue decrees, including arrest warrants and property seizures. The Freemen of Jordan, Montana, a group of violent extremists who forced an armed stand-off with government officials in 1996, went much further. They issued death warrants for local officials, crossing the line from rhetoric to terror.

Mark Pitcavage (2000) recently uncovered a new type of paperhanger, the right-wing redemption scheme. Redemption schemes are designed to bilk people out of money. Pitcavage says right-wing paperhangers use traditional fraud techniques, lacing them with patriotic language, secret government information, and talk of Jewish conspiracies. In one of these schemes, right-wing confidence people convinced victims that since the government abandoned the gold standard in 1933, the United States has had no real money. As a result, the President secretly authorized Delta Force to seize gold from other countries. When it arrives, each American will be entitled to several million dollars. To qualify, the frauds say, a person only needs to pay a $300 registration fee. One might think that nobody would be silly enough to believe such a story, but Pitcavage found that the scheme conned fellow right-wing extremists of more than $2,000,000.

Right-wing violence is also a problem. The primary group of right-wing violent extremists can be labeled "defenders." These people believe they are under siege from the forces of the Zionist Occupation Government (ZOG) or the New World Order. They arm themselves, read violent passages from the Bible, and wait for representatives of the federal government to show up on their doorsteps. The problem is that the "agent of ZOG" might be the mail carrier delivering the mail, or the local college student employed as a census taker. In the defender's world, this constitutes an attack, and the defender violently resists.

Attackers, the other type of violent offender, are overt. Not wanting to sit until the government acts, attackers want to take the battle to ZOG. They use standard terrorist tactics, including weapons violations, robbery, bombing, arson, ambush, and murder. They also use intimidation and threats against their enemies. Nihilistic attackers such as Buford Furrow and Benjamin Smith have broken away from their groups and struck out in rage. Furrow went into a Jewish center in Los Angeles and began shooting children. Smith drove through the suburbs of Chicago shooting nonwhites and interracial couples.

There is a more alarming trend, leaderless resistance. Small groups of armed extremists have broken up into cells with no centralized leadership. If domestic terrorism follows international trends, small groups like these are usually the first to commit acts of violence. The trend toward small-group decentralization is of some concern. Louis Beam, a Ku Klux Klansman and noted right-wing extremist, has encouraged local groups to work on their own. Whether Skinhead, militia, or Christian Identity, the purpose of the movement is to resist the intrusion of the federal government. Although much of this movement is based in rural communities, the philosophy is representative of Marighella's expressed ideal in *The Minimanual of the Urban Guerrilla*. The danger comes not from militias, but from small leaderless groups who take violent action.

As Brent Smith indicates, right-wing terrorists have often resorted to armed robbery to finance their campaigns. Stern points out that robberies are complemented by standoffs and militant resistance to arrest or government orders. Right-wing extremists, like the Freemen of Montana, also routinely threaten citizens and government officials. As the attack in Oklahoma City indicates, some small groups also engage in bombings. Leaderless resistance is a popular concept among right-wing extremists.

A new trend emerged after the sieges of Ruby Ridge and Waco. Old left-wing extremists and new right-wing extremists began to search for common ground. One philosophy, the Third Position, attempts to unite both extremes into one. Radicals (left-wing) and reactionaries (right-wing) found that they shared some things in common. They hate the government, they have no use for large corporations, and they distrust the media. The Third Position serves to blur the line between left and right by uniting former enemies around common themes. This becomes more apparent when examining the newest form of domestic terrorism, ecological violence.

ECOTERRORISM AND ANIMAL RIGHTS

The use of the term "ecoterrorism" in conjunction with animal rights or saving the environment is controversial because most people are in favor of the principle. That is, few people want to maim, injure, or harm animals, and even fewer people want to destroy the planet. Environmentalism is embraced across the political spectrum, and when it is associated with terrorism, it is bound to be controversial. Like the right-wing extremists, however, violent ecologists and animal rights advocates live in a world of their own making. Some of them cross the line from rhetoric to terror.

William Dyson (2000), a retired FBI agent who spent nearly 30 years working on domestic terrorism, says it is necessary to look at the way police officers classify crimes and the economic impact of violent ecological extremism to understand the full scope of ecoterrorism. Dyson contends most of the crimes are reported as localized vandalism. The significance of the total destruction is missed. Dyson says when the total economic impact of ecoterrorism is calculated, it demonstrates that the United States has been victimized by a long term terrorist campaign.

Bryan Denson and James Long (1999) come to a similar conclusion. After conducting a detailed study of ecological violence for *The Portland Oregonian*, Denson and Long found that damage from ecoterrorism reached into the millions of dollars. They conducted a 10-month review and considered crime only in excess of $50,000. Cases that could not be linked to environmental groups were eliminated. They found 100 cases with very few successful law enforcement investigations.

According to Denson and Long, most violence has taken place in the American West. From 1995 to 1999, damages totaled $28.8 million. Crimes included raids against farms; destruction of animal research laboratories at the University of California in Davis and Michigan State University, threats to individuals, sabotage against industrial equipment, and arson.

Denson and Long say the movement began in England in the 1970s with the formation of the Animal Liberation Front (ALF). The violent ecology movement appeared by 1981, and both ideas spread to the United States. Ironically, the animal rights advocates and the ecologists detested one another. Each group thought they were fighting for a different goal. The movements took root in the American West.

As was the case with the right-wing, a novel served to inspire the ecoterrorists. *The Monkey Wrench Gang,* a 1975 novel by Edward Abbey, told the story of a group of ecologists who were fed up with industrial development in the West. Abbey is an environmental activist and not a hate-filled ideologue like William Pierce. His novel is a fictional account that has inspired others. In *The Monkey Wrench Gang,* the heroes drive through the Western states sabotaging bulldozers, burning billboards, and damaging the property of people they deem to be destroying the environment. (This is the same type of low-level terrorism German leftists used in the mid-1990s.) "Monkey wrenching" has become a key touchstone for ecoterrorism.

In the past decade, Denson and Long say, ecological and animal-rights extremists have united. Like right-wing counterparts, many of these groups merely engage in rhetoric, or they encourage disruptive behavior. They are known by a variety of names with a myriad of extremist causes. A brief review of the World Wide Web reveals a plethora of groups and ecological causes. The Earth Liberation Front (ELF), Earth First, and the Justice Department are interested in planetary preservation. The Animal Liberation Front, Animal Rights Militia, Band of Mercy, and Paint Panthers champion animal rights.

The violent groups, such as ELF and ALF, advocate and engage in economic damage. The rhetorical groups, such as the Church of Euthanasia, simply border on the bizarre, advocating suicide, sodomy, and cannibalism to voluntarily eliminate the earth's human population.

The violent ecoterrorists revel in telling tales of their exploits. Denson and Long say ELF uses anonymous communiqués. According to ALF's Web site (www.nocompromise.org/alf/alf.html), animal rights criminals have a system to publicize their activities. Like all terrorists, ecoterrorists try to create an aura of power through publicity. ALF takes it further, using the Web site as a training device. For example, tactics for raiding mink farms are given in great detail. Utilizing a four-part series, a writer tells readers the methods for establishing and operating a cell, procedures for obtaining funds, and directions for planning and carrying out operations.

The ecologists pride themselves on arson, and both groups seek economic destruction as their primary goal. They want to economically force land developers, ski lodges, farms, and research labs out of business. Denson and Long say ecoterrorists have been successful in altering industry practices.

Ecoterrorists are uncompromising, illogical extremists just like their right-wing counterparts. A review of their ideological literature shows they use ecology as a surrogate religion (White, 2000). Like all extremists, their positions are full of contradictions and virtual absurdities. For example, the Web site for the "we-use-no-animal-products" ALF tells people to use leather gloves when raiding a mink farm. It also compares people who eat meat with Nazis and describes farms as concentration camps. Apparently, ALF members are unaware that Adolf Hitler was a vegetarian.

BLACK HEBREW ISRAELITES

In the public version of the FBI's *Project Megiddo,* a report about possible religious and cult terrorism at the turn of the millennium, FBI analysts say that Black Hebrew Israelism has the potential to become a violent group (www.FBI.gov). Some critics have scoffed at this suggestion, saying the FBI overreacted to a set of beliefs. Others believe the FBI has identified dangerous violent religious trends. Before finishing the discussion of extremism in the United States, a brief look at Black Hebrew Israelism and the FBI's concern follows.

What is Black Hebrew Israelism? In a nutshell it is Christian Identity with an African twist. According to Tory Thorpe (1996) (www.blackomahaon line.com/blkheb.htm), Black Hebrew Israelites believe that the original Israelites were dark-skinned Africans. They migrated to Nigeria in the Jewish Diaspora and waited for God to fulfill promises to the Hebrews. The white slave trade interfered, however, and created a greater Diaspora of black African Israelites.

The mythology of Black Hebrew Israelites and their beliefs dates back to the Civil War. In the later part of the twentieth century, again like Christian Identity, it developed an elaborate theology to explain the status of African

Americans. For example, according to Yehuda Benyamin be Yisrael (www.thelawkeepers.org), whites conspired to cancel the relationship between Africa and God. Another source (metalab.unc.edu/nge/blacked/bl2.html) explains that curly hair is evidence of the divine origins of black skin. *The Original African Heritage Study Bible* is used to demonstrate that the Jews Moses led in the exodus from Egypt were black.

The theology of Black Hebrew Israelism does not constitute a need for law enforcement investigation or even curiosity, so when any police agency inquires about the belief system, it is bound to create controversy. The First Amendment grants freedom of religion, and anyone is free to believe the tenants of Black Hebrew Israelism. This is the reason some people criticized the FBI for examining the concept in *Project Megiddo.* But the FBI is not interested in religion; it is concerned with potential violence. Some segments of Black Hebrew Israelism have a history of cultic violence, and some have demonized non-African races. Like the potential violence in Christian Identity, this merits law enforcement's attention.

The most attention has been gained by the actions of Hulon Mitchell, Jr. According to court records (United States Court of Appeals, 11th Circuit, 1996), Hulon Mitchell and Linda Gaines moved to Miami, Florida, in 1979, and laid the foundation for a Black Hebrew Israelite cult known as the Nation of Yahweh. Mitchell told followers that God and Jesus were black and he had been chosen to lead blacks back to Israel. By 1980, he ordered followers to abandon their given names and assume Hebrew identities. Gaines became Judith Israel, and Mitchell took the name Yahweh ben Yahweh. (Yahweh is an anglicized version of the Hebrew tetragram YHWH, or the name of God.) Mitchell's new name could be translated as "God son of God."

By 1985, the Nation of Yahweh had become a cult. Mitchell built the Temple of Love and stationed armed guards around its entrance. Gaines controlled the income of all temple members, while Mitchell ruled his followers with an iron hand. Mitchell began expanding his theology, teaching that whites were devils and his followers were to kill them in the name of God. He created an internal group called the Brotherhood, and one could only obtain membership by killing a white person.

When some members tried to leave the group, they were beaten and beheaded. Over the next few years, Mitchell dispatched "Death Angels" to kill whites in the Miami area. The Death Angels were ordered to bring victims' severed body parts back to Mitchell as proof that the murders had taken place. After a five-month trial, Mitchell, Gaines, and some of the other followers were convicted under federal organized crime statutes.

Black Hebrew Israelism is indicative of the tension between believing and acting, and it presents a dilemma for those charged with security. The theology of Black Hebrew Israelism is not violent, and most of its adherents would never follow in Hulon Mitchell's footsteps. The problem for those charged with preventing violence, however, is that when a belief system degrades or demonizes another group, violence often follows. Any time extremist beliefs are fused with hatred, the community is at risk.

KEY CONCEPTS

1. Extremism is nothing new in American history. Right-wing extremism can be traced from the Whiskey Rebellion to extremist violence today.

2. Modern right-wing extremist thought is characterized by intolerant religious dogma, racism, and belief in conspiracies. Adherents follow one or more of the following ideas: white supremacy, survivalism, or extremist religious expression.

3. *The Turner Diaries* and *Hunter* are violent right-wing fantasy novels that embody the ideology of the extremist right.

4. Right-wing criminal behavior can be divided into violent and nonviolent forms. Violent offenders include defenders and attackers. Nonviolent offenses include disorderly conduct, paperhanging, and redemption schemes.

5. Radical ecologists and animal rights activists primarily engage in property destruction in the name of their causes. Their goal is economic disruption.

6. Black Hebrew Israelism is an African-American version of Christian Identity. It claims that black Africans were the original Israelites. One violent group, the Nation of Yahweh, demonized whites and called for their destruction.

FOOD FOR THOUGHT

A silent alarm has sounded a bank robbery, and a patrol car responds. You are the first patrol officer on the scene. As you pull into the parking lot, two white males with automatic weapons are holding three hostages at gunpoint. You have blocked their escape, and are in a position that seems to be safe from gunfire. One hostage is white, and the other two are African American. You are attempting to calm the situation while waiting for backup units and tactical support. The hostagetakers are screaming that they represent the power of Yahweh and the constitutional government of the occupied states. Would you talk to these people as if they were normal criminals? What line of reasoning would you use to keep the situation calm? When a commander arrives with negotiators, what advice might you give?

FURTHER READING

John George and Laird M. Wilcox, *American Extremists: Militias, Supremacists, Klansmen, Communists, and Others*

PART IV

*

Issues in
Modern Terrorism

15

Technological Terrorism and Weapons of Mass Destruction

Two terrorist incidents, the 1993 World Trade Center bombing in New York City, and the 1995 attack on the Tokyo subway system, have raised the alarm about the threat of technological terrorism. In New York City, terrorists placed a barrel full of poison chemicals in the vicinity of a car bomb they detonated in a parking garage underneath the World Trade Center. Fortunately, the heat from the bomb destroyed the chemicals before they could be dispersed. Tokyo was another matter. Fanatics from a religious cult released poison gas on a subway, hoping to create massive casualties. The gas did not spread effectively. However, 12 people died, and over 5,000 were injured. This type of threat raises several questions: What is technological terrorism? What are the dangers from weapons of mass destruction? How could terrorists utilize such weapons? What countermeasures can be taken? These issues are discussed in this chapter.

After reading this chapter, you should be able to:

1. Summarize Aum Shinrikyo's attack in Tokyo.
2. Define and describe technological terrorism.
3. Discuss U.S. vulnerability to technological terrorism.
4. Describe security problems in the U.S. energy industry.
5. Describe the threat posed by nuclear, biological, and chemical terrorism.
6. Outline the threat of cyberterrorism.
7. Discuss possible responses to technological terrorism.

AUM SHINRIKYO

On March 20, 1995, Tokyo was subjected to a technological terrorist attack from a radical religious sect. Members of a religious cult, the Aum Shinrikyo or Aum Supreme Truth, released a poisonous gas, sarin, into the crowded subway system. The act involved criminal terrorism for psychological gratification, but it had a deadly twist. The terrorists were not individuals seeking social release, or some nebulous form of political revenge; they were members of an organized religious cult trying to destroy the Japanese government. Unintentionally reflecting the theories of Carlos Marighella, the gas attack was designed to produce chaos, and the terrorists hoped to seize power in the resulting confusion.

Every modern civilization has spawned some form of violence in the name of either religion or a surrogate ideology, and the presence of cult violence in the modern world is not surprising. The world was shocked in 1977, when hundreds of people committed suicide at the command of Jim Jones, a charismatic charlatan who manipulated his followers in a religious cult. In 1993, Vernon Wayne Howell (also known as David Koresh) managed to burn or shoot most of his devotees when federal agents closed in on his compound outside of Waco, Texas. Other cults have been less aggressive, simply requiring that followers sign over their financial assets to the local messianic figure. Aum Shinrikyo represented an alarming change in the pattern. Cult members were instructed to attack and conquer the world. They were to begin with Tokyo.

According to the U.S. Department of State (1996), the poison gas attack in the Tokyo subway was the first large-scale use of chemical agents by terrorists. Diplomatic officials estimated that cult members hoped to destabilize the Japanese government and seize power in the confusion. Aum Shinrikyo terrorists struck five subway trains simultaneously, killing 12 people and sending approximately 5,500 victims to hospitals for treatment. Subsequent investigations by Japanese police linked Aum Shinrikyo to a previous gas attack in 1994, which killed seven and injured 500 people (Muir, 1999).

D. W. Brackett (1996) paints the best and most comprehensive portrait of Aum Shinrikyo. Brackett argues that it is very difficult to grasp the entire event, because many differing layers of Japanese bureaucracy describe the attack from differing perspectives. In synopsis, Brackett finds the group gravitated around a charismatic leader, Shoko Asahara. Aum Shinrikyo planned murders and dress rehearsals prior to the subway attack, and developed a mechanism for funding, developing, and supporting a weapon of mass destruction (WMD) program. All of this came, not from a nation-state, but from a religiously motivated terrorist group.

Investigative reporters David Kaplan and Andrew Marshall (1996) paint a less objective portrait than Brackett, but their work reveals the same frightening infrastructure behind the seemingly misdirected incident. According to Kaplan and Marshall, the Tokyo attack was not a random action; it was synchronized to produce enormous casualties. As Aum Shinrikyo terrorists exposed their gas containers, they were to create a gas cloud that was to have enveloped five different trains converging on a single station. Aum Shinrikyo

terrorists believed the cloud would leave the subway cars, creating a mass conglomeration of poison gas in downtown Tokyo. Fortunately, the incident produced minimal fatalities.

The technology behind the attack was impressive, according to both
Brackett and Kaplan and Marshall. The terrorists used sarin gas, a deadly, odor-
less, colorless gas developed by Nazi researchers in World War II. They carried
containers of chemicals that would produce the gas when exposed to air, and
placed their packets under their seats in innocent-looking packages. Each terrorist punctured his lethal container just before 8:00 A.M., and sarin gas clouds
began working their way through the subway cars with immediate results.

Kaplan and Marshall say that though the technology was frightening, the
background of the terrorists causes even more alarm. These people were not
misfits or youths in search of a purpose, and they did not become true believers as a result of social failure. The terrorists represented some of the best and
brightest minds in the country. They included a middle-aged surgeon, three
physicists, and an electrical engineer. They were bright enough to plan and
carry out an act of technological terrorism.

Shoko Asahara, the leader of Aum Shinrikyo, developed a strange religion
loosely based on Hinduism and Buddhism. In reality, according to Brackett, he
became a messianic figure to his followers. Armed with divine expectations,
Asahara convinced his followers that he, and he alone, was worthy to interpret
the truth. As the cult grew in the early 1990s, Asahara solidified his hold over
the group. He gained control of immense personal wealth and developed his
messianic status to the point of unquestioned authority. Asahara was successful
because he blended charismatic leadership with economic power, but Asahara
did not stop with money. He used his wealth to move into cyberspace, and
Aum Shinrikyo became a high-tech cult.

Kaplan and Marshall point out that Aum Shinrikyo combined technology
with a variety of modern devices. The cult internationalized as Aum Shinrikyo
sought scientists and weapons from disenfranchised people in the former
Soviet Union. The cult established a financial network throughout the West,
and formed links with Japanese organized crime syndicates. It recruited the
intelligentsia, promising renewed purpose in a new world. Cult members
underwent military training, brainwashing, drug-induced religious devotions,
and weapons production. The cult was also not satisfied with small arms. Using
its members' technical skills and its financial resources, Asahara's followers
began building technological weapons. Aum Shinrikyo had a single goal: to
purify the world and dominate it within the confines of Asahara's revelations.

Kaplan and Marshall are highly critical of the Japanese police, claiming they
failed to intervene or understand the seriousness of the cult when they first
became aware of it. Their criticism may have merit, but the investigation after
the subway poison gas attack was thorough. It revealed production facilities
and an infrastructure designed to produce mass death. Although sensationalized
at times, Kaplan and Marshall also point out that the network was hardly localized around cult facilities. Aum Shinrikyo had developed an international support base, and it planned international operations.

Brackett has a more thorough analysis of the Japanese police and the social constraints that influence their investigations. Brackett argues that arrest in Japan is tantamount to a guilty verdict in the United States. Therefore, the Japanese police are reluctant to make an arrest until they are sure that the suspect is guilty. This social restriction played in Asahara's hands.

One of the most disturbing threats from Aum Shinrikyo is its attempt to combine religious eschatology with violence and technology. (Eschatology refers to the final experiences or the end times of humanity. See Chapter 4.) Gunther Lewy (1974) argues that the combination of violence and eschatology is dangerous because it gives warriors a cosmic sense of justice. Because they are fighting with a direct link to their concept of a divinity, eschatological warriors are particularly murderous, believing their actions enjoy holy sanctification. The case of Aum Shinrikyo proves Lewy's point.

There is another disturbing aspect beyond the utilization of religion. History demonstrates that religious violence is nothing new, but technology is another matter. In the case of Aum Shinrikyo, religion not only incorporated violence, but it also used technology. Terrorist groups often threaten technological attacks, but they are reluctant to use them. The reason is that terrorists tend to be rational creatures. If they engage in technological terrorism, they generally realize that they are planting the seeds for their destruction. For example, after the subway attack, the police dismantled Aum Shinrikyo—both physically and organizationally. Technological terrorism is not a path to victory for the rational actor (Jenkins, 1987, 1996).

As mentioned in Chapter 4, the problem of holy warriors—religious zealots in direct contact with the truth—is that rationality is no barrier to action for them. If one argues that the potential murder of thousands in the Tokyo subway system would bring the full wrath and weight of the Japanese political system on the group responsible for the action, religious zealots could dismiss the arguments. They would say the logic of potential retribution is a political argument. Zealots are responding with a divine proclamation, and religious terrorists believe they receive their instructions from God. When a religion of love is transformed into a doctrine of hate, the results are deadly. Technological destruction makes potential scenarios even more frightening, and given the human tendency to follow false messiahs, one will probably witness more cult terrorism from groups like Aum Shinrikyo.

TECHNOLOGICAL TERRORISM

Several analysts of terrorism (for example, Crenshaw, 1977; Clark, 1980; Wardlaw, 1982; Jenkins, 1983; Kupperman, 1985b; White, 1986b; Sloan, 1995; and Laqueur, 1996 and 1999) have raised concerns about technological terrorism. Essentially, technological terrorism is the use of a weapon of mass destruction or an attack on technological systems designed to create massive chaos in an act of terrorism. It can involve two principle actions. Terrorists may employ a WMD, or they might also use a railroad car full of chemicals as a type of chemical bomb, or simply program a virtual bomb in a computer network. Sophisticated terrorists might do both in a coordinated attack.

A few years ago, most analysts believed such attacks were unlikely. Brian Jenkins (1987) summarizes this view. Jenkins says it is difficult to create a WMD. The complexity of WMDs and the technical expertise needed to ensure that the weapon produces maximum casualties serve as a deterrent to their use. In addition, Jenkins believes there is little reward for the use of WMDs. Once they were employed, governments would unleash the full extent of their power on the offending group. The public, no doubt, would fully support such government actions. In short, there is no political payoff in WMDs.

Walter Laqueur (1999) argues this view is no longer warranted. Religious fanatics do not look for political payoffs in the same way as do political terrorists. Religious terrorists are more prone to use technological attacks than terrorists in the past. Technological terrorism has been a growing concern among security experts as a result.

Brian Clark (1980) sounded an early warning about technology and terrorism. Clark believes the importance of terrorism has been understated. Clark writes that terrorism is a weapon used to obtain a criminal or political goal, and it will become a problem that will make many other social problems shrink to insignificance. Clark claims political terrorism will emerge as the foremost problem in the world when terrorists begin to take advantage of technology.

Clark argues that terrorism has crossed the threshold into a technocratic age. Clark wrote his book to demonstrate the potential magnitude of the problem, and to charge the American government with insufficient preparation. He also wanted to demonstrate the political and social implications of large-scale technological terrorism. In short, his book was designed to be a warning.

Clark levels three charges against technological industries. First, nuclear waste material is not adequately protected and can easily be stolen. Second, he believes that chemical production facilities are vulnerable and chemical and biological weapons (CBW) can be stolen in a manner similar to nuclear waste. Third, Clark feels that the transportation system for dangerous chemical and nuclear agents lacks proper safeguards. Halstead and Ballard's (1997) study of antiterrorist problems in the nuclear waste industry demonstrates that current problems are more severe than when Clark first spoke of them 20 years ago. These areas leave the United States vulnerable to technological attack.

Clark acknowledges that his view is not accepted by all, citing comments by J. Bowyer Bell to show the other side. Clark admits that many analysts do not believe terrorism is extremely significant. However, he rejects their arguments on the basis of the coming threats from technology. Clark says the potential lethality of technology has rendered those arguments meaningless. Terrorism will become supremely important through the use of technology. In Clark's mind, it is only a matter of time.

Examine Clark's view closely. What would have happened had Aum Shinrikyo been more successful with its use of sarin gas? Now that a group has tried a technological attack, do you think there will be others? How do you think a government would respond to the deaths of several thousand people after a technological attack? Although the world has experienced horrible technological accidents, nuclear meltdowns in Russia, and gas leaks in India, no terrorist group has successfully managed a technological act. If Clark is correct, it is coming.

U.S. VULNERABILITY
TO TECHNOLOGICAL TERRORISM

The United States is the most technologically advanced superpower in the world. Technology has opened new doors to the future, which many Americans have taken for granted. Other national competitors have taken advantage of the United States's nonchalant attitude toward technology at times, but the United States stands as one of the masters of new industrial and technological techniques. Along with Japan and Western Europe, the United States is a technologically oriented society.

The irony of U.S. success with technology is that the country has become vulnerable to attacks on technology and by technology. One does not have to agree with Brian Clark's political position to understand that the United States is dependent on technology. While the military has taken precautions to shield defense and weapons systems from interference, civilian industry has fallen behind. Given U.S. dependence on technology, this has created a window of opportunity for terrorists.

There is no clear way to react to the problem of technological vulnerability. Some analysts, like Halstead and Ballard (1997), have called for rigid new safeguards and massive new security efforts. Others believe a calm assessment of potential threats is more in order (Heim, 1984). Analysts do not agree about the extent of the threat, and most of them focus on weapons of mass destruction. A study by B. J. Berkowitz et al. (1972) was one of the first to examine the implications of mass destruction weapons in the hands of terrorists. Its conclusion was that civil chaos would result. According to the study, several attempts were made by radical groups to employ some level of CBW attack from 1967 to 1970. Although this information is dated, the Aum Shinrikyo attack in Tokyo demonstrates the reality of the threat.

The Berkowitz study points to several areas of vulnerability. Metropolitan water supplies are subject to contamination. Although poisons would dissipate in a large volume of water, general public reaction would be one of panic. In addition, criminal organizations have attempted to produce chemical weapons for extortion and assassination. Berkowitz and his colleagues also point out attempts to steal or produce CBWs in Europe and the United States.

Robert Mullen (1978) also examines modern society's vulnerability to technological weapons. The capacity for mass destruction is a recent historical development. In the past, killing many people required many people to do the killing. Technology has changed this. Mass destruction terrorism can be inferred from CBWs and nuclear weapons.

Mullen states that terrorism based on massively destructive weapons involves skills that few terrorist groups possess. Technical weapons require technical skills and support networks. Many groups lack these capacities, but Mullen says the past may not be indicative of the future. The capability for mass destruction exists.

Robert Kupperman and Darrell Trent (1979) deal with some of the issues posed by technological threats. Kupperman (1985b) examines the issue again, with a specific focus on organizational responses to technological threats, and he describes the potential threat that technological terrorism poses for the United States. Both Kupperman and Trent strike a middle ground, however, between complacently ignoring the problem and overreacting to it.

In Kupperman and Trent's analysis, responsible policies should be developed to meet the potential threat. The response should be one of policy analysis and application. Industrial and technological safeguards will work only if they are accompanied by proper emergency procedures. Kupperman and Trent suggest models for restructuring U.S. federal bureaus and emergency planning networks.

Unlike many analysts, Kupperman and Trent believe the analytical literature on terrorism to be fairly complete. They do not see the need to add to the theoretical body of knowledge. Instead, they argue that Walter Laqueur has appropriately described the historical and social background of terrorism and that Brian Jenkins has adequately analyzed current and future trends. The only gap in the literature is in the area of technology.

The authors were trying to get policy moving in the direction of counterterrorism; technology provided their motivation for writing. Kupperman and Trent believe the problem of technological terrorism has generally been ignored and the U.S. government is woefully underprepared to deal with a technological threat. Accordingly, they describe several horrifying potential scenarios for terrorism (without giving terrorists clues on weapons construction or utilization). They hope the devastating nature of the scenarios will grab policymakers' attention.

Kupperman and Trent believe that social deterrents are insufficient to rule out the use of mass destruction weapons. Increased possession of nuclear and chemical weapons has been accompanied by their use or threatened use. Nation-states have legitimized the use of mass destruction weapons, hence paving the way for terrorists to adopt them. The analysts conclude that it is time to start realizing the truly destructive nature of such weapons.

The most common type of terrorist weapon is a bomb. It has been historically popular, it is easy to deliver, and it poses a difficult puzzle for police to solve. Kupperman and Trent say that when groups mature, they move toward more sophisticated weaponry, but in their initial stages, groups find that bombs are cheap and effective tools. Kupperman and Trent state that the danger is an enhancement of bombs through CBWs or nuclear capacities. Recent experience demonstrates that even sophisticated conventional bombs can destroy civilian aircraft.

Kupperman and Trent argue either type of weapon can be used for psychological impact, and they predict the public would react with panic if either nuclear or CBW agents were introduced by terrorists. They believe that because nuclear bombs are difficult to make or steal, terrorists would achieve the same psychological impact by spreading radioactive materials. If accompanied by an effective means to spread the toxins, chemical and biological weapons have a similar potential.

Attacks on technological targets are another way to achieve mass destruction without the need for technological weapons. In addition, Kupperman and Trent point to the ability of terrorists to paralyze the economy by attacking targets necessary for production and service. Electrical power grids are important from this standpoint, and the most likely targets are transmission lines and transformers. Gas and petroleum lines are even more vulnerable, and conventional and nuclear power plants present tempting targets. They also consider the vulnerability of computer networks.

In Kupperman and Trent's analysis, counterterrorism must begin with a reorganization of the federal bureaucracy. Without discussing the specifics for each agency, their recommendations can be summarized in two steps. First, the analysts want a few key federal agencies to have definite responsibility for emergency situations. The role of individual agencies should be spelled out in policy guidelines, and bureaucratic managers should be held responsible for their agencies' abilities to deal with potential terrorism.

In their second series of recommendations, Kupperman and Trent want the government to develop realistic management plans to coordinate the response of its various units. There is a need to develop a small, knowledgeable crisis staff to direct operations in the event of a technological attack. According to the researchers, it is not necessary to become preoccupied with the counterterrorist functions of each agency because mass destruction terrorism is a low-probability occurrence. However, preparing for an event with key managers can serve as both a deterrent and a practical method to restore normalcy in the event of an attack.

Some security specialists have focused on the idea of prevention. Indeed, it comprises the philosophy of such organizations as the American Society for Industrial Security. Prevention of technological terrorism is a corollary to safeguarding technological materials. Robert Kindilien (1985) makes this argument with reference to the nuclear power industry. Enhanced security will reduce the risk of losing dangerous material and waste. American industry is currently vulnerable to such losses. Kindilien says it is necessary to assess risks and attack them with an aggressive security system.

Another point about the vulnerability of the United States has been raised by many analysts. If a mass destruction threat developed, the initial public reaction would probably be one of panic. A fear of chemical weapons and radioactivity pervades popular culture. If the American public believed a major city was in jeopardy, there is reason to believe fear would sweep the nation. In a climate of fear, cherished liberties can be destroyed.

Russell Ayers (1975) and John Barton (1980) have raised this issue. In this sense, the corollary to technological terrorism is another threat. In reacting to potential mass destruction, security and police powers would be increased. In many societies, this has been closely correlated with a decline in civil liberties. The ideal function of the American justice system is to protect individual rights, but historically, in times of panic, the government and the police have forgotten this. There is good reason to believe that technological terrorism would create panic, and civil rights often fall by the wayside in such situations.

Another potential target of technology and terrorism is the energy industry. Oil and gas are the United States's chief means of energy. An article placed in an addendum to the Kupperman and Trent analysis raises the problem of securing the energy industry. The analysis claims the transportation and storage of fossil fuels is not as safe as people tend to assume.

SECURITY PROBLEMS
IN THE ENERGY INDUSTRY

The United States relies on energy to support its technology, and the interruption of energy supplies could be construed as a national security threat. If a nation or terrorist group could shut off U.S. energy, it could close down major portions of the economy. Secure energy production, transportation, and storage are all critical to the United States.

Kupperman and Trent state that electrical systems are quite vulnerable. Attacks on key power transformers could stop the flow of electricity to large segments of the country for quite some time. Damage to key generating facilities would also have long-term effects. Currently, the threat is localized. Power stations and transformers have been subject to industrial sabotage, but this has had only local, short-term effects.

Maynard Stephens (1979, pp. 220–223) assesses the vulnerability of U.S. oil and natural gas systems. Stephens argues the interruption of oil and gas delivery would have the most devastating economic impact of any attack on energy. The reason is that oil and gas form the United States's greatest source of energy. Seventy-five percent of U.S. energy needs are filled by oil and gas. Although electrical power grids have backup supplies, no method of continuing service is available if oil and gas lines are destroyed.

According to Stephens, the efficiency of the systems is the major problem. Industry and government planners designed U.S. pipelines for maximum flow and distribution of the product. As a result, oil and gas are channeled over hundreds of miles in a highly efficient and concentrated set of pipelines. But this very efficiency has weakened the security of the system: An attack on a major line would magnify the scope of the attack.

Stephens's main worry is the lack of federal and state concern about protecting the gas and petroleum industries. He claims the government has taken almost no protective measures. Stephens says because domestic terrorism in the United States has not often been manifested, threats to the oil and gas industries appear to be abstract.

Things have changed since Stephens's article appeared. Not only has the United States been subject to domestic terrorism, but also some of it has been supported by foreign governments. Kupperman and Trent appear to have been correct. In the early stages—the World Trade Center and Oklahoma City, for example—the primary weapon has been the bomb. More sophisticated attacks can be expected in the future. The oil and gas distribution systems are perfect targets. Transportation centers and parts are next in line.

To illustrate the point, consider a situation like the 1991 Persian Gulf War. American heavy equipment for the war was shipped through ports along the Atlantic seaboard and the Gulf of Mexico. Assume you are a Middle Eastern leader and the United States is preparing a Desert Storm–style operation against your country. You do not have conventional military forces cable of stopping the United States, but you have several terrorist training camps in your country and links to international terrorist structures inside the United States. What could you do?

If you had the technological sophistication, it would be relatively easy to strike the United States. If you could cause sufficient explosions in the ports at Houston, Charleston, Norfolk, and New York, you would limit American capacity to move heavy equipment to the Middle East. If this was combined with attacks on the electrical power grid and gas pipelines, your efforts would be more effective. Finally, a few well-placed bombs like that in Oklahoma City would cause general panic.

This hypothetical scenario is not designed to make you paranoid, and if it did happen, it probably would not end with a devastating defeat of the United States. In addition, any nation that would attempt such an undertaking would require extensive planning and coordination, something far beyond the leadership capacity of a street thug like Saddam Hussein. If it did happen, however, it would isolate military forces in the region and hamper their supply lines. In the opening stages of Desert Storm, it could have resulted in thousands of American casualties. Therefore, policies and emergency plans must begin to anticipate U.S. technological vulnerability. If terrorism is approached as a legal problem, a national defense role for federal, state, and local police agencies must be recognized.

THE THREAT OF NUCLEAR TERRORISM

The most frequently discussed aspect of future terrorism is nuclear attack, and it seems to have a psychological impact far more frightening than other scenarios. This may be due to the widespread fear of nuclear weapons, or to the fact that a greater body of knowledge on the topic is available to the general public. Regardless, it is frequently impossible to discuss the future of terrorism without examining the potential impact of nuclear weapons or radioactive material (Sanz, 1992).

One of many analysts who have addressed the question of nuclear terrorism, B. David (1985) makes four critical points about the issue. First, nuclear terrorism and chemical and biological weapon terrorism are usually discussed together. Second, true nuclear terrorism requires either a difficult production process or the theft of radioactive materials or weapons; CBW agents are easier to produce and obtain. Third, a key to responding to nuclear terrorism is to discern the motivation of a group that might be willing to use weapons of mass destruction. Finally, there are still social sanctions against employing such weapons.

Martha Crenshaw (1977) raises other points. First, Crenshaw is concerned about the proliferation of nuclear materials on an international level. She believes the abundance of nuclear materials increases the likelihood of nuclear terrorism.

More than two decades after Crenshaw's analysis, the nuclear issue still dominates segments of the international agenda. President Clinton signed a United Nations–sponsored antinuclear treaty in 1996, but some nations, such as India, refused to support the ban. The collapse of the Soviet Union also made active nuclear weapons available to terrorist groups.

Crenshaw also expresses concern about the spread of the nuclear power industry. The number of nuclear power plants increases the potential for attacks on power-generating stations and the theft of waste material. Terrorists who lack the ability to build or buy nuclear weapons can simply obtain nuclear waste from a generating station and detonate it. This would produce a ground-level "nuclear" blast, complete with fallout.

Brian Jenkins (1975, 1980, 1986, 1987) has approached the question of nuclear terrorism cautiously and provides several answers. He gave his first answer in 1975, admitting that his conjectures were purely speculative. His answer has been slightly revised through the years, but his initial response has been partially validated by nearly three decades of developments in terrorism. Basically, Jenkins says we do not know whether terrorists will use nuclear weapons but we have no reason to assume that they will automatically evolve in that direction.

Jenkins says nuclear terrorism is possible, but he is reluctant to see it as a major threat. He believes terrorists are rational creatures, and nuclear terrorism is irrational. Nuclear weapons would not work in low-level operations, and once the weapons were deactivated, there would be no incentive for governments to continue to honor any negotiated promises. Social restraints tend to make nuclear devices impractical.

However, the possibility of nuclear terrorism cannot be dismissed. Jenkins points out that many Americans believe nuclear terrorism is more likely than a nuclear war. Trends in nuclear-related terrorism have reinforced public beliefs. Jenkins equates attacks on nuclear facilities with nuclear terrorism, and his data indicate that attacks on the nuclear industry and on weapons facilities are declining. Yet attacks continue, accompanied by the general trend toward an increased level of violence. If nuclear terrorism is not inevitable, it is certainly not impossible.

Nuclear terrorism could take a variety of forms. Jenkins says terrorists could attack nuclear facilities and use the entire area as a weapon. They could also simply steal material or ask a ransom for it. Terrorists could fabricate a nuclear hoax, and the ensuing panic might be as dangerous as a threatened explosion. In the simplest case, terrorists could spread radioactive material; in the most complex case, they might detonate a device. More recently, British sources (Ryan, 1996) indicate that the Russian Mafia has attempted to sell live nuclear weapons and supporting technology on the black market. The term nuclear terrorism is used frequently, but for a variety of potential activities.

Several people have commented on Jenkins's position. Paul Leventhal and Yonah Alexander (1986, pp. 33–53) recorded a speech by Jenkins on nuclear terrorism and some experts' reactions to it. One member of the audience, David Mabry of the U.S. Department of State, agreed with Jenkins about the rationalism of terrorists. Mabry said terrorists do not kill for the sake of killing; they have a political motivation for their actions.

Mabry disagrees with Jenkins's assessment of the probability of nuclear terrorism. Given the increasing violence of terrorist groups, the lure of nuclear terrorism is becoming too great. State sponsors of terrorist groups have greater access to nuclear weapons, further increasing the possibility of such terrorism. Mabry was convinced that Iran and Libya would not hesitate to use nuclear weapons in a terrorist incident. Finally, because bombing is the most popular terrorist act, nuclear bombing might simply be viewed as its logical extension.

Yural Ne'eman, a physics professor and former Israeli cabinet minister, also disagreed with Jenkins. He was critical of Jenkins's reluctance to distinguish attacks on nuclear facilities from the use of nuclear materials in terrorism. Ne'eman said they are not the same thing and they certainly are not positively correlated. Therefore, declining rates of attacks on nuclear facilities had no connection with the probability of a use of nuclear material in terrorism.

Ne'eman also believed most terrorism was state-sponsored. Far from the individual groups that Jenkins imagined, Ne'eman saw most terrorists as an extension of national governments. Ne'eman agreed with Mabry that Iran and Libya were prime candidates for the use of nuclear weapons. He also added Iraq to the list and completely dismissed Jenkins's notion that terrorists would be somehow constrained by a sense of morality.

Larry Collins and Dominique Lapierre (1980) wrote a terrorist thriller titled *The Fifth Horseman* that featured fictional state-sponsored technological terrorism. The premise of the book is that Moamar Khadaffy has managed to construct a hydrogen bomb. He places the weapon in New York City by clandestinely shipping it to the United States with a semiautonomous terrorist group. An army of bureaucrats, emergency personnel, and police officers search for the device while Khadaffy negotiates with the U.S. president about

Libyan demands. The United States is paralyzed in its response for a variety of diplomatic reasons.

The premise of the novel is exciting, and the book is fun to read. In the real world, however, the scenario poses some problems. If a nation was to sponsor nuclear terrorism against the United States, it would run the risk of full American military reprisal. Mass destruction could obviously be construed as an act of war; American military forces have been deployed for terrorist events of far less significance than a nuclear explosion. This refers back to the policy debate between legality and defense.

The United States has undertaken efforts to prepare for technological terrorism. According to Christopher Dobson and Ronald Payne (1982b, pp. 51–76), an array of federal agencies has joined forces to combat all acts of domestic terrorism. Donald A. DeVito and Lacy Suiter (1987, pp. 416–432), both directors of state emergency planning agencies, suggest that the Federal Emergency Management Agency (FEMA) be used as the clearinghouse for bureaucratic coordination. They say terrorism demands emergency planning. FEMA has taken a leading role in preparing for effective interaction among local, federal, and state governments. It is supported by a variety of federal regulatory bodies and law enforcement agencies.

BIOLOGICAL AND CHEMICAL TERRORISM

Chemical and biological agents might well be the weapons of choice should terrorists use weapons of mass destruction. FEMA (1998) gives several reasons. First, biological and chemical agents are easier to produce than nuclear weapons or radioactive material. Second, as many as 26 nations appear to have developed chemical weapons, and 12 more nations are seeking to do so. In addition, 10 other nations have biological weapons programs. Finally, chemical and biological agents are easier to transport and utilize than nuclear weapons. Chemical and biological weapons are relatively easy to use, they are available, and they are mobile. Have they become, as some people argue, the poor person's nuclear bomb?

To answer this question, look at the nature of each agent. Ron Purver (1995) offers an outstanding summary of open source information on chemical and biological agents. Purver says biological weapons are based on microorganisms and poisons produced by plants and animals. Most of the weapons terrorists would use have been classified as agents that would produce fever, a plague, or some other type of infectious disease. Some of the agents are extremely lethal, while others would be used to incapacitate people. Purver also says some terrorism analysts fear the development of a genetically engineered disease.

Chemical agents are not as lethal as biological agents, and they are easier to control. The four common types of chemical weapons are: nerve agents, blood agents, choking agents, and blistering agents (see Table 15.1). Nerve agents

Table 15.1 Chemical and Biological Agents

Types of Chemical Agents	Types of Biological Agents
Nerve	Natural poisons (ricin, saxitoxin, venom)
Blood	Viruses
Choking	Salmonella, botulism, anthrax
Blistering	Plagues

SOURCES: Canadian Intelligence Service, and the Organisation for the Prohibition of Chemical Weapons.

enter the body through contaminated food or water, air, or contact with skin. They cause uncontrolled body fluids to flow from openings in the body and induce muscle spasms. In high doses, victims can go into convulsions, and death may come from the evacuation of body fluids within a matter of minutes. Sarin is a common type of nerve weapon. Blood agents are absorbed through breathing and are carried through the body by breathing. They cause lethal damage by reacting with enzymes in the body. Hydrogen cyanide, the gas used in Nazi concentration camps, is a blood agent. Choking chemicals, such as chlorine gas, attack the lungs and prevent people from breathing. These agents cause the walls of the lungs to flood with mucus, and the victim literally drowns in the secretions. Blistering agents are liquids or gases that burn the skin. The mustard gas used in World War I is a blistering agent (Organisation for the Prohibition of Chemical Weapons, 2000).

There are many advantages for terrorists who would like to use chemical or biological weapons. John Deutch (1996), former Director of the Central Intelligence Agency, believes the availability of chemical and biological weapons and the ease with which they can be transported make them the weapon of choice for terrorists who want to use WMDs. Jessica Stern (1998) says terrorists may use chemical and biological agents with crude delivery systems. In addition, Stern points out that the resulting panic caused by the use of such horrendous weapons will increase the aura of the group employing them.

While these weapons are horrific, many analysts feel they are inadequate substitutes for nuclear weapons. The reason is that there are more disadvantages than advantages. Leonard Cole (1996), one of the leading experts in the field of chemical and biological weapons, points out that these weapons are difficult to control.

Biological weapons virtually have no controls, and once they are introduced, the group using the weapon might well become a victim. For example, if a terrorist group was able to start a black plague epidemic in a major city, how could it stop the spread of the disease? In addition, it takes time for a biological agent to work. It must incubate, then spread from person to person. Most biological agents are destroyed by weather and sunlight. The agents that can survive, such as concentrated anthrax, are so lethal that they would threaten to contaminate their users for decades. According to Cole, biological weapons are unreliable.

Chemical weapons are more readily controlled, but they are not as lethal. The FBI's Larry Mefford (1996) shows that chemical weapons are best used in a confined area. They would be an excellent choice for an attack on a building, but their effectiveness in mass destruction is limited. Despite these disadvantages, one should not assume that these weapons will not be used. Terrorists have access to chemical and biological weapons, they have used them, and will probably use them again.

Stephen Bowers and Kimberly Keys (1998) offer a sobering analysis of the likelihood of continued chemical and biological terrorism. Like many other analysts, Bowers and Keys believe the recent infusion of racism and religion in terrorist activities has changed the structure of modern terrorism. Religious zealots are more interested in destruction than the aura created by media coverage. Chemical and biological agents are attractive to such people.

Bowers and Keys propose a three-step methodology for approaching terrorism and technology. First, they argue that group profiling and behavioral analysis has been a powerful tool for counterterrorism. To paraphrase a popular witticism among psychology professors, nothing predicts future behavior like past behavior. Bowers and Keys recommend that law enforcement and defense agencies aggressively analyze the behavior of terrorist groups in order to predict future behavior. Second, like Doug Bodrero, they recommend constant monitoring of social indicators. Terrorist groups do not develop overnight; they are produced by social forces. Law enforcement personnel must constantly monitor the social climate that produces violence. Finally, Bowers and Keys state a key point. Security personnel must share information. The days of FBI, CIA, and ATF rivalries are long gone. WMD threats make agency rivalries superfluous.

Law enforcement and the military can learn quite a bit about responding to WMDs from the firefighting service. Firefighters have dealt with chemical spills and biological disasters for decades. They have systems to identify and contain contaminated areas. Indeed, they already employ the biological and chemical detection systems used by the armed forces. Law enforcement, security, and military personnel can find a wealth of information on response at the National Fire Academy in Emmitsburg, Maryland.

CYBERTERRORISM

On January 22, 2000, President Clinton announced a billion dollar plan to fight cyberterrorism. The first question that came to many analysts of terrorism minds was: Is there a cyberterrorism? The answer is not clear. Former FBI counterterrorism specialist William Dyson (2000) perhaps gives the best answer. Dyson says computer terrorism is not a form of terrorism, but terrorists may use computers during the commission of terrorist acts.

Terrorists may use computers in a number of ways. Yael Shahar (1997) envisions scenarios where viruses are implanted in an enemy's computer. He also predicts "logic bombs" that lie dormant for years until they are instructed to overwhelm a computer system. Shahar also believes bogus chips can be sold to sabotage an enemy's computer network. Trojan horses can have a malevolent code to destroy a system, while back doors allow terrorists to enter "secure" systems. Shahar also believes conventional attacks such as overloading an electrical system serve to threaten computer security.

Michael Whine (1999) agrees with Shahar's conclusions, claiming that computer technology is attractive to terrorists for several reasons. Computers allow groups to remain connected, while allowing covert discussions and anonymity. Computer networks are also much less expensive and work intensive than the secretive infrastructures necessary to maintain terrorist groups. Computers also allow terrorists to reach their audiences with little effort. Whine concludes that computers are a force multiplier for terrorist groups.

Bowers and Keys (1998) believe cyberterrorism appears to be a threat because of the nature of modern society. Cyberterrorists may attack the infrastructure. In other words, they can destroy the underpinnings of the social base. Bowers and Keys believe this happens in terms of information flow. Since modern Western society functions on information, cyberterrorists threaten to interrupt or confuse the flow of information. Imagine, they say, an attack on the banking industry through the flow of fund information. Such an attack could completely devastate a society.

Bowers and Keys believe the ability of cyberterrorists to disrupt the economic system is matched by their ability to destroy confidence in social institutions. Cyberterrorists could make an audience feel as if their world is falling apart. Cyberterrorists can target health institutions as well as government services and businesses. They may even attack defense establishments.

By the same token, Bowers and Keys say cyberterrorism belongs to a broader category called "information warfare." Dyson (2000) agrees with all of these conclusions, and adds that terrorists even use the computer to train other terrorists. There is no doubt that computers are vulnerable to crime, and terrorists do use and will continue to use computers. In addition, Tiffany Danitz and Warren Strobel (1999) indicate that political activists can use the Internet as a command-and-control mechanism. Computer security is a necessity in commerce, government, and personal affairs. Terrorists, enemy military forces, criminals, hackers, and others will use computers to their advantage at the expense of others.

This chapter has presented the most depressing aspect of modern terrorism, the megadeath and destruction that can be wrought by terrorists using technology. Yet, Dyson's point needs to be considered. Computers are tools used by terrorists. WMDs and other forms of technology represent the same thing. Perhaps there is no technological terrorism, but there are terrorists who will use technological weapons. Regardless of the terminology, it is a frightening scenario.

KEY CONCEPTS

1. Aum Shinrikyo's attack on the Tokyo subway system in 1995 focused world attention on the problem of weapons of mass destruction and terrorism. The cult's attack combined the two most deadly factors in modern terrorism: religious fanaticism and weapons that could produce massive deaths.

2. Technological terrorism is any form of terrorism that uses modern technology. It may include WMDs, computers, and the transformation of technological infrastructures into temporary weapons.

3. The United States is vulnerable to technological attack on two levels. Its infrastructure may be destroyed for a period of time, or it may be attacked with a technological weapon.

4. The fuel and energy distribution systems in the United States are vulnerable targets. Oil and gas are more vulnerable than electricity, because it is more difficult to reroute petroleum products if sections of the distribution system are incapacitated.

5. Cyberterrorism is probably a misused term. Terrorists may use computers in terrorist acts. Such acts include the disruption of services, attacks on infrastructures including the defense system, and placing cyberbombs in selected information systems. Terrorists currently use computers for training and sharing information.

FOOD FOR THOUGHT

Assume you are in charge of security in a major urban hospital, and victims from a biological terrorist attack are arriving. What precautions would you need to take? Think about things like quarantining patients, protecting the staff, decontaminating rooms and equipment, obtaining and securing antidotes, and monitoring the spread of disease. Do you think the same techniques would be applicable in a chemical or nuclear attack? What additional actions would you take in these circumstances?

FURTHER READING

CSIS Global Organized Crime Project, *Cybercrime, Cyberterrorism, and Cyberwarfare*

Jessica Stern, *The Ultimate Terrorists*

Eric Taylor, *Lethal Mists: An Introduction to the Natural and Military Sciences of Chemical, Biological Warfare and Terrorism*

16

Terrorism
and the Media

One of the most controversial current topics of terrorism analysis is the way print and electronic media cover terrorist acts. Police and other government forces operate with a set of objectives diametrically opposed to the goals of reporters covering an event. In addition, experts have heatedly debated the effects of electronic coverage on terrorism, and there are several competing schools of thought on the effectiveness and impact of newspaper coverage. Regardless of which side one favors, reporting terrorism will remain controversial because the media has become part of the terrorist event. The purpose of this chapter is to summarize some of the issues inherent in the relationship between the media and terrorism.

After reading this chapter, you should be able to:

1. Outline the three positions on the relationship of the media to terrorist events.

2. Explain contagion theory within the context of terrorism and the media.

3. Using the findings of Schmid and de Graaf, discuss terrorism as a form of political communication.

4. Discuss the problems of censorship and the First Amendment to the U.S. Constitution.

SECURITY FORCES VERSUS REPORTERS

Within the ranks of everyday police or military operations, it is not uncommon to hear many statements criticizing the media. Chiefs of police and military commanders generally do not respect media figures and reporters, and their attitudes are reflected by their line personnel. Specialized command units are often created in police agencies to portray a favorable image to reporters, and U.S. military forces have been assigned to public relations.

Reporters, newspapers, and television news teams are generally not trusted. Police and security forces officially represent the social order, and they are charged with the maintenance of stability. They see themselves as servants of the public interest in the United States and other Western democracies. Additionally, they believe they make decisions for the public good. They perceive themselves to be the forceful extension of democracy.

Richard Schaffert (1992) provides the best quantitative analysis of terrorism and the media. He concludes that democracies can lower the amount of terrorism by implementing some form of media control, and such actions do not endanger democracy. He points to the United Kingdom, the Federal Republic of Germany, and Italy as examples. However, the United States has two problems with this approach. First, terrorism seems to be distant; Americans do not mind media exploitation of violence. Second, the American media is not driven by truth; it is driven by market domination. This leads to sensationalistic reporting.

Members of the media have two competing and often contradictory roles. They control the flow of information while simultaneously making the news entertaining enough to "sell." M. Cherif Bassiouni (1981) points out the potential conflict these competing purposes bring to terrorist scenarios. The police or security forces are charged with bringing the situation to a successful conclusion. Their job is primarily to preserve order and protect lives. The press has the job of transmitting information while making the story interesting to the consumer. During live coverage, the media must also facilitate interaction between the scene and the audience.

Bassiouni (1982) argues that the police must respond to terrorist situations by lessening their drama and psychological impact. News producers, however, see the drama of terrorism as the perfect attention grabber. Bassiouni notes that terrorism defies security force goals while catering to the goals of the media. The issue of terrorism heightens the animosity between the police and the media. It is a reflection of a deeper conflict between those in government and those in the media.

Government officials seldom enjoy having their decisions analyzed and criticized to a mass audience, but that is one of the major functions of media presentations. Tensions run high in terrorist situations, especially when the event is ongoing or when hostages are involved. Television and newspaper reporters usually arrive at the scene of a terrorist incident within minutes of security forces. Distrust and distaste often dominate their interactions from the start.

This predicament gives rise to three different points of view about terrorism and the media. First, some members and supporters of the press see the media as a quasi-Constitutional force keeping the government in check. A second group wants to limit press coverage during terrorist events. These people see the media as terrorism's ally. A third faction feels the opposite is true: The media may exploit terrorism, but they rarely convey messages favorable to terrorists.

Some members of the news media have no intention of endangering lives or escalating terrorism. Abraham Miller (1982, pp. 133–147) points to internal codes controlling journalistic excess. These guidelines indicate that news organizations expect their reporters to behave responsibly. Under no circumstances are they to interfere with security forces or to assist terrorists, even inadvertently.

Journalists, interestingly enough, seem to fear manipulation by terrorists as much as they do government control. The media claim to have the right to have access to and report all findings. Some analysts and government officials feel this right hampers governmental decision making. Reporters have defended their position by saying that in a democracy, all the people have a right to influence decision making. They can only do this, some media defenders have claimed, when they are given unrestricted information.

Several analysts of terrorism vehemently disagree with the position taken by the media. According to Yonah Alexander (1984, pp. 135–150), terrorism is a new type of struggle, and terrorists have made the media their ally. Modern terrorists view communication as a potential weapon, and they seek to exploit it by eliciting media exposure. Willingly or unwillingly, the media have become the tool of terrorism.

Other critics have gone further than Alexander. For example, Norman Podhoretz (1981) says modern reporters are in subtle, informal collusion with terrorists. Podhoretz says terrorists and journalists are in business for mutual benefits. The media do not consciously conspire with terrorists, but they play to each other's needs. Yoel Cohen (1983) shares this view. He says the PLO would not exist if it was not for media coverage and media sympathy. The media, in turn, make a profit by reporting PLO violence.

In separate works, J. Bowyer Bell (1978a) and H. H. A. Cooper (1977a, pp. 140–156) agree that the media produced terrorist theater. The drama of terrorism makes for great news stories: It is filled with action and is entertaining. In this sense, the press has become an ally of terrorism. Yet, both Bell and Cooper question the effectiveness of this relationship. Subsequent research has indicated the coverage of terrorism is not helpful to terrorist groups. Terrorists want to use the media for propaganda purposes, but the media focus on violence. News reports rarely explain the causes of the terrorists, and they almost never portray terrorism in a favorable light.

Quite a bit of research indicates the press makes a poor terrorist ally. Gabriel Weimann (1983) found that reporting terrorist events increases the public's knowledge about terrorism but builds little sympathy for terrorists. Michael Kelly and Thomas Mitchell (1981) also learned that news reports focus mainly on violence, which paints a negative picture of terrorism. L. John

Martin (1985) agrees, implying that a negative media image causes terrorist propaganda efforts to backfire.

Other researchers have questioned the effectiveness of the electronic and printed media in serving the needs of terrorists. David Paletz, Peter Fozzard, and John Ayanian (1982a, 1982b) conducted two studies on the way the media handles terrorism. They examined coverage of the Red Brigades, IRA, and FALN by both television and newspapers. In their television study, the researchers focused on the three major American network nightly news programs. They searched for the method of reporting, as well as any biases. They concluded that television generally ignores the motivations for violence, focusing instead on the activity itself.

The method of coverage used by network television was found to have a negative effect on terrorism. The purpose of terrorism is to communicate a message about its goals and objectives. Network television does not do this. In fact, the audience is appalled by terrorist violence. Paletz et al. conclude television engenders no sympathy for terrorists because coverage clearly portrays terrorism as an illegitimate form of violence.

Paletz et al. approached newspapers in a similar manner. In an analysis of the *New York Times,* they found a coverage pattern similar to that of television. Although the *New York Times* provided greater depth in the issues surrounding the terrorist event, the acts of terrorism were generally delegitimized. They also found another trend in press coverage: It tended to legitimize the government instead of the terrorists.

Far from being a tool for terrorism, the media served the interests of the government. Paletz et al. claim the perspectives of news stories depend on the source, and in the majority of terrorist stories examined, governments were the source. Reporters are under pressure to produce quickly, so over 75 percent of their stories came from government sources. This meant reporters also picked up the labels that government sources applied to the terrorists. The terrorists seldom fared well.

THE CONTAGION EFFECT
OF MEDIA COVERAGE

Some analysts are not as concerned about the content of press coverage as they are about its role in spreading terrorist violence. Does the coverage of terrorism inspire more violence? In other words, is it contagious? Some analysts believe it is. This has been a hotly debated issue leading to discussions of censorship.

Allan Mazur (1982) is convinced that media reports have a suggestive effect on violent behavior. His study compares bomb threats in the nuclear industry with the amount of press coverage nuclear power plants received. He begins by noting that news reports of suicides increase the actual number of suicides, and he wonders whether he might find a similar pattern in the nuclear industry.

Mazur examined bomb threats against nuclear power facilities from 1969 to 1980, comparing them with the amount of coverage devoted to nuclear power on television and in newspapers. He found the number of threats proportionately matched the number of news stories. When coverage increased, bomb threats increased, and the converse was also true. When coverage decreased, bomb threats decreased.

Mazur concludes the media can affect public behavior through suggestion. Coverage of problems in the nuclear industry seems to suggest there is a need for a general public response. Some people choose to make their statements violently. He is not sure whether the media alone causes the response or whether their reports combine with another factor. He is positive about the contagion effect, however.

M. Cherif Bassiouni (1981) locates the problem of contagion in the arena of police-media relations. He believes media coverage has several contagious effects. Media reports promote fear and magnify the threat in the public mind. That fear spreads. The media also influence the way terrorists select their targets; to spread violence, terrorists select targets for maximum publicity. The media have become the vehicle for the psychological impact of terrorism. From this standpoint, terrorism is contagious: Media-reported terrorism causes more terrorism.

Bassiouni applies the contagion hypothesis to criminal and political terrorism. He believes researchers have not derived any conclusive data, but the contagion theory is popularly accepted, especially in law enforcement circles. Although the evidence remains inconclusive, Bassiouni decides that there must be some basis to the contagion theory.

Philip Schlesinger (1981) is not willing to go quite so far. He believes the contagion theory is merely a hypothesis of terrorist researchers. Schlesinger does not reject the notion that terrorism can be contagious, but he denies that current evidence proves the point. Schlesinger argues that contagion theory is used to support censorship and analysts who subscribe to it are attempting to force their opinions on those who can control the media.

TERRORISM AS A FORM
OF COMMUNICATION

One of the most comprehensive research studies on terrorism and the media comes from Alex Schmid and Janny de Graaf (1982), two noted terrorist analysts from the Netherlands. They say the lack of understanding of the media's role in terrorism is due to a lack of research. They sought to provide information by conducting a systematic study of the relationship between the media and insurgent terrorism.

The purpose of the study was to examine the links among terrorist violence, the Western news media, and the political actors. Schmid and de Graaf hoped such information would help bring peaceful resolutions to violent

situations. Their study has been hailed as a landmark of empirical research on terrorism and the media.

They began their examination by looking at the nineteenth century Western anarchists, whose violence, they argue, resulted from political frustration. The anarchists were frustrated because they could not make their voices heard. Anarchists began using violence to communicate their political stance and force governments to respond to their demands. They found that resorting to violence publicized their presence.

Schmid and de Graaf say the twentieth century changed the nature of insurgent terrorism. In the nineteenth century, terrorists had used selective assassination; in the twentieth century, they opened a new technological arsenal of weapons. In addition, their choice of victims changed from selected government or industrial symbols to neutrals selected at random. This policy enhanced the communicative ability of terrorism, especially when it was combined with the revolution in the electronic media.

Modern communications and the mass media have helped shape the nature of modern conflict. Schmid and de Graaf argue that in the past, warring parties limited their strategy to major battlefields. Rapid communications, however, allow reporters to travel to the war zone and bring the battlefield to the general public. As a result, public opinion has become a major aspect of modern warfare, and mobilizing public opinion is deemed a necessary strategy to achieve victory. This attitude is reflected in terrorism.

Some terrorist groups have successfully exploited this factor, whereas others have been less opportunistic. Schmid and de Graaf believe that the way the media is used depends on the cultural conventions of a country. In Latin America, they argue, terrorists routinely seize broadcasting stations because government censorship is common. The Palestinian fedayeen, on the other hand, have taken full advantage of the Western press. The United States is a media-saturated nation, and the American media generally give any type of terrorist a forum. In Western Europe, terrorists use the media in an attempt to build public empathy.

The relationship does not only benefit the terrorists. Schmid and de Graaf state that the media have been able to exploit terrorists for their own needs. It is difficult to define terrorism, but the media have done so by applying labels to terrorist actions. They are selective about calling violent events terrorism, but when they do, the public is provided with a de facto definition. The media labels terrorism and covers it according to its own needs.

Schmid and de Graaf identify several motives behind Western news coverage of terrorism. The two leading reasons are the commercial profits obtained by reporting sensationalized violence and the public's inherent interest in terrorism. People also turn to the media for vicarious experiences, so terrorism has become a form of thrilling entertainment. Audiences also enjoy the rebellious aspects of terrorism and may safely identify with these rebels. Finally, television routinely favors violent over nonviolent stories.

The Western news media have few moral qualms about their desire to report terrorism because they have appeared themselves as neutral purveyors of information. Schmid and de Graaf point to the irony of this belief. They write that the thesis of a news story depends on the source. Stories generally reflect the source's perspective. The press is far from objective, in part because it is manipulated by its sources. Ironically, the greatest source of terrorist information is the government. Therefore, most Western news items reflect a governmental perspective.

Still, no one element—governmental or terrorist—has managed to control the media entirely. This situation has resulted in many types of outcomes from media reports on terrorism. Relatively minor violence may be exacerbated. The act of reporting may change the character of what is being reported. In hostage situations, reports may jeopardize operations and lives. The media may magnify the threat of terrorism to the government, and conversely, reports of violence may encourage more terrorism. Quite often, the public identifies with neither the government nor the terrorists but focuses on the victims. Given this myriad of possible effects, Schmid and de Graaf believe the media have a responsibility to the public.

Schmid and de Graaf place the blame for increased terrorism on the media. They conclude violence breeds violence. Terrorists learn their tactics and copy methods from the mass media. Media coverage also serves as a motivation for terrorism. The most serious outcome is that violence seems to increase during media coverage. The mass media have become the perfect instrument of violent communication.

Schmid and de Graaf conclude the media must live up to their responsibility to Western civilization. Their job is not simply to report; they should become effective agents of positive social change. Their job should be to illustrate social problems and positive solutions, rather than engaging in competition for the public's attention. Schmid and de Graaf suggest specially elected regulatory bodies should be created to ensure that the media follow this path.

CENSORSHIP AND FREEDOM
OF THE PRESS

The questions raised by Schmid and de Graaf ultimately lead to questions of censorship. Few officials want direct censorship of the press, but many agree with British terrorist expert Major General Richard Clutterbuck (1975) that the press should be a neutral factor. Officials and conservative analysts do not want to limit free speech and writing, but they are very concerned about the media playing into the hands of terrorists. Therefore, it is not surprising to hear calls for varying degrees of media control.

Schmid and de Graaf devote a chapter to the issue of censorship. They argue the original purpose of free speech was to allow a person to present a view. With the rise of capitalism in the 1800s and the late nineteenth century's corporate consolidation of the media, newspapers and eventually television news assumed the responsibility for protecting individual freedom of speech. Freedom from censorship came to equal the media's right to report the news.

In today's society, the control of information is far more important than it was in the past. Schmid and de Graaf argue the media have been given a very powerful position in the modern world as the gatekeepers of public information. The media are responsible to the large corporate conglomerates that own them. Because their reporting and interpretations have the potential to cause disasters, Schmid and de Graaf suggest it might be appropriate to hold the media accountable to another, more disinterested source.

Attitudes toward censorship tend to take one of three forms. A small minority of analysts have suggested some form of governmental control. Another group has urged the media to develop more stringent internal guidelines. A third group has argued the media are already bound by internal controls that serve established governments.

Christopher Kehler, Greg Harvey, and Richard Hall (1982) discuss the first two viewpoints from a Canadian perspective. A free press is an unquestioned Canadian right, deriving from a cultural history shared with the United States.

Still, Kehler et al. argue some form of media regulation is necessary because media coverage of terrorist events endangers lives. In some instances, the press has negotiated with terrorists, press corps members have entered lines of fire and secured zones, and hostage rescue forces have been pictured on live television as they moved in for an assault. They feel the government has a legal right to regulate, but it would be better if the broadcast industry developed responsible standards of its own. Internal regulation is more beneficial than governmental regulation.

At the same time, they point out the public does have a passive system to redress injuries that result from negligent news coverage. When the media behave negligently, victims have the right to sue. There is little history of such cases because the concept is in its embryonic stage. But if media news coverage violates standards of responsible reporting and someone is injured as a result, a tort claim may be pursued.

Juanita Jones and Abraham Miller (1979) suggest that government restrictions on dissemination of news do not violate the press's rights during emergency conditions. They compare hostage situations against the backdrop of the First Amendment to the U.S. Constitution, and view the problem through case-law history. They argue this is not an abstract problem; lives hang in the balance during hostage crises. They believe reporting and the freedom to report are not the only critical concerns in such crises: The impact of the media on the event, and media interference with police operations, have also become central issues.

Jones and Miller say the press could legally be excluded from certain areas during hostage situations, especially when police procedures call for secrecy in an attempt to save lives. However, the U.S. Supreme Court will not allow blanket denial through a set of preconditions. Limitations to access are supported only when they are justified by the circumstances. A total or standard ban on news access is not acceptable.

Hostage situations especially bear out the point. Jones and Miller say the police have a right to place restrictions on the press. The media's behavior at a hostage incident is a matter of conduct, not speech. Denial of access and specific regulations for the protection of hostages are acceptable, and such actions have been upheld in the courts. It is a form of censorship acceptable under the First Amendment, and it denies neither free speech nor free press.

Jones and Miller demonstrate that they are not trying to stop reporting. Miller's (1982) additional work provides further evidence of this. The researchers believe the police only want the media to behave in a responsible manner. The police can help encourage this by providing the media with realistic and timely information. If the police and media could come to an understanding of each other's positions, Jones and Miller believe many confrontational issues could be mollified.

Taking a different view, Philip Schlesinger (1981) argues the media in Western democracies favor government stability. Schlesinger centers his argument on the concept of legitimization. He states the media have worked to delegitimize terrorist violence.

Schlesinger examines the role of security forces in Northern Ireland. He concludes the British press has acted "responsibly" in terms of covering the government's position. That is, the press has supported the government while condemning antigovernment violence. He feels such actions only reflect "responsibility" as defined by the government.

Schlesinger argues that terrorism is approached by the media on official and unofficial levels. Language is crucial, because it can serve to either support or deny the legitimate right of a political position to exist. Officially, media language is used to criminalize terrorism. Unofficially, it can serve to criminalize the issue that motivates terrorists.

The language of news reporting has become secondary to the way in which governments have been portrayed by the media. Schlesinger says that when the first incidents of modern terrorism started to break out in Northern Ireland, reporters went to locations and tried to print and broadcast objective reports. Such reports were often as critical of government policy as they were of terrorists. This enraged the government, especially the security forces engaged in dangerous activities.

The government soon came to Richard Clutterbuck's conclusion that the media was a neutral weapon. It could be used for or against terrorism, and the best way to take advantage of the weapon was to cooperate with the media. Schlesinger says this process was accompanied by strong pressures for the press to behave within guidelines deemed to be responsible by the government. It has evolved into a de facto form of censorship, and the British government has found an ally in the press.

Shane Kingston (1995) stands in vehement disagreement with Schlesinger. Kingston argues that terrorism caters to the media. In the early days of modern terrorism, it was fairly easy to manipulate television because any event was an unfolding drama. Television producers, however, became more sophisticated and countered terrorist manipulations. Yet, Kingston says, the terrorists also became more adept at using the press. Using Ireland as a case study, Kingston says the IRA presents itself positively.

Schlesinger's conclusions are not readily accepted. Some distinguished terrorist experts have scoffed at his suggestions, whereas others who believe the media ends up being sympathetic to governmental authority structures reject the notion that the power of the media has been compromised. Schlesinger's position is one of many controversial aspects surrounding the media and terrorism. Even voluntary guidelines are subject to scrutiny from those who think they should be stronger, as well as those who think they should not exist at all. Noam Chomsky and Edward Herman (1977, p. 85) point out that control of the media can legitimize government terrorism. Abraham Miller believes others are aware of this, including police chiefs.

Regardless of the analytical positions taken about the media, security forces are faced with practical problems during terrorist events. Joseph Scanlon (1981, 1982) addresses the issue, suggesting some practical guidelines for operating with the media during a terrorist incident. Scanlon believes that if reporters are treated honestly and given the whole story, they will usually avoid interfering with police and security measures.

Scanlon focuses on the problem of terrorism as a live event. He does not feel the majority of reporters are irresponsible, but argues that media presence is a tactical consideration and often interferes with the successful resolution of the event.

Scanlon gives several suggestions for managing the media during a terrorist incident. The media should be pooled and given valid information. He emphasizes the media should be given as much information as possible, with the understanding that critical tactical items cannot be used until their publication or broadcast poses no threat to the public. If members of the media threaten operations or lives, they should be detained until their reporting no longer endangers an event. Scanlon is hesitant to recommend the use of police power against the media, however, and he believes media actions during terrorist events should be voluntary.

Western governments tend to approach the media with fear and mistrust. In terrorist incidents, police and military forces reflect this attitude. When lives hang in the balance, security forces should be able to expect cooperation from the media. After the event, however, the media are free to analyze and give critical opinions. This is a cherished aspect of freedom, and it is something that many terrorists would like to take from us.

KEY CONCEPTS

1. Members of the media and security forces often seem to be at odds when responding to terrorist events. Security forces want to restore the scene, investigate, and eliminate terrorism. Media sources want to tell the story, and they function in a highly competitive environment.

Sensational drama increases the attraction of the story to readers and viewers.

2.   Some researchers believe media reporting of terrorism encourages people to join the violence. This is known as contagion theory; it means these researchers believe terrorist violence is contagious.

3.   Schmid and de Graaf conclude that various media give terrorism a forum. As a result, terrorism is a form of political communication.

4.   Censorship is the most controversial area of media relations. A few analysts advocate direct censorship, but the majority of them favor voluntary controls. It may be possible to invoke some internal control without violating individual rights and freedoms, but such methods are controversial because they foster private media cooperation with the government.

FOOD FOR THOUGHT

Imagine you are the law enforcement scene commander at a convenience store robbery, where the robbers have taken the customers and clerk hostage. A local television station is broadcasting the event live through a telephoto lens, and the robbers are watching the coverage on a television inside the store. What actions should you take? Can you ask the station to stop broadcasting? Can you force them to do so? Could you use live television coverage to your advantage without the cooperation of the station? If the hostage-takers say they want to negotiate with the media, would you let them do so? List the things that might happen if you do.

FURTHER READING

Alex P. Schmid and Janny F. A. de Graaf, *Violence as Communication*

Abraham Miller, *Terrorism, the Media, and the Law*

Richard W. Schaffert, *Media Coverage and Political Terrorists: Quantitative Analysis*

17

✳

Policy, Liberty, Security, and the Future

Many analysts have speculated about the future of terrorism, and many political leaders have wondered what should be done about it. This chapter introduces some of the issues facing the political leaders who must deal with terrorism. Two specifics are focused on: questions about policy and speculations about the future. Unfortunately, this chapter raises many difficult issues and solves few of them. The purpose of this chapter is to alert one to some of the real-world dilemmas facing policymakers and those responsible for security.

After reading this chapter, you should be able to:

1. Define the dilemma regarding criminal justice and defense policy.
2. Summarize the issues raised by Admiral Stansfield Turner.
3. Explain the policy problems caused by weapons of mass destruction.
4. Discuss the role of civil liberties in counterterrorist policies.
5. Outline the issues involved in utilizing military force against terrorism.
6. Describe the way police secrecy hinders an effective counterterrorist response.
7. Summarize Stinson's analysis of security measures.

TOWARD A COUNTERTERRORIST POLICY

Terrorism is a nebulous form of conflict. It is conceptualized on the continuum discussed in Chapter 1, but policymakers must move beyond the conceptual stage. They must take action to prevent or strike back at terrorism. The question is, how should they do it? Is terrorism a criminal or military problem? Should terrorism be countered with military force, international and domestic laws, or a combination of both? Can political leaders employ non-Constitutional standards to apprehend terrorists? The answers to these questions are not easy, and the agencies charged with counterterrorism have a multitude of answers. In short, counterterrorist policies present a dilemma.

To help illustrate the dilemma, consider World War II (1939–1945). At the beginning of the war, German General Heinz Guderian introduced a new style of fighting, a style many French, British, American, and Russian generals did not understand. His method of fighting was called the "Lightning War," or the Blitzkrieg, and it was waged with a tank army, or a Panzerwaffe. In World War I (1914–1918), belligerent armies had fought and died for dozens of yards. Guderian's mechanized soldiers moved at 30 miles per hour, and sometimes advanced 50 miles in a single day! After France fell in a few weeks in 1940, and German forces advanced 500 miles into Russia in 1941, no one would have suggested sending the FBI to Berlin with arrest warrants for Guderian and his boss, Adolph Hitler. The United States handled the problem by following Constitutional standards and legally declaring war.

Herein lies the problem. The United States and other Western states pride themselves on being nations governed by law. They feel all social problems should be governed by the laws of the civil state, and even such barbarous acts as war fit into this legal framework. The U.S. Constitution allows the government to take extraordinary actions when the Congress of the United States formally declares war, but there are two policy problems posed by this logic. First, it assumes that acts of war can be legally rationalized. (In fact, after World War II, Allied military police did arrest Guderian, and he was sentenced to prison by an Allied court in Nürnberg.) Second, if we are being attacked by military means, do we respond with civil police or military forces? On some levels, terrorism threatens our legalistic views of conflict.

Some of the practical problems are approached by looking at the Middle East. The United States and Western Europe have often been stymied by transnational terrorism from that region. After 1967, Western security forces began to grow accustomed to attacks on innocent, unfortified civilian targets, and they began to prepare civilian police responses. They did not believe, however, that terrorists could attack well-fortified military targets. The terrorist group Islamic Jihad changed Western minds. In response to the 1982 Israeli invasion of Lebanon, Islamic Jihad shocked the West by attacking not only fortified Israeli military positions, but also multinational peacekeeping forces. The attacks were so effective that U.S. Marines were forced to retreat. Some experts in the West had always believed terrorists were too weak to engage in such tactics; suicide bombers in Lebanon proved them wrong. As a result, some analysts began speaking of terrorism as a mode of warfare.

This posed a problem. It seemed to be safe to argue that attacks on military positions were acts of war, but what if the troops being attacked were not under the rules of war? Furthermore, what if the troops were simply innocent victims or symbolic targets? What of civilian attacks? If a self-styled terrorist military organization attacked a civilian target, such as an airplane, was this also an act of war?

Robert Kupperman (1988b) of the Georgetown Institute for Strategic Studies was interviewed on NBC's *Today* show in December 1988 following the bombing of an American passenger plane over Scotland. Although it was a typically brief television interview, Kupperman managed to make a critical point. He stated that the United States faced two policy choices when dealing with transnational terrorism from the Middle East. It had to be approached either as a justice problem—meaning investigation, arrest, and punishment—or as a national security problem.

Had NBC given Kupperman more time to elaborate, his analysis would have been most interesting. The United States has long been in search of a policy to deal with this kind of terrorism. In the years following Kupperman's comments, U.S. counterterrorist policies have ranged from naval bombardments to FBI arrests outside the country. After the Pan Am bombing over Scotland, for example, U.S. courts issued two arrest warrants for fugitive terrorists hiding in Libya. So, one might say, this is a criminal justice policy. However, since it takes 35 to 50 supporters to keep a single terrorist in the field, will two warrants solve the problem? Kupperman's excellent point remains unsolved.

If the problem of transnational terrorism is a military one, however, then different military policies will need to be developed to counter terrorist threats. For example, to counter international terrorist threats, the U.S. president needs a variety of military options within his role as commander-in-chief. Larry Cable (1987) states that more innovative policies need to be found for counterterrorism. According to Cable, conventional concepts of conflict will not work.

Several options for unconventional responses are possible. Americans have supported naval attacks, air strikes, commando raids, and quick wars. They have not supported assassinations, long counterinsurgency wars, or U.S. support of undemocratic governments involved in a counterterrorist campaign. Yet, these problems are only superficial. The central question is if American interests are attacked by a foreign terrorist group, is this an act of war? If the answer is yes, a corollary question is if the attack occurs on American soil, do we continue to respond with military force, or do we handle it as a criminal investigation? The only thing one can say is the United States has been consistently inconsistent with its answer.

On one level, Americans seem to favor handling international terrorists as organized criminals. U.S. Senate hearings on the hijacking of a cruise ship, the *Achille Lauro,* concluded that hijacking was a violation of international law (U.S. House of Representatives, 1985); Congress expanded the enforcement power of the FBI as a result. The FBI was granted power to forcibly seize suspected terrorists menacing Americans in other countries, charge them with violation of American laws, and bring them to the United States for trial (U.S. Senate, 1985).

The law granting the FBI that power was tested in March 1989. In a unique trial, Fawaz Younis was charged with air piracy. He was allegedly the leader of a group of hijackers who took over a Royal Jordanian Airlines flight on June 11, 1985. Americans were aboard the flight, which gave the FBI power to arrest him under the 1985 law.

On September 13, 1987, Younis was lured aboard a yacht in the Mediterranean by secret agents. They informed him that the yacht contained arms and ammunition for an upcoming terrorist campaign. The agents sought Younis's support and direction. Younis boarded the boat to find a surprise: Instead of the promised terrorists, Israeli agents greeted him. Later, after an alleged unconstitutional interrogation, FBI agents welcomed Younis to the free world. He was charged and convicted of violation of American criminal law.

Interestingly, the defense did not base its case on a challenge of the law that allowed an extrajurisdictional arrest with no other government's cooperation. It also did not complain that Younis had been kidnapped by FBI agents. Instead, the defense argued that Younis was innocent because he was only following the orders of Al-Amal, the Lebanese Shiite militia. The defense did not question U.S. authority to arrest on the charge of air piracy. In another twist, the U.S. government relocated 14 witnesses from the Middle East, gave them legal alien status, and hid them, under the U.S. Marshals Service Witness Protection Program.

This policy has not been without its critics. Some analysts strongly disagree with the use of American law enforcement power outside American territory. Aside from the fact that its legality was questionable, it opened a Pandora's box of potential policy disasters. These analysts straightforwardly argue to keep American police at home.

Larry Cable (1987) has suggested a practical approach to the problem. He says it is not necessary to define every terrorist incident as either a violation of law or a matter of national security. States use force when relating to one another, and terrorism is nothing new. Cable argues the amount and type of force used are critical in determining the type of response. He feels a competent intelligence-gathering network should provide information to democratic decision-making bodies. The use of force in international relations must be understood apart from rhetoric about criminal justice or low-intensity conflict.

Grant Wardlaw (1988, pp. 237–259) comes to a similar conclusion. He argues the concept of terrorism is nebulous at best, and it is not always defined juridically. Some terrorist incidents demand an immediate, clear-cut political response. When judging how to respond to an incident, policymakers must examine the type of terrorism, as well as the nature of the threat posed by the particular group. Wardlaw believes the West, especially the United States, has overstated the dangers of terrorism and the difficulty of controlling it.

Even though individual acts of terrorism are horrific, Wardlaw argues, it is necessary to avoid overstating their importance. Major powers may feel psychologically threatened by terrorism, but they are often being challenged by minor powers too weak to play the international relations game by traditional rules. Unless a nation's approach to terrorism is well-defined and discerning, Wardlaw believes, policies would degenerate into ideological dogma and be nonfunctional.

STANSFIELD TURNER'S SEARCH
FOR SOLID GROUND

Retired U.S. Navy Admiral Stansfield Turner, former director of the Central Intelligence Agency, reflects the frustration associated with ideological dogma and counterterrorist rhetoric. Turner (1991) states that the United States will continue to experience failure in counterterrorist policies until it replaces rhetoric with flexible policy responses. He argues that dogmatic statements are counterproductive. For example, U.S. "policy" claims that we do not negotiate with terrorists, when the opposite is true. Turner says we frequently negotiate with terrorists, and he demonstrates it with an examination of U.S. foreign policy from the days of the Barbary pirates to the Iran-Contra affair. Turner asks policymakers to search for a set of flexible responses designed to meet a variety of scenarios.

Turner states that six tactics are demanded by those who want to take proactive measures against terrorists: Repealing the presidential ban on assassination, launching punitive military attacks, engaging in covert action, prioritizing hostage rescue operations, improving intelligence, and censoring the media. Most of these tactics involve activities that violate legal norms in the West. Turner advocates more legalistic tactics—economic pressure, defensive security, negotiations, and legal recourse.

Critics maintain that Turner is too soft on terrorism. Turner responds to such criticism by looking at the record. The most rhetorically militant president in the last two decades of the twentieth century, Ronald Reagan, only used a proactive option once, in a raid against Libya. In every other instance, Turner says, Reagan responded with the legalistic approach, including negotiations with revolutionary Iran. Rhetoric has emotional appeal, but policy demands pragmatic action.

Turner suggests several practical steps for countering terrorism, realizing that each case is unique. To guide policy, Turner says that assassinations are not acceptable in American democracy. They may seem like a quick step to a final solution, but they do not work in the long run. Most Americans are frightened by presidential "dirty tricks," and they would not ultimately support an assassination decision. In addition, once a leader was assassinated, there is no assurance that the replacement would be any better. Turner says assassination is not an American option.

Military attack, a real option, is an action that should be used sparingly. Turner says there is a fine line between "never" and "always." An example follows to illustrate his point—an analogy not used by Turner. Assume that terrorists blew up an American airplane, killing hundreds in the process. The subsequent investigation reveals that the XYZ terrorist organization did it, and they openly operated in country ABC. At this point, it would be time to consider attacking ABC. Before doing so, certain questions require answering. Can the terrorists be hit? Will there be civilian casualties? How will our allies feel about such a strike? Will Americans be killed? Will Americans be captured in the attack? Many other questions must be addressed, and even when they are all answered, any military option is dangerous. Events can always escalate.

The former CIA director has other recommendations. Turner believes the United States should become involved in covert operations, as well as hostage rescue efforts. However, he equates these with military actions and states that they should be used sparingly. Citing the First Amendment, he believes self-restraint is all that the government can expect from the media. He endorses economic sanctions, although it usually takes a long time to produce results, and he states that making deals is an option to be considered. He urges a path of legal restraint, arguing that it reflects the democratic values of the American people.

Turner also makes a critical comment about improving human intelligence. (Human intelligence is the information that agents obtain without using satellites, radios, and other technological devices.) He feels governmental commissions recommending improved human intelligence systems do not understand the world of intelligence. The director of central intelligence, for example, always tries to improve human intelligence-gathering systems. It is just not that easy to do. It takes quite a bit of time to build a network of informants, and most Americans are easily identified when they try to establish them. Turner says that even when they are employed, it is very difficult to predict future terrorist events. Turner argues that we should make every effort to increase human intelligence systems, but they cannot be considered a panacea for countering terrorist groups.

It is important to realize the theme of his work. Turner argues that the United States needs some type of counterterrorist policy beyond rhetoric. One may like or dislike his points, but his thesis is correct. Dennis Pluchinsky (1992) also adds a note for academics.

Pluchinsky says many academic analysts attempt to formulate or analyze policy as part of their basic research. Although this practice is laudable, Pluchinsky says it is not very practical. Professors do not make policy, but presidents, state department officials, and intelligence directors do. Pluchinsky asks academics to move away from policy analysis and focus on the need to gather basic information. Pluchinsky says policymakers need that information, and academic analysts would serve much better if they concentrated on providing basic information. He urges American researchers to focus on gathering information and analyzing its meaning or—to paraphrase political analyst Aaron Wildavsky—to speak plain truth to power.

WEAPONS OF MASS DESTRUCTION: PREDICTING THE FUTURE

Technological terrorism is one of the more frightening scenarios one can imagine. Modern societies are susceptible to two methods of technological terror. The first is the employment of mass destruction weapons or the conversion of an industrial site—for example, a chemical plant—into a massively lethal instrument through sabotage. The other method is to attack a source that supplies technology or energy. The results of either type of attack could be catastrophic. Technology looms as a potentially sinister partner in the evolution of terrorism.

The Aum Shinrikyo attack in the Tokyo subway system was a dramatic event. Although it failed to produce the intended number of casualties, massive death was just a few heartbeats away. The attack also represents a line of demarcation. Terrorists have attacked technological targets in the past, but until Tokyo, they had not used weapons of potential mass destruction. Terrorists have crossed the line separating terrorism from mass destruction. Technology and terrorism are a dangerous tandem, and the future is unknown. Policymakers cannot rest on the assumption, "Well, they have never done it before," and they must take massive disasters into account.

Several years ago, Grant Wardlaw (1982, pp. 173–184) made a good point about the future. He wrote that prediction is an occupation fraught with uncertainty and danger. Keeping that the unsure nature of futuristic analysis in mind (it is an educated guessing game), Wardlaw maintained that it is necessary and important to speculate about future trends in terrorism. In fact, Wardlaw argues that speculation should be an activity of as many analysts as possible.

Other analysts have shared Wardlaw's concern for the future of political violence. Richard Falk and Samuel Kim (1984) approach the problem strategically. They view the threat as one not so much of localized violence but of a social failure to think about all forms of violence from a global perspective. Walter Laqueur has speculated about a "Sarajevo effect," in which a terrorist incident expands into a war. (He referred to the assassination of the Austrian Archduke in Sarajevo in August 1914, which led to the start of World War I.) J. Bowyer Bell (1985, pp. 41–52) also raises this point. Bell says a single terrorist act is usually unlikely to create a major war, but the practice of terrorism can be a prelude to greater conflict.

In almost all speculations, analysts eventually turn their attention to technology (see Box 17.1). According to Wardlaw, the greatest danger looming in

---

BOX 17.1   Brian Clark's Thesis

Technology creates new opportunities for terrorism.

Technology will make terrorism a major problem of the future.

America is especially vulnerable to technological terrorism.

American bureaucracies have failed to take protective measures against technological terrorism.

SOURCE: Brian Clark (1980), *Technological Terrorism*, Old Greenwich, CT: Devin-Adair.

---

the future of terrorism is the potential destructive power of modern weaponry. Instruments of mass destruction could be used to produce the ultimate form of terrorism. Wardlaw says the essential question is whether terrorists will use such weapons. If they do, the face of terrorism and the nature of governmental response to the problem will change.

Wardlaw says trends in modern terrorism are disturbing because of the increasingly nihilistic spirit among terrorist groups. Groups that engage in thrill killing and devalue human life may not be deterred by the prospect of massive deaths. Many terrorist groups are calling for worldwide revolution, but this is not a concrete goal. Faced with this fact, individual terrorists are abandoning their national and group identifications to focus on abstract reasons for violence. Wardlaw argues that technology in the hands of such people is volatile. Although Wardlaw made these statements in 1982, the next two decades proved that he was absolutely correct.

Wardlaw was not the first to predict the potentially devastating effects of technology and terrorism; many other analysts have raised the issue (see Box 17.2 for a summary of speculations on terrorism). The literature focuses on (1) attacks on technological installations, (2) the use of chemical and biological weapons (CBW), and (3) the use of radioactive material and nuclear weapons. Nuclear terrorism seems to dominate the literature, but terrorism in any of these areas could produce devastating effects.

OUTLAWING TERRORISM:

THE THREAT TO CIVIL LIBERTIES

At first glance, it appears that a legal approach to terrorism would not be too controversial. Laws are passed by legislative assemblies in keeping with democratic traditions. For the most part, concepts of constitutionality and individuals' rights are emphasized. Judicial review is incorporated into most antiterrorist legislation, except for the most extreme cases. Terrorism treated as a criminal act rather than a political behavior seems to be compatible with the democratic process.

BOX 17.2 Analysts Speculate on the Future of Terrorism	
ANALYST	**VIEW**
Grant Wardlaw	Nihilism is increasing among terrorist groups. Technology offers the ultimate weapon.
Walter Laqueur	There is danger of a "Sarajevo effect": A single incident could spread to war.
J. Bowyer Bell	A "Sarajevo effect" probably will not develop from terrorism. Incidents need to be placed in perspective.
Robert Kupperman	Planning for technological terrorism is essential.
Brian Jenkins	Terrorism will continue as a mode of conflict. Social deterrents may eliminate technological terrorism.
Paul Wilkinson	Western democracies may have to accept minimal levels of terrorism.

The controversy about antiterrorist legislation arises from concerns about civil liberties. The legal solution has become controversial, because some critics have maintained that governments have overreacted to the problem of terrorism. They have argued that antiterrorist legislation is based on a political agenda, rather than on an objective assessment of the terrorist threat.

The potential destructive power of technological weapons brings civil liberties to the forefront. The essential policy question becomes, Is there a point where civil liberties can be curtailed in the name of public safety? Some analysts believe that WMD threats necessitate such safeguards. Other analysts say this is an overreaction.

David Kopel and Joseph Olson (1996) fear antiterrorist legislation will be used to empower law enforcement or the military against the civilian population. They say Americans are concerned with "terrorist anxiety," and the atmosphere is conducive to overregulation of society. They argue that this is a misperception of the current situation because the level of terrorism is dropping. Furthermore, there is no terrorist crisis. The laws used to regulate criminal behavior have worked quite well against terrorism. They believe the popular perception of the current situation is dangerous.

Kopel and Olsen use historical and legal arguments to bolster their case. Historically, laws focusing on social regulation in the face of public fear have been used to repress people. When such laws are enforced, they go far beyond the original intention of legislative bodies. For example, Kopel and Olson cite U.S. Attorney General A. Mitchell Palmer during the 1919 Red Scare. Palmer conducted raids and arrests against things he deemed un-American, all in the name of anticommunism. Many of his actions violated both the Constitution and the spirit of criminal legislation. Kopel and Olson also argue that more recent British policies in Ireland represent the same type of overreaction to terrorism.

Kopel and Olson argue that overreaction to terrorism can bring censorship, criminalization of political activity, and militarization of the police. They also fear military forces will be used to enforce civilian laws, a violation of the Constitution. They fear extensive government eavesdropping, expanded surveillance, and expanded powers for warrantless searches and arrests. This could be accompanied by centralized law enforcement efforts, and even secret trials. Kopel and Olson point to history to demonstrate their case.

Kopel and Olson find dangers in antiterrorist legislation, but one of the methods of countering terrorism in Western society has been to focus on the illegality of its actions. Several Western governments have attempted to regulate terrorism by legal means. Examples of this are the Emergency Powers and Prevention of Terrorism acts in Great Britain and Northern Ireland. The Spanish have also invoked a form of emergency legislation to deal with the Basques, and the Germans have enacted a variety of laws in their efforts against terrorism. Serious debate about the issue rose in the U.S. Congress in 1995. The basis for these actions is a belief in the efficacy of the legal system.

Among the staunchest critics of antiterrorist legislation is Beau Grosscup (1987). He is not as concerned with the overreaction of specific legislation, such as the Emergency Powers Act in Ireland, as he is with the whole concept behind such legislation. Grosscup believes antiterrorist legislation reflects the political will of a philosophical paradigm he calls neoconservatism. According to Grosscup, neoconservatism emerged from the Thatcher and Reagan governments and expanded in the 1990s. If Grosscup is correct, the Democratic Party in the Clinton administration embraced forms of neoconservatism in countering both crime and terrorism.

Neoconservatives believe most social problems, including terrorism, have been caused by a breakdown of cherished values and the permissiveness of liberal politics. The agenda of neoconservatism has been to return society to a more orderly course. This necessarily involves legislation of some moral issues to ensure the success of the neoconservative agenda.

Conservative analysts, too, have expressed concern about antiterrorist legislation, not so much from an acceptance of Grosscup's thesis but from fear of losing civil liberties (McFarlane, 1985). Some members of the British government have been critical of measures in Northern Ireland, fearing the limitations on freedom imposed by antiterrorist legislation. Former CIA Director William Webster issued several warnings about the danger of overreacting to terrorism at the expense of American liberties. Such warnings from conservative politicians hardly fit Grosscup's theories of neoconservatism.

The empirical voice of Christopher Hewitt (1984) has noted that terrorism decreases when terrorists are placed in jail. Whether this means that antiterrorist legislation is needed is another issue, however. If jailed terrorists do not engage in terrorism, the process of getting them into jail is still subject to question. The debate centers on two unresolved issues. First, should terrorists be jailed under special laws, or should they be charged with standard criminal violations? Second, have WMDs changed the equation to merit special laws?

THE USE OF MILITARY FORCE
AGAINST TERRORISM

Military units have come into play against terrorism in four ways. First and most frequently, military force has been used as an extension of police force. Second, when terrorist groups are supported by countries or when they operate from specific geographic areas, military force has been used to strike terrorist bases. Third, military force has seen the evolution of counterterrorist commando units. These have been used primarily in hostage rescue operations, but they have also been employed as specialized strike units. Finally, with the threat of destruction from WMDs, specialized military responses have been developed for a technological attack.

The assumption behind the use of military force is a belief that the terrorist problem has become too great for the state's civil power. When military forces are employed, governments feel that civilian police forces and the courts are no longer capable of dealing with violence. The terrorists have grown too strong, and police power must be augmented.

Four factors are at the heart of controversy over military counterterrorist activities. First, in Western democracies, civil governments have an aversion to the use of military force to ensure domestic peace. The function of the military is not to enforce civil law. In some places, such as the United States, the use of the military in a police role is outlawed.

The second factor is a history of overreaction on the part of military forces. In Latin America, for example, the use of military power to back civil power is often associated with the rise of repression. When military force is used to augment police power, the manner in which it is employed and the duration of its use becomes critical.

Another controversial aspect of military power is the use of armed forces in retaliatory strikes and in specialized tactical units. Once again, ideology often dominates the arguments for and against such retaliation. One side claims that retaliatory strikes deter terrorism by setting an example; the other believes revenge ultimately creates more terrorism.

There is another area in which military force is the focus of policy debate. When specialized commando units are employed against terrorists, they raise questions concerning the proper use of force and the role of the military. Few question the deployment of elite hostage rescue units; the debate concerns unconventional military tactics designed to strike at terrorist groups.

No unit better illustrates this last issue than the Twenty-second Special Air Service (SAS) Regiment operating within the British Army. According to John Akehurst (1982), the SAS evolved from the British commando units of World War II. P. Dickens (1983) says that after World War II, SAS tactics evolved to meet changing military threats. James Ladd (1986) and Tony Geraghty (1982) say SAS tactics were designed to offer unconventional military solutions to nontraditional military threats. As the threat of international terrorism grew after World War II, the SAS began to focus on counterterrorist strategies.

By 1975, the SAS had developed state-of-the-art hostage rescue techniques and methods for protecting dignitaries. Geraghty says these functions were developed in the Counter Revolutionary Warfare Wing. Bodyguards and hostage-rescue units began to pattern themselves after the SAS, and SAS troops and advisers were involved in several spectacular hostage rescue raids from 1977 to 1980. Their activities have been strongly applauded throughout the West.

Special Air Service activities have another aspect, however. Geraghty notes that the SAS was sent to Northern Ireland around 1975. They have remained there for several years, and they have also been deployed against the IRA in other parts of Europe. Geraghty says the SAS mission has been shrouded in secrecy, and its troops have learned to fight a most unconventional war. Christopher Dobson and Ronald Payne (1982a, pp. 19–50) believe the SAS has become extremely effective against the IRA by intimidating terrorists.

The SAS became the master of the counterterrorist ambush, and the IRA was completely taken aback by its tactics. Whereas the IRA understood the practices of the regular troops and of the RUC under the Emergency Powers Act, the SAS presented a more frightening reality of counterterrorist warfare. The IRA could not compete with the SAS.

Many IRA terrorists were never able to reach their own ambush areas when the SAS was in the countryside. The IRA began to claim that the SAS was a "killer squad," and an example of British terrorism. They had to say something; they were certainly no match for the SAS. SAS policies were ruthless and frightening to the IRA. Unlike the police, SAS troopers often killed terrorists during IRA operations. Individuals were shot while picking up weapons or planting car bombs. IRA "roadblocks" were destroyed by SAS ambushes. In 1987, the IRA planned to strike an RUC station for the purpose of killing several police officers. Unknown to the terrorists, intelligence sources knew of the plot, and the police were replaced by SAS troopers in RUC uniforms. Few of the would-be murderers from the IRA left the area alive.

One of the most widely reported events was an SAS ambush on Gibraltar in 1988. Three alleged members of the IRA were involved in a plot to set off a bomb during a parade. As they were making preparations, according to news reports, undercover SAS personnel ambushed the terrorists. The terrorists were killed by well-aimed small arms fire. According to all three major American television networks, one of the terrorists was shot repeatedly after falling to the ground.

The unconventional warfare tactics of the SAS have raised a storm of controversy. Supporters quickly point to the deplorable terrorism of the IRA and the inability of ordinary security forces to make proactive strikes against the terrorists. Critics take a different view. The clear implication of many critics is that SAS policies are acceptable under wartime conditions, but since the IRA represents a threat to civil peace, it should be countered by civil law. Unsurprisingly, Irish republicans lead the critics of the SAS. Denis Faul and Raymond Murray (1976b) claim the SAS is a death squad.

Grant Wardlaw (1982, pp. 87–102) examines the role of the military in counterterrorist operations, paying particular attention to the SAS. According to Wardlaw, a police force is more suitable for counterterrorist operations than are military units. The police have been better prepared for these activities in Western societies than in others because their organizations have been militarized. The police can adopt military training and tactics when extra power is needed, while still maintaining their orientation to civil law.

Wardlaw acknowledges that sometimes the police simply cannot handle a terrorist situation. The threat may become too great, or the police may not be prepared for a rapidly developing terrorist threat. In these cases, the military should be brought in subject to civil regulations, norms, and controls. Wardlaw believes the use of military force often exaggerates the threat of terrorism. He also shares others' concerns about the use of military force to enforce civil law. Military force may be required at times, but its use should be minimized.

Peter Kraska (1996) points to another controversial tendency. In the United States, Kraska says the police have created strong paramilitary units since the standoffs at Waco and Ruby Ridge. He believes the American police have conceptualized the urban environment as a war zone, and the growth of police special weapons units exemplifies the trend. As a result, not only terrorism, but also most social problems, are militarized. Kraska argues it is a cultural force. If he is correct, the trend goes far beyond law enforcement's tactical approach to terrorism, and it signifies the antithesis of efforts such as community-based policing.

SECRECY AND SHARED INFORMATION

Another controversial aspect of counterterrorism is directly related to the internal workings of police agencies. This issue is hidden from those unfamiliar with police operations, and it is not generally discussed by analysts of terrorism. It is also closely related to the abilities of the police to respond to crime. Stated simply, the police are reluctant to share information inside and outside their organizations. This attitude has a negative impact on all criminal investigations, and the effects spill over into counterterrorism.

Abraham Blumberg (1979) believes the problem originates with the bureaucratic nature of modern policing. Blumberg maintains that police agencies exhibit all the characteristics of bureaucracies: They are highly centralized hierarchical structures under rigid authority. Routine patrols cannot be regulated in such an environment, but routine management at the police station can. Information becomes the basis for such regulation, and control of information translates into power. Therefore, to obtain and maintain power, police officers develop a fetish for secrecy.

Peter Manning (1976) explains how secrecy maintains social power. Manning says the police claim to have a monopoly on understanding and controlling social violence. When the reality of police work is examined, however, they can do neither. If the police admit they can neither explain nor control crime, they would lose public confidence and support; to avoid this, they act as if they can. Manning calls this the "manipulation of appearances." The police manipulate their activities to give the appearance that they control violence. The weakness of their position is camouflaged by perpetual secrecy and lying. The police learn to gather information and then to hide it.

Secrecy is dysfunctional for conducting counterterrorism. Aside from the fact that it could be used to cover unauthorized repression, secrecy hampers the police in their response to terrorism. Manning argues that investigative capacity is directly linked to the ability to gather and use information. Secrecy works against the effective use of information. This issue has not been the subject of extensive public debates, but it is a key internal police dilemma.

The effectiveness of sharing counterterrorist information can be demonstrated through the activity of European police agencies in INTERPOL. A variety of factors was responsible for the recent decline of European terrorism, but it is interesting to note that the decline was accompanied by a willingness of police agencies to share information. Organizationally, governments provided more incentives for sharing rather than hoarding information. As the European Union moves to open Europe's borders, national police agencies must create new methods of sharing information.

STINSON'S ANALYSIS OF SECURITY

James Stinson, a security specialist and frequent counterterrorist consultant to the U.S. government, has conducted a number of studies of terrorist tactics, and was the principal investigator of several Middle Eastern bombings. He has compared the methods of tactical assaults on targets with the defensive measures used to protect them. His conclusions have sparked a heated debate among security experts.

Stinson (1984) argues the United States tends to approach counterterrorism in the same way it does crime prevention. For the past 20 years, American police agencies have preached that it is necessary to deny criminals the opportunity to commit a crime. In terms of physical security, this approach means it is necessary to add security measures to potential targets. For example, merchants might add additional locks, special doors, alarm systems, or even security guards to protect their assets. This process is known as target hardening.

Counterterrorism has been approached the same way. Stinson argues Americans have come to equate security with fortification. Targets are physically hardened to prevent terrorist assaults. Many analysts have cautioned against such an approach because it allows terrorists to maintain the initiative. Their feeling is that terrorists who encounter a hardened target will simply seek a weaker one. Stinson agrees with this conclusion, but he offers a more provocative analysis.

According to Stinson, target hardening has very little effect on the success or failure of a terrorist assault. This result is not because terrorists shy away from hardened targets, but rather because terrorists have a very high success rate in attacks on extremely secure targets. Stinson suggests physical security has very little to do with stopping terrorist threats. He supports his analysis with sobering data based on the bombings of several American military and diplomatic installations in the Middle East. When no physical security was present, terrorists had no problem attacking the target. Stinson says they enjoyed a 100 percent success rate. Yet when heavy security was present, including barricades, identification checkpoints, armed guards, surveillance systems, and interdiction teams, terrorists successfully attacked their targets 85 percent of the time. In other words, maximum security reduces the probability of assaults by 15 percent.

There is another opinion, and it can be gleaned from the analysis of the terrorist attack on U.S. forces at Dhahran, Saudi Arabia. On June 25, 1996, a lone truck laden with explosives was parked beside an outer perimeter fence. The resulting explosion killed 19 U.S. service personnel and injured dozens more. In September 1996, the Senate Armed Services Committee listened to an independent analysis on the incident, then questioned officials about the report's conclusions. The report claimed that security was lax.

General John Shalikashvili, former chair of the Joint Chiefs of Staff, and Secretary of Defense William Perry offered testimony to the senators. Some of the senators questioned the type of security in place at Dhahran before the attack, and they argued that proper defensive measures were lacking. Secretary Perry admitted there had been shortcomings and accepted blame for the incident. General Shalikashvili pointed out that even with increased security, terrorist attacks will occur in the future.

Did the findings imply that Stinson is wrong and that increased security will prevent successful terrorist attacks? The answer is yes and no. On the affirmative side, increased security would have minimized the loss of life at Dhahran. Simply moving the security fence farther from residences, for example, would have saved more American lives. On the negative side, increased security would not have stopped the attack. As General Shalikashvili said, attacks will continue. Security can minimize casualties, not prevent attacks.

Stinson's argument is not to abandon physical security but to enhance it with other measures. Stinson argues that defensive systems need to be proactive; target-hardening techniques for the most part are passive. He suggests the concept of target hardening has to be expanded beyond physical security. He believes behavioral models should be used to help predict potential targets. He also feels intelligence systems should concentrate on identifying and interdicting terrorists before they are able to strike. Stinson thinks this approach would reduce terrorism.

Aside from the brief review of Dhahran, critics of Stinson's approach point to two other problems. First, prediction is difficult. Predictive behavior models for terrorist activities provide intelligence, but in no way are they sophisticated enough to pinpoint the detailed probabilities needed to counteract an assault. Just as it is impossible to predict the types of people who will become terrorists, it has not been possible to develop a predictive model of terrorist groups.

The second controversial aspect of Stinson's remarks hinges on the meaning of "success." For example, the Macheteros once fired a rocket at the FBI office in San Juan. The office was fortified, and there was very little damage. The Macheteros held this to be a major victory against imperialism, but the janitors who cleaned up a few pieces of broken glass thought it only a mess. The extent of terrorist successes is highly debatable. Stinson's critics argue that physical security measures make people feel safe, and when people feel safe from terrorism, terrorists can have no victory.

Stinson's findings have been examined and debated within the security community. At first glance, he seems to be highly critical of physical security. (A security executive once complained to me, "Stinson thinks 85 percent of what I do is worthless!") This is not the case, however, because proactive security does not imply that target hardening should be abandoned. Stinson simply suggests that passive security be reinforced with active security. Despite the initial reactions, this view hardly seems controversial.

Stinson's suggestions also seem worthwhile. General Shalikashvili predicted there will be more attacks against United States interests. In 2000, the *USS Cole* was attacked by suicidal religious fanatics in Aden, a harbor in the country of Yemen. Unfortunately, the attack proves once again that General Shalikashvili's prediction is correct.

KEY CONCEPTS

1. The United States has yet to determine whether terrorism is a criminal justice issue or a matter of national defense.

2. Turner believes the United States must develop a rational, flexible response to terrorism. The country cannot effectively operate with catch phrases and zero-tolerance policies.

3. Weapons of mass destruction have changed the impact that terrorists may have on policy. As a result, it is important to develop models to reasonably predict terrorist behavior.

4. Simply outlawing terrorism may not be a viable solution. Laws to restrict terrorists also restrict the general population, frequently destroying civil liberties.

5. At times, law enforcement is not able to counteract terrorists, and they rely on military help. When military forces are used against terrorists, however, it militarizes the problem. When this happens, military forces have not always limited their response within the guidelines of civil and criminal law.

6. In order to be effective, security systems must be both active and passive.

FOOD FOR THOUGHT

Technological disasters do happen. In 1947, there was a massive firestorm in Texas City, Texas after an oil tanker fire ignited a refinery. In 1984, a chemical leak caused by a disgruntled employee in a Union Carbide plant killed thousands of people in Bhopal, India. If you were an emergency planner, what could you learn from these tragedies? Could you use similar response techniques? What is the difference between response and prevention? What policy issues should you consider if you want to stop a disaster before it happens?

FURTHER READING

George Buck, *Preparing for Terrorism: An Emergency Services Guide*

Appendix:
An Introductory
Dictionary of Extremism

A ny study of terrorism requires a working knowledge of groups, and this appendix is designed to get you started. What follows is a "quick and dirty" synopsis of some of the leading extremist and terrorist movements in the world.

Please keep a few warnings in mind before assuming that you can always identify a terrorist group. First, the world of political extremism changes overnight, and groups continually come and go. No list is ever quite finished, and you should not assume that any list of terrorist groups is complete. This list is simply a quick historical glance at terrorist groups.

Second, the most up-to-date listing of terrorist groups is on the Internet. To get more complete profiles, use "terrorist group" as a keyword on your favorite search engine. But remember, even the Internet may not be up-to-date. It is quite possible to read about a terrorist operation and be unable to find any reference to the group involved in the attack.

With those limitations in mind, this appendix will help begin to identify terrorist groups. Groups are listed in alphabetical order. The information was taken from the following sources:

1. *Patterns of Global Terrorism*, U.S. Department of State

2. *Terrorist Groups Profiles*, http://vislabwww.nps.navy.mil/~gmgoncal/
   tgp.htm

3. *The Directory of International Terrorism*, George Rosie

4. *Encyclopedia of Terrorism and Political Violence,* John Thackrah
5. *False Patriots and Klanwatch,* Joe Roy (editor)
6. *Guerrilla and Terrorist Organizations,* Peter Janke
7. *TPW: Terrorist Group Index,* http://www.site.gmu.edu/~cdibona/grpindex.html (This site is no longer available.)

GROUPS

Abu Nidal Organization (ANO)—One of the deadliest terrorist groups in the world, the Abu Nidal Organization is headquartered in Libya, with bases in Palestine and Lebanon. The group was founded in 1974 by Sabri al-Banna, code-named Abu Nidal. It is a splinter group from the Palestinian Liberation Organization and rejects peace with Israel. It frequently targets other Arab groups.

Abu Sayyaf Group (ASG)—An Islamic extremist group formed in 1991 in the Philippines. It separated from the Moro National Liberation Front.

Alex Boncayao Brigade (ABB)—A death squad of the Philippine Communist Party.

Al-Fatah—*See* Palestinian Liberation Organization.

Al-Gamaat al-Islamiyya (The Islamic Group, IG)—An Islamic fundamentalist group operating exclusively inside Egypt.

Al-Jihad—*See* Jihad Group. (Do not confuse with Islamic Jihad.)

Al-Qaeda—The Base. A multinational terrorist organization operated by Osama bin Ladin.

American Nazis—Any number of neo-Nazi groups operating in the United States. They are primarily affiliated with white supremacy and Christian Identity. They may also be involved with Creatorism and Nordic Christianity.

Angry Brigade—A British animal rights group operating between 1968 and 1971.

Arab Revolutionary Brigades—*See* Abu Nidal Organization.

Arab Revolutionary Council—*See* Abu Nidal Organization.

Argentine Anti-Communist Alliance (Triple A)—A death squad operating in Argentina from 1972 to 1981.

Armed Forces of National Liberation (FALN)—A Puerto Rican nationalist group. Spawned in the early 1950s, FALN maintains relations with other Puerto Rican terrorist groups such as the Organization of Volunteers for Revolution (OVRP), the Peoples Revolutionary Commando (CRP), and the Armed Forces of Popular Resistance (FARP).

Armed Forces of National Resistance (FARN)—A Salvadorian guerrilla group formed in 1974, the FARN was absorbed by the FMLN.

Armed Forces of Popular Resistance (FARP)—*See* Armed Forces of National Liberation.

Armed Islamic Group (GIA)—An Algerian extremist group, the GIA seeks to overthrow the Algerian government and replace it with an Islamic state.

Armed Resistance Unit—A left-wing American group that branched from the waning left-wing movement in the early 1980s. All the group's members belonged to other terrorist organizations. The group was defunct by 1985.

Armed Revolutionary Nuclei (NAR)—An Italian fascist group operating between 1977 and 1982.

Aryan Nations—A white supremacy, Christian Identity group formerly based in Hayden Lake, Idaho. The Southern Poverty Law Center won a suit against the group in 2000 and closed its operations. It now functions as the Aryan National Alliance.

Baader Meinhof Gang—*See* Red Army Faction.

Basque Nation and Liberty (ETA)—One of the largest terrorist groups in Europe, the ETA emerged from the Basque region in Spain in the 1950s. By 1968, it forced the Spanish government to declare a state of emergency, and it continued to increase operations until 1984. Popularity for the ETA waned between 1984 and 1994, but terrorists attempted to increase activities again in 1996. The ETA is a nationalistic terrorist group.

Black Guerrilla Family—An American revolutionary group from the West Coast in the late 1970s. Some members went on to join other leftist movements in the 1980s.

Black June—*See* Abu Nidal Organization.

Black Liberation Army—An American left-wing revolutionary group. Primarily active from 1978 to 1985, it combined with white leftist groups.

Black September—A terrorist wing of the Palestinian Liberation Organization established in 1970. Yasser Arafat abandoned Black September in the late 1980s. The name was resurrected by Abu Nidal.

Bruder Schweigen—*See* the Order.

Bruder Schweigen Strike Force II—*See* the Order.

Christian Identity—An American extremist religion proclaiming white supremacy.

Christian Patriots Defense League—An American Christian Identity group located in Illinois and Missouri.

Chukaku-Ha (Nucleus or Middle Core Faction)—A left-wing revolutionary group operating in Japan since 1957.

Church of Jesus Christ Christian—The Christian Identity church of Aryan Nations. Richard Butler leads the church from the new Aryan National Alliance.

Common Law Court—Any number of local American right-wing organizations that claim authority to interpret the Constitution.

Common Law Movement—An American right-wing philosophy guiding many militia groups. Most adherents want society to be governed by the English common law they choose to recognize, and they claim jurisdiction over local, state, and federal legal institutions.

Communist Combat Cells (CCC)—A fighting Communist revolutionary group in Belgium. It allied with other Communist groups between 1984 and 1987 but faded away owing to weakness.

Covenant, the Sword, and the Arm of the Lord—An American Christian Identity group that formed a survivalist compound in north Arkansas. The group disbanded after a raid by Bureau of Alcohol, Tobacco, and Firearms agents in 1985.

Creatorism—*See* Church of the Creator.

Democratic Front for the Liberation of Palestine (DFLP)—The DFLP is a Marxist splinter group that broke from the Popular Front for the Liberation of Palestine in 1969. The group split again in 1991, with moderates joining Yasser Arafat and militants following Nayif Hawatmah.

Dev Sol (Devrimci Sol)—A fighting Communist group in Turkey formed in 1978. Dev Sol attempted to unify with other European leftist groups from 1984 to 1987 but abandoned the plan. Unlike most other leftist groups, Dev Sol remained active in the 1990s.

Direct Action (AD)—A fighting Communist revolutionary group in France. It allied with other Communist groups between 1984 and 1987, spearheading a movement for unity among revolutionaries. It had faded by 1990 because of weakness.

Ellalan Force—*See* Liberation Tigers of Tamil Eelam.

Elohim City—A right-wing American survivalist settlement in Oklahoma.

Evan Mecham Eco-Terrorist International Conspiracy (EMETIC)—Formed in 1985 satirically using the name of a conservative Arizona governor, EMETIC is an ecological terrorist group. The group is known for tree spiking and sabotage, and it represents a new trend in domestic terrorism.

Farabundo Marti Front for National Liberation (FMLN)—A Salvadorian coalition of five leftist guerrilla groups and two Marxist terrorist groups, the FMLN formed in the late 1970s. In 1992, the FMLN signed a peace agreement with the government.

Fatah Revolutionary Council—*See* Abu Nidal Organization.

February 28 Popular Leagues (LP-28)—A Salvadorian guerrilla group formed in 1977, the LP-28 was absorbed by the FMLN.

Federation of Associations of Canadian Tamils—*See* Liberation Tigers of Tamil Eelam.

First October Anti-Fascist Resistance Group (GRAPO)—A fighting Communist revolutionary group in Spain that formed around 1974. It attempted to ally with other Communist groups between 1984 and 1987 but was unsuccessful.

Freeman—Any number of American right-wing, common-law extremists. The most noted group was arrested in Jordan, Montana, after refusing to respond to summons by law enforcement officers in 1995.

Front for United Popular Action (FAPU)—A Salvadorian guerrilla group formed in 1974, the FAPU was absorbed by the FMLN.

Gadsen Minutemen—A right-wing American militia.

Ghost Buster Commando—A right-wing Salvadorian death squad operating from 1985 to 1992.

Gun Owners of America (GOA)—An American political association of right-wing gun owners.

HAMAS (Islamic Resistance Movement)—Formed in 1987, Hamas is an outgrowth of the Muslim Brotherhood. The group operates in Palestine, Israel, and Jordan, and it has frequently attacked Israel, Palestinian moderates, and PLO rivals.

Harakat ul-Ansar (HUA)—A Pakistani group formed in 1993, fighting to incorporate the Indian state of Kashmir into Pakistan.

Hizbollah (Party of God)—A radical Shia group formed in Lebanon after the Israeli invasion. Its large size (several thousand) allows Hizbollah to operate as a militia. It has been involved in several attacks against American interests in the Middle East and has infrastructures in Europe, Africa, South America, and the United States.

Invisible Empire—*See* Ku Klux Klan.

Irgun Zvai Leumi (the Irgun)—A Jewish terrorist group operating against Palestinians in Palestine from 1945 to 1947. It emerged from the Stern Gang.

Irish National Liberation Army (INLA)—A militant Irish terrorist group formed from dissatisfied Official IRA members. Members of INLA have generally favored violent revolution. *See* Irish Republican Army.

Irish Republican Army (IRA)—One of two nationalistic terrorist organizations in Ireland, the IRA is one of the largest terrorist groups in the world. The Provisional IRA was established after the formation of the Irish free state. It fights for a united Ireland without regard to the form of government. The Official IRA was born in

Dublin in the 1916 Easter Rebellion. It is a Marxist group favoring a socialist state. The Officials have exhibited less violent tendencies than the Provisionals in recent years.

Islamic Jihad—A militant Palestinian group closely allied with Hizbollah. It began as a clearinghouse for terrorist groups in Lebanon in 1982, but emerged as a militia-style group by 1991. The group is committed to the destruction of Israel and the creation of an Islamic Palestinian state. Islamic Jihad is also known as the Palestine Islamic Jihad (PIJ).

Jammat ul-Fuqra—An Islamic purification movement, most Fuqra cells are located in North America, with many in the United States.

Japanese Red Army (JRA)—A fighting Communist group from Japan with international links, the JRA is responsible for attacks from the Middle East to the Far East, as well as an attempted attack in the United States. It is believed to be headquartered in Lebanon.

Jewish Defense League—An American Zionist group based in New York City. It is closely allied with other militant Jewish groups.

Jihad Group—An Egyptian Islamic extremist group, the Jihad Group seeks to overthrow the government of Egypt and replace it with an Islamic state. (Do not confuse this group with Islamic Jihad.)

Kach and Kahane Chai—A militant Jewish group fighting for the restoration of the biblical state of Israel.

Khmer Rouge—*See* Party of Democratic Kampuchea.

~~**Knights of the Ku Klux Klan**—*See* Ku Klux Klan.~~

Ku Klux Klan—Any number of American white supremacy groups growing after the Civil War. The major groups include the Invisible Empire, the Knights of the Ku Klux Klan, United Klans of America, and the National Knights of the Ku Klux Klan.

Kurdistan Workers' Party (PKK)—A Marxist group of Turkish Kurds formed in 1974, the PKK seeks to develop an independent Marxist state in southeastern Turkey.

Lautaro Faction of the Popular Action Movement—*See* Lautaro Youth Movement.

Lautaro Youth Movement (MJL)—An anti-U.S. group in Chile advocating overthrow of the Chilean government. The MJL is also known as the Lautaro Popular Rebel Forces.

Leaderless Resistance—An informal confederation of right-wing American extremists. Apparently coined by Louis Beam, Leaderless Resistance is more of a concept than an organization. It is closely related to Carlos Marighella's theory of violence.

Liberation Tigers of Tamil Eelam (LTTE or Tamil Tigers)—An ethnic revolutionary group in Sri Lanka, the LTTE was formed in 1976 and began terrorist operations in 1983. The LTTE has grown beyond terrorism at times and has been able to wage guerrilla war.

M-19—A Colombian terrorist group formed around 1977. Activities of M-19 peaked in 1988 and dwindled in the early 1990s.

Macheteros—A Puerto Rican revolutionary group operating in the eastern United States and Puerto Rico.

Manual Rodriguez Patriotic Front (FPMR)—Founded in 1983 as the armed wing of the Chilean Communist Party and one of Chile's most active terrorist groups.

May 19th Communist Organization (M19CO)—Formed from black and white left-wing radicals around 1968, the M19CO became one of the leading revolutionary organizations in the United States. It lasted well into the 1980s, and members remained ideologically active while in prison. It was a clearinghouse and a focal point for most left-wing and Puerto Rican terrorist groups from 1981 to 1986.

Michigan Militia—*See* Militia.

Militia—Any number of American paramilitary extremist groups formed after 1994, militias are usually grouped around right-wing issues, and they are highly individualistic. They typically center on the following issues: taxes, white supremacy, Christian Identity, gun control, abortion, or survivalism. Militias claim legitimacy through the Second Amendment of the U.S. Constitution and claim to represent the Constitutional rights of individuals.

Militia of Montana (MOM)—The original militia founded by John Torchmann in 1994, MOM spawned militias in other parts of the United States. *See* Militia.

Minutemen—*See* Militia.

MJL—*See* Lautaro Youth Movement.

Montoneros—A left-wing Perónist group operating in Argentina from 1975 to 1979.

Morazanist Patriotic Front (FPM)—A leftist Honduran group that began attacking U.S. civilian and military personnel in 1988.

MRTA—*See* Tupac Amaru Revolution Movement.

Mujahadin—Guerrillas resisting the Soviet invasion of Afghanistan from 1970 to 1979. The term is also used to describe any warrior resisting non-Islam power.

Mujahadin-e Khalq Organization (MEK)—An Iranian revolutionary group combining Marxism and Islam.

National Alliance—An American right-wing extremist organization headquartered in West Virginia and based on white supremacy.

National Knights of the Ku Klux Klan—*See* Ku Klux Klan.

National Liberation Alliance (ALN)—A Brazilian terrorist group operating from 1968 to 1972. Its founder and leader was the famed terrorist Carlos Marighella.

National Liberation Army (Bolivian) (ELN)—A Bolivian terrorist group trying to model a rural revolution in the Guevara style.

National Liberation Army (Colombian) (ELN)—A Colombian leftist guerrilla group formed in 1963, the ELN has been relatively inactive since ending peace talks in 1992.

National Liberation Movement (MLN)—*See* Tupamaros.

The New Peoples Army (NPA)—A Maoist guerrilla group in the Philippines formed in 1969, the NPA uses selective terrorism to support guerrilla operations.

New World Liberation Front—An American left-wing group operating on the West Coast in the late 1970s. It was closely associated with the Tribal Thumb and the Black Guerrilla Family.

Nordic Christianity—An American extremist religion proclaiming white supremacy and incorporating Norse traditions in Christianity. It is also known as Odinism.

Northern Michigan Militia—*See* Militia.

Odinism—*See* Nordic Christianity.

Omega 7—An anti-Castro Cuban group that operated in the United States from 1975 to the late 1980s.

Orden—A right-wing Salvadorian death squad. Among its thousands of victims was the Archbishop Oscar Romero, who was murdered while serving the Eucharist.

The Order—An American right-wing terrorist group that engaged in a number of high-profile crimes in the mid-1980s. It was followed by the Silent Brotherhood (Bruder Schweigen) Strike Force II.

Organization of the Oppressed on Earth—*See* Hizbollah.

Organization of Volunteers for Revolution (OVRP)—*See* Armed Forces of National Revolution.

Palestine Islamic Jihad (PIJ)—*See* Islamic Jihad.

Palestine Liberation Front (PLF)—A splinter group from the Popular Front for the Liberation of Palestine–General Command, the PLF formed under Abu Abbas in the mid-1980s. The group split again in 1991 into pro-Libyan and pro-Syrian factions.

Palestinian Liberation Organization (PLO)—A confederacy of Palestinian groups formed in 1964. Soon dominated by Yasser Arafat, the PLO established many branches, including groups that engaged in terrorism. Its military branch, al-Fatah, was staffed by fedayeen (holy warriors). Arafat branched away from terrorism in the 1980s, although several groups involved in the PLO maintained a terrorist campaign. In 1993, the PLO formally renounced terrorism.

Party of Democratic Kampuchea (Khmer Rouge)—Communist guerrillas in Kampuchea (Cambodia).

Patriot Movement—A description of American extremist right-wing philosophy. Patriots are frequently involved in militias. Christian Patriots usually follow the beliefs of Christian Identity, Nordic Christianity, Creatorism, or Free wheeling Fundamentalism.

Peoples Revolutionary Army (Argentina) (ERP)—A left-wing terrorist group operating in Argentina from 1969 to 1980.

Peoples Revolutionary Army (El Salvador) (ERP)—A Salvadorian terrorist group formed in 1971, the ERP was absorbed by the FMLN.

Peoples Revolutionary Army of the Armed Forces of National Resistance (ERP-FARN)—A Salvadorian terrorist group that broke away from FARN in 1975. ERP-FARN was absorbed by the FMLN.

Peoples Revolutionary Commando (CRP)—*See* Armed Forces of National Liberation.

PKK—*See* Kurdistan Workers' Party.

Popular Forces of Liberation (FPL)—A Salvadorian Communist guerrilla group formed in 1970, the FPL was absorbed by the FMLN.

Popular Front for the Liberation of Palestine (PFLP)—A Marxist terrorist group formed in 1967 under the direction of George Habash. In 1993, the PFLP broke with Yasser Arafat, rejecting the Palestinian Liberation Organization's attempts to make peace with Israel.

Popular Front for the Liberation of Palestine–General Command (PFLP-GC)—Split from the Popular Front for the Liberation of Palestine in 1968, the PFLP-GC formed under Ahmad Jabril. Its purpose was to wage a more aggressive campaign against Israel and establish closer links with Syria.

Popular Front for the Liberation of Palestine–Special Command (PFLP-SC)—A Marxist Palestinian group formed by Abu Salim in 1979, the PFLP-SC has specialized in attacks in Western Europe.

Popular Revolutionary Block (BPR)—A Salvadorian guerrilla group formed in 1974, the BPR was absorbed by the FMLN.

Popular Struggle Front (PSF)—A radical Palestinian group based in Syria led by Samir Ghosheh, the PSF is internally divided over the 1993 attempt to make peace with Israel.

Popular Vanguard of the Revolution (UPR)—A Brazilian terrorist group operating from about 1967 to the early 1970s, the UPR was closely allied with the National Liberation Alliance.

Posse Comitatus—An American white supremacy group formed in Wisconsin in the mid-1970s, the group has incorporated tax protest and Christian Identity in its message. It was a forerunner to various paramilitary movements in the 1990s.

Red Army Faction (RAF)—A German group and the largest and most successful Communist fighting group in Europe. The RAF was dominated by Ulricke Meinhof and Andreas Baader from 1968 to 1974, given the alternative name of the Baader-Meinhof Gang. After a series of setbacks, the RAF joined an alliance among fighting Communist groups between 1984 and 1987. The alliance failed, and the RAF declared peace in 1992. Several actions continue in the name of the RAF.

Red Brigades (BR)—An Italian fighting Communist group that reached its zenith between 1970 and 1982. It was known for its decentralized organizational structure and attacks on prominent people. It joined the alliance among Communist fighting groups between 1984 and 1987 but faded because of lack of support.

Red Hand Commandos (The Red Hand)—An Irish unionist terrorist organization that carries out vigilante attacks on Irish republicans.

Revolutionary Armed Forces of Colombia (FARC)—Established in 1966 as the military wing of the Colombian Communist Party.

Revolutionary Justice Organization—*See* Hizbollah.

Revolutionary Organization 17 November (17 November)—A radical leftist group in Greece formed in 1975, 17 November attacks NATO, Turkish, and European Union targets.

Revolutionary Organization of Socialist Muslims—*See* Abu Nidal Organization.

Revolutionary Peoples Liberation Party—*See* Dev Sol.

Sendero Luminoso—*See* Shining Path.

Sheriff's Posse Comitatus—*See* Posse Comitatus.

Shining Path—A Peruvian guerrilla organization founded in the late 1960s by Professor Abimael Guzman, the Shining Path combined guerrilla operations with ruthless terrorist attacks. Most leaders were arrested by 1995, but small operations began again in 1996.

Sikh Terrorism—Terrorism sponsored by some religious Sikhs in India for the purpose of establishing an independent Sikh state.

Silent Brotherhood—*See* the Order.

Skinheads—A white supremacy movement in Europe, the United States, and South Africa. It is primarily a white youth gang movement.

Stern Gang—A Jewish terrorist group operating against Palestinians before World War II.

Symbionese Liberation Army—An American left-wing revolutionary group made famous by the kidnapping of Patricia Hearst.

Tamil Tigers—*See* Liberation Tigers of Tamil Eelam.

Texas Constitutional Militia—*See* Militia.

The Tribal Thumb—*See* New World Liberation Front.

Tupac Amaru Revolutionary Movement (MRTA)—A Marxist revolutionary group in Peru formed in 1983. Most members were jailed by 1996, but terrorists from the group made headlines by seizing the Japanese embassy in Lima in December 1996.

Tupac Katari Guerrilla Army (EGTK)—A Bolivian group targeting U.S. interests in Bolivia.

Tupamaros—The prototype of the modern urban terrorist group that operated in Uruguay from 1963 to 1972. Founded by Raul Sendic, the Tupamaros embodied the revolutionary principles of Carlos Marighella, and the group served as a model for terrorists and extremists throughout the world. Most of the Tupamaros were murdered in a wave of government repression in 1972.

Ulster Defense Association (UDA)—A large Irish unionist organization, it allegedly supports several unionist terrorist organizations. The UDA has extensive membership and actively promotes militant Protestantism.

Ulster Freedom Fighters (UFF)—An Irish unionist terrorist organization, the Ulster Freedom Fighters mimic the tactics of the Provisional IRA.

Ulster Volunteer Force (UVF)—An Irish unionist terrorist organization formed after 1969. It specializes in assassination of suspected IRA members.

United Freedom Front (UFF)—A left-wing American revolutionary group that operated until 1985. Unlike most left-wing groups, the United Freedom Front survived the 1970s and allied with other left-wing groups. The group was especially noted for bombings.

United Klans of America—*See* Ku Klux Klan.

United States Militia Association—*See* Militia.

Vampire Killer 2000—An American right-wing newsletter and plan for restoring "Constitutional" government. *See* Militia.

Vipers—A militant militia movement in Arizona that allegedly planned a bombing campaign.

The Weather Underground—A left-wing American group that emerged from the Students for a Democratic Society's Weathermen. The group was defunct by 1985.

White Warriors Union—A Salvadorian death squad.

Wolf Packs—An American right-wing extremist term for small groups of activists operating below the militia level.

Wolverine Brigade—A militia group in Michigan. *See* Militia.

World Church of the Creator—Any number of American right-wing extremist churches created by Ben Klassen. Creatorists are deistic, believing that a creator has called them to preserve their race. They frequently employ the acronym RAHOWA for "Racial Holy War." Matt Hale is the self-proclaimed leader of the WCOTC.

World Tamil Association—*See* Liberation Tigers of Tamil Eelam.

Selected Bibliography

This bibliography contains selected citations from all editions of *Terrorism: An Introduction.*

Abbey, Edward. (1975). *The Monkey Wrench Gang.* Salt Lake City: Roaming the West.

ABC News. (1998). "John Miller Interview with Osama bin Laden." http://abcnews.co.com/sections/world/DailyNews/terror_1stperson_980612.html

Adams, James. (1986). *The Financing of Terror.* New York: Simon & Schuster.

Addis, Karen K. (1992). "Profiling for Terrorists." *Security Management* May: 27–33.

Akehurst, John. (1982). *We Won a War.* London: Russell.

Albats, Yevgenia. (1995). *KGB: State Within a State: The Secret Police and Its Hold on Russia's Past, Present, and Future.* London: Tauris.

Alexander, Yonah. (1976). "From Terrorism to War: The Anatomy of the Birth of Israel." In Yonah Alexander (ed.), *International Terrorism.* New York: Praeger.

Alexander, Yonah. (1984). "Terrorism, the Media, and the Police." In Henry Han (ed.), *Terrorism, Political Violence and World Order.* Landham, MD: University of America Press.

Alexander, Yonah. (1994). *Middle Eastern Terrorism: Current Trends and Future Prospects.* New York: Hall.

Alexander, Yonah, and Alan O'Day (eds.). (1984). *Terrorism in Ireland.* New York: St. Martin's.

Alexander, Yonah, and Kenneth A. Myers (eds.). (1982). *Terrorism in Europe.* New York: St. Martin's.

Al-Marayati, Salam. (1994, June 27). "The Rising Tide of Hostile Stereotyping of Islam." *Washington Report on Middle East Affairs.* http://www.washington-report.org/backissues/0694/94006027.htm.

Anderson, James H. (1995). "The Neo-Nazi Menace in Germany." *Studies in Conflict and Terrorism* 18: 39–46.

Andics, Helmut. (1969). *Rule of Terror*. New York: Holt, Rinehart & Winston.

Animal Liberation Front. (2000). Homepage. http://www. nocompromise.org/alf/alf.html.

Anonymous. (n.d.). *The Last Letter of Gordon Kahl*. Cohotah, MI: The Mountain Church.

Arquilla, John, and David Ronfeldt. (1999). "The Advent of Netwar: Analytic Background." *Studies in Conflict and Terrorism* 22: 193–206.

Aryan Nations. (n.d.). *The Death of the White Race*. Hayden Lake, ID: Aryan Nations.

Ayers, Russell W. (1975). "Policing Plutonium: The Civil Liberties Fallout." *Harvard Civil Rights–Civil Liberties Law Review* 10: 369–403.

Bahgat, Gawdat. (1994). "Democracy in the Middle East: The American Connection." *Studies in Conflict and Terrorism* 17: 87–96.

Bahgat, Gawdat. (1999). "Iran and Terrorism: The Transatlantic Response." *Studies in Conflict and Terrorism* 22: 141–152.

Baker, Mary, and Edward Wood. (1998). *The Criminal Justice Terrorism and Conspiracy Bill*. London: House of Commons Library.

Bakunin, Mikhail. (1987). "Revolution, Terrorism, Banditry." Reprinted in Walter Laqueur and Yonah Alexander (eds.), *The Terrorism Reader*. New York: Meridian.

Barkun, Michael. (1997). *Religion and the Racist Right: The Origins of the Christian Identity Movement*. Chapel Hill: University of North Carolina Press.l

Barton, John H. (1980). "The Civil Liberties Implications of a Nuclear Emergency." *New York University Review of Law and Social Change* 10: 299–317.

Bass, Gail, and Brian Jenkins. (1983). *A Review of Recent Trends in International Terrorism and Nuclear Incidents Abroad*. Santa Monica, CA: Rand.

Bassiouni, M. Cherif. (1981). "Terrorism and the Media." *Journal of Criminal Law and Criminology* 72: 1–55.

Bassiouni, M. Cherif. (1982). "Media Coverage of Terrorism." *Journal of Communication* 32: 128–143.

Bassiouni, M. Cherif (ed.). (1983). *Terrorism, Law Enforcement, and the Mass Media*. Rockville, MD: National Criminal Justice Reference Service.

Baumel, Judith Tydor. (1999). "Kahane in America: An Exercise in Right-Wing Urban Terror." *Studies in Conflict and Terrorism* 22: 311–329.

Beam, Louis. (1985). *Klan Alert*. Hayden Lake, ID: Aryan Nations.

Becker, Jillian. (1977). *Hitler's Children*. Philadelphia: Lippincott.

Becker, Jillian. (1984). *The PLO*. New York: St. Martin's.

Beckwith, Charlie, and Donald Knox. (1985). *Delta Force*. New York: Dell.

Bell, J. Bowyer. (1974). *The Secret Army: A History of the IRA, 1916–1970*. Cambridge, MA: MIT Press.

Bell, J. Bowyer. (1975). *Transnational Terror*. Washington, DC: American Enterprise Institute.

Bell, J. Bowyer. (1976). "Strategy, Tactics, and Terror: An Irish Perspective." In Yonah Alexander (ed.), *International Terrorism*. New York: Praeger.

Bell, J. Bowyer. (1978a). "Terrorist Scripts and Live Action Spectaculars." *Columbia Journalism Review* 17: 47–50.

Bell, J. Bowyer. (1978b). *A Time of Terror*. New York: Basic.

Bell, J. Bowyer. (1985). "Terrorism and the Eruption of Wars." In Ariel Merari (ed.), *On Terrorism and Combating Terrorism*. Landham, MD: University of America Press.

Bell, J. Bowyer, Jr. (1995). "The Irish Republican Army Enters an End Game: An Overview." *Studies in Conflict and Terrorism* 18: 153–174.

Bell, J. Bowyer. (1998). "Ireland: The Long End Game." *Studies in Conflict and Terrorism* 21: 5–28.

Bell, J. Bowyer, and Ted Robert Gurr. (1979). "Terrorism and Revolution in America." In Hugh D. Graham and Ted Robert Gurr (eds.), *Violence in America.* Newbury Park, CA: Sage.

Berard, Stanley, (1985). "Nuclear Terrorism: More Myth Than Reality." *Air University Review* 36: 30–36.

Beres, Louis. (1979). *Terrorism and Global Security.* Boulder, CO: Westview.

Beres, Louis. (1980). *Apocalypse: Nuclear Catastrophe in World Politics.* Chicago: University of Chicago Press.

Beres, Louis. (1983). "Subways to Armageddon." *Society* 20: 7–10.

Berkowitz, B. J., et al. (1972). *Superviolence: The Civil Threat of Mass Destruction Weapons.* Santa Monica, CA: Advanced Concepts Research.

Berlet, Chip. (1998). "Dances with Devils." Political Research Associates. http://www.publiceye.org/Apocalyptic/Dances_with_Devils_1.html; http://www.publiceye.org/Apocalyptic/Dances_with_Devils_2.htm.

Bermudez, Joseph S., Jr. (1990). *Terrorism: The North Korean Connection.* New York: Crane Russak.

Berthelsen, John. (1996, May 9). "Room with No View." *Far Eastern Economic Review,* p. 159.

Bill, James A., and Carl Leiden. (1984). *Politics in the Middle East.* Boston: Little, Brown.

Blumberg, Abraham S. (1979). *Criminal Justice: Issues and Ironies.* New York: New Viewpoints.

Bodansky, Yoseff. (1986a). *The Rise of Terrorism in the USA.* Unpublished manuscript, The Maldon Institute.

Bodansky, Yoseff. (1986b, September). *Terrorism in America.* Paper presented at EITWAT (Equalization on the War Against Terrorism), New Orleans, LA.

Bodansky, Yoseff. (1999). *Bin Laden: The Man Who Declared War on America.* Rocklin, CA: Forum.

Bodrero, D. Douglas. (1999). *Project Megiddo Y2K Paranoia: Extremists Confront the Millenium.* Tallahassee, FL: Institute for Intergovernmental Research.

Bodrero, D. Douglas. (2000). *State Roles, Community Assessment, and Personality Profiles.* Tallahassee, FL: Institute for Intergovernmental Research.

Bolz, Francis. (1984, May). *Hostage Negotiation Training.* Grand Rapids, MI: Grand Rapids Police Department.

Bolz, Francis A., and E. Hershey. (1980). *Hostage Cop.* New York: Rawson, Wade.

Bonner, Raymond. (1984). *Weakness and Deceit: U.S. Policy and El Salvador.* New York: Times Books.

Bouchat, Clarence J. (1996). "A Fundamentalist Islamic Threat to the West." *Studies in Conflict and Terrorism* 19: 339–352.

Bowers, Stephen R., and Kimberly R. Keys. (1998, May). "Technology and Terrorism: The New Threat for the Millenium." *Conflict Studies.*

Boyce, D. G. (1984). "Water for the Fish, Terrorism and Public Opinion." In Yonah Alexander and Alan O'Day (eds.), *Terrorism in Ireland.* New York: St. Martin's.

Brackett, D. W. (1996). *Holy Terror: Armageddon in Tokyo.* New York: Weatherhill.

Bright, John. (1981). *A History of Israel,* (3rd Ed.) Philadelphia: Westminster.

Brockman, James R. (1988). *The Violence of Love: The Pastoral Wisdom of Archbishop Oscar Romero.* San Francisco: Harper & Row.

Brown, David J., and Robert Merrill. (1993). *Violent Persuasions: The Politics and Imagery of Terrorism.* Seattle: Bay Press.

Bruce, S. (1993). "Fundamentalism, Ethnicity, and Enclave." In Martin E. Marty and R. Scott Appleby (eds.), *Fundamentalisms and the State.* Chicago: University of Chicago Press.

Bruce, Steve. (1995). "Paramilitaries, Peace, and Politics: Ulster Loyalists and the 1994 Truce." *Studies in Conflict and Terrorism* 18: 187–202.

Buchanan, Paul G. (1987). "The Varied Faces of Domination: State Terror, Economic Policy, and Social Rupture During the Argentine 'Proceso,' 1976–1981." *American Journal of Political Science* 31: 336–380.

Buck, George. (1998). *Preparing for Terrorism: An Emergency Services Guide.* Albany: Delmar Publishing.

Bullion, Alan J. (1995). *India, Sri Lanka, and the Tamil Crisis, 1976–1994: An International Perspective.* London: Pinter.

Bureau of Alcohol, Tobacco, and Firearms, U.S. Department of the Treasury. (1994). *Report on Waco.* Washington, DC: ATF.

Bureau of Alcohol, Tobacco, and Firearms, U.S. Department of the Treasury. (1995). *Violent White Supremacist Groups.* Washington, DC: ATF.

Burton, Anthony. (1976). *Urban Terrorism.* New York: Free Press.

Butler, Ross E. (1976). "Terrorism in Latin America." In Yonah Alexander (ed.), *International Terrorism.* New York: Praeger.

Byman, Daniel. (1998). "The Logic of Ethnic Terrorism." *Studies in Conflict and Terrorism* 21: 149–169.

Cabezas, Omar. (1985). *Fire from the Mountain.* New York: Crown.

Cable, Larry. (1986, November). *Soviet Low-Intensity Operations and NATO.* Paper presented at the International Studies Association Section on Military Studies Conference, Harvard University, Cambridge, MA.

Cable, Larry. (1987). *Piercing the Mists: Intelligence and Policy in Constrained Lethality and Ambiguous Conflicts.* Paper presented at the International Studies Association Section on Military Studies Conference, Atlanta.

Cameron, Gavin. (1999). "Multi-track Microproliferation: Lessons from Aum Shinrikyo and Al Qaida." *Studies in Conflict and Terrorism* 22: 277–309.

Campbell, Joseph. (1949). *The Hero with a Thousand Faces.* New York: MJF Books.

Campbell, Joseph. (1985). *The Inner Reaches of Outer Space: Metaphor as Myth and Religion.* New York: A. van der Marck.

Campbell, Joseph with Bill Moyer. (1998). *The Power of Myth.* New York: Doubleday.

Carment, David, Patrick James, and Donald J. Puchala (eds.), (1998). *Peace in the Midst of Wars: Preventing and Managing International Ethnic Conflicts.* Columbia: University of South Carolina Press.

Chomsky, Noam, and Edward S. Herman. (1977). *The Washington Connection and Third World Fascism.* Boston: South End Press.

Christman, Henry M. (ed.). (1987). *Essential Works of Lenin.* New York: Dover.

Chubin, Shahram. (1987). "Iran and Its Neighbours: The Impact of the Gulf War." *Conflict Studies* 204: 1–20.

Clark, Brian. (1980). *Technological Terrorism.* Old Greenwich, CT: Devin-Adair.

Clark, Robert. (1979). *The Basques.* Reno: University of Nevada Press.

Clark, Robert. (1984). *The Basque Insurgents.* Madison: University of Wisconsin Press.

Cloward, Richard, and Lloyd Ohlin. (1960). *Delinquency and Opportunity.* New York: Free Press.

Clutterbuck, Richard C. (1975). *Living with Terrorism.* London: Faber & Faber.

Clutterbuck, Richard C. (1980). *Guerrillas and Terrorists.* Athens: Ohio University Press.

Coates, James. (1987). *Armed and Dangerous: The Rise of the Survivalist Right.* New York: Hill & Wang.

Cobban, Helene. (1984). *The Palestine Liberation Organization: People, Power, and Politics.* Cambridge: Cambridge University Press.

Cohen, Yoel. (1983, February). "The PLO: Guardian Angels of the Media." *Midstream:* 7–10.

Cohn, Norman. (1957). *The Pursuit of the Millennium.* London: Secker & Warburg.

Cole, Leonard A. (1996). "The Specter of Biological Weapons." *Scientific American.* http://sciam.com/1296issue/1296cole.html.

Collier, George Allen. (1994). *Basta!: Land and the Zapatista Rebellion in Chiapas.* Oakland, CA: Institute for Food and Development Policy.

Collins, Larry, and Dominique Lapierre. (1973). *O Jerusalem.* New York: Pocket Books.

Collins, Larry, and Dominique Lapierre. (1980). *The Fifth Horseman.* New York: Avon.

Committee of the States Assembled in Congress. (ca. 1985). *Special Orders.* Unpublished manuscript.

Coogan, Tim Pat. (1971). *The IRA.* London: Fortune.

Cook, Schura. (1982). "Germany: From Protest to Terrorism." In Yonah Alexander and Kenneth A. Myers (eds.), *Terrorism in Europe.* New York: St. Martin's.

Cooper, H. H. A. (1977a). "Terrorism and the Media." In Yonah Alexander and Seymour Finger (eds.), *Terrorism: Interdisciplinary Perspectives.* New York: John Jay.

Cooper, H. H. A. (1977b). "What Is a Terrorist? A Psychological Perspective." *Legal Medical Quarterly* 1: 8–18.

Cooper, H. H. A. (1978). "Terrorism: The Problem of the Problem Definition." *Chitty's Law Journal* 26: 105–108.

Corcoran, James. (1995). *Bitter Harvest: The Birth of Paramilitary Terrorism in the Heartland.* New York: Penguin.

Cornwell, Bernard. (1997). *The Winter King: A Novel of Arthur.* New York: St. Martin's.

Corrado, Raymond, and Rebecca Evans. (1988). "Ethnic and Ideological Terrorism in Western Europe." In Michael Stohl (ed.), *The Politics of Terrorism.* New York: Dekker.

Costigan, Giovani. (1980). *A History of Modern Ireland.* Indianapolis, IN: Bobbs-Merrill.

Covenant, the Sword, and the Arm of the Lord. (1982). *Defense Manual.* Zorapath-Horeb, AR: CSA.

Cox, Robert. (1983). "Total Terrorism: Argentina, 1969 to 1979." In Martha Crenshaw (ed.), *Terrorism, Legitimacy, and Power.* Middletown, CT: Wesleyan University Press.

Coyle, Harold W. (1992). *Trial by Fire.* New York: Pocket Books.

Cranston, Alan. (1986). "The Nuclear Terrorist State." In Benjamin Netanyahu (ed.), *Terrorism: How the West Can Win.* New York: Avon.

Crenshaw, Martha. (1977). "Defining Future Threats: Terrorists and Nuclear Proliferation." In Yonah Alexander and Seymour Finger (eds.), *Terrorism: Interdisciplinary Perspectives.* New York: John Jay.

Crenshaw, Martha (ed.). (1983). Terrorism, Legitimacy, and Power. Middletown, CT: Wesleyan University Press.

Criss, Nur Bilge. (1995). "The Nature of PKK Terrorism in Turkey." *Studies in Conflict and Terrorism* 18: 17–38.

Crossan, John Domonic. (1999). *The Birth of Christianity: Discovering What Happened in the Years Immediately after the Execution of Jesus.* San Francisco: Harper San Francisco.

Crozier, Brian. (1975). "Terrorist Activity: International Terrorism." Hearings Before the Subcommittee to Investigate the Administration of the Internal Security Act and Other Internal Security Laws of the Committee on the Judiciary, 79th Congress, 1st session, Washington, DC: U.S. Senate.

CSIS Global Organized Crime Project (William H. Webster, project chair). (1998). *Cybercrime . . . Cyberterrorism . . . Cyberwarfare: Averting an Electronic*

Waterloo. Washington, DC: Center for Strategic and International Studies.

Danitz, Tiffany, and Warren P. Strobel. (1999). "The Internet's Impact on Activism: The Case of Burma." *Studies in Conflict and Terrorism* 22: 257–269.

David, B. (1985). "The Capability and Motivation of Terrorist Organizations to Use Mass-Destruction Weapons." In Ariel Merari (ed.), *On Terrorism and Combating Terrorism.* Landham, MD: University Press of America.

Debray, Regis. (1967). *Revolution in the Revolution?* Westport, CT: Greenwood.

Deerin, James B. (1978). "Twilight War." In *Northern Ireland: A Role for the United States?* (Report by two members of the Committee on the Judiciary, U.S. Congress, based on a fact-finding trip to Northern Ireland, the Irish Republic, and England; 95th Congress, August/September.) Washington, DC: Government Printing Office.

Denson, Bryan. (2000, February 10). "Saboteurs Target High Tech Crops." *The Portland Oregonian.* http://www.oregonlive.com/cgi-bin/printer/printer.cgi.

Denson, Bryan, and James Long. (1999, September 26). "Ecoterrorism Sweeps the American West." *The Portland Oregonian.* http://www.oregonlive.com/cgi-bin/printer/printer.cgi.

Denson, Bryan, and James Long. (1999, September 27). "Ideologues Drive the Violence." *The Portland Oregonian.* http://www.oregonlive.com/cgi-bin/printer/printer.cgi.

Denson, Bryan, and James Long. (1999, September 28). "Terrorist Acts Provoke Change in Research, Business, Society." *The Portland Oregonian.* http://www.oregonlive.com/cgi-bin/printer/printer.cgi.

Denson, Bryan, and James Long. (1999, September 29). "Can Sabotage Have a Place in a Democratic Community?" *The Portland Oregonian.* http://www.oregonlive.com/cgi-bin/printer/printer.cgi.

Der Spiegel. (1980, October 6), pp. 37–46.

de Silva, Marik. (1996, May 5). "Sunshine over Jaffna." *Far Eastern Economic Review,* p. 159.

Deutch, John M. (1996). "Speech May 23, 1996." Conference on Nuclear, Biological, Chemical Weapons Proliferation and Terrorism. Central Intelligence Agency. http://fas.org/irp/cia/product/dci_speech_052396.html.

DeVito, Donald A., and Lacy Suiter. (1987). "Emergency Management and the Nuclear Terrorism Threat." In Paul Leventhal and Yonah Alexander (eds.), *Preventing Nuclear Terrorism.* Lexington, MA: Lexington Books.

Dickens, P. (1983). *SAS: The Jungle Frontier.* London: Arms & Armour.

Dobson, Christopher, and Ronald Payne. (1982a). *Counterattack: The West's Battle Against the Terrorists.* New York: Facts on File.

Dobson, Christopher, and Ronald Payne. (1982b). *The Terrorists.* New York: Facts on File.

D'Oliviera, Sergio. (1973). "Uruguay and the Tupamaro Myth." *Military Review* 53: 25–36.

Dunn, Seamus and Valerie Morgan. (1995). "Protestant Alienation in Northern Ireland." *Studies in Conflict and Terrorism* 18: 175–185.

Dworkin, Ronald. (1986). *Nunca Mas: The Report of the Argentine National Commission on the Disappeared.* New York: Farrar, Straus & Giroux.

Dyson, William E. (2000). *An Overview of Terrorism.* Tallahassee, FL: Institute for Intergovernmental Research.

Dyson, William E. (2001). *Terrorism: An Investigator's Handbook.* Cincinnati: Anderson Publishing.

Ehrenfeld, Rachel. (1986, September). *Narco-Terrorism.* Paper presented at EITWAT (Equalization in the War Against Terrorism) conference, New Orleans, LA.

Ehrenfeld, Rachel. (1990). *Narcoterrorism.* New York: Basic Books.

Ehteshami, Anoushiravan. (1995). *After Khomeini: The Iranian Second Republic.* London: Routledge.

Eliade, Mircea. (1961). *Myths, Dreams, and Mysteries: The Encounter Between Contemporary Faiths and Archaic Realities.* Translated by Philip Mairet. San Francisco: Harper.

Emerson, Steven A. (1994). *Jihad in America.* Public Broadcasting System.

Emerson, Steven A., and Cristina Del Sesto. (1991). *Terrorist: The Inside Story of the Highest Ranking Iraqi Terrorist Ever to Defect to the West.* New York: Villard.

Erlich, Reuven. (1998). "Hizballah Leaders: Terrorism Against Israel to Continue Even After IDF Withdrawal." Institute for Counter-Terrorism. http://www.ict.org.il/home.htm.

Ezeldin (Izz al-Din), Ahmed (Ahmad). (1991). *Global Terrorism: An Overview.* Chicago: University of Illinois Office of International Criminal Justice.

Falk, Richard A., and Samuel S. Kim. (1984). "World Order Studies: New Directions and Orientations." In Henry Han (ed.), *Terrorism, Political Violence, and World Order.* Landham, MD: University Press of America.

Fall, Bernard B. (1967). *Ho Chi Minh on Revolution.* New York: Praeger.

Fanon, Frantz. (1982). *The Wretched of the Earth.* New York: Grove.

Fanon, Frantz. (1980, originally 1965). *A Dying Colonialism.* London: Writers and Readers.

Farrell, William R. (1990). *Blood and Rage: The Story of the Japanese Red Army.* Lexington, MA: Lexington Books.

Faul, Denis, and Raymond Murray. (1976a). *Majella O'Hare Shot Dead by British Army.* Dungannon, Northern Ireland: St. Patrick's Academy.

Faul, Denis, and Raymond Murray. (1976b). *SAS Terrorism: The Assassin's Glove.* Dungannon, Northern Ireland: St. Patrick's Academy.

Federal Bureau of Investigation. (2000). "Terrorism in the United States." http://www.fbi.gov/publish/terror/terrusa.htm.

Federal Bureau of Investigation. (2000). "U.S. Embassy Bombings Summary." http://www.fbi.gov/majcase/eastafrica/summary.htm.

Federal Emergency Management Agency (FEMA). (1998). "Background: Terrorism." http://www.fema.gov/library/terror.htm.

Fellner, Jamie. (1988, February). "Invitation to a Murder: Colombian Death Squad Message." *Harper's,* pp. 58–59.

Fernandez, Ronald. (1987). *Los Macheteros: The Wells Fargo Robbery and the Violent Struggle for Puerto Rican Independence.* Upper Saddle River, NJ: Prentice Hall.

Finch, Phillip. (1983). *God, Guts, and Guns.* New York: Seaview Putnam.

Finn, John E. (1987). "Public Support for Emergency (Anti-Terrorist) Legislation in Northern Ireland: A Preliminary Analysis." *Terrorism* 10: 113–124.

Flackes, William D. (1989). *Northern Ireland: A Political Directory.* St. Paul, MN: Blackstaff.

Fleming, Marie. (1982). "Propaganda by the Deed: Terrorism and Anarchist Theory in Late Nineteenth-Century Europe." In Yonah Alexander and Kenneth A. Myers (eds.), *Terrorism in Europe.* New York: St. Martin's.

Fleming, Peter A., Michael Stohl, and Alex P. Schmid. (1988). "The Theoretical Utility of Typologies of Terrorism: Lessons and Opportunities." In Michael Stohl (ed.), *The Politics of Terrorism.* New York: Dekker.

Forrest, Frank R. (1976). "Nuclear Terrorism and the Escalation of International Conflict." *Naval War College Review* 29: 12–27.

Fox, Jonathan. (1999). "Do Religious Institutions Support Violence or the

Status Quo?" *Studies in Conflict and Terrorism* 22: 119–139.

Fraser, James, and Ian Fulton. (1984). *Terrorism Counteraction. FC 100-37.* Fort Leavenworth, KS: U.S. Army Command and General Staff College.

Freedman, Lawrence, et al. (1986). *Terrorism and International Order.* New York: Routledge & Kegan Paul.

Gal-or, Noemi (ed.). (1991). *Tolerating Terrorism in the West: An International Survey.* London: Routledge.

Gates, Mahlon E. (1987). "The Nuclear Emergency Search Team." In Paul Leventhal and Yonah Alexander (eds.), *Preventing Nuclear Terrorism.* Lexington, MA: Lexington Books.

Gay, Oonagh. (1998). *The Northern Ireland Bill: Implementing the Belfast Agreement.* London: House of Commons Library.

George, Alexander. (1991). *Western State Terrorism.* New York: Routledge, Chapman & Hall.

George, John, and Laird M. Wilcox. (1996). *American Extremists: Militias, Supremacists, Klansmen, Communist, and Others.* Amherst, NY: Prometheus Books.

Geraghty, Tony. (1982). *Inside the SAS.* New York: Ballantine.

Gibson, James William. (1994). *Warrior Dreams: Paramilitary Culture in Post-Vietnam America.* New York: Hill & Wang.

Gilio, María Esther. (1972). *The Tupamaros.* London: Secker & Warburg.

Gillespie, Richard. (1980). "A Critique of the Urban Guerrilla in Argentina, Uruguay, and Brazil." *Conflict Quarterly* 1: 39–53.

Goren, Roberta. (1984). *The Soviet Union and Terrorism.* Winchester, MA: Allen & Unwin.

Graham, Hugh D., and Ted Robert Gurr. (1979). *Violence in America: Historical and Comparative Perspectives.* Newbury Park, CA: Sage.

Greer, Steven. (1995). "De-centralised Policing in Spain: The Case of the Autonomous Basque Police." *Policing and Society* 5: 15–36.

Grosscup, Beau. (1987). *The Explosion of Terrorism.* Far Hills, NJ: New Horizons.

Guelke, Adrian. 1998. *The Age of Terrorism and the International Political System.* New York: St. Martin's.

Guevara, Ernesto (Che). (1968). *Reminiscences of the Cuban Revolutionary War.* New York: Monthly Review Press.

Gunaratna, Rohan. (1998). "International and Regional Implications of the Sri Lankan Tamil Insurgency." http://www.ict.org.il/.

Gupta, Dipak K., Harinder Singh, and Tom Sprague. (1993). "Government Coercion of Dissidents: Deterrence or Provocation?" *Journal of Conflict Resolution* 37: 301–339.

Gurr, Ted Robert. (1970). *Why Men Rebel.* Princeton, NJ: Princeton University Press.

Gurr, Ted Robert. (1988a). "Some Characteristics of Political Terrorism in the 1960s." In Michael Stohl (ed.), *The Politics of Terrorism.* New York: Dekker.

Gurr, Ted Robert. (1988b). "Political Terrorism in the United States: Historical Antecedents and Contemporary Trends." In Michael Stohl (ed.), *The Politics of Terrorism.* New York: Dekker.

Hacker, Frederick J. (1976). *Crusaders, Criminals, and Crazies.* New York: Norton.

Hadawi, Sami. (1967). *Bitter Harvest: Palestine Between 1914–1967.* New York: New World Press.

Halstead, Robert J., and James David Ballard. (1997). *Nuclear Waste Transportation Safety and Security Issues.* http://www.state.nv.us.nucwaste.

Hamilton, Iain. (1971). "From Liberalism to Extremism." *Conflict Studies* 17: 5–17.

Hamm, Mark (ed.). (1994). *Hate Crime: International Perspectives on Causes and Control.* Cincinnati: Anderson.

(Although not cited in this book, Hamm's *Skinheads* is the definitive work on the American skinhead movement.)

Han, Henry H. (ed.). (1984). *Terrorism, Political Violence, and World Order.* Landham, MD: University Press of America.

Hanauer, Laurence S. (1995). "The Path to Redemption: Fundamentalist Judaism, Territory, and Jewish Settler Violence in the West Bank." *Studies in Conflict and Terrorism* 18: 245–270.

Harik, Judith. (1997). "Syrian Foreign Policy and State/Resistance Dynamics in Lebanon." *Studies in Conflict and Terrorism* 20: 249–265.

Harris, John W. (1987). "Domestic Terrorism in the 1980s." *FBI Law Enforcement Bulletin* 56: 5–13.

Harris, Jonathan. (1983). *The New Terrorism.* New York: Simon & Schuster.

Harris, Marvin. (1990). *Our Kind: Who We Are, Where We Came From, and Where We Are Going.* New York: Harper Collins.

Harris, Wesley. (1998). *Burglary for the Patrol Officer.* Longview, TX: Rough Edge Publications.

Harvey, Neil. (1994). *Rebellion in Chiapas: Rural Reforms, Campesino Radicalism, and the Limits to Salinismo.* San Diego: University of California at San Diego.

Hasselbach, Ingo. (1996, February 10). "My Days as a Neo-Nazi." *Guardian Weekend,* pp. 12ff.

Hasselbach, Ingo, and Tom Reiss. (1996). *Fuhrer-Ex: Memoirs of a Former Neo-Nazi.* New York: Random House.

Hastings, Max. (1970). *Barricades in Belfast.* New York: Taplinger.

Heikal, Mohammed. (1975). *The Road to Ramadan.* London: Collins.

Heim, M. (1984). "Reason As a Response to Nuclear Terrorism." *Philosophy Today* 28: 300–307.

Heinzen, Karl. (1987). "Murder." Reprinted in Walter Laqueur and

Yonah Alexander (eds.), *The Terrorism Reader.* New York: Meridian.

Herman, Edward. (1983). *The Real Terror Network.* Boston: South End Press.

Hewitt, Christopher. (1984). *The Effectiveness of Anti-Terrorist Policies.* Landham, MD: University Press of America.

Hibbert, Christopher. (1999). *The Days of the French Revolution.* New York: Morrow.

Hiro, Dilip. (1987). *Iran Under the Ayatollahs.* London: Routledge & Kegan Paul.

History Channel. (2000). "100 Years of Terror." Four Part Series. New York: A&E Television Networks.

Hodges, Donald C. (1976). *Argentina, 1943–1976.* Albuquerque: University of New Mexico Press.

Hoffman, Bruce. (1995). "Holy Terror: The Implications of Terrorism Motivated by a Religious Imperative." *Studies in Conflict and Terrorism* 18: 271–284.

Hoffman, Bruce. (1999). *Inside Terrorism.* New York: Columbia University Press.

Hoffman, Bruce, and David Claridge. (1999). "Illicit Trafficking in Nuclear Materials." *Conflict Studies.* January/February 1999.

Holden, Richard. (1985, March). *Historical and International Perspectives on Right-Wing Militancy in the United States.* Paper presented at the annual meeting of the Academy of Criminal Justice Sciences, Las Vegas, NV.

Holden, Richard. (1986). *Postmillennialism as a Justification for Right-Wing Violence.* Gaithersburg, MD: International Association of Chiefs of Police.

Holden, Richard. (1999, March). *Illuminati, Bilderbergers, and the Trilateral Commission: The New World Order and Global Conspiracies.* Paper presented at the Academy of Criminal Justice Sciences annual meeting, Orlando, FL.

Holeck, Carl. (1985). *The Re-establishment of a Constitutional Republic Known As*

These United States of America. Omaha, NE: Constitutional Party.

Horchem, Hans-Josef. (1985). "Political Terrorism: The German Perspective." In Ariel Merari (ed.), *On Terrorism and Combating Terrorism.* Frederick, MD: University of America Press.

Horchem, Hans-Josef. (1986). "Terrorism in West Germany." *Conflict Studies* 186.

Hourani, Albert. (1997). *A History of the Arab Peoples.* Cambridge, MA: Belknap Press.

House of Commons: Northern Ireland Affairs Committee. (1998). *Composition, Recruitment and Training of the RUC.* London: The Stationary Office.

Hunker, Jeffrey. (1999). "Combating Cyberterrorism." ABC News. http://www.abcnews.go.com/sections/tech/DailyNews/terror990203_chat.html.

Huntington, Samuel P. (1993). "The Clash of Civilizations?" *Foreign Affairs* 72: 22–49.

Huntington, Samuel P. (1996). *The Clash of Civilizations and the Remaking of World Order.* New York: Simon & Schuster.

Institute for Counter-Terrorism. (2000a). "Al-Gama'a al-Islamiyya (the Islamic Group, IG)." http://www.ict.org.il/inter_ter/orgdet.cfm?orgid=18.

Institute for Counter-Terrorism. (2000b). "al-Jihad, Islamic Jihad, New Jihad Group, Vanquards of Conguest, Tala' i' al Fatah." http://www.ict.org.il/inter_ter/orgdet.cfm?orgid=12.

Institute for Counter-Terrorism. (2000c). "ETA Attacks Continue in Spain." http://www.ict.org.il?spotlight/det.cfm?id=455.

Institute for Counter-Terrorism. (2000d). "Partiya Karkeren Kurdistan (Kurdistan Workers' Party PKK). http://www.counterror.org.il/inter_ter/orgdet.cfm?orgid=20.

International Security Council. (1986). *State Sponsored Terrorism.* Tel Aviv: ISC.

Israeli Foreign Ministry. (1996, April 11). "Hizbullah." http://www.israel-mfa.gov.il.

Israeli Foreign Ministry. (1998). "Iran and Hizbullah." http://www.ict.org.il/home.htm.

Ivianski, Zeev. (1988). "The Terrorist Revolution: Roots of Modern Terrorism." In David C. Rapoport (ed.), *Inside Terrorist Organizations.* New York: Columbia University Press.

Iyad, Abu. (1978). *My Home, My Land: A Narrative of the Palestinian Struggle.* New York: Times Books.

Jackson, Geoffrey. (1972). *Peoples' Prison.* London: Faber & Faber. (Published in the United States in 1974 as *Surviving the Long Night,* New York: Vanguard.)

Janke, Peter. (1974). "Terrorism in Argentina." *Royal United Service Institute for Defence Studies Journal* (September): 43–48.

Janke, Peter. (1983). *Guerrilla and Terrorist Organizations.* New York: Macmillan.

Jenkins, Brian. (1975). *Will Terrorists Go Nuclear?* Santa Monica, CA: Rand. (Original predictions.)

Jenkins, Brian. (1983). *New Modes of Conflict.* Santa Monica, CA: Rand.

Jenkins, Brian. (1984, November). *The Who, What, When, Where, How, and Why of Terrorism.* Paper presented at the Detroit Police Department Conference on "Urban Terrorism: Planning or Chaos?", Detroit.

Jenkins, Brian. (1985). *International Terrorism: The Other World War.* Santa Monica, CA: Rand.

Jenkins, Brian. (1987a, July/August). "The Future Course of International Terrorism." *The Futurist,* pp. 8–13.

Jenkins, Brian, and Gail Bass. (1983). *A Review of Recent Trends in International Terrorism and Nuclear Incidents Abroad.* Santa Monica, CA: Rand.

Jenkins, Brian M. (1996). "Introduction." In D.W. Brackett (ed.), *Armageddon in Tokyo.* New York: Weatherhill.

Jenkins, Brian Michael. (1980). "Nuclear Terrorism and Its Consequences." *Society,* July/August: 5–16.

Jenkins, Brian Michael. (1986). "Is Nuclear Terrorism Plausible?" In Paul Leventhal and Yonah Alexander (eds.), *Nuclear Terrorism.* New York: Pergamon.

Jenkins, Brian Michael. (1987b). "Will Terrorists Go Nuclear?" In Walter Laqueur and Yonah Alexander (eds.), *The Terrorism Reader.* New York: Meridian. (Original predictions with comments and revisions.)

Jeurgensmeyer, Mark (ed.). (1992). *Violence and the Sacred in the Modern World.* London: Frank Cass.

Johnpoll, Bernard K. (1976). "Perspectives on Political Terrorism in the United States." In Yonah Alexander (ed.), *International Terrorism.* New York: Praeger.

Johnson, James Turner. (1997). *The Holy War Idea in Western and Islamic Traditions.* University Park: Penn State University Press.

Joll, James. (1980). *The Anarchists.* Cambridge, MA: Harvard University Press.

Jones, Juanita, and Abraham Miller. (1979). "The Media and Terrorist Activity: Resolving the First Amendment Dilemma." *Ohio Northern University Law Review* 6: 70–81.

Joshi, Manoj. (1996). "On the Razor's Edge: The Liberation Tigers of Tamil Eelam." *Studies in Conflict and Terrorism,* 19: 19–42.

Juergensmeyer, Mark. (1988). "The Logic of Religious Violence." In David C. Rapoport (ed.), *Inside Terrorist Organizations.* New York: Columbia University Press.

Kansas Bureau of Investigation. (1984). *Special Report by the Crime Analysis Unit on the Posse Comitatus.* Unpublished manuscript.

Kaplan, David, and Andrew Marshall. (1996). *The Cult at the End of the World: The Incredible Story of Aum from the Subways of Tokyo to the Nuclear Arsenals of Russia.* New York: Crown.

Kaplan, David E. (1997). "Terrorism's Next Wave." *U.S. News Online.* http://www.usnews.com/usnews/issue971117/17weap.htm.

Karmon, Ely. (1999). "Terrorism in Turkey: An Analysis of the Principal Players." Institute for Counter-Terrorism. http://www.counterror.org.il/articles/articledet.cfm?articleid+74

Kehler, Christopher P., Greg Harvey, and Richard Hall. (1982). "Perspectives on Media Control in Terrorist-Related Incidents." *Canadian Police Journal* 6: 226–243.

Kellen, Konrad. (1979). *Terrorists: What Are They Like? How Some Terrorists Describe Their World and Actions.* Santa Monica, CA: Rand.

Kelley, Kevin. (1982). *The Longest War.* Westport, CT: Hill.

Kelly, Michael J., and Thomas H. Mitchell. (1981). "Transnational Terrorism and the Western Press Elite." *Political Communication and Persuasion* 1: 269–296.

Ketcham, Christine C., and Harvey J. McGeorge. (1986). "Terrorist Violence: Its Mechanics and Countermeasures." In Neil C. Livingstone and Terrell E. Arnold (eds.), *Fighting Back.* Lexington, MA: Heath.

Khalidi, Ahmad S. (1995). "Security in a Middle East Settlement: Some Components of Palestinian National Security." *International Affairs* 71: 1–18.

Khatami, Siamak. (1997). "Between Class and Nation: Ideology and Radical Basque Ethnonationalism." *Studies in Conflict and Terrorism* 20: 395–417.

Kibble, David. G. (1996). "The Threat of Militant Islam: A Fundamental Reappraisal." *Studies in Conflict and Terrorism* 19: 353–364.

Kindilien, Robert E. (1985). "Nuclear Plants Confront Modern Terrorism." *Security Management* 29: 119–120.

Kingston, Shane. (1995). "Terrorism, the Media, and the Northern Ireland

Conflict." *Studies in Conflict and Terrorism* 18: 203.

Kittel, G. (1964). *The Theological Dictionary of the New Testament,* vol II, Δ–H. Grand Rapids, MI: Eerdmans.

Klassen, Ben. (1986). *The White Man's Bible.* Costa Mesa, CA: Noontide Press.

Koch, Peter, and Kai Hermann. (1977). *Assault at Mogadishu.* London: Corgi.

Kopel, David B., and Joseph Olson. (1996). *Preventing a Reign of Terror: Civil Liberties Implications of Terrorism Legislation.* Oklahoma City University Law Review. http://www.12i.org/SuptDocs/Crime/Preventing_a_Reign_of_Terror.htm.

Korn, David A. (1995). *Interview with Abdullah Ocalan.* http://kurdstruggle.org/index.shtml.

Kraska, Peter B. (1996). "Enjoying Militarism: Political/Personal Dilemmas in Studying U.S. Police Paramilitary Units." *Justice Quarterly* 13: 405–429.

Kropotkin, Peter. (1987). "The Spirit of Revolt." In Walter Laqueur and Yonah Alexander (eds.), *The Terrorism Reader.* New York: Meridian.

Kupperman, Robert. (1985a). CBS television interview.

Kupperman, Robert. (1985b). "Government Response to Mass Destruction Threats." In Ariel Merari (ed.), *On Terrorism and Combating Terrorism.* Landham, MD: University Press of America.

Kupperman, Robert. (1988a). CNN television interview.

Kupperman, Robert. (1988b, December). NBC Today interview.

Kupperman, Robert, and Darrell Trent (eds.). (1979). *Terrorism: Threat, Reality, and Response.* Stanford, CA: Hoover Institute.

Kurz, Anat. (1994). "Palestinian Terrorism—The Violent Aspect of a Political Struggle." In Yonah Alexander (ed.), *Middle Eastern Terrorism: Current Threats and Future Prospects.* New York: Hall.

Kushner, Harvey W., and Benjamin Jacobson. (1998). "Financing Terrorist Activities Through Coupon Fraud and Counterfeiting." *Counterterrorism and Security International* 5 (Summer): 10–12.

Labrousse, Alain. (1973). *The Tupamaros.* Harmondsworth, England: Penguin.

Ladd, James. (1986). *SAS Operations.* London: Hale.

LaFeber, Walter. (1983). *Inevitable Revolutions.* New York: Norton.

Laffin, John. (1987). *The PLO Connections.* London: Corgi.

Lake, Peter. (1984). Video files of the Ontario Provincial Police made available to the author through the courtesy of the Detroit FBI office.

Lakos, Amos. (1986). *International Terrorism: A Bibliography.* Boulder, CO: Westview.

Lakshmanan, Indria. (2000). "The Face of Terror that Only Zealots See." *The Boston Globe.* http://www.smh.com.au:80/news/0007/22/text/world11.html.

Langguth, A. J. (1978). *Hidden Terrors.* New York: Pantheon.

Laqueur, Walter. (1976). *Guerrilla: A Historical and Critical Study.* Boston: Little, Brown.

Laqueur, Walter. (1987). *The Age of Terrorism.* Boston: Little, Brown.

Laqueur, Walter. (1996, September/October). "Postmodern Terrorism: New Rules for an Old Game." *Foreign Affairs.*

Laqueur, Walter. (1999). *The New Terrorism: Fanaticism and the Arms of Mass Destruction.* New York: Oxford University Press.

Laqueur, Walter, and Yonah Alexander (eds.). (1987). *The Terrorism Reader.* New York: Meridian.

Lasky, Melvin J. (1975, May 11). "Andreas and Ulricke." *New York Times Magazine,* pp. 73–81.

Lee, Alfred McClung. (1983). *Terrorism in Northern Ireland.* New York: General Hall.

Lesser, Ian O. (ed.). (1999). *Countering the New Terrorism.* Santa Monica, CA: Rand.

Leventhal, Paul, and Yonah Alexander (eds.). (1986). *Nuclear Terrorism.* New York: Pergamon.

Leventhal, Paul, and Yonah Alexander (eds.). (1987). *Preventing Nuclear Terrorism.* Lexington MA: Lexington Books.

Lewy, Gunther. (1974). *Religion and Revolution.* New York: Oxford University Press.

Livingstone, Neil C. (1986). "Death Squads." *World Affairs* 116: 239–248.

Livingstone, Neil C., and Terrell E. Arnold (eds.). (1986). *Fighting Back.* Lexington, MA: Heath.

Llora, Francisco, Joseph M. Mata, and Cynthia L. Irvin. (1993). "ETA: From Secret Army to Social Movement: The Post-Franco Schism of the Basque Nationalist Movement." *Terrorism and Political Violence* 5: 106–134.

MacDonald, Andrew (William Pierce). (1985). *The Turner Diaries.* Arlington, VA: National Vanguard.

MacDonald, Andrew. (William Pierce). (1989). *Hunter: A Novel.* Hillsboro, WV: National Alliance.

MacDonald, Ronald. (1972). "Electoral Politics and Uruguayan Political Decay." *International Economic Affairs* 26: 24–45.

Mallin, J. "Terrorism As a Military Weapon." *Air University Review* 28.

Manning, Peter K. (1976). *Police Work: The Social Organization of Policing.* Cambridge, MA: MIT Press.

Marighella, Carlos. (1969). *The Minimanual of the Urban Guerrilla.* Unpublished copy of the U.S. Army Military Intelligence School.

Marighella, Carlos. (1971). *For the Liberation of Brazil.* Translated by John Butt and Rosemary Sheed. Harmondsworth, England: Pelican.

Martens, Frederick T. (1996). "New Russians, Old Cons, and the Transition to a Market Economy: Reflections from Abroad." *Criminal Organizations* 10: 4–5.

Martin, L. John. (1985). "The Media's Role in International Terrorism." *Terrorism* 8: 44–58.

Marty, Martin, and Scott Appleby. (1993). *Fundamentalisms and the State.* Chicago: University of Chicago Press.

Massie, Robert K. (1991). *Dreadnought: Britain, Germany and the Coming of the Great War.* New York: Random House.

Mauvel, Marlon. (2000, March 21). "Center Closing as Hunt for Rudolph Scales Down." *Atlanta Journal-Constitution.*

Mazur, Allan. (1982). "Bomb Threats and the Mass Media: Evidence for a Theory of Suggestion." *American Sociological Review* 47: 407–410.

McClintok, Michael. (1992). *Instruments of Statecraft: U.S. Guerrilla Warfare, Counterinsurgency, and Counter-terrorism, 1940–1990.* New York: Pantheon.

McFarlane, Robert C. (1985). "Terrorism and the Future of Free Society." *Terrorism* 8: 315–326.

McGuire, Maria. (1973). *To Take Arms: A Year in the Provisional IRA.* London: Macmillan.

McKinley, Michael. (1984). "The International Dimensions of Terrorism in Ireland." In Yonah Alexander and Alan O'Day (eds.), *Terrorism in Ireland.* New York: St. Martin's.

Mefford, Larry. (1996, August). "Canaries in Cages: Responding to Chemical Biological Incidents." *FBI Law Enforcement Bulletin* 20.

Mehrota, O. N. (2000). "Ethnic Strife in Sri Lanka." Institute for Defence Studies and Analyses, India. http://www.ict.org.il/home.htm.

Melman, Yossi. (1986). *The Master Terrorist.* New York: Avon.

Merari, Ariel (ed.). (1985). *On Terrorism and Combating Terrorism.* Frederick, MD: University Publications of America.

Merkl, Peter. (1986). *Political Violence and Terror.* Berkeley: University of California Press.

Micklus, Edward F. (1993). *Terrorism, 1988–1991: A Chronology of Events and Selectively Annotated Bibliography.* Westport, CT: Greenwood.

Miller, Abraham. (1982). *Terrorism, the Media, and the Law.* New York: Transnational.

Miller, David. (1984). *Anarchism.* London: Dent.

Monti, D. J. (1980). "The Relation Between Terrorism and Domestic Civil Disorders." *Terrorism 4:* 123–141.

Moss, Robert. (1972). *Urban Guerrillas.* London: Temple Smith.

Moxon-Browne, Edward. (1987). "Spain and the ETA." *Conflict Studies* 201.

Moxon-Browne, Edward (ed.). (1994). *European Terrorism.* New York: Hall.

Muir, Angus M. (1999). "Terrorism and Weapons of Mass Destruction: The Case of Aum Shinrikyo." *Studies in Conflict and Terrorism* 22: 79–91.

Mullen, Robert K. (1978). "Mass Destruction and Terrorism." *Journal of International Affairs* 32: 63–89.

Mullendore, Kristine, and Jonathan R. White. (1996, March). *Legislating Terrorism: Justice Issues and the Public Forum.* Paper presented at the Academy of Criminal Justice Sciences Annual Meeting, Las Vegas, NV.

Mullins, Eustace. (1984). *The Secret Holocaust.* Hayden Lake, ID: Aryan Nations.

National Advisory Committee on Criminal Justice Standards and Goals. (H. H. A. Cooper et al., eds.) (1976). *Report of the Task Force on Disorders and Terrorism.* Washington, DC: Government Printing Office.

National Public Radio. (1988, December). Report on Aryan Nations' links with the Skinheads.

Nechaev, Sergey. (1987). "Catechism of the Revolutionist." In Walter Laqueur and Yonah Alexander (eds.), *The Terrorism Reader.* New York: Meridian.

Nelson, Anthony. (1986). *Terrorism: The Intelligence System.* U.S. Defense Intelligence Agency, unpublished manuscript.

Netanyahu, Benjamin. (1986). *Terrorism: How the West Can Win.* New York: Avon. (Revised editions published 1995 and 1997.)

New York Times News Service. (1996, August 25). "American Terrorist: Just an Average Joe with a Bomb." *Grand Rapids Press.*

Newsweek. (November 4, 1974), p. 53.

Nice, David C. (1988). "Abortion Clinic Bombings As Political Violence." *American Journal of Political Science* 32: 178–195.

Nima, Ramy. (1983). *The Wrath of Allah.* London: Pluto.

Noble, Kerry. (1998). *Tabernacle of Hate: Why They Bombed Oklahoma City.* Ontario: Voyageur Publishing.

Norton, Augustus, and Martin Greenberg (eds.). (1979). *Studies in Nuclear Terrorism.* Boston: Hall.

Nunn, Sam, and John W. Warner. (1987). "U.S.–Soviet Cooperation in Countering Nuclear Terrorism: The Role of Risk Reduction Centers." In Paul Leventhal and Yonah Alexander (eds.), *Preventing Nuclear Terrorism.* Lexington, MA: Lexington Books.

Nusse, Andrea. (1999). *Muslim Palestine: The Ideology of Hamas.* London: Harwood Academic Publications.

O'Day, Alan (ed.). (1994). *Dimensions of Irish Terrorism.* New York: Hall.

O'Donnell, Guillermo. (1973). *Modernization and Bureaucratic-Authoritarianism.* Berkeley: University of California Press.

Office of International Criminal Justice. (1996, May–June). "Interpol Tries to Curb Spread of Russian Mafia in Europe." *Criminal Organizations.*

Organization for the Prohibition of Chemical Weapons. (2000). "Nerve Agents: Lethal Organo-Phosphorus Compounds Inhibiting Cholonest-erase." http://www.opcw.nl/chemhaz/nerve.htm.

Pace, Eric. (1984, September 21). "Car Bombing Has Become Favored Tactic of Terrorists in the Middle East." *New York Times,* p. A13.

Paletz, David L., Peter A. Fozzard, and John Z. Ayanian. (1982a). "The IRA, the Red Brigades, and the FALN in the New York Times." *Journal of Communication* 32: 162–171.

Paletz, David L., John Z. Ayanian, and Peter A. Fozzard. (1982b). "Terrorism on Television News: The IRA, the FALN, and the Red Brigades." In William C. Adams (ed.), *Television Coverage of International Affairs.* Norwood, NJ: Ablex.

Paz, Reuven. (1998). "Is There an 'Islamic Terrorism'?" Institute for Counter-Terrorism. http://www.ict.org.il/.

Paz, Reuven. (2000). "Hamas's Lesson from Lebanon." Institute for Counter-Terrorism. http://www.ict.org.il/home.htm.

PBS Front Line. (1998). "Hunting bin Laden." http://www.pbs.org/wgbh/pages/frontline/shows/binladen/.

Pearlstein, Richard M. (1991). *The Mind of the Political Terrorist.* Wilmington, DE: SR Books.

Peleg, Ilan. (1988). "Terrorism in the Middle East: The Case of the Arab-Israeli Conflict." In Michael Stohl (ed.), *The Politics of Terrorism.* New York: Dekker.

Phillips, Kevin P. (2000). *The Cousins' Wars: Religion, Politics, and the Triumph of Anglo America.* New York: Basic Books.

Pipes, Daniel. (1983). *In the Path of God: Islam and Political Power.* New York: Basic Books.

Pisano, Vittorfranco S. (1987). *The Dynamics of Subversion and Violence in Contemporary Italy.* Stanford, CA: The Hoover Institute.

Pictcavage, Mark (1999). *Anti-Government Extremism: Origins, Ideology, and Tactics.* Tallahassee, FL: Institute for Intergovernmental Research.

Pitcavage, Mark. (1999). *Current Activities and Trends.* Tallahassee, FL: Institute for Intergovernmental Research.

Pitcavage, Mark. (2000). *Right-Wing Scams.* Tallahassee, FL: Institute for Intergovernmental Research.

Pluchinsky, Dennis. (1982). "Political Terrorism in Western Europe: Some Themes and Variations." In Yonah Alexander and Kenneth A. Myers (eds.), *Terrorism in Europe.* New York: St. Martin's.

Pluchinsky, Dennis. (1986). "Middle Eastern Terrorist Activity in Western Europe: A Diagnosis and Prognosis." *Conflict Quarterly* 3: 5–26.

Pluchinsky, Dennis. (1993). "Germany's Red Army Faction: An Obituary." *Studies in Conflict and Terrorism* 16: 135–157.

Pockrass, Robert M. (1985, March). *Out and About: The Royal Ulster Constabulary and the Campaign Against Terrorism.* Paper presented at the annual meeting of the Academy of Criminal Justice Sciences, Las Vegas, NV.

Pockrass, Robert M. (1987). "Terroristic Murder in Northern Ireland: Who Is Killed and Why." *Terrorism* 9: 341–357.

Podhoretz, Norman. (1981). "The Subtle Collusion." *Political Communication and Persuasion* 1: 84–89.

Poland, James M. (1988). *Understanding Terrorism: Groups, Strategies, and Responses.* Upper Saddle River, NJ: Prentice Hall.

Pollit, Mark M. (2000). "Cyberterrorism—Fact of Fantasy?" http://cs.georgetown.edu/~denning/infosec/pollitt.html

Porzecanski, Arturo C. (1973). *Uruguay's Tupamaros.* New York: Praeger.

Post, Jerrold M. (1987). "Rewarding Fire with Fire: Effects of Retaliation on Terrorist Group Dynamics." *Terrorism* 10: 23–36.

Purver, Ron. (1995). "Chemical and Biological Terrorism: The Threat According to Open Literature." Canadian Intelligence Service. http://www.csis-scrs.gc.ca/eng/misdocs/tabintre.html.

Quarles, Chester L. (1991, January). "A Pause in Terror." *Security Management:* 27–30.

Quigley, Robert C. (1991, January). "Terror Marches On." *Security Management*: 31–40.

Randal, Jonathan C. (1984). *Going All the Way.* New York: Vintage.

Ranstorp, Magnus. (1998). "Interpreting the Broader Context and Meaning of Bin-Laden's Fatwa." *Studies in Conflict and Terrorism* 21: 321–330.

Rapoport, David C. (ed.). (1988). *Inside Terrorist Organizations.* New York: Columbia University Press.

Rashad, Ahmad. (1996). "The Truth About Hamas." http://www.iap.org/politics/misc/truth.html.

Raufer, Xavier. (1993). "The Red Brigades: Farewell to Arms." *Studies in Conflict and Terrorism* 16: 313–325.

Reese, John. (1986, September). Unpublished briefing presented at EITWAT (Equalization in the War Against Terrorism), New Orleans, LA.

Reeve, Simon. (1999). *The New Jackals: Ramzi Yousef, Osama bin Ladin, and the Future of Terrorism.* Boston: Northeastern University Press.

Reich, Walter, and Walter Laqueur (eds.). (1998). *Origins of Terrorism: Psychologies, Ideologies, Theologies, States of Mind.* Princeton: Woodrow Wilson Center.

Reuters. (1996, April 12). "Israel Arch Foe Hizbollah Tough Nut to Crack." http://www.nando.net/newsroom/nt/412rwhoiz.html.

Reuters. (1996, April 21). "Israeli Intervention in Lebanon is Latest of Many." http://www.nando.net/newsroom/nt/421/many.html.

Ridgeway, James. (1995). *Blood in the Face: The Ku Klux Klan, Aryan Nations, Nazi Skinheads, and the Rise of the White Culture.* New York: Thunders.

The Road Back. (n.d.) *Macaba.* (Suspected publication of Ku Klux Klan, ca. 1985).

Rojahn, Christoph. (1998). "Left-Wing Terrorism in Germany: The Aftermath of Ideological Violence." *Conflict Studies* October 1998.

Ronfeldt, David. (1999). "Netwar Across the Spectrum of Conflict: An Introductory Comment." *Studies in Conflict and Terrorism* 22: 189–192.

Rose, Richard. (1971). *Governing Without Consensus: An Irish Perspective.* Boston: Beacon.

Rosen, M. Daniel. (1982, March). "At War with the Red Brigades." *Police Magazine*: 42–48.

Rosenbaum, David M. (1977). "Nuclear Terror." *International Security* 1: 140–161.

Rosie, George. (1987). *The Directory of International Terrorism.* New York: Paragon House.

Ross, Jeffery Ian. (1999). "Beyond the Conceptualization of Terrorism: A Psychological-Structural Model of the Causes of This Activity." In Craig Summers and Eric Markusen (eds.), *Collective Violence: Harmful Behavior in Groups and Governments.* New York: Rowen and Littlefield.

Roy, Joe. (1996). *False Patriots: The Threat of Antigovernment Extremists.* Montgomery, AL: Southern Poverty Law Center.

Royal Ulster Constabulary. (1996). "Policing Northern Ireland." http://www.nics.gov.uk/ruc/ruchome.htm.

Rubenstein, Richard E. (1987). *Alchemists of Revolution.* New York: Basic Books.

Rubin, Barry M. (1991). *Terrorism and State Politics.* New York: St. Martin's.

Russell, Charles A., and Bowman H. Miller. (1978). "Profile of a Terrorist." In J. D. Elliot and L. K. Gibson (eds.), *Contemporary Terrorism.* Gaithersburg, MD: International Association of Chiefs of Police.

Ryan, Peter. (1996). Unpublished personal notes shared with the author.

Saltman, Richard B. (1983). *The Social and Political Thought of Michael Bakunin.* Westport, CT: Greenwood.

Sanz, Timothy L. (1992, Winter). "Nuclear Terrorism: Selected Research Materials." Low Intensity Conflict and Law Enforcement: 1.

Sapp, Allen. (1985, March). *Basic Ideologies of Right-Wing Extremist Groups in America.* Paper presented at the annual meeting of the Academy of Criminal Justice Sciences, Las Vegas, NV.

Sapp, Allen. (1986). *The Nehemiah Township Charter: Applied Right-Wing Ideology.* Paper presented at the annual meeting of the Academy of Criminal Justice, Orlando, FL.

Sapp, Allen D. (1999). *Terrorist Use of Weapons of Mass Destruction: Current Realities and Future Considerations.* Paper presented at the Academy of Criminal Justice Sciences Annual Meeting, March 1999, Orlando, FL.

Sargent, Lyman Towed (ed.). (1995). *Extremism in America.* New York: New York University Press.

Scanlon, Joseph. (1981). "Coping with the Media: Police Media Problems and Tactics in Hostage Taking and Terrorist Incidents." *Canadian Police College Journal* 5: 129–148.

Scanlon, Joseph. (1982). "Domestic Terrorism and the Media: Live Coverage of Crime." *Canadian Police College Journal* 8: 154–178.

Scarman, Leslie. (1972). *Violence and Civil Disturbance in Northern Ireland in 1969.* Belfast: Her Majesty's Stationery Office.

Schaffert, Richard W. (1992). *Media Coverage and Political Terrorists: A Quantitative Analysis.* New York: Praeger.

Schevill, Ferdinand. (1922). *The History of the Balkan Peninsula: From the Earliest Times to the Present.* New York: Harcourt, Brace, and Co.

Schiller, David T. (1987). "Germany's Other Terrorists." *Terrorism* 9: 87–99.

Schiller, David T. (1988). "A Battlegroup Divided: The Palestinian Fedayeen." In David C. Rapoport (ed.), *Inside Terrorist Organizations.* New York: Columbia University Press.

Schlapentokh, Dmitry. (1998). *The Counter-Revolution in Revolution: Images of Thermidor and Napoleon at the Time of the Russian Revolution and Civil War.* New York: St. Martin's.

Schlesinger, Philip. (1981). "Terrorism, the Media and the Liberal-Democratic State: A Critique of Orthodoxy." *Social Research* 48: 74–99.

Schmid, Alex P. (1983). *Political Terrorism: A Research Guide to Concepts, Theories, Data Bases, and Literature.* New Brunswick, CT: Transaction.

Schmid, Alex P., and Janny F. A. de Graaf. (1982). *Violence as Communication.* Newbury Park, CA: Sage.

Schweitzer, Yoram. (2000). "Suicide Terrorism: Development and Characteristics." Institute for Counter-Terrorism. http://www.ict.org.il/home.htm.

Scotti, Tony. (1983). "Is the Media Really Covering Terrorism?" *TVI Journal* 4: 2–4.

Seale, Patrick. (1992). *Abu Nidal: A Gun for Hire.* New York: Random House.

Segaller, Stephen. (1987). *Invisible Armies: Terrorism into the 1990s.* San Diego: Harcourt Brace Jovanovich.

Seger, Karl A. (1991, April). "Is America Next?" *Security Management*: 31–38.

Shahar, Yael. (1997). "Information Warfare." Institute for Counter-Terrorism. http://www.ict.org.il/articles/articledet.cfm?articleid=13.

Shahar, Yael. (1998). "Osama bin Ladin: Marketing Terrorism." Institute for Counter-Terrorism. http://www.ict.org.il/articles/articledet.cfm?articleid=42.

Shaked, Emmanuel. (1986, September). *A Review of Counterterrorist Operations, Including Hostage Rescue.* Paper presented at EITWAT (Equalization in the War Against Terrorism), New Orleans, LA.

Sharif, Idris. (1995). *The Success of Political Terrorist Events: An Analysis of Terrorist Tactics and Victim Characteristics 1968 to 1977.* Landham, MD: University Press of America.

Shelley, Louise. (1994). "The Sources of Soviet Policing." *Police Studies* 17: 49–69.

Shultz, Richard. (1984). "The Role of External Forces in Promoting and Facilitating Internal Conflict." In Stephen J. Cimbala (ed.), *National Security Strategy.* New York: Praeger.

Silker, Laura, and Allen Little. (1996). *Yugoslavia: Death of a Nation.* New York: TV Books.

Simpson, John, and Jana Bennett. (1985). *The Disappeared and the Mothers of the Plaza.* New York: St. Martin's.

Sinn Fein. (1996). http://www.serve.com/rm/sinnfein/index.html.

Sloan, Stephen. (1981). *Simulating Terrorism.* Norman: University of Oklahoma Press.

Sloan, Stephen. (1995). *Terrorism: How Vulnerable is the United States?* U.S. Army War College. http://www.kimsoft.com/korea/terror.htm.

Smith, Brent L. (1994). *Terrorism in America: Pipe Bombs and Pipe Dreams.* Albany: State University of New York Press.

Smith, M. L. R. (1998). "A Still Distant Prospect: Processing the Peace in Northern Ireland." *Studies in Conflict and Terrorism* 21: 363–367.

Stanton, Bill. (1991). *Klanwatch: Bringing the Ku Klux Klan to Justice.* New York: Grove Weidenfeld.

Stephens, Hugh. (1987, September). *Maritime Defense at Home: The Influence of Jurisdictions.* Paper presented at the International Studies Association Section on Military Studies, Atlanta, GA.

Stephens, Hugh. (1997). *The Texas City Disaster, 1947.* Austin: University of Texas Press.

Stephens, Maynard M. (1979). "The Oil and Natural Gas Industries: A Potential Target of Terrorists." In Robert Kupperman and Darrell Trent (eds.), *Terrorism: Threat, Reality, and Response.* Stanford, CA: Hoover Institute.

Sterling, Claire. (1986). *The Terror Network.* New York: Dell.

Stern, Jessica. (1998). "The Prospect of Domestic Bioterrorism." *Emerging Infectious Diseases.* Center for Disease Control and Prevention. http://www.cdc.gov/ncidod/eid/vol5no4/stern.htm.

Stern, Jessica. (1999). *The Ultimate Terrorists.* Cambridge, MA: Harvard University Press.

Stern, Kenneth S. (1996). *A Force on the Plain: The American Militia Movement and the Politics of Hate.* New York: Simon & Schuster.

Stevenson, William. (1976). *Ninety Minutes at Entebbe.* New York: Bantam.

Stille, Alexander. (1995). *Excellent Cadavers: The Mafia and the Death of the First Italian Republic.* London: Cape.

Stinson, James. (1984, November). *Assessing Terrorist Tactics and Security Measures.* Paper presented at the Detroit Police Department Conference on "Urban Terrorism: Planning or Chaos?" (See also James Stinson [1981]. Unconventional Threat Assessment: The Role of Behavioral Sciences in Physical Security. DNA-TR-83-32. Washington, DC: Defense Nuclear Agency.)

Stockton, Ronald R. (1993). "The Israeli-Palestinian Conflict." http://www.umich.edu/ainet/cmenas/studyunits/israeli-palestinian_conflict/.

Stoffa, Adam Paul. (1995). "Special Forces, Counterterrorism, and the Law of Armed Conflict." *Studies in Conflict and Terrorism* 18: 47–65.

Stohl, Michael (ed.). (1988). *The Politics of Terrorism* (3rd ed.). New York: Dekker.

Suall, Irwin, and David Lowe. (1987). "Special Report: The Hate Movement Today: A Chronicle of Violence and Disarray." *Terrorism* 10: 345–364.

Taheri, Amir. (1987). *Holy Terror.* Bethesda, MD: Adler & Adler.

Taubman, Philip. (1984, September 21). "U.S. Said to Know Little About Group Despite Intelligence Efforts." *New York Times,* p. A13.

Taylor, Eric R. (1998). *Lethal Mists: An Introduction to the Natural and Military Sciences of Chemical, Biological Warfare and Terrorism.* Commack, NY: Nova Science Publisher.

Taylor, Maxwell, and Helen Ryan. (1988). "Fanaticism, Political Suicide, and Terrorism." *Terrorism* 11: 91–111.

Tessler, Mark. (1994). *A History of the Israeli-Palestinian Conflict.* Bloomington: Indiana University Press.

Thackrah, John. (1987). *Encyclopedia of Terrorism and Political Violence.* London: Routledge & Kegan Paul.

Thomas, Hugh. (1977). *The Cuban Revolution.* New York: Harper & Row.

Thomas, Mark. (1995, November 24). "The Watchman: A Publication of the Pennsylvania Christian Posse Comitatus." http://www.stormfront.org/watchman/terror.html.

Thorpe, Tory. (1996). "Black Hebrew Israelites." http://www.blackomahaonline.com/blkheb.htm.

Thorton, Thomas P. (1964). "Terror As a Weapon of Political Agitation." In H. Eckstein (ed.), *Internal War.* New York: Free Press.

Tillich, Paul. (1957). *The Dynamics of Faith.* New York: Harper Torch.

Time. (1987, November 23): 37.

Tololyan, Kachig. (1988). "Cultural Narrative and the Motivation of the Terrorist." In David C. Rapoport (ed.), *Inside Terrorist Organizations.* New York: Columbia University Press.

Trevino, Jose A. (1982). "Spain's Internal Security: The Basque Autonomous Police Force." In Yonah Alexander and Kenneth A. Myers (eds.), *Terrorism in Europe.* New York: St. Martin's.

Trojanowicz, Robert C., Bonnie Busqueroux, Victor E. Kappeler, and Larry K. Ganines. (1998). *Community Policing: A Contemporary Perspective.* Cincinnati: Anderson Publishing.

Trundle, Robert C., Jr. (1996). "Has Global Ethnic Conflict Superseded Cold War Ideology?" *Studies in Conflict and Terrorism* 19: 93–107.

Tula, Maria Teresa. (1994). *Hear My Testimony: Maria Teresa Tula, Human Rights Activist of El Salvador.* Translated by Lynn Stephen. Boston: South End Press.

Turner, Stansfield. (1991). *Terrorism and Democracy.* Boston: Houghton Mifflin.

Turvey, Brent E., Diana Tamlyn, and W. Jerry Chisum. (1999). *Criminal Profiling: An Introduction to Behavioral Evidence Analysis.* San Diego: Academic Press.

United Kingdom. (1980). *Northern Ireland (Emergency Provisions) Act 1980.* London: Her Majesty's Stationery Office.

United Nations. (2000). "Terrorism." http://www.inlink.com/~civitas/mun/res9596/terror.htm.

U.S. Congress. (1984). "Recent Developments in Colombian Narcotics Control." Hearings Before the Committee on Foreign Affairs. Washington, DC: Government Printing Office.

U.S. Congress. (1986). *Omnibus Diplomatic Security and Antiterrorism Act.* Washington DC: Government Printing Office.

U.S. Congress. (1995). *Omnibus Counterterrorism Act.* Washington, DC: Government Printing Office.

U.S. Court of Appeal. (1996). Eleventh Circuit, No. 92-4473. "United States of America, Plaintiff-Appellee v. Robert Louis Beasley et al." http://www.law.emory.edu.11circuit/jan96/92-4773.man.html.

U.S. Department of Defense. (1983). *Report of the DOD Commission on the Beirut International Terrorist Act, October*

23, 1983. Washington, DC: Government Printing Office.

U.S. Department of Defense. (2000). "Terrorist Group Profiles." http://www.periscope.usni.com/demo/terms/t0000282.html.

U.S. Department of State. (1981). "Press Release." In Marvin E. Gettleman et al. (eds.), *El Salvador.* New York: Grove.

U.S. Department of State. (1985, March 5). "Combating International Terrorism." *(Policy Circular 667).* Washington, DC: Government Printing Office.

U.S. Department of State. (1985–1996). *Patterns of Global Terrorism.* Washington, DC: Government Printing Office.

U.S. Department of State. (1986). *Human Rights in Nicaragua.* Washington, DC: Government Printing Office.

U.S. Department of State. (1999). *Patterns of Global Terrorism: 1999.* http://www.state.gov/www/global/terrorism/1999report/appb.html.

U.S. Department of State. (2000). *Patterns of Global Terrorism.* http://www.state.gov/www/global/terrorism/2000report/appb.html.

U.S. Drug Enforcement Administration. (1985). "Cocaine Review." *The Quarterly* (DEA quarterly intelligence trends) 12: 8–14.

U.S. House of Representatives. (1980). *FBI Oversight.* Hearings before the House Subcommittee on Civil and Constitutional Rights. Washington, DC: U.S. House of Representatives.

U.S. House of Representatives. (1980, December 9). *Increasing Violence Against Minorities.* Hearings before the Subcommittee on Crime. Washington, DC: U.S. House of Representatives.

U.S. House of Representatives. (1985). *Aftermath of the Achille Lauro Incident.* Hearing before the Committee on Foreign Affairs and Its Subcommittee on International Operations. Washington, DC: U.S. House of Representatives.

U.S. Marshals Service. (1988). Unpublished circular for domestic terrorism briefing.

U.S. Senate. (1985). *Bills to Authorize Prosecution of Terrorists and Others Who Attack U.S. Government Employees and Citizens Abroad.* Hearing before the Subcommittee on Security and Terrorism of the Committee of the Judiciary. Washington, DC: U.S. Senate.

U.S. Senate. (1995). *Comprehensive Terrorism Prevention Act, SB 735.* (See Mullendore and White, 1996.)

Uris, Leon. (1976). *Trinity.* Garden City, NY: Doubleday.

Usher, Grahaun. (1995). *Palestine in Crisis: The Struggle for Peace and Political Independence After Oslo.* East Haven, CT: Pluto Press.

Waldmann, Peter. (1986). "Guerrilla Movements in Argentina, Guatemala, Nicaragua, and Uruguay." In Peter Merkle (ed.), *Political Violence and Terror.* Berkeley: University of California Press.

Walker, Samuel. (1985). *Sense and Nonsense About Crime: A Policy Guide.* Pacific Grove, CA: Brooks/Cole.

Wallach, Janet, and John Wallach. (1992). *Arafat in the Eyes of the Beholder.* Rocklin, CA: Prima.

Walter, Jess. (1995). *Every Knee Shall Bow: The Truth and Tragedy of Ruby Ridge and the Randy Weaver Family.* New York: HarperCollins.

Wann Alle Bruder Schweigen. (n.d.). Cohoctah, MI: The Mountain Church.

Wardlaw, Grant. (1982). *Political Terrorism: Theory, Tactics, and Counter-Measures.* London: Cambridge University Press.

Wardlaw, Grant. (1988). "Terror as an Instrument of Foreign Policy." In David C. Rapoport (ed.), *Inside Terrorist Organizations.* New York: Columbia University Press.

Warner, Philip. (1972). *The Special Air Service.* London: Kimber.

Waxman, Dov. (1998, April). "The Islamic Republic of Iran: Between

Revolution and Realpolitik." *Conflict Studies.*

Waxman, Dov. (1998, August). "Turkey's Identity Crises: Domestic Discord and Foreign Policy." *Conflict Studies.*

Wege, Carl Anthony. (1991). "The Abu Nidal Organization." *Terrorism* 14: 59–66.

Wege, Carl Anthony. (1994). "Hizbollah Organization." *Studies in Conflict and Terrorism* 17: 151–164.

Weimann, Gabriel. (1983). "Theater of Terror: Effects of Press Coverage." *Journal of Communication* 33: 38–45.

Weinberg, Leonard. (1986). "The Violent Life: Left and Right Wing Terrorism in Italy." In Peter Merkl (ed.), *Political Violence and Terror.* Berkeley: University of California Press.

Weisband, Edward, and Damir Roguly. (1976). "Palestinian Terrorism: Violence, Verbal Strategy, and Legitimacy." In Yonah Alexander (ed.), *International Terrorism.* New York: Praeger.

Western Front. (n.d.). *The Hidden Tyranny.* Sacramento, CA: Western Front.

Western Goals Foundation. (ca. 1984). *No Place to Hide.* n.p.: Western Goals Foundation.

Whine, Michael. (1999). "Cyberspace—A New Medium for Communication, Command, and Control by Extremists." *Institute for Counter-Terrorism.* http://www.ict.org.il/articles/articledet.cfm?articleid=76

White, Jonathan R. (1986a, November). *The Development of Offensive Strategies in Counterterrorism.* Paper presented at the International Studies Association Section on Military Studies Conference, Harvard University, Cambridge, MA.

White, Jonathan R. (1986b). *Holy War: Terrorism As a Theological Construct.* Gaithersburg, MD: International Association of Chiefs of Police.

White, Jonathan R. (1995, June). *The Militia Movement.* Paper presented at the Midwest-Atlantic-Great Lakes

Organized Crime Law Enforcement Network, Baltimore, MD.

White, Jonathan R. (1996). Selected non-confidential material used at a briefing of the North Dakota Bureau of Criminal Investigation. Devil's Lake and Minot, ND.

White, Jonathan R. (1997). "Militia Madness: Extremist Interpretations of Christian Doctrine." *Perspectives: A Journal of Reformed Thought* 12: 8–12.

White, Jonathan R. (2000). *The Religious Roots of Criminal Behavior.* Tallahassee, FL: Institute for Intergovernmental Research.

White, Jonathan R. (2001). "Political Eschatology: A Theology of Antigovernment Extremism." *American Behavioral Scientist* 44: 937–956.

Wickham-Crowley, Timothy P. (1992). *Guerrillas and Revolution in Latin America: A Comparative Study of Insurgents and Regimes Since 1956.* Princeton, NJ: Princeton University Press.

Wickstrom, James. (1983). "Memorial Day Sermon." (Source unknown; taped by Posse Comitatus.)

Wieviorka, Michel. (1993). *The Making of Terrorism.* Chicago: University of Chicago Press.

Wiggins, Michael E. (1985, March). *The Relationship of Extreme Right-Wing Ideologies and Geographical Distribution of Select Right-Wing Groups.* Paper presented at the annual meeting of the Academy of Criminal Justice Sciences, Las Vegas, NV.

Wiggins, Michael E. (1986, March). *The Turner Diaries: Blueprint for Right-Wing Extremist Violence.* Paper presented at the annual meeting of the Academy of Criminal Justice Sciences, Orlando, FL.

Wilkinson, Paul. (1974). *Political Terrorism.* New York: Wiley.

Wilkinson, Paul. (1986). "Trends in International Terrorism and the American Response." In Lawrence Freedman et al. (eds.), *Terrorism and International Order.* London: Routledge & Kegan Paul.

Wilkinson, Paul. (1994). *Terrorism: British Perspectives.* New York: Hall.

Willrich, Mason, and Theodore Taylor. (1974). *Nuclear Theft: Risks and Safeguards.* Cambridge, MA: Ballinger.

Winchester, James H. (1974, July). "Kidnapping Unlimited." *Reader's Digest,* pp. 70–74.

Winchester, Simon. (1974). *Northern Ireland in Crisis.* New York: Holmes & Meier.

Windsor, Phillip. (1986). "The Middle East and Terrorism." In Lawrence Freedman et al. (eds.), *Terrorism and International Order.* London: Routledge & Kegan Paul.

Wolf, John B. (1981). *Fear of Fear.* New York: Plenum.

Woodcock, George. (1962). *Anarchism: A History of Liberation Ideas and Movements.* Harmondsworth, England: Penguin.

Woodham-Smith, Cecil. (1962). *The Great Hunger.* New York: Harper & Row.

World Church of the Creator. (1999). "WCOTC Membership Manual." http://www.rahowa.com/manual.htm.

Wright, Jeffery W. (1984). *Terrorism: A Mode of Warfare.* FC 100-37. Fort Leavenworth, KS: U.S. Army Command and General Staff College.

Wright, Robin. (1986). *Sacred Rage.* New York: Touchstone.

Wright, Robin. (1989). *In the Name of God: The Khomeini Decade.* New York: Simon & Schuster.

Wright, Thomas C. (1991). *Latin America in the Era of the Cuban Revolution.* New York: Praeger.

Wynia, Gary W. (1986). *Argentina.* New York: Holmes & Holmes.

Yodfat, Aryeh Y., and Yuval Aron-Ohanna. (1981). *PLO Strategy and Tactics.* London: Croom Helm.

Zanni, Michele. (1999). "Middle Eastern Terrorism and Netwar." *Studies in Conflict and Terrorism* 22: 247–256.

Index

Abbasids, 93
Abbey, Edward, 233
abortion clinic bombing, 43, 217
abortion clinic violence, 43, 217, 218, 219
Abu Abbas, 139, 290
Abu Ibrahim, 139, 215
Abu Jihad, 137, 144
Abu Nidal, 37, 135, 139, 141, 143, 144,
    145, 146, 147, 148, 150, 151, 156, 164,
    215, 285, 286, 287, 291
Abu Nidal Organization, 285
Abu Sayyaf Group, 285
Academy of Criminal Justice Sciences, 40
Act of Union (United Kingdom), 81
Adams, James, 16, 31, 40, 41, 42, 45.
Afghanistan, 56, 93, 162, 163, 164, 167,
    168, 215
Afghans (Osama bin Ladin's mujahidin), 163,
    164, 165, 167
Africa, 113, 287
African Civilization, 49
Ai, 51
al-Adnani, Tamim, 216
al-Ail, Ghana, 148
Albania, 48, 168
Alex Boncayo Brigade, 285
Alexander III, 73
Alexander, Yonah, 95, 98, 250, 258
ALF. *See* Animal Liberation Front.
Al-Gamaat al-Islamiyya, 285
Algeria, 41, 113, 152, 165, 168, 170
Al-Marayati, Salam, 74
Amal, 155, 270
ambush, 114, 138, 232, 278
American Civil War, 5, 83, 221, 222, 234
American Institute of Theology, 59
American Nazis, 285
American Revolution, 66, 67, 76, 77, 221
American Society for Industrial Security, 246
anarchism, 69, 70, 71, 72, 135, 221
anarchists, 5, 65, 69, 70, 71, 72, 74, 75, 76,
    78, 85, 90, 185, 219, 261
anarchy, 69, 141
Anderson, John, 5

Anglo-Irish Peace Accord, 90, 193, 194,
    196, 197
Anglo-Israelism, 59, 222, 224
Anglo-Persian Oil Company, 107
Angry Brigade, 285
Animal Liberation Front, 20, 43, 213, 233
animal rights, 220, 232, 233, 234, 236
Animal Rights Militia, 233
anti-Semitism, 59, 60, 184, 226
apocalypse, 53
apocalyptic cults, 59
Apprentice Boys, 81, 87
Arab Revolt, 92, 99
Arab Revolutionary Brigades, 285
Arab Revolutionary Council, 285
Arafat, Yasser, 136, 137, 138, 139, 140, 141,
    142, 143, 144, 145, 146, 150, 151, 159,
    160, 161, 286, 288
Argentina, 96, 118
Argentine Anti-Communist Alliance, 285
Arizona Vipers, 228, 229
Arkansas, 223
Armageddon, 54
Armed Forces of National Liberation, 212,
    259, 285, 288
Armed Forces of National Resistance, 285
Armed Forces of National Revolution, 288
Armed Forces of Popular Resistance, 285
Armed Islamic Group, 168, 170, 285
Armed Resistance Unit, 285
Armed Revolutionary Nuclei, 286
arson, 16, 17, 126, 219, 232, 233, 234
Aryan Congress, 224
Aryan National Alliance, 286
Aryan Nations, 59, 222, 224, 286
Asahara, Shoko, 240, 241, 242
Asia, 113
Assad, Hafez, 101
Atef, Mohammed, 166
ATF. *See* Bureau of Alcohol, Tobacco, and
    Firearms.
Atlanta, 1996 Olympics, 43
Aum Shinrikyo, 37, 239, 240, 241, 242, 243,
    244, 255, 273